Authors

Randall I. Charles
Professor Emeritus
Department of Mathematics
San Jose State University
San Jose, California

Jennifer Bay-Williams
Professor of Mathematics Education
College of Education and Human Development
University of Louisville
Louisville, Kentucky

Robert Q. Berry, III
Associate Professor of Mathematics Education
Department of Curriculum, Instruction and Special Education
University of Virginia
Charlottesville, Virginia

Janet H. Caldwell
Professor of Mathematics
Rowan University
Glassboro, New Jersey

Zachary Champagne
Assistant in Research
Florida Center for Research in Science, Technology, Engineering, and Mathematics (FCR-STEM)
Jacksonville, Florida

Juanita Copley
Professor Emerita, College of Education
University of Houston
Houston, Texas

Warren Crown
Professor Emeritus of Mathematics Education
Graduate School of Education
Rutgers University
New Brunswick, New Jersey

Francis (Skip) Fennell
L. Stanley Bowlsbey Professor of Education and Graduate and Professional Studies
McDaniel College
Westminster, Maryland

Karen Karp
Professor of Mathematics Education
Department of Early Childhood and Elementary Education
University of Louisville
Louisville, Kentucky

Stuart J. Murphy
Visual Learning Specialist
Boston, Massachusetts

Jane F. Schielack
Professor of Mathematics
Associate Dean for Assessment and Pre K-12 Education,
College of Science
Texas A&M University
College Station, Texas

Jennifer M. Suh
Associate Professor for Mathematics Education
George Mason University
Fairfax, Virginia

Jonathan A. Wray
Mathematics Instructional Facilitator
Howard County Public Schools
Ellicott City, Maryland

PEARSON

Glenview, Illinois   Boston, Massachusetts   Chandler, Arizona   Hoboken, New Jersey

Mathematicians

Roger Howe
Professor of Mathematics
Yale University
New Haven, Connecticut

Gary Lippman
Professor of Mathematics and Computer Science
California State University, East Bay
Hayward, California

ELL Consultants

Janice R. Corona
Independent Education Consultant
Dallas, Texas

Jim Cummins
Professor
The University of Toronto
Toronto, Canada

Common Core State Standards Reviewers

Debbie Crisco
Math Coach
Beebe Public Schools
Beebe, Arkansas

Kathleen A. Cuff
Teacher
Kings Park Central School District
Kings Park, New York

Erika Doyle
Math and Science Coordinator
Richland School District
Richland, Washington

Susan Jarvis
Math and Science Curriculum Coordinator
Ocean Springs Schools
Ocean Springs, Mississippi

Velvet M. Simington
K-12 Mathematics Director
Winston-Salem/Forsyth County Schools
Winston-Salem, North Carolina

Copyright © 2016 by Pearson Education, Inc., or its affiliates. All Rights Reserved. Printed in the United States of America. This publication is protected by copyright, and permission should be obtained from the publisher prior to any prohibited reproduction, storage in a retrieval system, or transmission in any form or by any means, electronic, mechanical, photocopying, recording, or otherwise. For information regarding permissions, request forms from the appropriate contacts within the Pearson Education Global Rights & Permissions Department. Please visit www.pearsoned.com/permissions/.

PEARSON, ALWAYS LEARNING, SCOTT FORESMAN, PEARSON SCOTT FORESMAN, and **enVision**math are exclusive trademarks owned by Pearson Education, Inc. or its affiliates in the U.S. and/or other countries.

Unless otherwise indicated herein, any third-party trademarks that may appear in this work are the property of their respective owners and any references to third-party trademarks, logos or other trade dress are for demonstrative or descriptive purposes only. Such references are not intended to imply any sponsorship, endorsement, authorization, or promotion of Pearson's products by the owners of such marks, or any relationship between the owner and Pearson Education, Inc. or its affiliates, authors, licensees or distributors.

Common Core State Standards: Copyright © 2010. National Governors Association Center for Best Practices and Council of Chief State School Officers. All rights reserved.

ISBN-13: 978-0-328-82741-1
ISBN-10: 0-328-82741-X

PEARSON

7 16

Digital Resources

You'll be using these digital resources throughout the year!

Go to PearsonRealize.com

MP

Math Practices Animations to play anytime

Learn

Visual Learning Animation Plus with animation, interaction, and math tools

Practice Buddy

Online Personalized Practice for each lesson

Assessment

Quick Check for each lesson

Games

Math Games to help you learn

ACTIVe-book

Student Edition online for showing your work

Solve

Solve & Share problems plus math tools

Glossary

Animated Glossary in English and Spanish

Tools

Math Tools to help you understand

Help

Another Look Homework Video for extra help

eText

Student Edition online

PEARSON realize™ Everything you need for math anytime, anywhere

Hi, we're here to help you. Let's have a great year!

KEY

Major Cluster

Supporting Cluster

Additional Cluster

The content is organized to focus on Common Core clusters.

For a list of clusters, see pages F15–F18.

Digital Resources at PearsonRealize.com

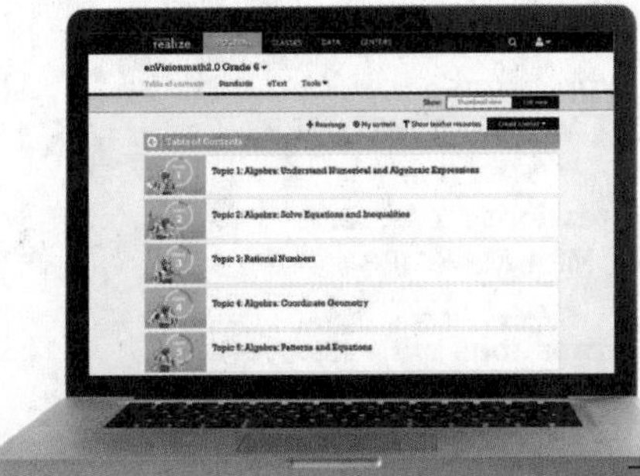

And remember your eText is available at PearsonRealize.com!

Contents

TOPICS

PearsonRealize.com

Algebraic expressions contain at least one variable and can have 1 or more terms.

$$12r + \frac{r}{2} - 19$$

TOPIC 1 Algebra: Understand Numerical and Algebraic Expressions

© Pearson Education, Inc. 6

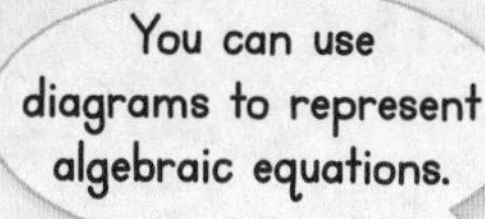

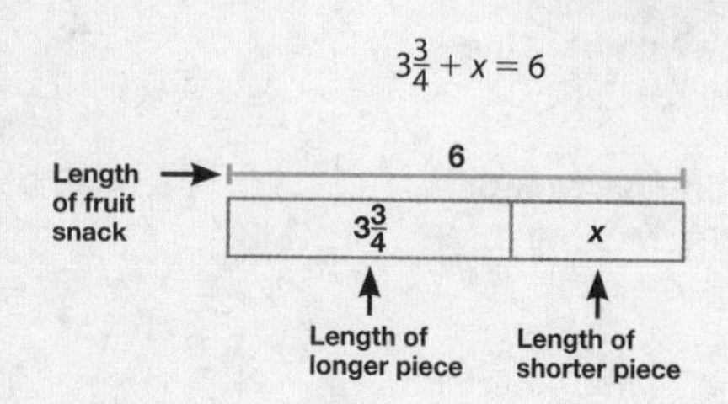

TOPIC 2 Algebra: Solve Equations and Inequalities

Rational numbers, like integers, can be negative or positive. You can use a number line to help you compare and order rational numbers.

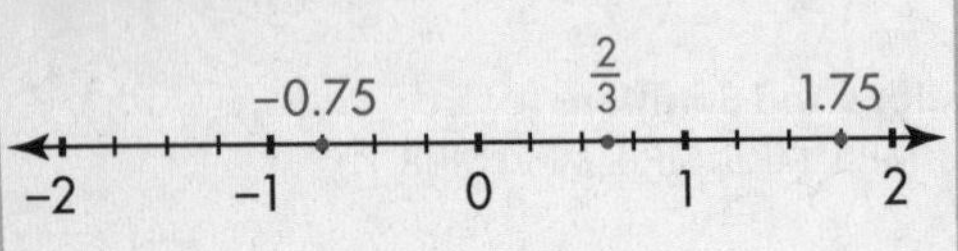

TOPIC 3 Rational Numbers

© Pearson Education, Inc. 6

You can use the math structure found on the coordinate plane to solve problems.

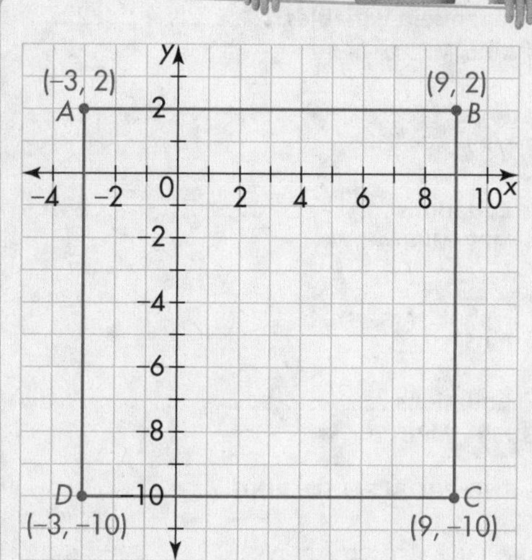

TOPIC 4 Algebra: Coordinate Geometry

TOPIC 5 Algebra: Patterns and Equations

© Pearson Education, Inc. 6

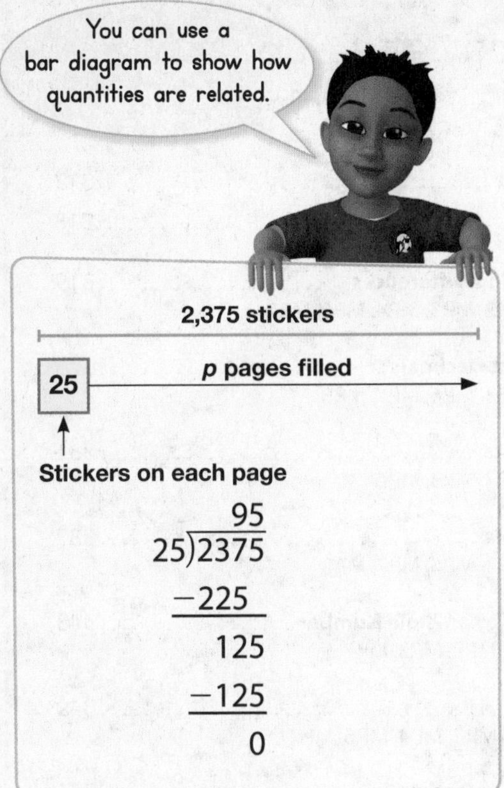

TOPIC 6 Fluently Divide Whole Numbers

You use place value structure when you compute with decimals.

$$\begin{array}{rl} \overset{1\,2}{0.36} & \leftarrow \text{2 decimal places} \\ \times \quad 4 & \leftarrow \underline{+\,0 \text{ decimal places}} \\ \hline 1.44 & \leftarrow \text{2 decimal places} \end{array}$$

$$\begin{array}{r} 220 \\ 0.16\overline{)35.20} \\ -32 \\ \hline 32 \\ -32 \\ \hline 0 \end{array}$$

TOPIC 7 Fluently Add, Subtract, Multiply, and Divide Decimals

© Pearson Education, Inc. 6

TOPIC 8 Common Factors and Multiples

KEY

- Major Cluster
- Supporting Cluster
- Additional Cluster

The content is organized to focus on Common Core clusters.

Dear Families,

The standards on the following pages describe the math that students will learn this year. The greatest amount of time will be spent on standards in the major clusters.

Grade 6 Common Core Standards

Common Core Standards for Mathematical Content

DOMAIN **6.RP**
RATIOS AND PROPORTIONAL RELATIONSHIPS

MAJOR CLUSTER **6.RP.A**

Understand ratio concepts and use ratio reasoning to solve problems.

6.RP.A.1 Understand the concept of a ratio and use ratio language to describe a ratio relationship between two quantities.

6.RP.A.2 Understand the concept of a unit rate a/b associated with a ratio $a{:}b$ with $b \neq 0$, and use rate language in the context of a ratio relationship.[1]

6.RP.A.3 Use ratio and rate reasoning to solve real-world and mathematical problems, e.g., by reasoning about tables of equivalent ratios, tape diagrams, double number line diagrams, or equations.

6.RP.A.3a Make tables of equivalent ratios relating quantities with whole-number measurements, find missing values in the tables, and plot the pairs of values on the coordinate plane. Use tables to compare ratios.

6.RP.A.3b Solve unit rate problems including those involving unit pricing and constant speed.

6.RP.A.3c Find a percent of a quantity as a rate per 100 (e.g., 30% of a quantity means 30/100 times the quantity); solve problems involving finding the whole, given a part and the percent.

6.RP.A.3d Use ratio reasoning to convert measurement units; manipulate and transform units appropriately when multiplying or dividing quantities.

DOMAIN **6.NS**
THE NUMBER SYSTEM

MAJOR CLUSTER **6.NS.A**

Apply and extend previous understandings of multiplication and division to divide fractions by fractions.

6.NS.A.1 Interpret and compute quotients of fractions, and solve word problems involving division of fractions by fractions, e.g., by using visual fraction models and equations to represent the problem.

Common Core Standards for Mathematical Content

ADDITIONAL CLUSTER **6.NS.B**

Compute fluently with multi-digit numbers and find common factors and multiples.

6.NS.B.2 Fluently divide multi-digit numbers using the standard algorithm.

6.NS.B.3 Fluently add, subtract, multiply, and divide multi-digit decimals using the standard algorithm for each operation.

6.NS.B.4 Find the greatest common factor of two whole numbers less than or equal to 100 and the least common multiple of two whole numbers less than or equal to 12. Use the distributive property to express a sum of two whole numbers 1–100 with a common factor as a multiple of a sum of two whole numbers with no common factor.

MAJOR CLUSTER **6.NS.C**

Apply and extend previous understandings of numbers to the system of rational numbers.

6.NS.C.5 Understand that positive and negative numbers are used together to describe quantities having opposite directions or values (e.g., temperature above/below zero, elevation above/below sea level, credits/debits, positive/negative electric charge); use positive and negative numbers to represent quantities in real-world contexts, explaining the meaning of 0 in each situation.

6.NS.C.6 Understand a rational number as a point on the number line. Extend number line diagrams and coordinate axes familiar from previous grades to represent points on the line and in the plane with negative number coordinates.

6.NS.C.6a Recognize opposite signs of numbers as indicating locations on opposite sides of 0 on the number line; recognize that the opposite of the opposite of a number is the number itself, e.g., $-(-3) = 3$, and that 0 is its own opposite.

6.NS.C.6b Understand signs of numbers in ordered pairs as indicating locations in quadrants of the coordinate plane; recognize that when two ordered pairs differ only by signs, the locations of the points are related by reflections across one or both axes.

6.NS.C.6c Find and position integers and other rational numbers on a horizontal or vertical number line diagram; find and position pairs of integers and other rational numbers on a coordinate plane.

6.NS.C.7 Understand ordering and absolute value of rational numbers.

6.NS.C.7a Interpret statements of inequality as statements about the relative position of two numbers on a number line diagram.

6.NS.C.7b Write, interpret, and explain statements of order for rational numbers in real-world contexts.

6.NS.C.7c Understand the absolute value of a rational number as its distance from 0 on the number line; interpret absolute value as magnitude for a positive or negative quantity in a real-world situation.

6.NS.C.7d Distinguish comparisons of absolute value from statements about order.

6.NS.C.8 Solve real-world and mathematical problems by graphing points in all four quadrants of the coordinate plane. Include use of coordinates and absolute value to find distances between points with the same first coordinate or the same second coordinate.

DOMAIN 6.EE
EXPRESSIONS AND EQUATIONS

MAJOR CLUSTER **6.EE.A**

Apply and extend previous understandings of arithmetic to algebraic expressions.

6.EE.A.1 Write and evaluate numerical expressions involving whole-number exponents.

6.EE.A.2 Write, read, and evaluate expressions in which letters stand for numbers.

6.EE.A.2a Write expressions that record operations with numbers and with letters standing for numbers.

6.EE.A.2b Identify parts of an expression using mathematical terms (sum, term, product, factor, quotient, coefficient); view one or more parts of an expression as a single entity.

© Pearson Education, Inc. 6

Common Core Standards for Mathematical Content

6.EE.A.2c Evaluate expressions at specific values of their variables. Include expressions that arise from formulas used in real-world problems. Perform arithmetic operations, including those involving whole-number exponents, in the conventional order when there are no parentheses to specify a particular order (Order of Operations).

6.EE.A.3 Apply the properties of operations to generate equivalent expressions.

6.EE.A.4 Identify when two expressions are equivalent (i.e., when the two expressions name the same number regardless of which value is substituted into them).

MAJOR CLUSTER **6.EE.B**

Reason about and solve one-variable equations and inequalities.

6.EE.B.5 Understand solving an equation or inequality as a process of answering a question: which values from a specified set, if any, make the equation or inequality true? Use substitution to determine whether a given number in a specified set makes an equation or inequality true.

6.EE.B.6 Use variables to represent numbers and write expressions when solving a real-world or mathematical problem; understand that a variable can represent an unknown number, or, depending on the purpose at hand, any number in a specified set.

6.EE.B.7 Solve real-world and mathematical problems by writing and solving equations of the form $x + p = q$ and $px = q$ for cases in which p, q and x are all nonnegative rational numbers.

6.EE.B.8 Write an inequality of the form $x > c$ or $x < c$ to represent a constraint or condition in a real-world or mathematical problem. Recognize that inequalities of the form $x > c$ or $x < c$ have infinitely many solutions; represent solutions of such inequalities on number line diagrams.

MAJOR CLUSTER **6.EE.C**

Represent and analyze quantitative relationships between dependent and independent variables.

6.EE.C.9 Use variables to represent two quantities in a real-world problem that change in relationship to one another; write an equation to express one quantity, thought of as the dependent variable, in terms of the other quantity, thought of as the independent variable. Analyze the relationship between the dependent and independent variables using graphs and tables, and relate these to the equation.

DOMAIN **6.G**
GEOMETRY

SUPPORTING CLUSTER **6.G.A**

Solve real-world and mathematical problems involving area, surface area, and volume.

6.G.A.1 Find the area of right triangles, other triangles, special quadrilaterals, and polygons by composing into rectangles or decomposing into triangles and other shapes; apply these techniques in the context of solving real-world and mathematical problems.

6.G.A.2 Find the volume of a right rectangular prism with fractional edge lengths by packing it with unit cubes of the appropriate unit fraction edge lengths, and show that the volume is the same as would be found by multiplying the edge lengths of the prism. Apply the formulas $V = \ell w h$ and $V = b h$ to find volumes of right rectangular prisms with fractional edge lengths in the context of solving real-world and mathematical problems.

6.G.A.3 Draw polygons in the coordinate plane given coordinates for the vertices; use coordinates to find the length of a side joining points with the same first coordinate or the same second coordinate. Apply these techniques in the context of solving real-world and mathematical problems.

6.G.A.4 Represent three-dimensional figures using nets made up of rectangles and triangles, and use the nets to find the surface area of these figures. Apply these techniques in the context of solving real-world and mathematical problems.

Common Core Standards for Mathematical Content

DOMAIN **6.SP**
STATISTICS AND PROBABILITY

ADDITIONAL CLUSTER **6.SP.A**
Develop understanding of statistical variability.

6.SP.A.1 Recognize a statistical question as one that anticipates variability in the data related to the question and accounts for it in the answers.

6.SP.A.2 Understand that a set of data collected to answer a statistical question has a distribution which can be described by its center, spread, and overall shape.

6.SP.A.3 Recognize that a measure of center for a numerical data set summarizes all of its values with a single number, while a measure of variation describes how its values vary with a single number.

ADDITIONAL CLUSTER **6.SP.B**
Summarize and describe distributions.

6.SP.B.4 Display numerical data in plots on a number line, including dot plots, histograms, and box plots.

6.SP.B.5 Summarize numerical data sets in relation to their context, such as by:

6.SP.B.5a Reporting the number of observations.

6.SP.B.5b Describing the nature of the attribute under investigation, including how it was measured and its units of measurement.

6.SP.B.5c Giving quantitative measures of center (median and/or mean) and variability (interquartile range and/or mean absolute deviation), as well as describing any overall pattern and any striking deviations from the overall pattern with reference to the context in which the data were gathered.

6.SP.B.5d Relating the choice of measures of center and variability to the shape of the data distribution and the context in which the data were gathered.

[1]Expectations for unit rates in this grade are limited to non-complex fractions.

© Pearson Education, Inc. 6

Common Core Standards for Mathematical Practice

MP.1 MAKE SENSE OF PROBLEMS AND PERSEVERE IN SOLVING THEM.

Mathematically proficient students start by explaining to themselves the meaning of a problem and looking for entry points to its solution. They analyze givens, constraints, relationships, and goals. They make conjectures about the form and meaning of the solution and plan a solution pathway rather than simply jumping into a solution attempt. They consider analogous problems, and try special cases and simpler forms of the original problem in order to gain insight into its solution. They monitor and evaluate their progress and change course if necessary. Older students might, depending on the context of the problem, transform algebraic expressions or change the viewing window on their graphing calculator to get the information they need. Mathematically proficient students can explain correspondences between equations, verbal descriptions, tables, and graphs or draw diagrams of important features and relationships, graph data, and search for regularity or trends. Younger students might rely on using concrete objects or pictures to help conceptualize and solve a problem. Mathematically proficient students check their answers to problems using a different method, and they continually ask themselves, "Does this make sense?" They can understand the approaches of others to solving complex problems and identify correspondences between different approaches.

MP.2 REASON ABSTRACTLY AND QUANTITATIVELY.

Mathematically proficient students make sense of quantities and their relationships in problem situations. They bring two complementary abilities to bear on problems involving quantitative relationships: the ability to *decontextualize*—to abstract a given situation and represent it symbolically and manipulate the representing symbols as if they have a life of their own, without necessarily attending to their referents—and the ability to *contextualize*, to pause as needed during the manipulation process in order to probe into the referents for the symbols involved. Quantitative reasoning entails habits of creating a coherent representation of the problem at hand; considering the units involved; attending to the meaning of quantities, not just how to compute them; and knowing and flexibly using different properties of operations and objects.

MP.3 CONSTRUCT VIABLE ARGUMENTS AND CRITIQUE THE REASONING OF OTHERS.

Mathematically proficient students understand and use stated assumptions, definitions, and previously established results in constructing arguments. They make conjectures and build a logical progression of statements to explore the truth of their conjectures. They are able to analyze situations by breaking them into cases, and can recognize and use counterexamples. They justify their conclusions, communicate them to others, and respond to the arguments of others. They reason inductively about data, making plausible arguments that take into account the context from which the data arose. Mathematically proficient students are also able to compare the effectiveness of two plausible arguments, distinguish correct logic or reasoning from that which is flawed, and—if there is a flaw in an argument—explain what it is. Elementary students can construct arguments using concrete referents such as objects, drawings, diagrams, and actions. Such arguments can make sense and be correct, even though they are not generalized or made formal until later grades. Later, students learn to determine domains to which an argument applies. Students at all grades can listen or read the arguments of others, decide whether they make sense, and ask useful questions to clarify or improve the arguments.

MP.4 MODEL WITH MATHEMATICS.

Mathematically proficient students can apply the mathematics they know to solve problems arising in everyday life, society, and the workplace. In early grades, this might be as simple as writing an addition equation to describe a situation. In middle grades, a student might apply proportional reasoning to plan a school event or analyze a problem in the community. By high school, a student might use geometry to solve a design problem or use a function to describe how one quantity of interest depends on another. Mathematically proficient students who can apply what they know are comfortable making assumptions and approximations to simplify a complicated situation, realizing that these may need revision later. They are able to identify important quantities in a practical situation and map their relationships using such tools as diagrams, two-way tables, graphs, flowcharts and formulas. They can analyze those relationships mathematically to draw conclusions. They routinely interpret their mathematical results in the context of the situation and reflect on whether the results make sense, possibly improving the model if it has not served its purpose.

MP.5 USE APPROPRIATE TOOLS STRATEGICALLY.

Mathematically proficient students consider the available tools when solving a mathematical problem. These tools might include pencil and paper, concrete models, a ruler, a protractor, a calculator, a spreadsheet, a computer algebra system, a statistical package, or dynamic geometry software. Proficient students are sufficiently familiar with tools appropriate for their grade or course to make sound decisions about when each of these tools might be helpful, recognizing both the insight to be gained and their limitations. For example, mathematically proficient high school students analyze graphs of functions and solutions generated using a graphing calculator. They detect possible errors by strategically using estimation and other mathematical knowledge. When making mathematical models, they know that technology can enable them to visualize the results of varying assumptions, explore consequences, and compare predictions with data. Mathematically proficient students at various grade levels are able to identify relevant external mathematical resources, such as digital content located on a website, and use them to pose or solve problems. They are able to use technological tools to explore and deepen their understanding of concepts.

MP.6 ATTEND TO PRECISION.

Mathematically proficient students try to communicate precisely to others. They try to use clear definitions in discussion with others and in their own reasoning. They state the meaning of the symbols they choose, including using the equal sign consistently and appropriately. They are careful about specifying units of measure, and labeling axes to clarify the correspondence with quantities in a problem. They calculate accurately and efficiently, express numerical answers with a degree of precision appropriate for the problem context. In the elementary grades, students give carefully formulated explanations to each other. By the time they reach high school they have learned to examine claims and make explicit use of definitions.

MP.7 LOOK FOR AND MAKE USE OF STRUCTURE.

Mathematically proficient students look closely to discern a pattern or structure. Young students, for example, might notice that three and seven more is the same amount as seven and three more, or they may sort a collection of shapes according to how many sides the shapes have. Later, students will see 7×8 equals the well remembered $7 \times 5 + 7 \times 3$, in preparation for learning about the distributive property. In the expression $x^2 + 9x + 14$, older students can see the 14 as 2×7 and the 9 as $2 + 7$. They recognize the significance of an existing line in a geometric figure and can use the strategy of drawing an auxiliary line for solving problems. They also can step back for an overview and shift perspective. They can see complicated things, such as some algebraic expressions, as single objects or as being composed of several objects. For example, they can see $5 - 3(x - y)^2$ as 5 minus a positive number times a square and use that to realize that its value cannot be more than 5 for any real numbers x and y.

MP.8 LOOK FOR AND EXPRESS REGULARITY IN REPEATED REASONING.

Mathematically proficient students notice if calculations are repeated, and look both for general methods and for shortcuts. Upper elementary students might notice when dividing 25 by 11 that they are repeating the same calculations over and over again, and conclude they have a repeating decimal. By paying attention to the calculation of slope as they repeatedly check whether points are on the line through (1, 2) with slope 3, middle school students might abstract the equation $(y - 2)/(x - 1) = 3$. Noticing the regularity in the way terms cancel when expanding $(x - 1)(x + 1)$, $(x - 1)(x^2 + x + 1)$, and $(x - 1)(x^3 + x^2 + x + 1)$ might lead them to the general formula for the sum of a geometric series. As they work to solve a problem, mathematically proficient students maintain oversight of the process, while attending to the details. They continually evaluate the reasonableness of their intermediate results.

© Pearson Education, Inc. 6

Math Practices and Problem Solving Handbook

Math practices are ways we think about and do math.

Math practices will help you solve problems.

Math Practices

MP.1 Make sense of problems and persevere in solving them.

MP.2 Reason abstractly and quantitatively.

MP.3 Construct viable arguments and critique the reasoning of others.

MP.4 Model with mathematics.

MP.5 Use appropriate tools strategically.

MP.6 Attend to precision.

MP.7 Look for and make use of structure.

MP.8 Look for and express regularity in repeated reasoning.

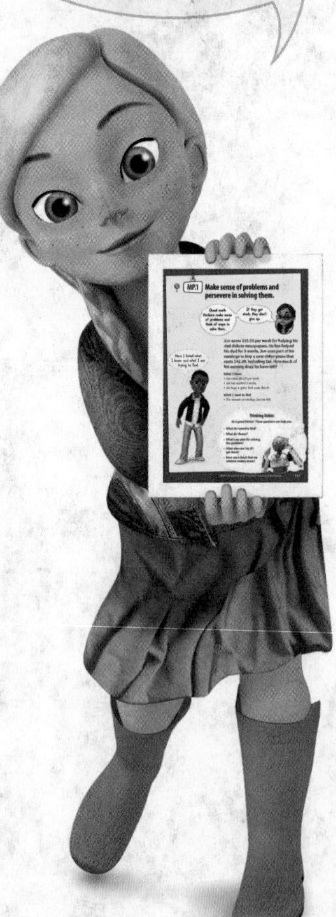

There are good Thinking Habits for each of these math practices.
MP.1 Make sense of problems and persevere in solving them.

© Pearson Education, Inc. 6

Make sense of problems and persevere in solving them.

If they get stuck, they don't give up.

Jon earns $15.50 per week for helping his dad deliver newspapers. He has helped his dad for 3 weeks. Jon uses part of his earnings to buy a new video game that costs $42.39, including tax. How much of his earnings does he have left?

Here I listed what I know and what I am trying to find.

What I Know:

- *Jon earns $15.50 per week.*
- *Jon has worked 3 weeks.*
- *Jon buys a game that costs $42.39.*

What I need to find:

- *The amount of earnings Jon has left.*

Thinking Habits

Be a good thinker! These questions can help you.

- What do I need to find?
- What do I know?
- What's my plan for solving the problem?
- What else can I try if I get stuck?
- How can I check that my solution makes sense?

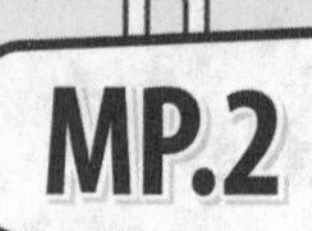

Reason abstractly and quantitatively.

Good math thinkers know how to think about words and numbers to solve problems.

I drew a bar diagram that shows how the quantities in the problem are related.

Jacie bought a 6-pack of juice drinks for $4.50. How much does each drink in the pack of juice cost?

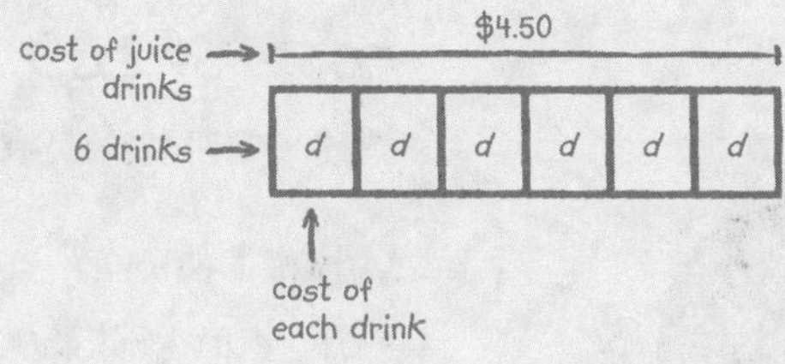

Thinking Habits

Be a good thinker! These questions can help you.

- What do the numbers and symbols in the problem mean?
- How are the numbers or quantities related?
- How can I represent a word problem using pictures, numbers, or equations?

© Pearson Education, Inc. 6

MP.3 Construct viable arguments and critique the reasoning of others.

Good math thinkers use math to explain why they are right. They can talk about the math that others do, too.

I wrote a clear argument with words, numbers, and symbols.

Jo said that when you multiply a nonzero whole number by a fraction less than 1, the product is always less than the whole number. Do you agree? Explain.

You can think of multiplying by a fraction less than one as finding a part of a whole group. So, the product of a nonzero whole number and a fraction less than one is always less than the whole number. For example:

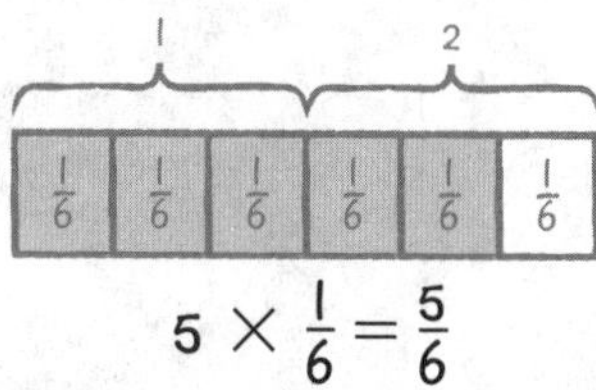

$5 \times \frac{1}{6} = \frac{5}{6}$

Thinking Habits

Be a good thinker! These questions can help you.

- How can I use numbers, objects, drawings, or actions to justify my argument?
- Am I using numbers and symbols correctly?
- Is my explanation clear and complete?
- What questions can I ask to understand other people's thinking?
- Are there mistakes in other people's thinking?
- Can I improve other people's thinking?
- Can I use a counterexample in my argument?

MP.4 Model with mathematics.

Good math thinkers choose and apply math they know to show and solve problems from everyday life.

Sally's dad is building shelving in his garage. He fills a 32.5-foot long wall with 6 identical shelves. How wide is each shelf?

I can use what I know about division to solve this problem. I drew a diagram to help.

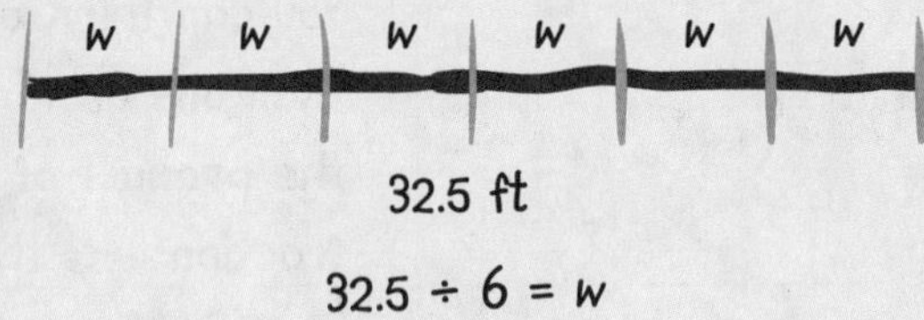

$32.5 \div 6 = w$

Thinking Habits

Be a good thinker! These questions can help you.

- How can I use math I know to help solve the problem?
- How can I use pictures, objects, or an equation to represent the problem?
- How can I use numbers, words, and symbols to solve the problem?

© Pearson Education, Inc. 6

Use appropriate tools strategically.

Good math thinkers know how to pick the right tools to solve math problems.

I decided to use unit cubes to show how I could fill the box.

Alex has a pencil box that is 9 inches long, 6 inches wide, and 3 inches high. What is the volume of his pencil box?

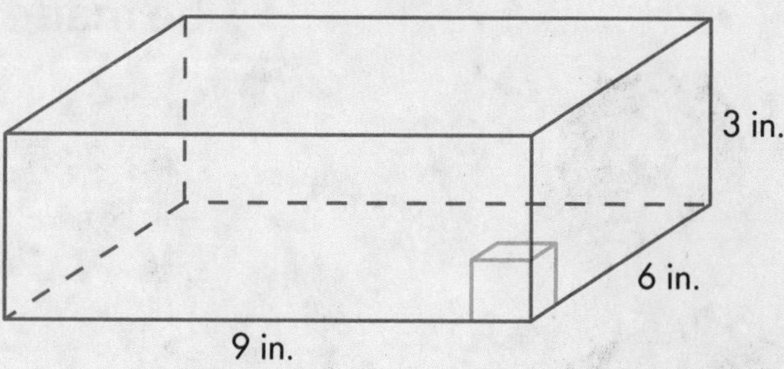

Thinking Habits

Be a good thinker! These questions can help you.

- Which tools can I use?
- Why should I use this tool to help me solve the problem?
- Is there a different tool I could use?
- Am I using the tool appropriately?

Attend to precision.

Good math thinkers are careful about what they write and say, so their ideas about math are clear.

I was precise with my work and the way that I wrote my solution.

A party planner says that $\frac{2}{3}$ pound of chicken should be made for each person at a party. There will be 8 people at a dinner party. How much chicken should be made for the party?

$$8 \times \frac{2}{3}$$
$$= 8 \times 2 \times \frac{1}{3}$$
$$= 16 \times \frac{1}{3}$$
$$= \frac{16}{3}$$
$$= 5\frac{1}{3}$$

$5\frac{1}{3}$ pounds of chicken should be made for the party.

Thinking Habits

Be a good thinker! These questions can help you.

- Am I using numbers, units, and symbols appropriately?
- Am I using the correct definitions?
- Am I calculating accurately?
- Is my answer clear?

© Pearson Education, Inc. 6

MP

Look for and make use of structure.

Good math thinkers look for patterns in math to help solve problems.

I used place-value structure to multiply a decimal and solve this problem.

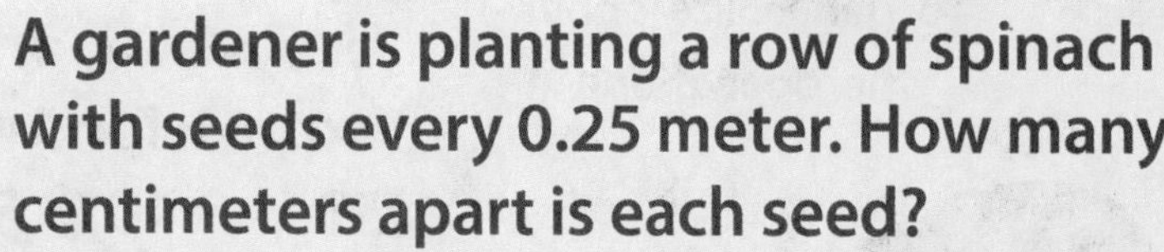

A gardener is planting a row of spinach with seeds every 0.25 meter. How many centimeters apart is each seed?

1 m = 100 cm

0.25×10^2
$= 0.25 \times 100$
$= 25$

Each *seed* is 25 centimeters apart.

Thinking Habits

Be a good thinker! These questions can help you.

- What patterns can I see and describe?
- How can I use the patterns to solve the problem?
- Can I see expressions and objects in different ways?
- What equivalent expressions can I use?

Look for and express regularity in repeated reasoning.

Good math thinkers look for things that repeat, and they make generalizations.

I used reasoning to generalize about the operations.

Use <, >, or = to compare the expressions without calculating.
534 ÷ 10 ◯ 534 × 10

534 ÷ 10 < 534 × 10
because the result of dividing a number by 10 is *less* than the result of multiplying the *same* number by 10.

Thinking Habits

Be a good thinker! These questions can help you.

- Are any calculations repeated?
- Can I generalize from examples?
- What shortcuts do I notice?

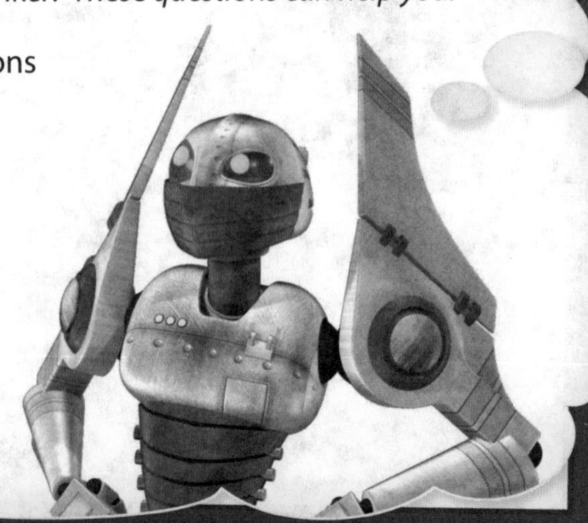

© Pearson Education, Inc. 6

Math Practices and Problem Solving Handbook

Problem Solving Guide

Math practices can help you solve problems.

Make Sense of the Problem

Reason Abstractly and Quantitatively

- What do I need to find?
- What given information can I use?
- How are the quantities related?

Think About Similar Problems

- Have I solved problems like this before?

Persevere in Solving the Problem

Model with Math

- How can I use the math I know?
- How can I represent the problem?
- Is there a pattern or structure I can use?

Use Appropriate Tools Strategically

- What math tools could I use?
- How can I use those tools strategically?

Check the Answer

Make Sense of the Answer

- Is my answer reasonable?

Check for Precision

- Did I check my work?
- Is my answer clear?
- Did I construct a viable argument?
- Did I generalize correctly?

Some Ways to Represent Problems

- Draw a Picture
- Make a Bar Diagram
- Make a Table or Graph
- Write an Equation

Some Math Tools

- Objects
- Grid Paper
- Rulers
- Technology
- Paper and Pencil

Math Practices and Problem Solving Handbook

Problem Solving Recording Sheet

Name Carlos

Teaching Tool 1

Problem Solving Recording Sheet

Problem:
One of the Thorny Devil lizard's favorite foods is ants. It can eat up to 45 ants per minute. How long would it take it to eat 1,080 ants? Express your answer in seconds.

MAKE SENSE OF THE PROBLEM

Need to Find
How many seconds it takes the Thorny Devil to eat 1,080 ants

Given
The Thorny Devil lizard can eat 45 ants per minute.

PERSEVERE IN SOLVING THE PROBLEM

Some Ways to Represent Problems

- ☐ Draw a Picture
- ☑ Make a Bar Diagram
- ☐ Make a Table or Graph
- ☑ Write an Equation

Some Math Tools

- ☐ Objects
- ☐ Grid Paper
- ☐ Rulers
- ☐ Technology
- ☑ Paper and Pencil

Solution and Answer

1,080 ÷ 45

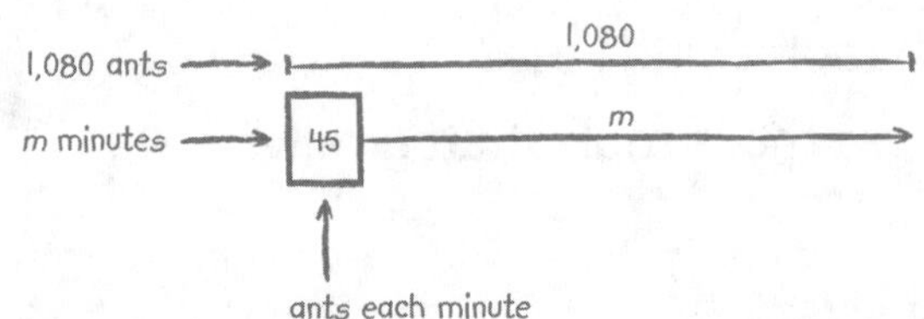

It takes 24 minutes for the lizard to eat 1,080 ants. There are 60 seconds in each minute.
24 × 60 = 1,440

Answer:
The Thorny Devil lizard would take 1,440 seconds to eat 1,080 ants.

CHECK THE ANSWER

Check
1,440 ÷ 60 = 24 minutes
24 × 45 = 1,080

My answer is correct.

T1

© Pearson Education, Inc. 6

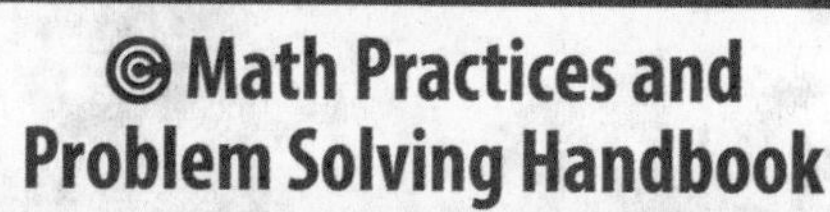

Math Practices and Problem Solving Handbook

Bar Diagrams

You can draw a **bar diagram** to show how the quantities in a problem are related. Then you can write an equation to solve the problem.

Add To

Draw this **bar diagram** for situations that involve *adding* to a quantity.

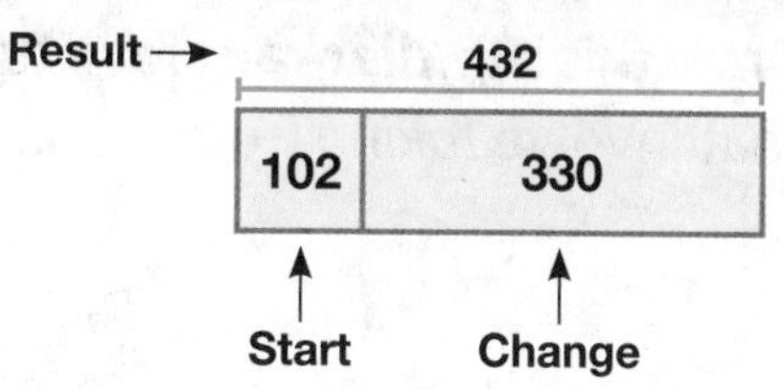

Result Unknown

Terence buys a bag of apples and a jar of peanut butter. How much did Terence spend in all?

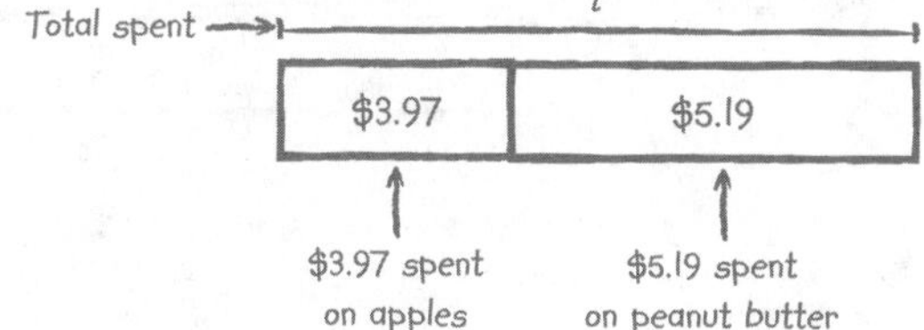

$\$3.97 + \$5.19 = t$

Terence spent $9.16 in all.

Start Unknown

Kari walked for a while on a trail in the park. Then she ran $1\frac{3}{8}$ miles to the end of the trail. How many miles did Kari walk?

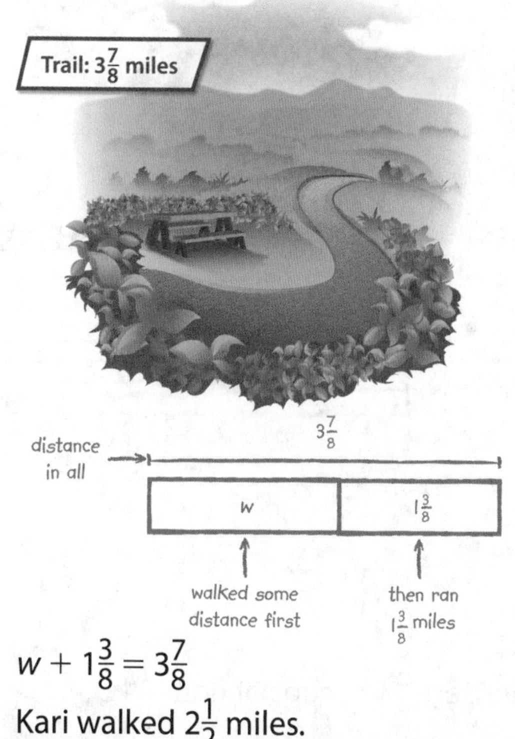

$w + 1\frac{3}{8} = 3\frac{7}{8}$

Kari walked $2\frac{1}{2}$ miles.

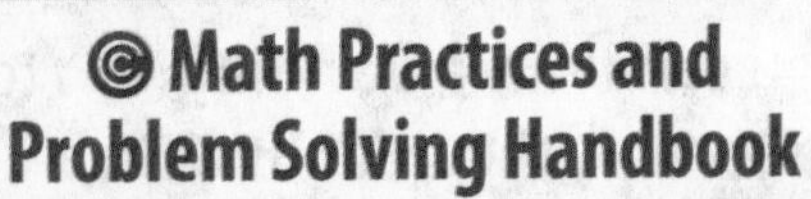

Bar Diagrams

You can use bar diagrams to make sense of addition and subtraction problems.

Take From

Draw this **bar diagram** for situations that involve *taking* from a quantity.

Start → 18,600

12,000	6,600
↑ Change	↑ Result

Result Unknown

Bristol had $15\frac{1}{4}$ cups of flour. She used some of the flour to make a pie. How many cups of flour are left?

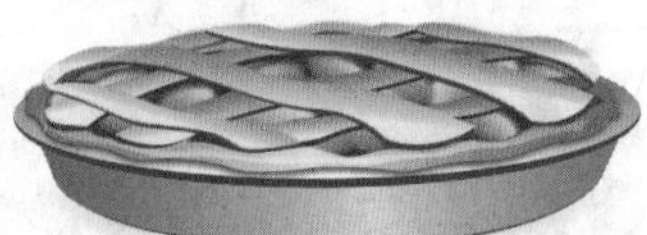

$3\frac{1}{3}$ cups of flour used

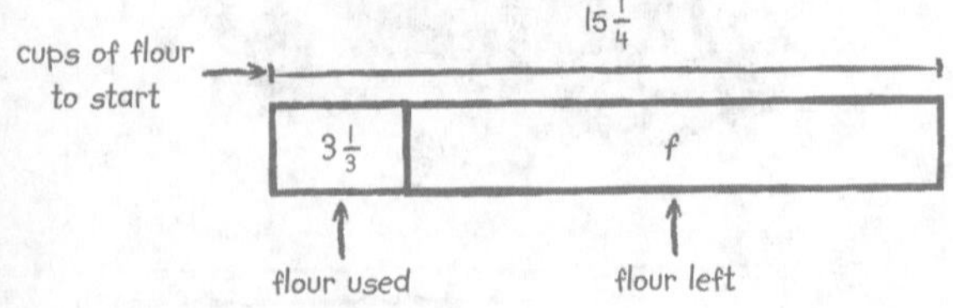

$15\frac{1}{4} - 3\frac{1}{3} = f$

There are $11\frac{11}{12}$ cups of flour left.

Start Unknown

Mr. Adkins used 2.4 gallons of gas doing errands on Saturday. Including the gas he has left, how many gallons of gas did he start with?

6.73 gallons of gas left

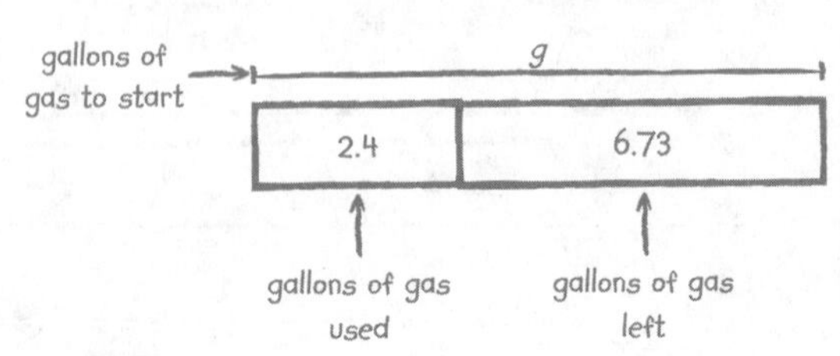

$g - 2.4 = 6.73$

Mr. Adkins started with 9.13 gallons of gas.

© Pearson Education, Inc. 6

The **bar diagrams** on this page can help you make sense of more addition and subtraction situations.

Put Together/Take Apart

Draw this **bar diagram** for situations that involve *putting together* or *taking apart* quantities.

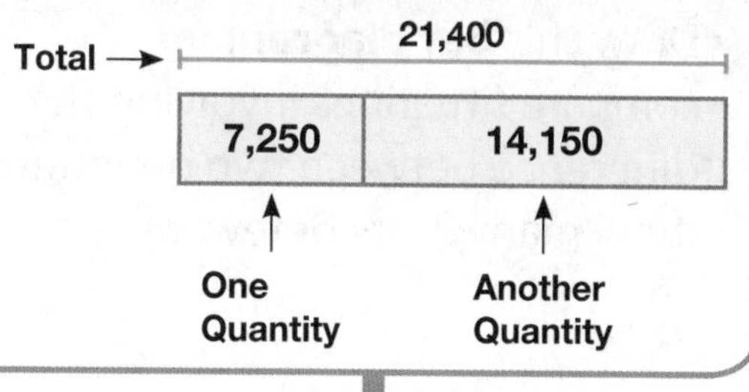

Whole Unknown

Joseph planted soybeans and corn in separate sections of his farm. How many acres did Joseph plant?

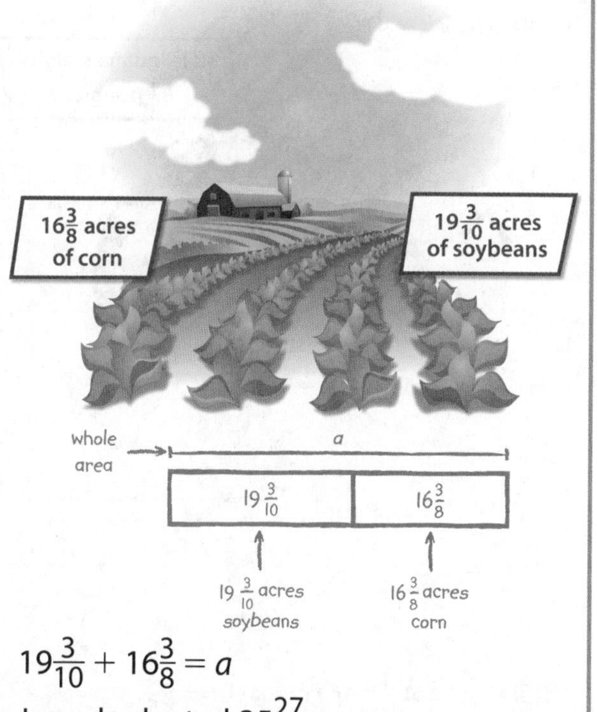

$19\frac{3}{10} + 16\frac{3}{8} = a$

Joseph planted $35\frac{27}{40}$ acres.

Part Unknown

Karyn's two beehives produced 64.9 pounds of honey. How much honey did the second hive produce?

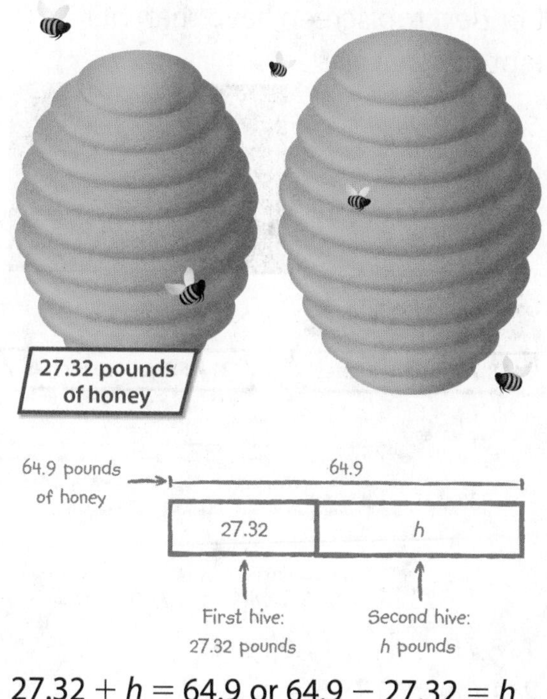

$27.32 + h = 64.9$ or $64.9 - 27.32 = h$

The second hive produced 37.58 pounds of honey.

Math Practices and Problem Solving Handbook

Bar Diagrams

Pictures help you understand. Don't trust key words in a problem.

Compare: Addition and Subtraction

Draw this **bar diagram** for *compare* situations involving the difference between two quantities (how many more or fewer.)

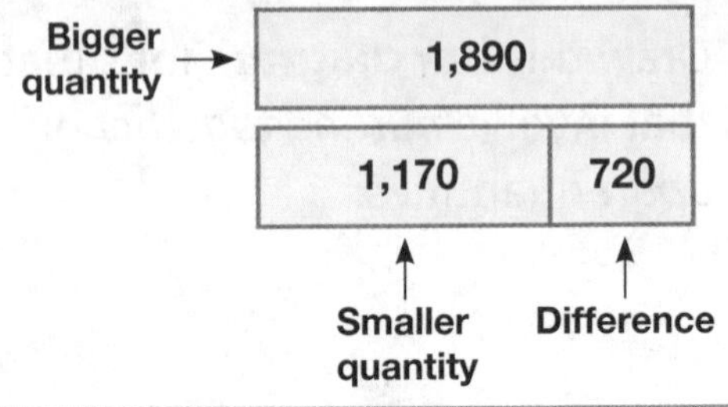

Difference Unknown

Sandi has a laptop computer and a desktop computer. How many more square inches of viewing space does her desktop screen have than her laptop screen?

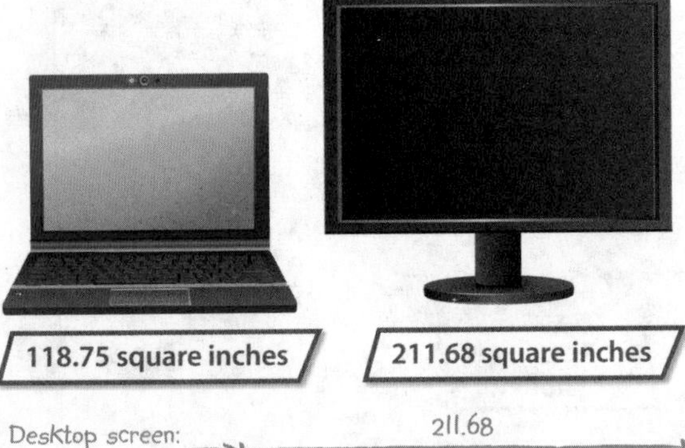

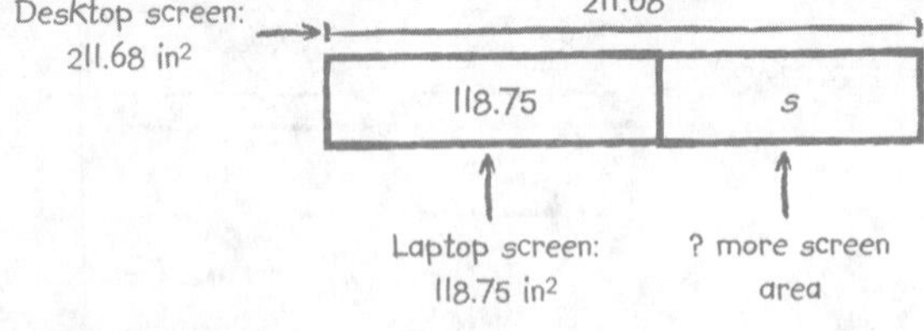

$118.75 + s = 211.68$ or
$211.68 - 118.75 = s$

The desktop screen has 92.93 in^2 more viewing space than the laptop screen.

Smaller Unknown

Jared has two green iguanas, a male and a female. The female weighs $4\frac{1}{10}$ pounds less than the male. How many pounds does the female iguana weigh?

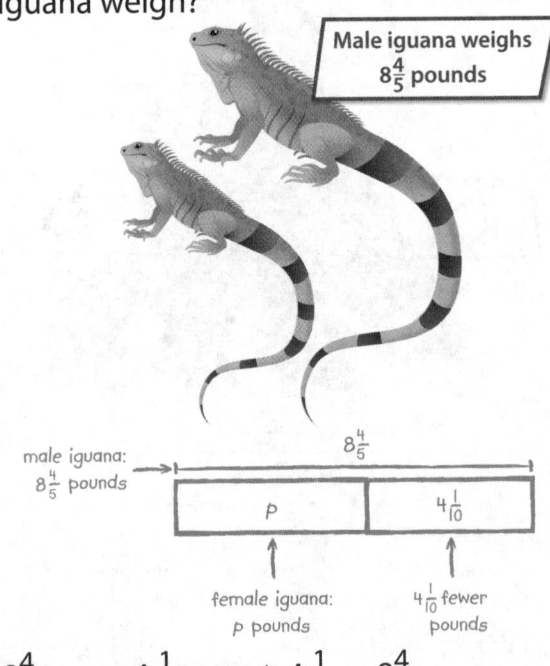

$8\frac{4}{5} - p = 4\frac{1}{10}$ or $p + 4\frac{1}{10} = 8\frac{4}{5}$

The female iguana weighs $4\frac{7}{10}$ pounds.

© Pearson Education, Inc. 6

The **bar diagrams** on this page can help you solve problems involving multiplication and division.

Equal Groups: Multiplication and Division

Draw this **bar diagram** for situations that involve *equal groups*.

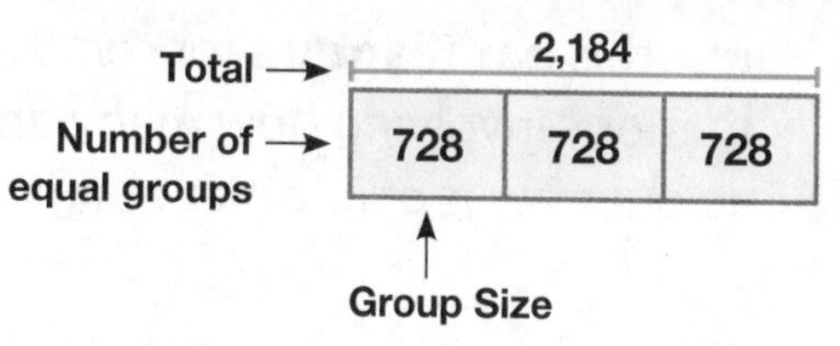

Number of Groups Unknown

Sierra's parents spent $390 on passes to the amusement park. How many passes did Sierra's parents purchase?

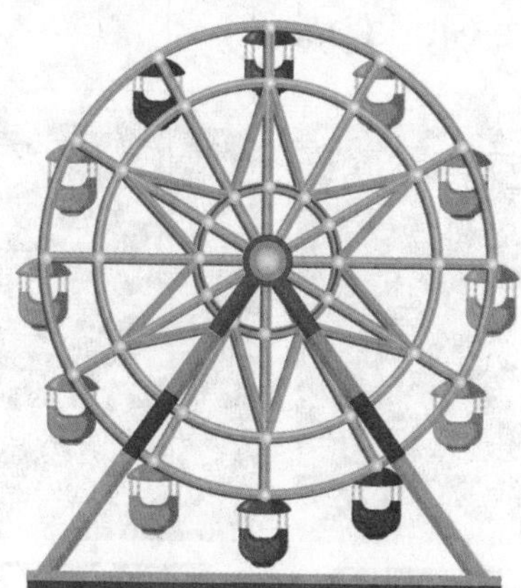

$65 for each pass

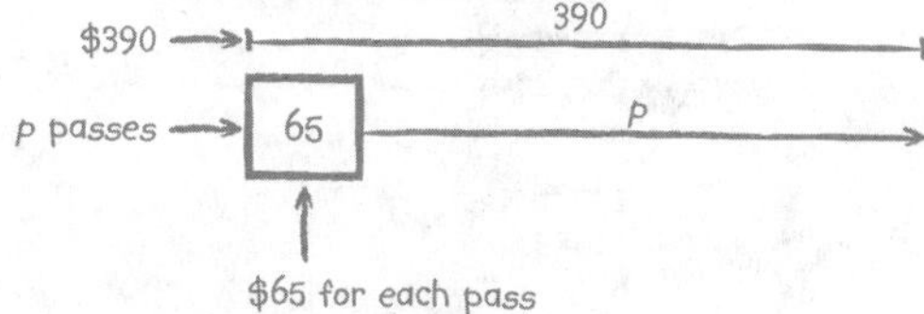

$p \times 65 = 390$ or $390 \div 65 = p$

Sierra's parents purchased 6 passes to the amusement park.

Group Size Unknown

With the money he has saved, Ben plans to go to 3 major league baseball games this summer. If he spends the same amount, how much can he spend at each game?

$133.47

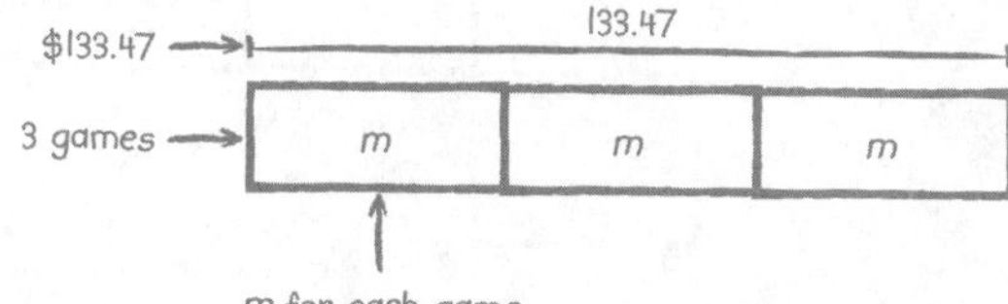

$3 \times m = 133.47$ or $133.47 \div 3 = m$

Ben can spend $44.49 at each game.

Math Practices and Problem Solving Handbook

Bar Diagrams

Bar diagrams can be used to show how quantities that are being compared are related.

Compare: Multiplication and Division

Draw this **bar diagram** for *compare* situations involving how many times one quantity is of another quantity.

	1,650			
Bigger quantity →	550	550	550	Multiplier: 3 times as many
Smaller quantity →	550			

Bigger Unknown

Marci's horse eats $2\frac{1}{4}$ bales of hay in a week. How many bales of hay do Craig's horses below eat in a week?

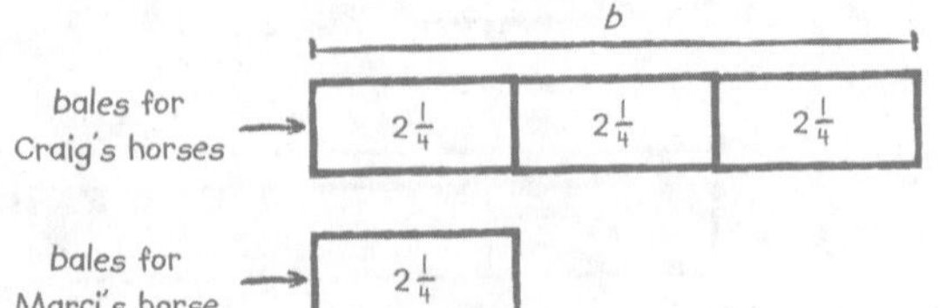

$2\frac{1}{4} \times 3 = b$ or $b \div 2\frac{1}{4} = 3$

Ben's horses eat $6\frac{3}{4}$ bales of hay in a week.

Multiplier Unknown

Tre bought a new book. Gloria bought the same book at a used bookstore. The price Tre paid is how many times the price Gloria paid?

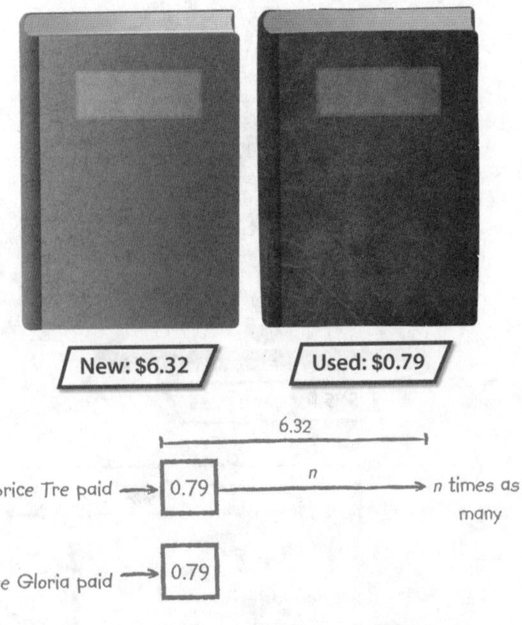

$0.79 \times n = 6.32$ or $6.32 \div 0.79 = n$

Tre paid 8 times as much as Gloria did for the book.

© Pearson Education, Inc. 6

Algebra: Understand Numerical and Algebraic Expressions

Essential Question: What are expressions and how can they be written and evaluated?

A food chain shows a path of energy moving through an ecosystem.

For example, plants capture the sun's energy and convert it to food energy. Then cows eat the plants.

So when I eat a hamburger, I am part of that food chain. Yum! Here's a project on food chains and food webs and algebraic expressions.

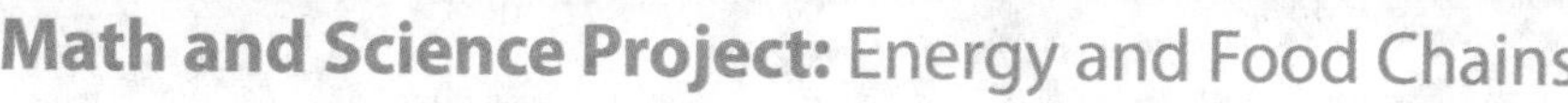

Math and Science Project: Energy and Food Chains

Do Research Use the Internet or other sources to learn more about how energy flows through food webs. Explain how you get energy, or calories, from sunlight. Find how much energy is lost at each level in a food chain. Show energy losses in a food chain that ends at your plate.

Journal: Write a Report Include what you found. Also in your report:

- Draw a food web from an ecosystem near your home.
- Label your food web with arrows to show how energy moves. Explain why the order is important.
- Write an algebraic expression to show the flow of energy through each part of a single food chain.

Name ______________________________

Review What You Know

Vocabulary

- formula
- order of operations
- numerical expression
- variable

Choose the best term from the box. Write it on the blank.

1. A(n) __________ is a rule that uses symbols to relate two or more quantities.
2. A(n) __________ is a mathematical phrase that includes numbers and at least one operation.
3. A quantity that is unknown may be represented by a(n) __________.

Numerical Expressions

Evaluate each numerical expression.

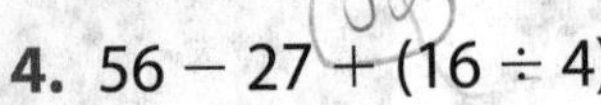
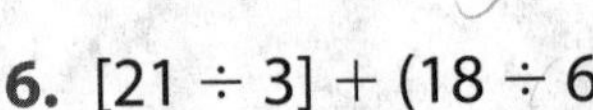

4. $56 - 27 + (16 \div 4)$
5. $94 - (5 \times 6) \div 6 \times 11$
6. $[21 \div 3] + (18 \div 6)$

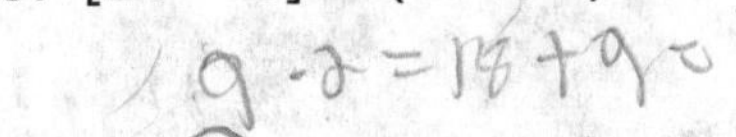

7. $2 \times 36 - (12 + 7)$
8. $12 \div (2 + 1) \times 15 \div 3$
9. $15 - (2 \times 3) \times 2 + 9$

Perimeter and Area

Use the formulas $P = 2\ell + 2w$ and $A = \ell w$, where ℓ is the length and w is the width, to find the perimeter, P, and the area, A, of each figure.

10. 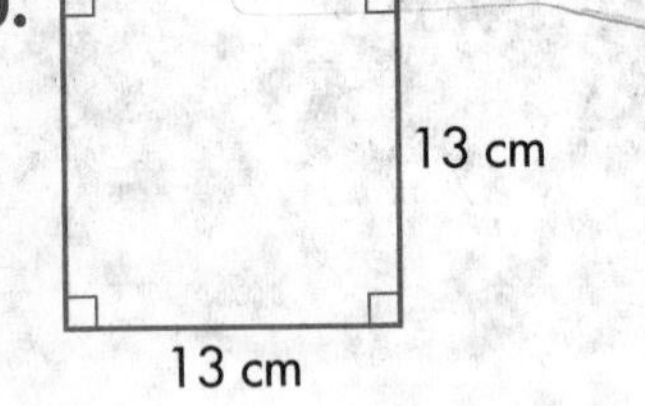

$P =$ __________

$A =$ __________

11. 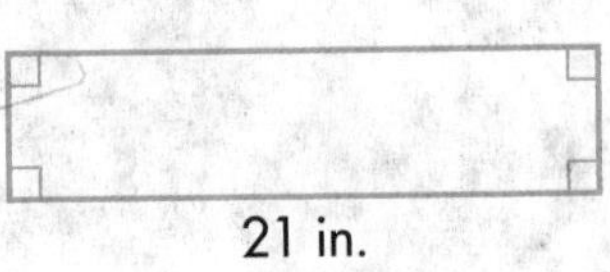

$P =$ __________

$A =$ __________

12. 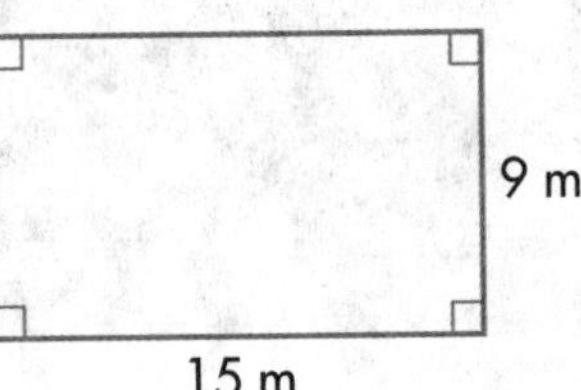

$P =$ __________

$A =$ __________

Operations and Expressions

13. How are the terms difference, sum, quotient, and product alike?

14. What does it mean to evaluate an expression?

© Pearson Education, Inc. 6

Name ______________________________________

Solve

Lesson 1-1
Exponents

I can …
write and evaluate numbers with exponents.

Content Standard 6.EE.A.1
Mathematical Practices MP.2, MP.3, MP.4, MP.7, MP.8

Solve & Share Fold a sheet of paper in half. The number of sections you see when it is unfolded is recorded in the chart. Continue folding the paper in half 4 more times. Record the number of sections each time. Describe any patterns you see in the table.

Look for relationships in the repeated multiplications.

Number of Folds	Number of Sections	Number of 2s
1	2	1
2	2 × 2 = 4	2
3	2 · 4 = 8	4
4	2 · 8 = 16	8
5	2 · 16 = 32	16

Look Back! **MP.7 Use Structure** How many sections will there be after 6 folds? 7 folds?

6 = 64
7 = 122

How Can You Write a Number Using Exponents?

A

The expression $2 \times 2 \times 2$ represents the number of cells after 1 hour if there is 1 cell at the start. How can you write this expression using exponents? How many cells will there be after 1 hour?

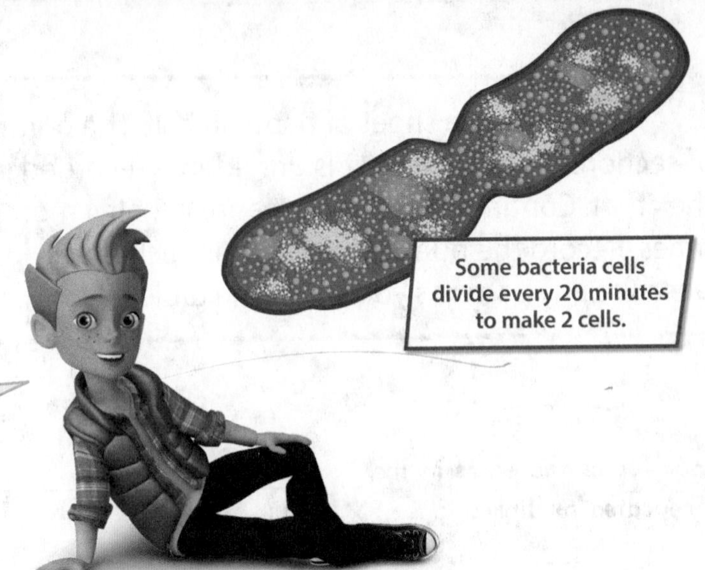

Some bacteria cells divide every 20 minutes to make 2 cells.
An exponent is a way to write a repeated multiplication expression.

B You can use an exponent to write repeated multiplication of a number.

The number that is repeatedly multiplied is the base. The exponent tells how many times the base is used as a factor.

$$\underbrace{2 \times 2 \times 2}_{\text{3 factors of 2}} = \underbrace{2^3}_{\text{power}}$$

(base → 2; exponent → 3)

A number that can be written using exponents is called a power.

C You can use repeated multiplication to evaluate, or find the value of a power.

Multiply the first two factors, 2 × 2 = 4. Then multiply that product by the last factor, 4 × 2 = 8.

$2^3 = 2 \times 2 \times 2 = 8$

There will be 8 cells after 1 hour.

Convince Me! ◎ **MP.4 Model with Math** Write an expression using repeated multiplication to show how many cells there would be after 2 hours. Then write the expression using an exponent. Evaluate your expression.

© Pearson Education, Inc. 6

Name ______

Practice Buddy Tools Assessment

Another Example

How can you evaluate 2^0?

Make a table and look for a pattern.

Power	2^0	2^1	2^2	2^3	2^4
Value	1	2	4	8	16

Each value equals the previous value multiplied by 2.

1 $\times 2 = 2$, so the value of 2^0 is 1.

You can generalize. Any non-zero number raised to an exponent of zero has a value of 1.

Guided Practice*

Do You Understand?

1. **MP.7 Look for Relationships** How many times is 4 used as a factor in the expression 4^5? Write the numerical expression as repeated multiplication.

5 times, 4·4·4·4·4

2. **MP.8 Generalize** Write any power, then evaluate the power.

$3^2 = 9$

$3 \cdot 3 = 9$

Do You Know How?

3. Write 81 as a repeated multiplication of 3s. Then write it as a power.

81·81·81
81^3

4. How would you write $\left(\frac{1}{2}\right)^3$ as repeated multiplication?

$\frac{1}{2} \cdot \frac{1}{2} \cdot \frac{1}{2}$

Parentheses are used when a fraction is raised to an exponent.

Independent Practice

In **5–7**, write the exponent for each expression.

5. $9 \times 9 \times 9 \times 9$ __4__

6. 1.2^9 __9__

7. $\frac{1}{6} \times \frac{1}{6} \times \frac{1}{6}$ __3__

In **8–10**, evaluate each power.

8. $0.6^2 =$ __.36__

9. $\left(\frac{1}{4}\right)^2 =$ __.0625__

10. $2^7 =$ __128__

*For another example, see Set A on page 69.

Math Practices and Problem Solving

11. **Number Sense** Explain why the expressions 10^0, 1^4, and 1×1.0^0 have the same value.

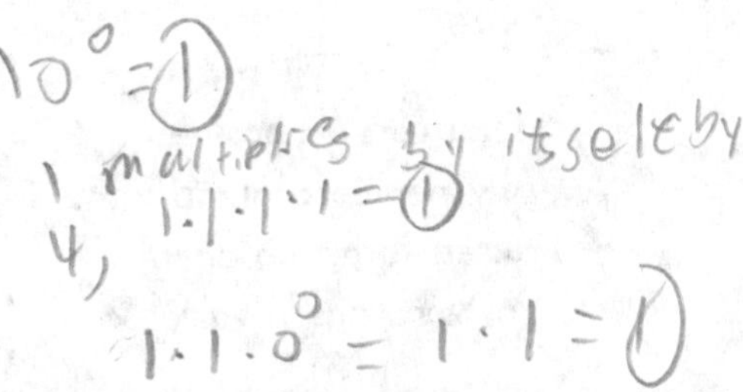

12. **MP.3 Construct Arguments** The same digits are used for the expressions 2^5 and 5^2. Explain how to compare the value of each expression.

13. **MP.3 Critique Reasoning** Kristen was asked to write each of the numbers in the expression $80{,}000 \times 25$ using exponents. Her response was $(8 \times 10^3) \times 5^2$. Was her response correct? Explain how you know.

14. **Algebra** Solve the equation $0.3^3 = n$.

15. Consider the equation $1{,}000{,}000 = 10^6$. Why is the number 10 used as the base to write 10^6?

16. **Higher Order Thinking** Zach invested \$50 and tripled his money in two years. Kayla also invested \$50, and after two years the amount was equal to 50 to the third power. Who had more money after two years? Explain.

Common Core Assessment

17. Which expression is **NOT** equal to 1,024?

Ⓐ 2^{10}

Ⓑ $5 \times 5 \times 5 \times 5$

Ⓒ 4^5

Ⓓ $4 \times 4 \times 4 \times 4 \times 4$

18. Which expression is equal to $\frac{1}{36}$?

Ⓐ $\frac{1}{3} \times \frac{1}{6}$

Ⓑ $\frac{1}{4} \times \left(\frac{1}{3}\right)^3$

Ⓒ $\left(\frac{1}{2}\right)^2 \times \left(\frac{1}{3}\right)^2$

Ⓓ $\frac{1}{2} \times \frac{1}{3} \times \frac{1}{3} \times \frac{1}{3}$

© Pearson Education, Inc. 6

Name ______________________

Homework & Practice 1-1
Exponents

Another Look!

Write $5 \times 5 \times 5 \times 5$ using an exponent. Then evaluate the expression.

$5 \times 5 \times 5 \times 5 = 5^4$ (exponent: 4; base: 5; power: 5^4)

Evaluate 5^4 using repeated multiplication.

$5^4 = 5 \times 5 \times 5 \times 5 = 625$

A calculator can be a useful tool to help you evaluate a power using repeated multiplication.

Press: 5 × 5 × 5 × 5 ENTER =

Display: 625

In **1–3**, write the base number for each expression.

1. 5^{12} ____ **2.** 1.2^2 ____ **3.** $\left(\frac{1}{3}\right)^4$ ____

In **4–6**, write the exponent for each expression.

4. $7 \times 7 \times 7 \times 7$ ____ **5.** $\left(\frac{2}{3}\right)^8$ ____ **6.** $0.5 \times 0.5 \times 0.5$ ____

In **7–12**, evaluate each expression.

7. $9^3 =$ ____ **8.** $\left(\frac{1}{4}\right)^3 =$ ____

9. $3^5 =$ ____ **10.** $\left(\frac{1}{8}\right)^3$ ____

11. $99^0 =$ ____ **12.** $1.5^2 =$ ____

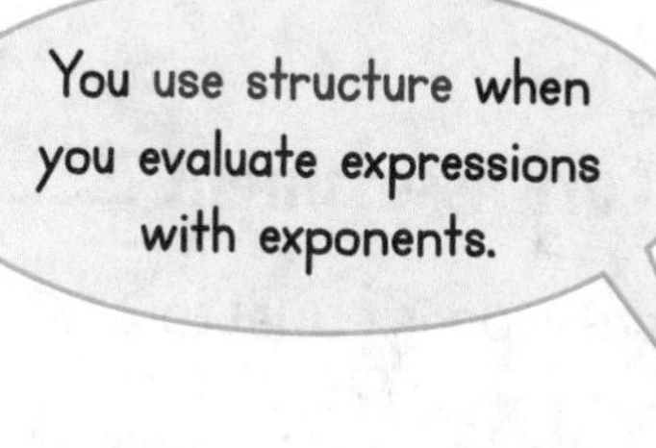

You use structure when you evaluate expressions with exponents.

13. © **MP.3 Construct Arguments** Is 0.3^4 equal to 0.9^2? Explain.

14. **Number Sense** What are two ways you can represent the number 27 using the number 3?

15. © **MP.2 Reasoning** What is the value of 1^{102}? What is the value of any power of 1? Justify your answer.

16. Humans can distinguish up to 18,400,000 individual dots called pixels on a typical computer display. Can a human distinguish pixels on a same-sized HDTV with 2×10^6 pixels? Explain.

17. **Higher Order Thinking** In case of an emergency, the school has a calling list so everyone is called in the least amount of time. Each of the first 3 people on the list calls another 3 people on the list. Then, each of the people in the second group calls another 3 people on the list, and so on. The 5th group of people will make 243 calls. Is this statement accurate? Explain.

18. © **MP.7 Use Structure** An investment of $1 is put in an account. Every 8 years, the money doubles. No additional money was added to the account. Would the expression $1 \times 2 \times 2 \times 2 \times 2 \times 2 \times 2$ correctly represent how much was in the investment account after 48 years? Explain.

© Common Core Assessment

19. Which expression is equal to 343?

Ⓐ 8^3

Ⓑ $6 \times 6 \times 6$

Ⓒ 7^3

Ⓓ $7 \times 7 \times 7 \times 7$

20. Which expression is **NOT** equal to 0.125?

Ⓐ 0.5^3

Ⓑ 0.5×3

Ⓒ $0.5 \times 0.5 \times 0.5$

Ⓓ 0.5×0.5^2

© Pearson Education, Inc. 6

Name ______________________

Solve

Lesson 1-2
Evaluate Numerical Expressions

I can ...
use the order of operations to evaluate numerical expressions with decimals and fractions.

Content Standards 6.EE.A.1, 6.EE.A.3
Mathematical Practices MP.1, MP.3, MP.4, MP.6, MP.7

Solve & Share

An airline company charges additional fees for bags that are over weight and size limits. For one flight, fees were charged for a total of 50 bags over the weight limit and 6 over-sized bags. Write and evaluate an expression to find the total amount in fees collected for that flight.

Remember to look for relationships. Use the order of operations to evaluate numerical expressions.

Overweight Bags	\$49 per bag
Oversized Bags	\$75 per bag

Look Back! **MP.4 Model with Math** Tamara was charged for two bags that were over the weight limit and another bag that was over the size limit. Write and evaluate a numerical expression to find how much Tamara was charged for her bags.

How Do You Evaluate Expressions?

A

Some expressions look difficult because they include parentheses and brackets. You can think of brackets as "outside" parentheses.

Evaluate the expression
$\frac{1}{2} \times 4^2 - [2 + (3.6 \div 0.9)]$.

Start with the inside parentheses first. Then do the rest of the calculations within the brackets.

Order of Operations

1. Evaluate parentheses and brackets from inside out.
2. Evaluate powers.
3. Multiply and divide from left to right.
4. Add and subtract from left to right.

B **What You Write**

Evaluate inside the parentheses.

$$\frac{1}{2} \times 4^2 - [2 + (3.6 \div 0.9)]$$

Evaluate inside the brackets.

$$\frac{1}{2} \times 4^2 - [2 + 4]$$

Evaluate the power.

$$\frac{1}{2} \times 4^2 - 6$$

Multiply or divide from left to right.

$$\frac{1}{2} \times \frac{16}{1} - 6$$

Add or subtract from left to right.

$$8 - 6$$

$$2$$

C **How to Use a Calculator**

3.6 ÷ 0.9 ENTER = Display: 4.

2 + 4 ENTER = Display: 6.

4 × 4 ENTER = Display: 16.

16 ÷ 2 ENTER = Display: 8.

8 − 6 ENTER = Display: 2.

Convince Me! **MP.6 Be Precise** Evaluate the expression $\frac{1}{8}(6^3 + [48 \div 6]) - 20$.

© Pearson Education, Inc. 6

Name ______

Guided Practice*

Practice Buddy Tools Assessment

Do You Understand?

1. MP.1 Make Sense and Persevere
Insert parentheses to make this number sentence true.

$80 \div 8 \times 5 + 4 = 90$

2. In the expression $(21 - 3) \times (7 + 2) \div (12 - 4)$, what operation should you perform last? Why?

Do You Know How?

In **3–6**, evaluate each expression.

3. $5^2 + (6.7 - 3.1)$

4. $(8.2 + 5.3) \div 5$

5. $[(7.3 + 3.6) - 4.7] + 1.8 - 2^2$

6. $\left[(11.2 + 8.8) \times \frac{1}{4}\right] - 1.8$

Independent Practice

Leveled Practice In **7–9**, use the order of operations to evaluate.

7. $4^2 - (3.1 + 6.4) + 4.5$

$4^2 -$ ___ $+ 4.5$

___ $-$ ___ $+ 4.5$

___ $+ 4.5$

___

8. $(8.7 + 3.3) \times \left(\frac{1}{2}\right)^2$

___ $\times \left(\frac{1}{2}\right)^2$

___ $\times$ ___

___

9. $157.8 - (3^2 + 6) \times 3$

$157.8 - ($___ $+ 6) \times 3$

$157.8 -$ ___ $\times 3$

$157.8 -$ ___

___

Be precise and record your work carefully when you evaluate numerical expressions.

In **10–12**, evaluate each expression.

10. $4.3 + (8.4 - 5.1)$

11. $4^3 - \left[(9.9 \div 3.3) \times \frac{1}{3}\right]$

12. $[2^3 \times (152 \div 8)] - 52$

*For another example, see Set B on page 69.

Math Practices and Problem Solving

13. **MP.7 Use Structure** How do you know which part of the numerical expression to evaluate first? Explain.
$(26 + 2.5) - [(8.3 \times 3) + (1^3 - 0.25)]$

14. **Math and Science** In an ecosystem, some animals get energy by eating plants. An elk can eat 20 pounds of plants each day. Write and evaluate an expression to find how many pounds of plants a herd of 18 elk can eat in one week.

15. **MP.4 Model with Math** Lillian bought four hairbrushes at \$3.99 each. She had a coupon for \$1 off. Her mom paid for half of the remaining cost. Write and evaluate a numerical expression to find how much Lillian paid toward the purchase of the hairbrushes.

16. **Higher Order Thinking** Frederick evaluates the numerical expression $[(53.7 + 37.2) - (3^3 + 3.8)] - 8.6$. He records the answer as 51.5. Lana evaluates the numerical expression $53.7 + 37.2 - 3^3 + 3.8 - 8.6$. She records the answer as 59.1. The expressions have the same numbers and operations. Explain how Frederick and Lana can both be correct.

Common Core Assessment

17. Draw lines to match each number on the right to the equivalent numerical expression on the left.

Expression	Number
$12.3 \times [(2 \times 1.7) + 6.6] - 2^3$	21
$2^4 \div [(3.2 \times 0.8) + 1.44]$	12
$6.2 + \left(3 \times \frac{1}{3} + 4.8\right)$	115
$[4 \times (9.6 \div 3)] + 8.2$	4

© Pearson Education, Inc. 6

Name ______________________

Help | Practice Buddy | Tools | Games

Homework & Practice 1-2

Evaluate Numerical Expressions

Another Look!

Use the order of operations to evaluate the expression $2.3^2 + [(9 \times 4) + 9] \times \left(\frac{1}{3}\right)^2$.

Order of operations is a set of rules used to evaluate expressions when there is more than one operation.

First, evaluate inside the parentheses. $2.3^2 + [(9 \times 4) + 9] \times \left(\frac{1}{3}\right)^2$ Evaluate inside any other grouping symbols, such as brackets. $2.3^2 + [36 + 9] \times \left(\frac{1}{3}\right)^2$	Then, evaluate any powers. $2.3^2 + 45 \times \left(\frac{1}{3}\right)^2$	Next, multiply or divide from left to right. $5.29 + 45 \times \frac{1}{9}$	Finally, add or subtract from left to right. $5.29 + 5$ The value of the numerical expression is 10.29.

In **1–3**, use the order of operations to evaluate.

1. $0.2^2 \div [7.9 - (4.1 + 1.8)]$

$0.2^2 \div [7.9 - \_\_\_\_]$

$0.2^2 \div \_\_\_\_$

$\_\_\_\_ \div \_\_\_\_$

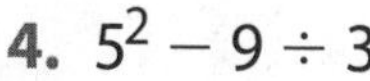

2. $(14.7 + 9.3) \times \left(\frac{1}{2}\right)^2$

$\_\_\_\_ \times \left(\frac{1}{2}\right)^2$

$\_\_\_\_ \times \_\_\_\_$

$\_\_\_\_$

3. $12.3 + (6^2 - 11.8) - 1$

$12.3 + (\_\_\_\_ - 11.8) - 1$

$12.3 + \_\_\_\_ - 1$

$\_\_\_\_ - 1$

$\_\_\_\_$

When expressions do not have grouping symbols, what is the first operation you evaluate?

In **4–12**, evaluate each expression.

4. $5^2 - 9 \div 3$

5. $8 + 6 - 2 \times 2 - 3^2$

6. $4^2 \div [(3.2 \times 2) + 1.6]$

7. $8 + (6 - 2) \times 2 - 3^2$

8. $[(12 \times 2^2) - (18.4 + 0.6)] + 3^2$

9. $\left[(19 + 1^5) \div \frac{1}{2}\right] + 5$

10. $4 \times (5 + 5) \div 20 + 6^2$

11. $5^2 - [(0.2 \times 8) + 0.4] \times \frac{1}{2}$

12. $36 \div 9 + 4 \times 5 - 3$

13. **MP.3 Critique Reasoning** Ivy's basketball team scored 38 points in the first game of the season. The next two games they scored a total of 77 points. For every point scored, \$0.50 is put in a jar to use for a party after the season. Ivy says you can use the expression $38 + 77 \times 0.5$ to find how much money is in the jar after the third game. Is she correct? Explain.

14. **Higher Order Thinking** A printing error in a math book removed the brackets and parentheses from a numerical expression. Rewrite the expression $3^2 + 7 \times 4 + 5$ with parentheses so that it is equivalent to 69.

15. Jessica bought a new computer for \$800. She put \$120 down and got a student discount of \$50. Her mother gave her $\frac{1}{2}$ of the balance for her birthday. Use the numerical expression to find the amount Jessica still owes for the computer.

$[800 - (120 + 50)] \div 2$

16. Luke needs a new fence around his garden, but the gate across the narrow end of the garden will not be replaced. Write and evaluate a numerical expression to find how many feet of fencing Luke needs.

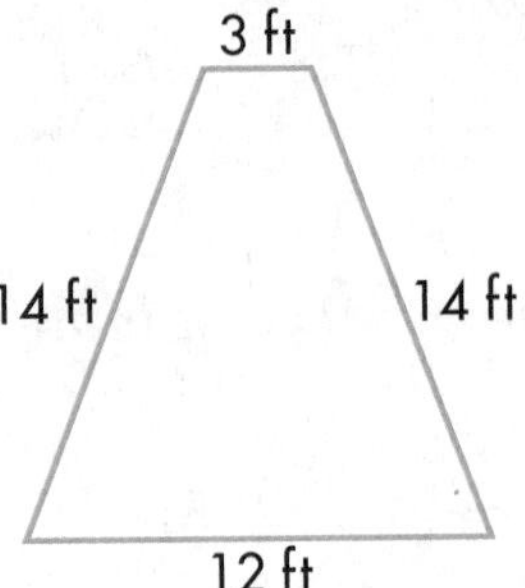

Common Core Assessment

17. Draw lines to match each number on the right to the equivalent expression on the left.

Expression	Number
$102.4 - [(2^3 \times 3) + 13.8] \div 7$	5
$\frac{1}{2} \times \left[(3^3 - 17) \div \frac{1}{6}\right] + 20$	25
$4 + [(1^6 \times 18) + 3]$	97
$[(7.21 \times 2) + 0.58] \div 3$	50

© Pearson Education, Inc. 6

Name ______________________________

Lesson 1-3
Use Variables to Write Expressions

I can ...
use variables to write algebraic expressions.

Content Standards 6.EE.A.2a, 6.EE.B.6
Mathematical Practices MP.1, MP.2, MP.4, MP.6, MP.7, MP.8

Solve & Share

The table shows the number of games the Hornets won and the number of games the Lynx won. Explain how you would complete the table for the Lynx if the Hornets won *n* number of games.

Look for a relationship and generalize the pattern for any number.

DATA

Games Won

Hornets	Lynx
3	5
6	8
9	11
n	

Look Back! MP.2 Reasoning Suppose the Lynx won g games. What mathematical expression could you write to show how many games the Hornets won?

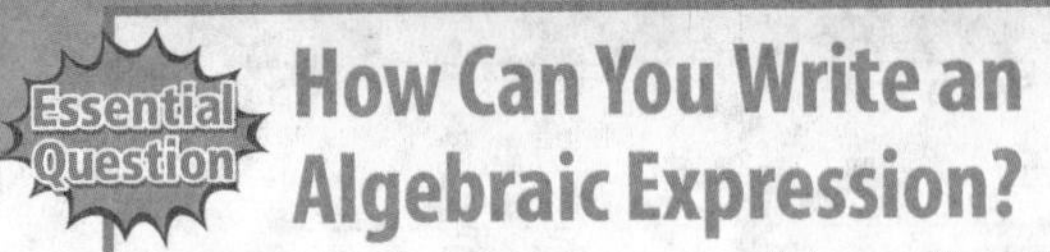

How Can You Write an Algebraic Expression?

A

Darius bought some comic books. How can you write an algebraic expression to represent the total cost of the comic books?

Use a variable to write an algebraic expression. A variable is a letter or symbol that represents an unknown quantity.

B Let $n =$ the number of comic books.

Each comic book costs $4.

Number of Comic Books	Total Cost($)
1	4×1
2	4×2
3	4×3
4	4×4
⋮	
n	$4 \times n$

C An algebraic expression is a type of math expression that has at least one variable and at least one operation.

The total cost of n comic books can be represented by the algebraic expression $4 \times n$.

D You can also use a solid dot (•), parentheses, or no symbol at all to write the expression $4 \times n$.

$4 \cdot n$ or $4(n)$ or $4n$

$4 \times n$, $4 \cdot n$, $4(n)$, or $4n$ are all ways to write the same expression.

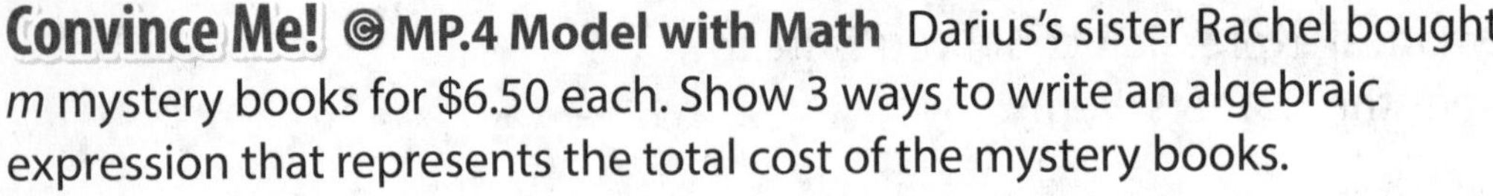

Convince Me! ◎ **MP.4 Model with Math** Darius's sister Rachel bought m mystery books for $6.50 each. Show 3 ways to write an algebraic expression that represents the total cost of the mystery books.

© Pearson Education, Inc. 6

Name ______________________________

Another Example

The table shows algebraic expressions that represent given situations.

Word Phrase	Operation	Algebraic Expression
five minutes more than time t	addition	$t + 5$
ten erasers decreased by a number n	subtraction	$10 - n$
six times a width w	multiplication	$6w$ or $6 \cdot w$ or $6(w)$
n nectarines divided by three	division	$n \div 3$ or $\frac{n}{3}$
4 times the quantity x plus 8	multiplication and addition	$4(x + 8)$

Guided Practice*

Do You Understand?

1. **MP.6 Be Precise** Identify the variable and the operation in the algebraic expression $\frac{6}{x}$.

2. **Vocabulary** Explain why $15 + \frac{1}{2}n$ is an algebraic expression.

Do You Know How?

In **3–5**, write an algebraic expression for each situation.

3. five less than y

4. four more than twice x

5. six times the quantity two x plus three y

Independent Practice

In **6–11**, write an algebraic expression for each situation.

6. 12 times a number g

7. the difference of a number m and 18

8. p pennies added to 22 pennies

9. 5 less than 3 times a number z

10. 22 divided by a number s

11. $12\frac{3}{4}$ less than the product of 7 and a number x

*For another example, see Set C on page 69.

Math Practices and Problem Solving

12. A float in the Tournament of Roses parade may use as many flowers as a florist sells in 6 years. If f is the number of flowers a florist sells in 1 year, write an algebraic expression to represent the number of flowers a float in the parade may use.

13. MP.1 Make Sense and Persevere A group of cows produced the same number of gallons, g, of milk each day for a week. Sara collected the milk for six days. Write an expression to show the number of gallons Sara did **NOT** collect.

14. Yuri walked p poodles and b bulldogs on Monday. He walked the same number of poodles and bulldogs each day Tuesday through Friday as he did on Monday. Write an algebraic expression to represent how many total dogs were walked in this 5-day period.

15. Higher Order Thinking Some students equally share 2 baskets of apples. Each basket has 12 apples. Write an algebraic expression to represent this situation. Then explain how you chose which variable and operations to use.

16. MP.4 Model with Math The figure is a regular octagon with side length s. Write two algebraic expressions that use different operations to represent the perimeter of the figure.

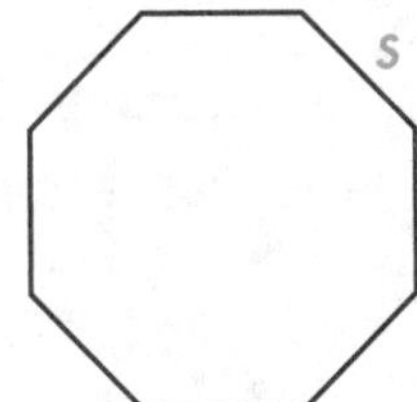

Common Core Assessment

17. Which algebraic expression could **NOT** represent the phrase below?

Four more than the product 3 times the number of c cats

Ⓐ $4 + 3c$

Ⓑ $(4 + 3)c$

Ⓒ $3 \cdot c + 4$

Ⓓ $(3 \times c) + 4$

18. Which phrase could be best represented by the algebraic expression $\frac{w}{4} - 4$?

Ⓐ the quotient of four and a number w

Ⓑ the difference between a number w and 4

Ⓒ four less than the quotient of w divided by 4

Ⓓ four less than a number w

© Pearson Education, Inc. 6

Name ______________________________

Homework & Practice 1-3

Use Variables to Write Expressions

Another Look!

A variable, written as a letter, represents a quantity that can change. You can use a variable to write an algebraic expression that has at least one operation.

Here are some word phrases and their corresponding algebraic expressions.

How can an algebraic expression represent a given situation?

Word Phrase	Variable	Operation	Algebraic Expression
ten **more than** a number b	b	Addition	$b + 10$
the **sum** of 8 and a number c	c		$8 + c$
five **less than** a number d	d	Subtraction	$d - 5$
15 **decreased by** a number e	e		$15 - e$
the **product** of 8 and a number f	f	Multiplication	$8f$
19 **times** a number g	g		$19g$
the quotient of a number h **divided by** 2	h	Division	$\frac{h}{2}$
50 **divided by** a number i	i		$50 \div i$

In **1–10**, write an algebraic expression for each situation.

Remember, an algebraic expression includes at least one variable and at least one operation.

1. 6 more than a number c

2. 2.5 less than a number d

3. 50 divided by a number f

4. twice a number n

5. 12 fewer than h hats

6. 4 times the sum of x and $\frac{1}{2}$

7. 6 less than the quotient of z divided by 3

8. Twice a number k plus the quantity s minus 2

9. 8 more than s stripes

10. 5 times the quantity m divided by 2

In **11–14**, use the chart at the right.

11. A pet store is having a pet fish sale. Lenny bought p platies and l loaches. Write an algebraic expression to represent the total cost of the fish.

12. **MP.4 Model with Math** Mr. Bolden bought g guppies and paid with a \$20 bill. Write an algebraic expression to represent how much change Mr. Bolden got back.

Pet Fish Sale

Fish	Price
Guppy	\$3
Loach	\$4
Platy	\$2
Tetra	\$5

13. **MP.1 Make Sense and Persevere** Ms. Wilson bought two bags of pet fish for her twin nieces. Each bag has g guppies and one tetra. She also bought one box of fish food that cost d dollars. Write an algebraic expression to represent how much she paid in all.

14. In 3 days the pet store sold 27 guppies. The store sold twice as many platies as guppies. Evaluate the expression below to find the dollar amount of sales of guppies and platies.

$27 \cdot 3 + (2 \cdot 27) \cdot 2$

15. **Higher Order Thinking** Describe a situation that can be represented by the algebraic expression $6b + w$.

Be sure to tell what quantities are represented by the variables, b and w.

Common Core Assessment

16. Which algebraic expression could represent the phrase below?

Six pencils less than p packs of pencils that have 5 pencils in each pack

Ⓐ $5p - 6$

Ⓑ $p - 6$

Ⓒ $5 \cdot (p - 6)$

Ⓓ $6 - 5p$

17. Which of the following is the variable in the algebraic expression $(6.5 + 2.2y) \div 3$?

Ⓐ 6.5

Ⓑ 2.2

Ⓒ y

Ⓓ 3

© Pearson Education, Inc. 6

Name ______________________________ Solve

Solve & Share

Look at the mathematical expression on the sign below. Use math language to write at least three statements that describe the expression or parts of the expression.

Lesson 1-4

Identify Parts of an Expression

I can ...
use specific math words to describe parts of mathematical expressions.

Content Standard 6.EE.A.2b
Mathematical Practices MP.1, MP.3, MP.4, MP.6

Remember to be precise. You already know the meanings of many math words.

Look Back! **MP.6 Be Precise** In the expression above, how are $4t$ and $(3 \div 2)$ alike and how are they different?

How Can You Describe the Parts of an Expression?

A

Each part of an expression that is separated by a plus or a minus sign is called a term.
How many terms does the expression have?
Describe the parts of the expression.

$$12r + \frac{r}{2} - 19$$

Remember that a fraction bar also means divide.

B

$12r + \frac{r}{2} - 19$ has three terms.

$12r + \frac{r}{2} - 19$ — terms

The terms are $12r$, $\frac{r}{2}$, and 19.

Because the expression includes a variable, r, it is an algebraic expression.

C

The first term, $12r$, is a product of two factors.

product: $12r$ — factors

A coefficient is the number that is multiplied by a variable.

12 is the coefficient of r.

$12r$ — coefficient

D

The second term, $\frac{r}{2}$, is written as a fraction and represents the quotient of r divided by 2.

quotient — $\frac{r}{2}$ — r: dividend, 2: divisor

The third term, 19, is a constant numerical value.

Convince Me! **MP.6 Be Precise** How many terms does the expression $r \div 9 + 5.5$ have? Explain.

© Pearson Education, Inc. 6

Name ______________________

Practice Buddy Tools Assessment

Guided Practice*

Do You Understand?

1. MP.6 Be Precise Could you describe the expression $2(3 + 4)$ as a product of two factors? Explain.

2. Which part of the expression $2(3 + 4)$ is the sum of two terms? Explain.

Do You Know How?

In **3** and **4**, use the expression $\frac{w}{4} + 12.5 - 7z$.

3. How many terms does the expression have?

4. Which part of the expression is a product of two factors? Describe its parts.

Independent Practice

Leveled Practice In **5–8**, tell how many terms each expression has.

5. $5 - g$

6. $3 + \frac{1}{2}b$

7. $\frac{v}{3} + 2 \cdot 5$

8. $16.2 - (3 \cdot 4) + (14 \div 2)$

In **9** and **10**, use the expression $5.3t - (20 \div 4) + 11$.

9. Which part of the expression is a quotient? Describe its parts.

10. Which part of the expression is a product of two factors? Describe its parts.

In **11** and **12**, use the expression $7(10 + 8) - 9$.

11. Which part of the expression represents a sum?

12. Which part of the expression represents a product? Identify the factors.

*For another example, see Set D on page 70.

Math Practices and Problem Solving

In **13** and **14**, use the table at the right.

13. **MP.4 Model with Math** Write an expression to show how much longer the round trip to San Diego is than the round trip to San Jose. How many terms does the expression have?

14. **MP.1 Make Sense and Persevere** Last month, a truck driver made 5 round trips to Los Angeles and some round trips to San Diego. Write an expression that shows how many round trips he made in all. Identify and describe the part of the expression that shows how many trips he made to San Diego.

DATA

Sacramento to ...	Round trip Distance (miles)
San Jose	236
Los Angeles	770
San Diego	1,012

15. **MP.3 Critique Reasoning** Anthony says that the expression *abc* has three terms because it uses three different variables. Critique Anthony's reasoning and explain whether he is correct.

16. **Higher Order Thinking** Write a numerical expression with a value of 45. The expression must include at least three terms, one power, and one set of parentheses.

Common Core Assessment

17. Use the expression below to complete the table. The first column lists parts of the expression. Identify the parts of the expression that correspond to the descriptions to complete the table.

$$y \div 3(4 - 2) + 5.5$$

Description of Part	Part
Variable	
Difference	
Product	
Constant numerical value	

© Pearson Education, Inc. 6

Name ____________________

Help | Practice Buddy | Tools | Games

Homework & Practice 1-4

Identify Parts of an Expression

Another Look!

How can you use math words to describe these expressions?

Expression	Description	Word Phrase
$4(7 + 11)$	This expression has two factors. One factor is 4, and the other is the sum $7 + 11$.	4 times the sum of 7 and 11
$\frac{x}{6}$	This expression has one term and is the quotient x divided by 6.	x divided by 6
$f - 3$	This expression has two terms and is the difference of f and 3.	3 less than f or f minus 3
$15g$	In this expression with one term, the coefficient of g is 15.	15 times a quantity g

In **1–4**, tell how many terms each expression has.

1. $4c + 7\frac{1}{2}$

2. $80.6 - 3p - q$

3. $(7 \cdot 2) \div s$

4. $100 + (8 \cdot 6) - 50 + 2$

In **5** and **6**, use the expression $1 + \frac{z}{3} + 2w$.

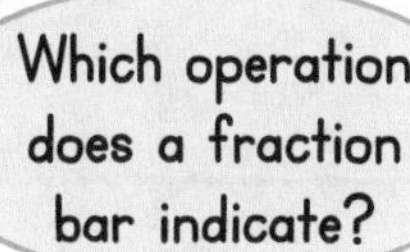
Which operation does a fraction bar indicate?

5. Which part of the expression is a quotient? Describe its parts.

6. Which part of the expression is a product of two factors? Describe its parts.

In **7** and **8**, use the expression $\frac{3}{4} + 3(14 - 7)$.

7. Which part of the expression represents a difference?

8. Which part of the expression represents a product? Identify the factors.

In **9** and **10**, use the menu at the right.

Lunch Menu
Sandwich $5
Soup $2
Salad $4
Juice
Drink .... $ 1

9. **MP.4 Model with Math** Write an expression to show the cost of 2 sandwiches, 2 drinks, and a salad. How many terms does your expression have?

10. **MP.6 Be Precise** The soccer team ordered 16 drinks and some sandwiches. Write an expression that shows the total cost of their order. Describe the expression and identify its parts.

11. **MP.3 Critique Reasoning** Mary says that the expression $\frac{a}{2}$ has no terms because there are no plus or minus signs. Explain if her reasoning is correct.

12. **Number Sense** Multiplying the expression $(x + y)$ by $\frac{1}{3}$ is the same as dividing it by which number?

13. **Higher Order Thinking** For $6 + 5(12 - 8)$, which word best describes the entire expression: sum, difference, product, or quotient? Explain your reasoning.

Common Core Assessment

14. Use the expression shown at the right to complete the table below. The first column lists parts of the expression. Complete the second column, identifying the parts of the expression that correspond to the descriptions.

$$3t - \frac{10}{(4 + 1)} - 2$$

Description of Part	Part
Coefficient	
Quotient	
Sum	
Product	

© Pearson Education, Inc. 6

Name ______________________________

Lesson 1-5
Evaluate Algebraic Expressions

I can ...
use substitution to evaluate algebraic expressions.

Content Standards 6.EE.A.2c, 6.EE.B.6
Mathematical Practices MP.2, MP.3, MP.4, MP.7, MP.8

Solve & Share Jason has 20 sports cards to start a collection. He can buy packs of cards to build his collection. How many cards will Jason have if he buys 3 packs of cards? If he buys 8 packs of cards? ***Solve this problem any way you choose.***

You can write an algebraic expression to structure the problem. If p = the number of packs Jason buys, "$20 + 12p$" tells the number of cards Jason will have.

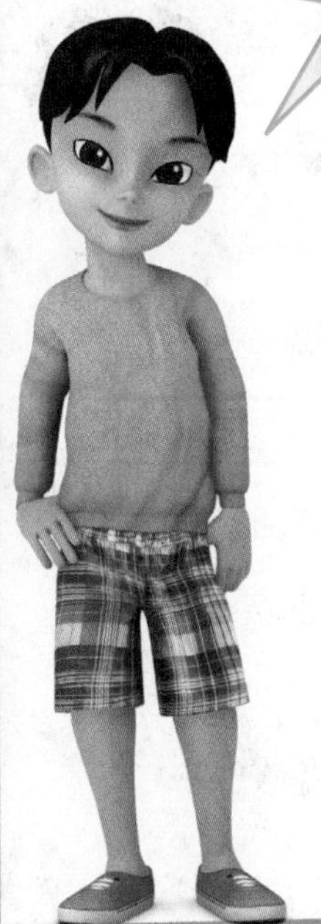

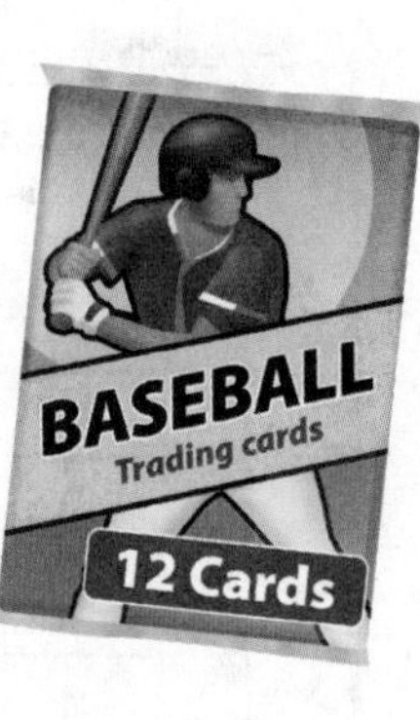

Look Back! **MP.8 Generalize** For which whole number values of p would evaluating the expression $12p + 20$ be a way of finding how many cards Jason will have if he buys p packs of cards?

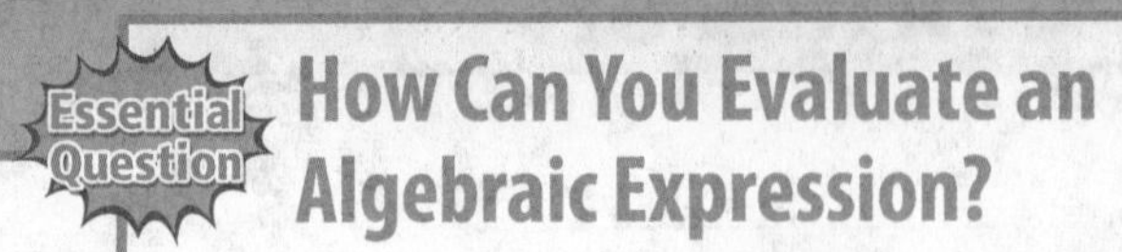

How Can You Evaluate an Algebraic Expression?

A

Erik collects miniature cars. He has one large case that has 20 cars. He also has 3 same-size, smaller cases filled with cars.

Let n = the number of cars in each smaller case.

Then the expression 20 + 3n represents the total number of cars that Erik has.

How many miniature cars does Erik have if each smaller case holds 10 cars? 12 cars? 14 cars?

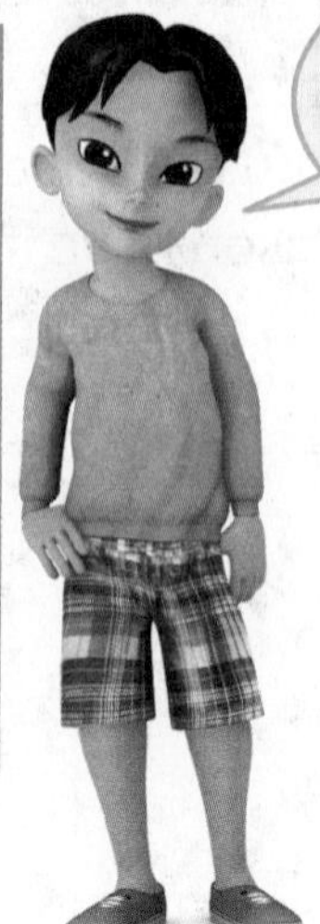

Remember, a variable can represent an unknown number or any number in a set of data.

B

Evaluate $20 + 3n$ when n equals 10, 12, or 14.
To evaluate an algebraic expression, use **substitution** to replace the variable with a number.

Substitute 10 for n.

$$20 + 3n$$
$$20 + 3(10)$$
$$= 20 + 30$$
$$= 50$$

If each smaller case holds 10 cars, Erik has 50 cars.

C

Substitute 12 for n.

$$20 + 3n$$
$$20 + 3(12)$$
$$= 20 + 36$$
$$= 56$$

If each smaller case holds 12 cars, Erik has 56 cars.

Substitute 14 for n.

$$20 + 3n$$
$$20 + 3(14)$$
$$= 20 + 42$$
$$= 62$$

If each smaller case holds 14 cars, Erik has 62 cars.

D

The table summarizes the values of $20 + 3n$ for each number of cars.

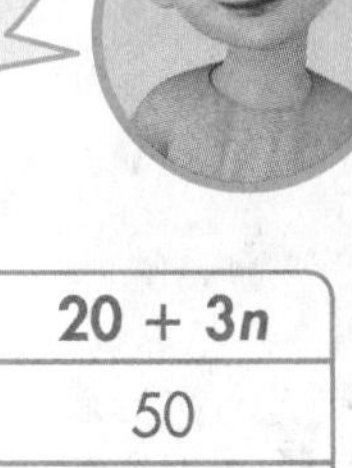

n	$20 + 3n$
10	50
12	56
14	62

Convince Me! **MP.7 Use Structure** Evaluate the expression $\frac{t}{5} + 13$ for each value of t shown in the table.

t	10	20	25
$\frac{t}{5} + 13$			

© Pearson Education, Inc. 6

Name ____________________

Practice Buddy   Tools   Assessment

Another Example

What is the value of $3a - 6b \div c + d^2$, when $a = 9$, $b = 8$, $c = 4$, and $d = 3$?

Evaluate the expression.

$$3a - 6b \div c + d^2 = 3(9) - 6(8) \div 4 + 3^2$$
$$= 24$$

Use substitution to replace each variable with its value.

Guided Practice*

Do You Understand?

1. **MP.3 Construct Arguments** Why is it important to use the order of operations to evaluate algebraic expressions?

2. **MP.2 Reasoning** In the problem on the previous page, are there any whole numbers that should not be part of a set of data used to evaluate $20 + 3n$? Explain.

Do You Know How?

In **3–6**, evaluate the expressions when $t = 8$, $w = \frac{1}{2}$, and $x = 3$.

3. $3t - 8$

4. $6w \div x + 9$

5. $t^2 - 12w \div x$

6. $5x - 2w + t$

Independent Practice

Remember to use order of operations.

Leveled Practice In **7–12**, evaluate each expression for $w = 5$, $x = 3$, $y = 4$, and $z = 8$.

7. $9x$

8. $3w + 6 \div 2x$

9. $w^2 + 2 + 48 \div 2x$

10. $x^3 + 5y \div w + z$

11. $9y \div x + z^2 - w$

12. $x^2 + 4w - 2y \div z$

*For another example, see Set E on page 70.

Math Practices and Problem Solving

In **13–15**, use the table at the right.

Vehicle	Week	Day
Small car	$250	$100
Medium car	$290	$110
Luxury car	$325	$120
Small van	$350	$150
Large van	$390	$170

13. MP.4 Model with Math Ms. White wants to rent a small car for a week. It will cost the weekly fee plus $0.30 per mile driven.

a. Let $m =$ the number of miles Ms. White drives during the week. Write an expression that shows the amount she will pay for the car.

b. Evaluate the expression you wrote to find how much she will pay if she drives 100 miles.

14. Mr. Black is renting a luxury car for one week and a few additional days, d. He does not have to pay a per-mile fee. Evaluate the expression $325 + 120d$ to find how much he will pay for an 11-day rental.

15. Number Sense For any of the vehicles listed in the table, how many days can you rent before it would be less expensive to rent for the week?

16. MP.3 Critique Reasoning Charlene says that the expression $5 + 3n$ can be evaluated by adding $5 + 3$ and then multiplying by the value of n. Do you agree? Explain.

17. Higher Order Thinking Explain how to evaluate the expression below for $d = 7$ using mental math. Then evaluate the expression.

$$(d \cdot 10^4) + (d \cdot 10^3) + (d \cdot 10^2) + (d \cdot 10^1) + (d \cdot 10^0)$$

Common Core Assessment

18. What is the value of $a^2 + 3b \div c - d$, when $a = 7$, $b = 8$, $c = 6$, and $d = 1$?

Ⓐ 52

Ⓑ 17

Ⓒ 9

Ⓓ 5

19. What is the value of $8b \div a - c^2 + d$, when $a = 2$, $b = 5$, $c = 3$, and $d = 9$?

Ⓐ 2

Ⓑ 5

Ⓒ 20

Ⓓ 23

© Pearson Education, Inc. 6

Name ______________________________

Help | Practice Buddy | Tools | Games

Homework & Practice 1-5

Evaluate Algebraic Expressions

Another Look!

Evaluate the expression $5a + 2b \div c - d^2$, when $a = 9$, $b = 6$, $c = 3$, and $d = 5$.

Use substitution to replace each variable with its value. Then use the order of operations to simplify.

$$5a + 2b \div c - d^2 = 5(9) + 2(6) \div 3 + 5^2$$
$$= 74$$

Be precise. Be careful to replace each variable with its specific value.

Leveled Practice In **1–8**, find the value of each expression when $a = \frac{1}{3}$, $b = 9$, $c = 5$, and $d = 10$.

1. $6a + 4$

2. $5a - \frac{2}{3}$

3. $5d \div c + 2$

4. $b^2 - 9a$

5. $12a + c - b$

6. $\frac{1}{2}d + c^2 - b$

7. $d^2 \div 2c - b + 3a$

8. $3c + b^2 \div 27a - d$

In **9** and **10**, evaluate each expression for the set of values given in each table.

9.

c	1	2	3
$28 - c^3 + 6$			

10.

d	28	49	63
$\frac{d}{7} - 3 + 10$			

In **11** and **12**, use the table at the right.

11. MP.4 Model with Math Tamera has a pet sitting business. The table shows how much she charges. Last week, she sat for one dog and for two cats.

Number of Pets	Per Day	Per Hour
One dog	\$20	\$7
Two dogs	\$25	\$9
One or two cats	\$15	\$6

a. Suppose she spent h hours sitting the dog and 2 days sitting the cats. Write an expression that shows how much she earned.

b. Evaluate the expression you wrote to find how much she earned if she sat 2 hours for the dog.

12. Number Sense For any of the pet sitting services listed in the table, how many hours can you purchase before it would be cheaper to pay for one day?

13. Conner is learning how to surf. He can pay \$65 for a basic training course and then rent a surfboard for \$6 per hour. He wrote the expression $65 + 6x$ to find out how much it would cost to go surfing. How much will it cost if he surfs for 4 hours?

14. Higher Order Thinking Rita and Janet signed up for two different dance classes. Rita's dance class charges \$20 plus \$8 per lesson. Janet's dance class charges \$12 per lesson. How many lessons will it take for Janet's class to cost the same amount as Rita's class? Explain how you decided.

Common Core Assessment

15. What is the value of $3g \div h^2 + k - n$, when $g = 12$, $h = 3$, $k = 10$, and $n = 1$?

Ⓐ 21

Ⓑ 16

Ⓒ 15

Ⓓ 13

16. What is the value of $\frac{1}{2}x + y^2 - 4z \div t$, when $x = 10$, $y = 4$, $z = 5$, and $t = 2$?

Ⓐ 3

Ⓑ 4

Ⓒ 11

Ⓓ 18

© Pearson Education, Inc. 6

Name ____________________

Solve

Lesson 1-6
Write Equivalent Expressions

Solve & Share Write an expression equivalent to $2(3x + 1)$. Explain why your expression is equivalent to $2(3x + 1)$. ***Solve this problem any way you choose.***

I can ...
use the properties of operations to write equivalent expressions.

Content Standards 6.EE.A.3, 6.EE.A.4
Mathematical Practices MP.3, MP.4, MP.7, MP.8

You can use properties of operations to construct arguments about math. Which properties of operations do you know?

Look Back! **MP.7 Look for Relationships** Write an expression equivalent to $2(3x - 1)$. Explain what this expression has in common with the expression in the problem above.

How Can You Write Equivalent Expressions?

A

Equivalent expressions have the same value regardless of the value that is substituted for the same variable in the expressions.

Use properties of operations to write equivalent expressions for 3(4x − 1) and 2x + 4.

Think about how you can use these properties of operations for any numbers *a*, *b*, or *c*.

Properties of Operations

Commutative Property

of Addition $a + b = b + a$

of Multiplication $a \times b = b \times a$

Associative Property

of Addition $(a + b) + c = a + (b + c)$

of Multiplication $(a \times b) \times c = a \times (b \times c)$

Distributive Property

$a(b + c) = a(b) + a(c)$

$a(b - c) = a(b) - a(c)$

B

Use the Distributive and Associative Properties to write an expression equivalent to $3(4x - 1)$.

$3(4x - 1) = 3(4x) - 3(1)$ ← Distributive Property

$= (3 \cdot 4)x - 3$ ← Associative Property of Multiplication

$= 12x - 3$

$12x - 3$ and $3(4x - 1)$ are equivalent expressions.

C

Use the Distributive Property in reverse order to write an expression equivalent to $2x + 4$. Look for a common factor of both terms that is greater than 1.

$2x + 4 = 2(x) + 2(2)$ ← Distributive Property

$= 2(x + 2)$ ← 2 is a common factor.

So $2(x + 2)$ is equivalent to $2x + 4$.

Equivalent expressions can be written in more than one way.

Convince Me! **MP.7 Use Structure** Write an expression that is equivalent to $3y - 9$.

© Pearson Education, Inc. 6

Name ___________

Practice Buddy | Tools | Assessment

Another Example

Are n^2 and $2n$ equivalent expressions?

You can use substitution to determine if two expressions are equivalent. For algebraic expressions to be equivalent, they must have the same value for *any* number substituted for the same variable. Since n^2 and $2n$ are not equivalent when $n = 1$, they are not equivalent expressions.

n	n^2	$2n$
0	0	0
1	1	2
2	4	4

Guided Practice*

Do You Understand?

1. **MP.7 Use Structure** Which property of operations could you use to write an equivalent expression for $y + \frac{1}{2}$? Write the equivalent expression.

2. **MP.8 Generalize** Are z^3 and $3z$ equivalent expressions? Explain.

Do You Know How?

In **3–5**, use properties of operations to complete the equivalent expressions.

3. $2(r + 3) =$ ____ $r +$ ____

4. $6(4s - 1) =$ ____ $s -$ ____

5. $8t + 2 = 2($ ____ $t +$ ____ $)$

Independent Practice

Leveled Practice In **6–8**, use properties of operations to complete the equivalent expressions.

6. $3(m + 3) =$ __ $m +$ __

7. $20n - 4m = 4($ __ $n -$ __ $m)$

8. $4\left(3p + 2\frac{1}{2}\right) =$ __ $p +$ __

In **9–16**, write equivalent expressions.

9. $3(x - 6)$

10. $2x + 10$

11. $8\left(2y + \frac{1}{4}\right)$

12. $5.7 + (3z + 0.3)$

13. $5w - 15$

14. $2x + 4y$

15. $10(y^2 + 2.45)$

16. $\frac{3}{4} \cdot (z^3 \cdot 4)$

*For another example, see Set F on page 70.

Math Practices and Problem Solving

In **17–19**, use the diagram at the right.

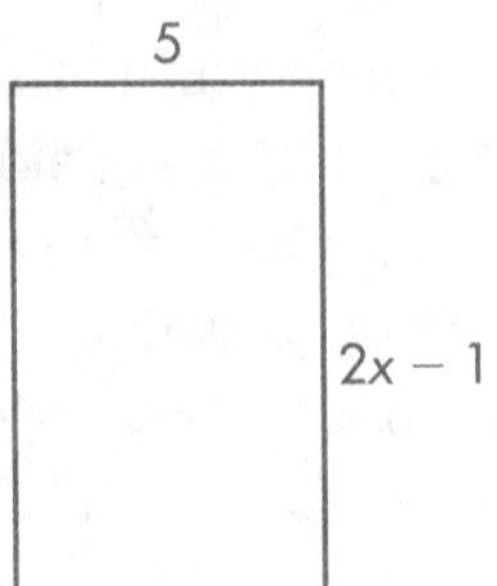

5
2x − 1

17. Write an algebraic expression to represent the area of the rectangle.

18. **MP.7 Use Structure** Use properties of operations to write an equivalent expression for the expression you wrote for Exercise 17.

19. What is the area of the rectangle, in square units, if $x = 5\frac{1}{2}$?

20. The science teacher ordered 7 magnifying glasses that cost \$1.25 each and 7 pairs of safety glasses that cost \$3.75 each. What was the total cost? Show how you know.

Can you use the Distributive Property?

21. **Vocabulary** What is a common factor of both terms that is greater than one in the expression $5y - 20$?

22. **MP.3 Critique Reasoning** Chris says that the expression $4n - 2$ can be written as $2(2n - 1)$. Do you agree? Explain.

23. **Higher Order Thinking** Write an expression that has only one term and is equivalent to the expression below.

$$(f \cdot g^2) + 5 - (g^2 \cdot f)$$

Common Core Assessment

24. Select each expression that is equivalent to $8.5 + (2s + 0.5)$.

- ☐ $(8.5 + 2s) + 0.5$
- ☐ $(8.5 + 0.5) + 2s$
- ☐ $9 + 2$
- ☐ $2(4.5 + s)$

25. Select each expression that is equivalent to $5(n + 4)$.

- ☐ $5n + 4$
- ☐ $5n + 20$
- ☐ $15 + 5n + 5$
- ☐ $5(n + 3) + 5$

© Pearson Education, Inc. 6

Name ______________________

Help Practice Buddy Tools Games

Homework & Practice 1-6
Write Equivalent Expressions

Another Look!

Write an expression equivalent to $2(5x + 7)$.

You can use the properties of operations to write equivalent expressions.

Use the Distributive Property.

$$2(5x + 7) = 2(5x) + 2(7)$$
$$= (2 \cdot 5)x + 14$$
$$= 10x + 14$$

Two algebraic expressions are equivalent if they have the same value when any number is substituted for the variable.

Properties of Operations

Commutative Property

of Addition	$a + b = b + a$
of Multiplication	$a \times b = b \times a$

Associative Property

of Addition	$(a + b) + c = a + (b + c)$
of Multiplication	$(a \times b) \times c = a \times (b \times c)$

Distributive Property

across Addition	$a(b + c) = a(b) + a(c)$
across Subtraction	$a(b - c) = a(b) - a(c)$

In **1–6**, use properties of operations to complete the equivalent expressions.

1. $5(m - 2) =$ ____ $m -$ ____

2. $24x + 18y = 6($ ____ $x +$ ____ $y)$

3. $2\left(9p - \frac{1}{2}\right) =$ ____ $p -$ ____

4. $8(2x - 3)$ and ____ $x - 24$

5. $5(3x - 9)$ and ____ $x -$ ____

6. $6(2x + 9)$ and ____ $x +$ ____

In **7–18**, use properties of operations to write equivalent expressions.

7. $3(6x - 7)$

8. $4(9x - 2)$

9. $6(8x + 1)$

10. $35x + 30$

11. $4(x + 7)$

12. $5x - 15y$

13. $6\left(3y - \frac{1}{2}\right)$

14. $1.6 + (2z + 0.4)$

15. $8w - 16$

16. $2.2x + 2.2$

17. $100(z^2 - 5.38)$

18. $8 \cdot \left(y^3 \cdot \frac{3}{4}\right)$

In **19–21**, use the sign at the right.

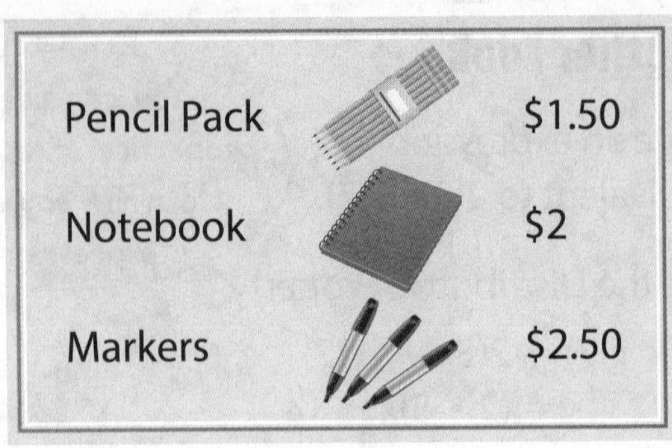
Pencil Pack $1.50
Notebook $2
Markers $2.50

19. **MP.4 Model with Math** Ms. Thomas ordered 5 pencil packs, *n* notebooks, and 5 sets of markers. Write an algebraic expression that represents the cost of Ms. Thomas's order.

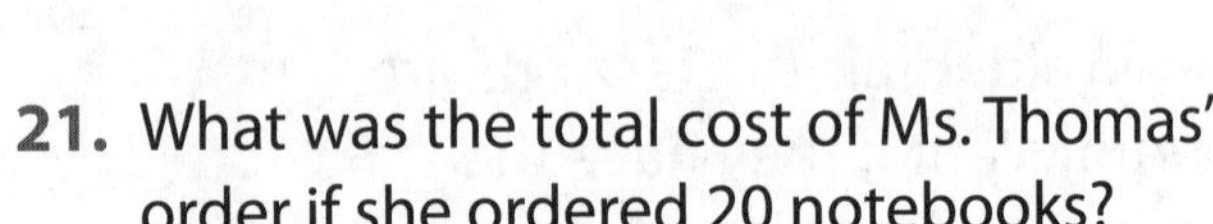

20. **MP.7 Use Structure** Use properties of operations to write an equivalent expression for the expression you wrote for Exercise 19.

21. What was the total cost of Ms. Thomas' order if she ordered 20 notebooks?

You can use properties of operations to write equivalent expressions in more than one way.

22. **MP.4 Model with Math** The formula for the perimeter of a rectangle is $2\ell + 2w$, where ℓ is the length and w is the width. How can you use the Distributive Property to write an equivalent expression for $2\ell + 2w$?

23. **Higher Order Thinking** Explain why the expression you wrote in Exercise 22 is easier to use than $2\ell + 2w$.

Common Core Assessment

24. Select each expression that is equivalent to $4\frac{1}{2} + \left(3t + 1\frac{1}{2}\right)$.

- ☐ $\left(4\frac{1}{2} + 3t\right) + 1\frac{1}{2}$
- ☐ $\left(4\frac{1}{2} + 1\frac{1}{2}\right) + 3t$
- ☐ $6 + 3t$
- ☐ $3(2 + t)$

25. Select each expression that is equivalent to $8x - 24$.

- ☐ $8(x - 3)$
- ☐ $8(x - 24)$
- ☐ $9(x - 3) - (x - 3)$
- ☐ $(5 + 3)x - 24$

© Pearson Education, Inc. 6

Name ______________________________

Solve

Lesson 1-7
Simplify Algebraic Expressions

I can ...
combine like terms in algebraic expressions.

Content Standards 6.EE.A.3, 6.EE.A.4
Mathematical Practices MP.1, MP.3, MP.4, MP.6, MP.7

Solve & Share

Write an expression equivalent to $x + 5 + 2x + 2$ by combining as many terms as you can. ***Solve this problem any way you choose.***

Use what you know about algebraic expressions and properties of operations to make sense of the problem.

Look Back! **MP.6 Be Precise** How do you know that the expression you wrote is equivalent to $x + 5 + 2x + 2$?

Learn Glossary

How Can You Combine Like Terms to Simplify Algebraic Expressions?

A

Terms that have the same variable part, such as y and 2y, are like terms. To simplify algebraic expressions you use properties of operations to write equivalent expressions that have no like terms and no parentheses.

Write simplified equivalent expressions for x + x + x and 2y − y.

Properties of Operations

Identity Property

of Addition $a + 0 = a = 0 + a$

of Multiplication $a \times 1 = a = 1 \times a$

Distributive Property

across Addition $a(b + c) = a(b) + a(c)$

across Subtraction $a(b - c) = a(b) - a(c)$

You can use the Identity Property of Multiplication to write x as $1x$.

B

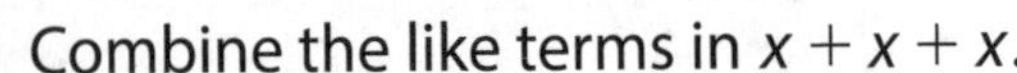

Combine the like terms in $x + x + x$.

$x + x + x$ ← All three terms are like terms.

$= 1x + 1x + 1x$ ← Identity Property of Multiplication

$= (1 + 1 + 1)x$ ← Distributive Property

$= 3x$

Shortcut: Add the coefficients, and write the common variable.

So $3x$ is equivalent to $x + x + x$.

C

Combine the like terms in $2y - y$.

$2y - y$ ← $2y$ and y are like terms.

$= 2y - 1y$ ← Identity Property of Multiplication

$= (2 - 1)y$ ← Distributive Property

$= 1y$ or y

Shortcut: Subtract the coefficients, and write the common variable.

So y is equivalent to $2y - y$.

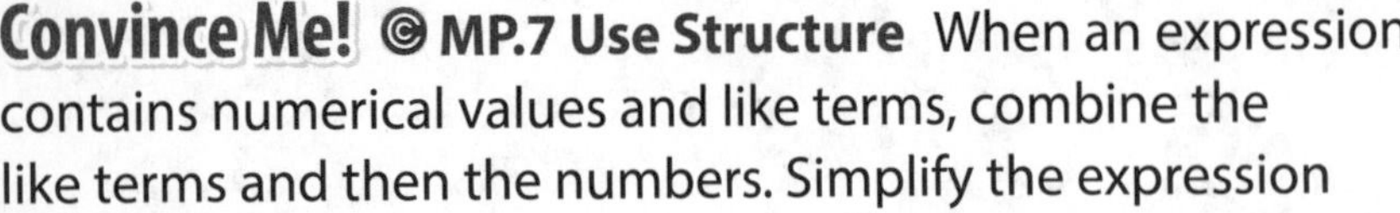

Convince Me! **MP.7 Use Structure** When an expression contains numerical values and like terms, combine the like terms and then the numbers. Simplify the expression $4z + 7 - z - 4$.

© Pearson Education, Inc. 6

Name ____________________

Guided Practice*

Do You Understand?

1. **MP.3 Construct Arguments** Explain why the expression $2y - y$ can be written as y.

2. Explain why the expressions $\frac{1}{2}x + \frac{1}{2}x$ and x are equivalent.

3. **MP.3 Critique Reasoning** Henry wrote $4z^2 - z^2$ as 4. Are $4z^2 - z^2$ and 4 equivalent expressions? Explain.

Do You Know How?

In **4–11**, simplify each expression.

4. $x + x + x + x$

5. $4y - y$

6. $3x + 8 + 2x$

7. $7y - 4.5 - 6y$

8. $4x + 2 - \frac{1}{2}x$

9. $3 + 3y - 1 + y$

10. $x + 6x$

11. $9y - 3y$

Independent Practice

In **12–23**, simplify each expression.

12. $2z + \frac{1}{4} + 2z$

13. $5 + 3w + 3 - w$

14. $5w - 5w$

15. $2x + 5 + 3x + 6$

16. $10y^2 + 2y^2$

17. $\frac{3}{4}z^3 + 4 - \frac{1}{4}z^3$

18. $3.4m + 2.4m$

19. $4.2n + 5 - 3.2n$

20. $5p^2 - 5 - 2p^2$

21. $q^5 + q^5 + q^5$

22. $3x + \frac{1}{4} + 2y + \frac{1}{4} + 7x - y$

23. $1.5z^2 + 4.5 + 6z - 0.3 - 3z + z^2$

For another example, see Set G on page 71.

Math Practices and Problem Solving

In **24–26**, use the diagram at the right.

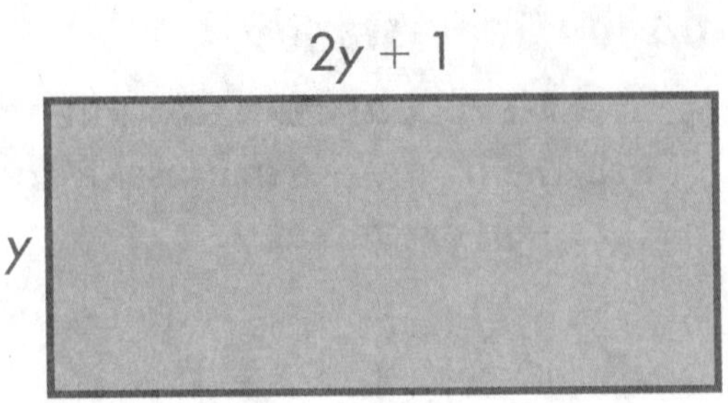

24. Write an algebraic expression for the perimeter of the rectangle.

25. **MP.7 Use Structure** Write an expression equivalent to the expression you wrote for Exercise 24.

26. What is the perimeter of the rectangle, in units, if $y = 2\frac{1}{2}$?

27. Rodney rewrote the expression $\frac{1}{2}(2x + 7)$ as $x + 3\frac{1}{2}$. Which property of operations did Rodney use?

28. **Number Sense** Give an example of a number, n, for which the inequality below is true.

$$n > n^2$$

29. **MP.3 Critique Reasoning** Thea said that the expressions $4x - 3x + 2$ and $x + 2$ are equivalent. Is Thea correct? Explain.

30. **Higher Order Thinking** Write an equivalent expression for the expression shown below.

$$\frac{a}{3} + \frac{a}{3} + \frac{a}{3}$$

Common Core Assessment

31. Write each expression below in the correct column in the table at the right to show whether the expression is equivalent to $2x + 7 + 6x - x$.

$2x + 13$
$7 + 7x$
$14x$
$7x + 7$

Equivalent to $2x + 7 + 6x - x$	NOT Equivalent to $2x + 7 + 6x - x$

© Pearson Education, Inc. 6

Name ____________________

Help Practice Buddy Tools Games

Homework & Practice 1-7

Simplify Algebraic Expressions

Another Look!

Simplify the expression $2x + 6 + 5x + 4$.

Like terms have the same variable part.
In this expression, $2x$ and $5x$ are like terms.

$2x + 6 + 5x + 4$
$= 2x + 5x + 6 + 4$ Commutative Property of Addition
$= 7x + 10$

$2x + 6 + 5x + 4 = 7x + 10$

You can combine like terms and then numbers to write equivalent expressions.

In **1–3**, combine like terms to complete the equivalent expressions.

1. $n + n + n = 1n + 1n + 1n$
$= (1 + \_\_ + \_\_)n$
$= \_\_$

2. $3n + 6 - n - 4 = (\_\_n - \_\_n) + 6 - 4$
$= \_\_n + \_\_$

3. $1\frac{1}{2}z^2 + 3\frac{1}{2} + 5z - 3 + 6z - \frac{1}{2}z^2$
$= (\quad z^2 - \quad z^2) + (\ z + \ z) + (\quad - \quad)$
$= \_\_z^2 + \quad z +$

You can combine like terms with fraction or decimal coefficients the same way you do whole number coefficients.

In **4–15**, simplify each expression.

4. $4y + 9y$

5. $3z + \frac{3}{4} - 2z$

6. $25 + 5w - 10 + w$

7. $7.7w - 4.6w$

8. $\frac{1}{2}x + \frac{1}{2} + \frac{1}{2}x + \frac{1}{2}$

9. $12y^2 - 6y^2$

10. $3z^3 + 2\frac{1}{4} - z^3$

11. $6.6m + 3m$

12. $100n - 1 - 25n$

13. $5x + \frac{1}{2} + 3y + \frac{1}{4} + 2x - 2y$

14. $p^2 + 2.3 + 3p^2$

15. $z^4 + z^4 + z^4 + z^4$

In **16–18**, use the sign at the right.

16. MP.4 Model with Math At a drive-thru restaurant, Casey's family ordered a small drink and m medium drinks. Anika's family ordered m medium drinks and a large drink. Write an algebraic expression that shows the total cost, in dollars, of both orders.

17. MP.7 Use Structure Combine like terms to write an expression that is equivalent to the expression you wrote for Exercise 16.

18. What was the total cost of the drinks in both orders if $m = 3$?

19. Jan rewrote the expression $\frac{1}{2}y \cdot 5$ as $5 \cdot \frac{1}{2}y$. Which property of operations did Jan use?

20. Number Sense Give an example of a number, n, for which the inequality below is true.

$$n^3 < n^2$$

21. MP.3 Critique Reasoning Manuel rewrote the expression $6x - x + 5$ as $6 + 5$. Are $6x - x + 5$ and $6 + 5$ equivalent expressions? Explain.

22. Higher Order Thinking Write an equivalent expression for the expression shown below.

$$\frac{b}{2} + \frac{b}{2}$$

Common Core Assessment

23. Write each expression below in the correct column in the table at the right to show whether the expression is equivalent to $\frac{1}{2}x + 4\frac{1}{2} + \frac{1}{2}x - \frac{1}{2}$.

$\frac{1}{2}x + 4$

$x + 4\frac{1}{2}$

$x + 4$

$x - 4$

Equivalent to $\frac{1}{2}x + 4\frac{1}{2} + \frac{1}{2}x - \frac{1}{2}$	NOT Equivalent to $\frac{1}{2}x + 4\frac{1}{2} + \frac{1}{2}x - \frac{1}{2}$

© Pearson Education, Inc. 6

Name ______________________________

Lesson 1-8
Equivalent Expressions

I can ...
identify equivalent algebraic expressions.

Content Standards 6.EE.A.3, 6.EE.A.4
Mathematical Practices MP.1, MP.3, MP.7, MP.8

Solve & Share Juwon made the table shown below. He says the table shows that $8n + 6$, $2(4n + 3)$, and $14n$ are all equivalent expressions. Do you agree? Explain your reasoning. ***Solve this problem any way you choose.***

n	8n + 6	2(4n + 3)	14n
1	$8(1) + 6$ $= 14$	$2(4 \cdot 1 + 3)$ $= 2(4 + 3)$ $= 2 \cdot 7$ $= 14$	$14(1)$ $= 14$

A table is a good way to make sense of the problem.

Look Back! MP.8 Generalize When a number is substituted for the same variable in two expressions, how many times must those two expressions have different values before you know they are not equivalent? Explain.

Essential Question

How Can You Identify Equivalent Expressions?

A

Which of the expressions below are equivalent? Explain how you know.

$8x - 4$

$4x$

$4(2x - 1)$

B One Way

Try some numbers!

Evaluate each expression for the same values of x.

Try $x = 1$.

$8x - 4 = 8 \cdot 1 - 4 = 4$
$4x = 4 \cdot 1 = 4$
$4(2x - 1) = 4(2 \cdot 1 - 1) = 4$

Try $x = 2$.

$8x - 4 = 8 \cdot 2 - 4 = 12$
$4x = 4 \cdot 2 = 8$
$4(2x - 1) = 4(2 \cdot 2 - 1) = 12$

$8x - 4$ and $4(2x - 1)$ name the same number regardless of the value of x, so they are equivalent.

C Another Way

You can use properties of operations to determine whether expressions are equivalent.

Use the Distributive Property to write $8x - 4$ as $4(2x - 1)$.

$$8x - 4 = 4(2x) - 4(1) = 4(2x - 1)$$

Properties of operations cannot be used to write $8x - 4$ or $4(2x - 1)$ as $4x$.

$8x - 4 \neq 4x$
$4(2x - 1) \neq 4x$

$8x - 4$ and $4(2x - 1)$ are equivalent expressions.

Convince Me! **MP.7 Use Structure** Which of the following expressions are equivalent? Explain how you know.

$10y + 5$

$15y$

$5(2y + 1)$

© Pearson Education, Inc. 6

Name ________________________________

Practice Buddy   Tools   Assessment

Guided Practice*

Do You Understand?

1. Are the expressions $3(y + 1)$ and $3y + 3$ equivalent for $y = 1$? $y = 2$? $y = 3$?

2. MP.3 **Construct Arguments** Are the expressions $3(y + 1)$ and $3y + 3$ equivalent for any value of y? Explain.

Do You Know How?

3. Complete the table below.

x	$12x - 6$	$3x + 3$	$6(2x - 1)$
1			
2			
3			

4. Which expressions in the table are equivalent?

Independent Practice

Leveled Practice In **5** and **6**, complete each table. Then circle the expressions that are equivalent.

5.

y	$9(y + 3)$	$9y + 27$	$9y + 3$
1			
2			
3			

6.

y	$4\frac{1}{2} + \left(2y - \frac{1}{2}\right)$	$\left(4\frac{1}{2} - \frac{1}{2}\right) + 2y$	$2(y + 2)$
1			
2			
3			

In **7–10**, identify which expressions are equivalent to the given expression.

7. $5(2x + 3)$
   a. $10x + 15$
   b. $5x + 15 + 5x$
   c. $10x + 8$

8. $4x - 8$
   a. $2(2x - 6)$
   b. $2(2x - 4)$
   c. $x - 8 + 3x$

9. $12x - 16$
   a. $9.6x - 16 + 2.4x$
   b. $3(3x - 5)$
   c. $4(3x - 4)$

10. $2\left(6x + \frac{1}{2}\right)$
   a. $12x + 2$
   b. $12x + 1$
   c. $6x + \frac{1}{2} + 6x + \frac{1}{2}$

*For another example, see Set H on page 71.

Math Practices and Problem Solving

In **11–13**, use the sign at the right.

11. Write an algebraic expression that represents each purchase.

a. Mr. Tonkery bought x number of soccer balls and 3 baseballs.

b. Dennis, Eddie, and Felix are on a baseball team. They each bought a baseball and x pairs of sweat socks.

12. **MP.1 Make Sense and Persevere** Suppose x has the same value in both of the expressions you wrote for Exercise 11. Are the two expressions you wrote equivalent? Explain.

13. **MP.3 Critique Reasoning** Wendy says that soccer balls cost $2\frac{1}{2}$ times as much as baseballs cost. Do you agree? Explain.

14. **MP.3 Critique Reasoning** Jamie says that the expressions $6x - 2x + 4$ and $4(x + 1)$ are not equivalent because one expression has a term that is subtracted and the other does not. Do you agree? Explain.

15. **Higher Order Thinking** Are the two expressions shown below equivalent? Explain.

$4(n + 3) - (3 + n)$ and $3n + 9$

Common Core Assessment

16. Which expression below is **NOT** equivalent to $6x + 12$?

Ⓐ $6(x + 2)$

Ⓑ $12 + 6x$

Ⓒ $3(2x + 4)$

Ⓓ $18x$

17. Which expression is equivalent to $4y + \frac{1}{2} - y + 2\frac{1}{4}$?

Ⓐ $4y + 2\frac{3}{4}$

Ⓑ $2\frac{3}{4} + 3y$

Ⓒ $3y + 2\frac{1}{2}$

Ⓓ $2\frac{3}{4} + 5y$

© Pearson Education, Inc. 6

Name ______________________

Homework & Practice 1-8

Equivalent Expressions

Another Look!

Which of the following expressions are equivalent? Explain how you know.

$2(5x + 7)$
$10x + 14$
$24x$

You can evaluate the expressions for the same values of x or use properties to determine whether the expressions are equivalent.

Expressions are equivalent if they name the same number or the same value regardless of the value of the variable.

Try $x = 2$.

$2(5x + 7) = 2(5 \cdot 2 + 7) = 34$
$10x + 14 = 10(2) + 14 = 34$
$24x = 24(2) = 48$

You can use properties of operations to determine whether expressions are equivalent.

$2(5x + 7) = 2(5x) + 2(7)$ Distributive Property
$= 10x + 14$

Properties of operations cannot be used to write $2(5x + 7)$ or $10x + 14$ as $24x$.

$2(5x + 7) \neq 24x$
$10x + 14 \neq 24x$

$2(5x + 7)$ and $10x + 14$ are equivalent expressions.

In **1** and **2**, complete each table. Then circle the expressions that are equivalent.

1.

y	$10y - 5$	$5y$	$5(2y - 1)$
1			
2			
3			

2.

y	$3y + 3.5 - y$	$1.5 + 2(1 + y)$	$3y + 2.5$
1			
2			
3			

In **3–6**, identify which expressions are equivalent to the given expression.

3. $5x + 5$

a. $10x + 5 - 5x$

b. $10x$

c. $5(x + 1)$

4. $12x - 10 - 6x$

a. $6x - 10$

b. $2(3x - 5)$

c. $16x - 8 - 2$

5. $\frac{1}{2}x + 3 + \frac{1}{2}x$

a. $\frac{1}{2}(x + 3)$

b. $x + 3$

c. $3x + 3 - x$

6. $3(3x - 1)$

a. $6x - 2$

b. $9x - 3$

c. $15x + 6 - 6x - 3$

In **7–9**, use the sign at the right.

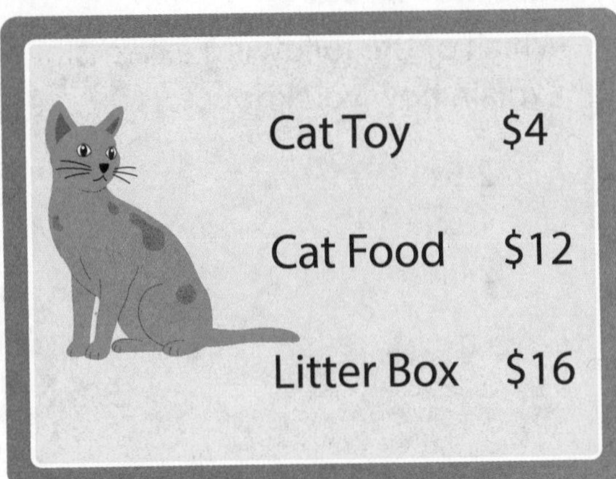

7. Write an algebraic expression that represents each purchase.

a. Ms. Martinez bought *x* number of litter boxes and 8 bags of cat food for the animal shelter.

b. Two sisters each bought 1 litter box, 10 cat toys, and *x* bags of cat food.

8. **MP.1 Make Sense and Persevere** Suppose *x* has the same value in both of the expressions you wrote for Exercise 7. Are the two expressions you wrote equivalent? Explain.

9. **MP.3 Construct Arguments** Which costs the most: 12 cat toys, 4 bags of cat food, or 3 litter boxes? Explain.

10. **MP.3 Critique Reasoning** Zach says that the expressions $6x - 36$ and $3(2x - 12)$ are equivalent because of the Distributive Property. Do you agree? Explain.

11. **Higher Order Thinking** Are the two expressions shown below equivalent? Explain.

$4n + 6m - 12k$ and $2(2n + 3m - 6k)$

Common Core Assessment

12. Which expression below is **NOT** equivalent to $9x + 3x - 12$?

Ⓐ $6(x - 2)$

Ⓑ $12x - 12$

Ⓒ $3(4x - 4)$

Ⓓ $4(3x - 3)$

13. Which expression is equivalent to $3\left(y + \frac{1}{4}\right)$?

Ⓐ $3y + 2\frac{3}{4} - 1$

Ⓑ $3y + \frac{3}{4} - y$

Ⓒ $\frac{3}{4} + 3y$

Ⓓ $\frac{3}{4} - 3y$

© Pearson Education, Inc. 6

Name ____________________

Solve

Lesson 1-9
Formulas

I can ...
use formulas to solve problems.

Content Standard 6.EE.A.2c
Mathematical Practices MP.3, MP.4, MP.5, MP.6, MP.8

Solve & Share You can use the formula $P = 4s$ to find the perimeter, P, of a square with side length s. What is the difference between the perimeters of a square with side length 1.2 inches and a square with side length 2.5 inches? ***Solve this problem any way you choose.***

You can use measuring tools to draw the squares and then to find their perimeters.

Look Back! **MP.8 Generalize** How can you use the formula to find the length of each side of a square that has a perimeter of 72 inches?

Essential Question How Can You Use Formulas to Solve Problems?

A

A formula is a rule that uses symbols to relate two or more quantities.

The simple interest formula, I = prt, can be used to find I, the simple interest charged on a loan where p is the principal amount, r is the interest rate, and t is the length of the loan in years.

Use the formula to find the interest on the loan.

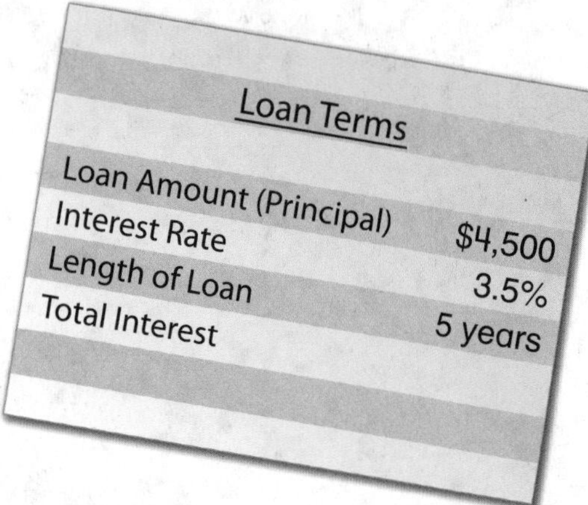

Loan Terms	
Loan Amount (Principal)	$4,500
Interest Rate	3.5%
Length of Loan	5 years
Total Interest	

A formula is used to generalize a relationship between quantities.

B

Step 1

Identify the values used in the formula.

$I =$ the unknown interest
$p =$ the principal loan amount, $4,500
$r =$ the interest rate, 3.5%
$t =$ time in years, 5

C

Step 2

Substitute the values in the formula and evaluate. 3.5% = 0.035

$$I = prt$$
$$= (4{,}500 \cdot 0.035 \cdot 5)$$
$$= 787.5$$

The interest charged on the loan is $787.50.

Convince Me! **MP.8 Generalize** How much interest is paid on a $10,000 simple interest loan with a rate of 5%, or 0.05, that is paid over 4 years? How do you know that you can use the formula above to solve this problem?

© Pearson Education, Inc. 6

Name

Practice Buddy Tools Assessment

Guided Practice*

Do You Understand?

1. Why are formulas useful?

2. MP.6 Be Precise Why is it important to define each variable used in a formula?

Do You Know How?

3. The formula $d = rt$ relates the distance, d, to the rate, r, and the time, t. A plane travels at a rate of 400 miles per hour. How far will the plane travel in 5 hours?

4. How long will it take a car traveling at a rate of 68 miles per hour to go 510 miles? Show how you know.

Independent Practice

In **5** and **6**, use the diagram of the cube to solve.

5. The formula $V = s^3$ can be used to find the volume, V, of the cube. The variable s represents the cube's equal length, width, and height dimensions. Find its volume.

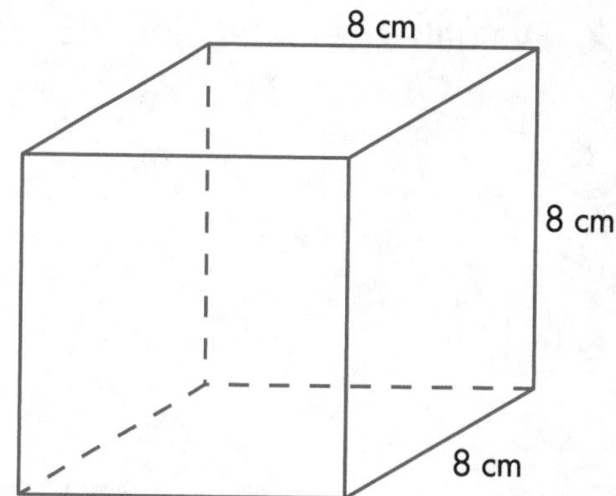

6. The formula $A = 6s^2$ can be used to find the total surface area of the cube. Find its total surface area. Show your work.

7. Myra's truck can travel 16 miles on 1 gallon of gasoline. How many gallons of gasoline will Myra need to travel 296 miles? Use the formula $\frac{d}{m} = g$, where m represents miles per gallon, d is distance traveled, and g is the number of gallons of gasoline used.

Be precise by using the correct units of measure for each quantity.

*For another example, see Set I on page 72.

Math Practices and Problem Solving

8. The formula $F = (C \times 1.8) + 32$ can be used to convert temperature in degrees Celsius, C, to degrees Fahrenheit, F. Use the formula to convert the temperature shown on the thermometer to degrees Fahrenheit. Show your work.

9. **MP.3 Construct Arguments** Could a thermometer that is marked in both °F and °C show the temperature as both 45°F and 13°C? Explain.

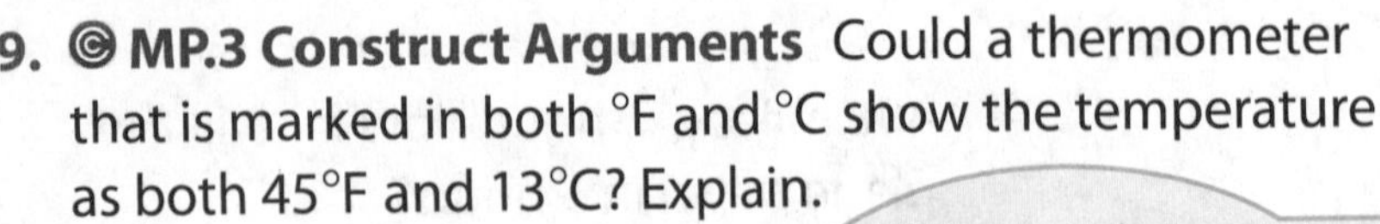

Substitute known values into a formula to find the missing value.

10. **Algebra** The formula to find the average grade, A, of three tests is $A = \frac{X + Y + Z}{3}$, where X, Y, and Z are the three test scores. Jules earned the scores 78, 90, and 81 on his last three tests. Use the formula to find his average test grade.

11. **Math and Science** The density, d, of an object can be found by using the formula $d = \frac{m}{v}$, where m is the mass of the object and v is its volume. What is the density of an object that has a mass of 65 grams and a volume of 8 cubic meters?

12. Evaluate the expression $7(3^2 + 5) - \left(\frac{81}{9}\right)$.

13. **Higher Order Thinking** Janie knows that she will pay \$696 of interest if she borrows \$5,800 at a rate of 4%, or 0.04. Show how to use the formula $I = prt$ to find whether it will take Janie 2 years, 3 years, or 4 years to pay off the loan.

Common Core Assessment

14. Jeremiah helps his neighbor with yard work for 6 hours each day for 15 days. His neighbor offers two payment options. Option 1 is to pay him \$4.50 for each hour worked. Option 2 is a final payment of \$350. Use the formula $p = 15 \times 4.50h$, where p is the total payment after 15 days and h is the hours worked each day, to decide which offer Jeremiah should choose. Justify your response.

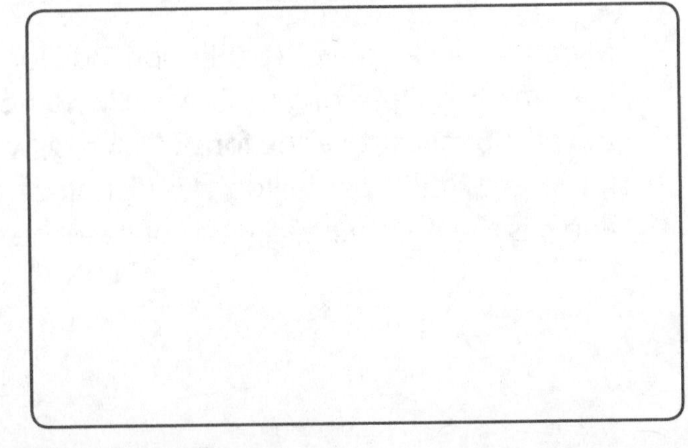

© Pearson Education, Inc. 6

Name ____________________

Help | Practice Buddy | Tools | Games

Homework & Practice 1-9

Formulas

Another Look!

To find a missing angle measure of a triangle, use the formula $a = 180 - (b + c)$, where a, b, and c are the angle measures of the triangle. Use the formula to find the measure of angle A.

A: $a°$; B: 30°; C: 62°

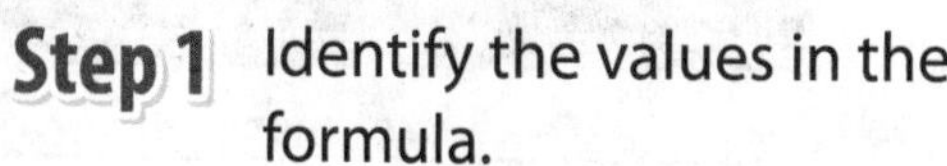

Step 1 Identify the values in the formula.

a = measure of angle A

$b = 30$

$c = 62$

Organize what you know, so you can use it to find the missing value.

Step 2 Substitute the values in the formula and evaluate.

$a = 180 - (30 + 62)$

$a = 180 - 92$

$a = 88$

The measure of angle A is 88°.

In **1** and **2**, let ℓ = the length of the rectangle and w = the width of the rectangle.

1. The formula to find the perimeter of a rectangle is $P = 2\ell + 2w$. Use the formula to find the perimeter of rectangle $LMNP$.

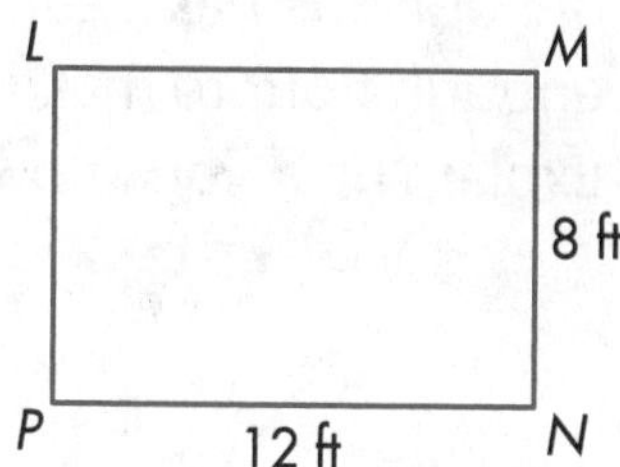

2. The formula $A = \ell w$ can be used to find the area of a rectangle. Use the formula to find the area of rectangle $LMNP$.

Formulas help you model problems and show how quantities are related.

In **3** and **4**, use the formula $a = \frac{(f - s)}{t}$, where a is the rate of acceleration, f is the final speed, s is the starting speed, and t is the time.

3. A racecar goes from 44 meters per second to 77 meters per second in just 11 seconds. What is the acceleration (in meters per second squared) of the racecar? Show how you know.

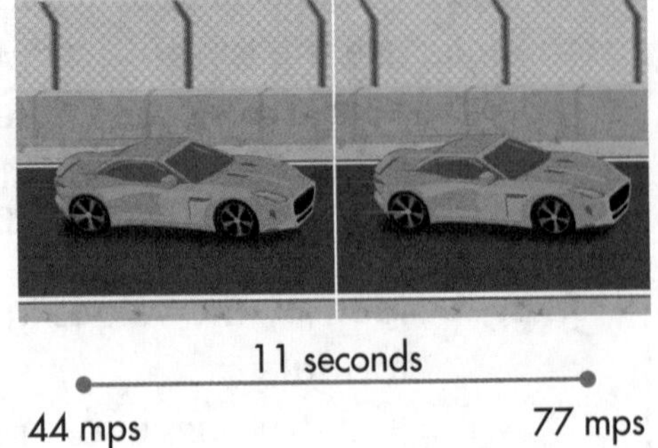

4. **MP.3 Construct Arguments** A popular car model accelerates from 0 to 26.9 meters per second in just 6.5 seconds. An advertisement for the car claims its rate of acceleration is 4 meters per second squared. Can you support this claim? Explain.

5. Jenna is baking two different types of cookies. One recipe requires $\frac{3}{4}$ cup of flour. The other recipe requires $\frac{1}{2}$ cup of flour. She has 2 cups of flour. Is this enough flour to make both recipes? Explain how you know.

6. **Higher Order Thinking** Jack writes the formula $P = 2\ell + 2w$ to find the perimeter, P, of a rectangle with length, ℓ, and width, w. Sandy says that she uses the formula $P = 2(\ell + w)$ to find the perimeter of a rectangle. Which formula is correct? Explain.

Common Core Assessment

7. A European furniture maker requires that dimensions of custom orders be given in centimeters. The rectangle at the right is a model of a tabletop. One foot is equal to about 0.3 meter. Use the formula $c = 0.3f \times 100$, where c is the measure in centimeters and f is the measure in feet, to find the dimensions of the rectangular tabletop in centimeters.

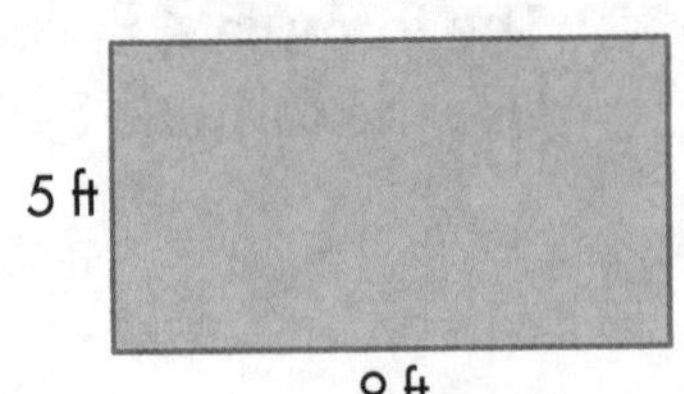

© Pearson Education, Inc. 6

Name ___

Solve & Share

Alicia says that $3(2b - 4)$ is equivalent to $6b - 12$. Benny says Alicia is correct but that he can think of three other expressions that are also equivalent to $3(2b - 4)$.

Think about the structure of the algebraic expression $3(2b - 4)$. Find three other equivalent algebraic expressions.

Math Practices and Problem Solving

Lesson 1-10

Look For and Use Structure

I can ...
look for and make use of structure to analyze algebraic expressions.

Mathematical Practices MP.7, MP.2, MP.3, MP.6
Content Standards 6.EE.A.3, 6.EE.A.2c

Thinking Habits

Be a good thinker!
These questions can help you.

- What patterns can I see and describe?
- How can I use the patterns to solve the problem?
- Can I see expressions and objects in different ways?
- What equivalent expressions can I use?

Look Back! **MP.7 Use Structure** Write two expressions that are equivalent to $8g + 2$.

Essential Question: How Can You Use Structure to Analyze Expressions?

A

This summer Vanna wants to charge twice as much for mowing and raking, but her expenses ($10 per weekend) will also double. The expression below can be used to find how much Vanna will make this summer mowing and raking x lawns in a weekend.

Job	Amount Earned for Each
Mowing the lawn	$20
Raking the cut grass	$5

$2(20x + 5x - 10)$

Write four equivalent algebraic expressions.

What do I need to do to solve this problem?

I need to analyze the structure of the algebraic expression and write four equivalent algebraic expressions.

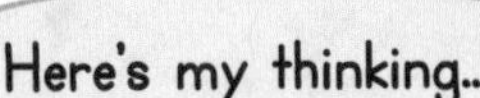

B **How can I use structure to solve this problem?**

I can

- find and describe patterns.
- use the patterns to solve the problem.
- see expressions and objects in different ways.
- use equivalent expressions.

C One way to analyze structure is to think about properties.

Use the Commutative Property.
$2(20x + 5x - 10) = (20x + 5x - 10)2$

Use the Distributive Property.
$$2(20x + 5x - 10) = 2(20x) + 2(5x) - 2(10)$$
$$= 40x + 10x - 20$$
$$= 50x - 20$$

Reordering or combining terms and simplifying expressions can make the expressions easier to evaluate.

Convince Me! **MP.7 Use Structure** Is there more than one way the Commutative Property can be used to write an algebraic expression equivalent to $2(20x + 5x - 10)$? Show how.

© Pearson Education, Inc. 6

Name

Practice Buddy Tools Assessment

Guided Practice*

MP.7 Use Structure

This summer, Patrick wants to triple the amount of time he spends training for sports. The chart shows how much time he spends training for sports during the school year. The expression below represents the total hours Patrick plans to spend training over x weeks in the summer.

$3(3x + 2x + x)$

Sport	Hours Spent Training Each Week During the School Year
Baseball	3
Football	2
Basketball	1

1. How can you use properties to write equivalent expressions?

2. Explain how you can use the expression to find the number of hours Patrick plans to spend training during the summer if $x = 9$. Then solve.

Independent Practice

MP.7 Use Structure

Yolanda is planning a party that will take place in three rooms. The expression below can be used to represent the total amount Yolanda will need to rent all three rooms for t hours. Let $t = 5$.

$(25t + 15) + (20t + 10) + 50t$

Room	Rental Fee (per hour)	Sound System Fee
1	\$25	\$15
2	\$20	\$10
3	\$50	no charge

3. How can you use a property to write an equivalent expression?

4. Explain how you can evaluate your expression and find the total rental cost Yolanda will pay. Then solve.

You use structure when you analyze expressions and determine what each part represents.

*For another example, see Set J on page 72.

Math Practices and Problem Solving

Common Core Performance Assessment

Construction Work
Mrs. Hayes hired Alex and Tyrone to build doghouses for her kennel service. She paid each worker a daily overtime bonus and an hourly wage. The project took two days to complete. Mrs. Hayes used the algebraic expression $2(10 + 7x) + 2(15 + 8x)$ to calculate the total amount she paid Alex and Tyrone for working x hours on each of the two days.

Worker	Overtime Bonus ($)	Hourly Wage ($)
Alex	10	7
Tyrone	15	8

5. **MP.6 Be Precise** How are each worker's earnings represented in the expression? Explain how you know.

6. **MP.3 Critique Reasoning** Is Mrs. Hayes's expression accurate? How did you decide?

When you are precise, you can state the meaning of symbols and clarify the meaning of quantities in an expression.

7. **MP.2 Reasoning** Which property can you use to write an equivalent expression? Explain.

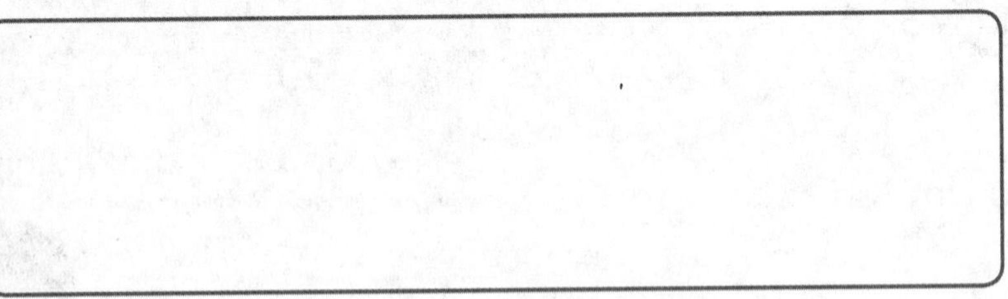

8. **MP.7 Use Structure** Explain how you can use an equivalent expression to find the total amount Mrs. Hayes paid Alex and Tyrone if each worked 9 hours each day.

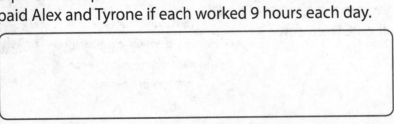

© Pearson Education, Inc. 6

Name ____________________

Homework & Practice 1-10

Look for and Use Structure

Another Look!

Shea sells bracelets at the Farmer's Market. For each bracelet she sells, she spends $1.50 on beads and $3.00 on hardware. She also pays $10 to rent her booth. The expression $4(1.50x + 3x) + 10$ represents her total expenses for selling x bracelets per day in four days. Write two equivalent expressions.

When you use structure, you can see different ways of writing an expression.

How can you use structure to solve the problem?

- I can simplify the algebraic expression by combining like terms.
- I can use properties of operations to write equivalent expressions and solve the problem.

Write two equivalent expressions.

By combining like terms, I can write this expression:

$$\begin{aligned} 4(1.50x + 3x) + 10 &= 4[(1.50 + 3)x] + 10 \\ &= 4(4.50x) + 10 \end{aligned}$$

By using the Distributive Property, I can write this expression:

$$\begin{aligned} 4(1.50x + 3x) + 10 &= 4(1.50x) + 4(3x) + 10 \\ &= (4 \cdot 1.50)x + (4 \cdot 3)x + 10 \\ &= 6x + 12x + 10 \end{aligned}$$

MP.7 Use Structure

Jose is training for a half-marathon. Each week he runs x miles per day for 5 days. For 3 days of the week, he runs at a speed of 8 minutes per mile. For 2 days he runs 7-minute miles. Jose uses the expression $4(3 \cdot 8x) + 4(2 \cdot 7x)$ to represent the amount of time, in minutes, that he runs in 4 weeks.

1. Which parts of Jose's expression describe the amount of time he spends running on a given day? Explain.

2. How can you use properties to write equivalent expressions?

Common Core Performance Assessment

Research Project

Josephine's math study group is doing a research project. There are 5 students in her group. In January, each group member surveyed *x* volunteers and gave a 10-minute presentation. Each volunteer completed a follow-up survey in May. Josephine wrote the expression $5(6x + 25x + 10)$ to represent the total time in minutes that her group spent surveying volunteers and giving presentations.

Time Spent Surveying Volunteers

Month	Survey Time
January	6
May	25

3. **MP.6 Be Precise** Which parts of the expression represent the time each group member spent surveying volunteers? Explain.

4. **MP.3 Critique Reasoning** Is Josephine's expression accurate? How did you decide?

When you critique reasoning, you explain why someone's thinking is correct or incorrect.

5. **MP.2 Reasoning** How can you use properties of operations to write an equivalent expression? Explain your reasoning.

6. **MP.7 Use Structure** Explain how you can use an equivalent expression to find the total time Josephine's group spent on the research project if each worked with 20 volunteers.

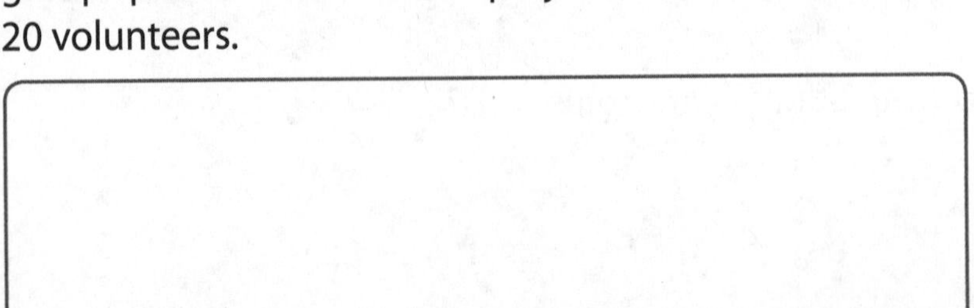

© Pearson Education, Inc. 6

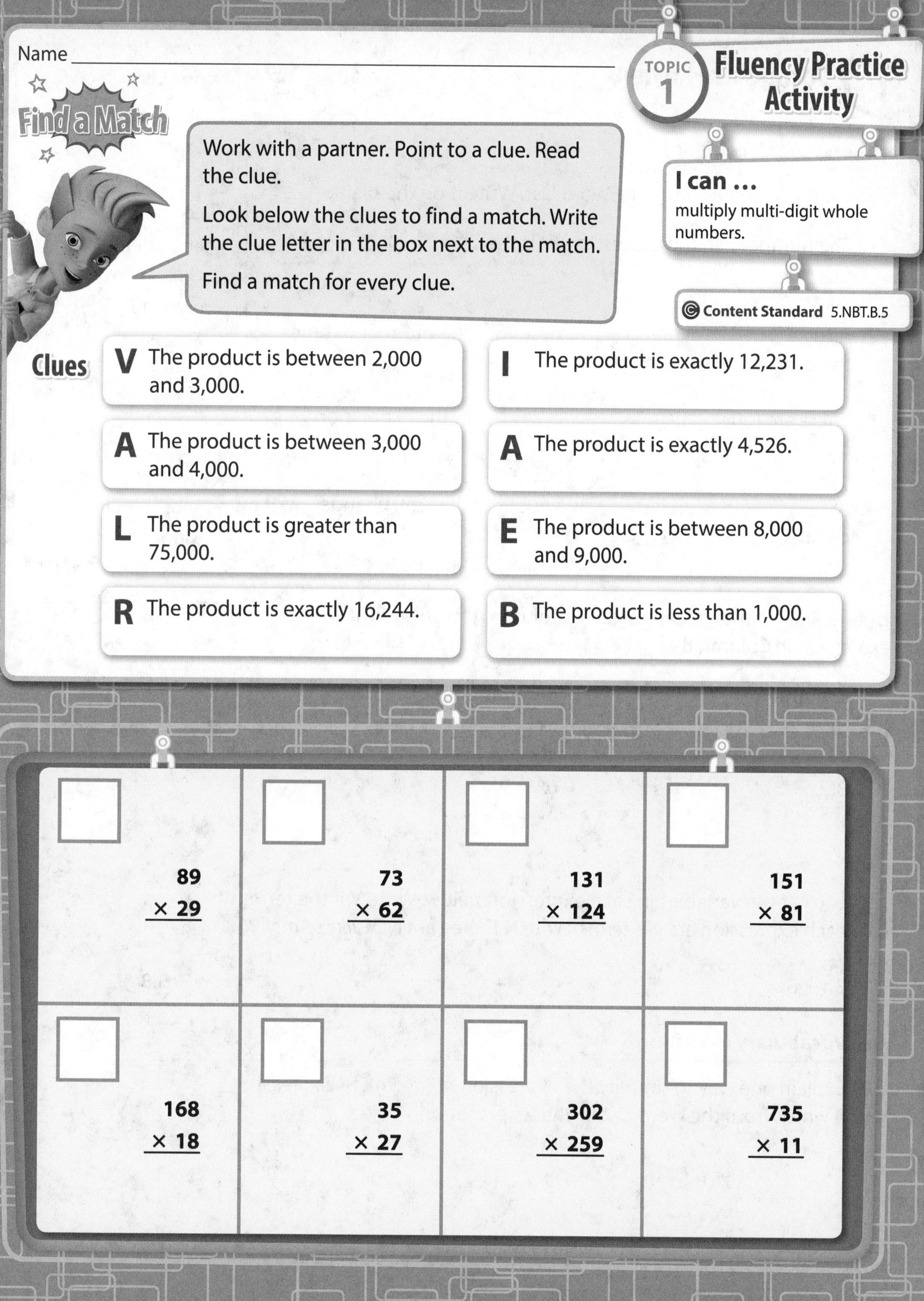

Name ____________________

Find a Match

TOPIC 1

Fluency Practice Activity

Work with a partner. Point to a clue. Read the clue.

Look below the clues to find a match. Write the clue letter in the box next to the match.

Find a match for every clue.

I can ...
multiply multi-digit whole numbers.

Content Standard 5.NBT.B.5

Clues

V The product is between 2,000 and 3,000.

I The product is exactly 12,231.

A The product is between 3,000 and 4,000.

A The product is exactly 4,526.

L The product is greater than 75,000.

E The product is between 8,000 and 9,000.

R The product is exactly 16,244.

B The product is less than 1,000.

☐ 89×29	☐ 73×62	☐ 131×124	☐ 151×81
☐ 168×18	☐ 35×27	☐ 302×259	☐ 735×11

Word List

- algebraic expression
- base
- coefficient
- equivalent expressions
- evaluate
- exponent
- formula
- like terms
- power
- simplify
- substitution
- terms
- variable

Understand Vocabulary

Choose the best term from the Word List. Write it on the blank.

1. The number 5 in the expression 5^3 is the ________________.

2. A(n) ________________ describes the number of times the base is used as a factor.

3. There are four ________________ in the expression $5k + 3 - 2k + 7$.

4. A ________________ is a quantity that can change or vary.

Draw a line from each expression in Column A to an *equivalent expression* in Column B.

Column A	Column B
5. $3x + 2$	$6x$
6. $7x - x$	$4(x - 2)$
7. $3(2x - 3)$	$6x - 9$
8. $x - 8 + 3x$	$4x + 3 - x - 1$

9. Look at the variables in each expression below. Write **Y** if the terms of each expression are *like terms*. Write **N** if they are NOT *like terms*.

$3a + 3z$ ____ $\frac{x}{3} + \frac{x}{4}$ ____ $4j - j + 3.8j$ ____

Use Vocabulary in Writing

10. Explain one way to simplify the expression $4(3q - q)$. Use at least 4 words from the Word List in your explanation.

© Pearson Education, Inc. 6

Name ______________________________

TOPIC 1

Reteaching

Set A pages 7–12

Evaluate 6^3.

6 is the base and 3 is the exponent.

6 is used as a factor 3 times.

$6 \times 6 \times 6 = 216$

Remember that any base number, except zero, with an exponent of 0 has a value of 1.

Evaluate each expression.

1. 9^2 **2.** 99^1 **3.** $3{,}105^0$

Set B pages 13–18

Use the order of operations to evaluate expressions with parentheses and brackets.

Order of Operations

1. Compute inside parentheses and brackets.
2. Evaluate terms with exponents.
3. Multiply and divide from left to right.
4. Add and subtract from left to right.

Remember that you can think of brackets as outside parentheses and evaluate the inside parentheses first.

Evaluate each expression.

1. $80 - 4^2 \div 8$

2. $92.3 - (3.2 \div 0.4) \times 2^3$

3. $\left[(2^3 \times 2.5) \div \frac{1}{2}\right] + 120$

4. $[20 + (2.5 \cdot 3)] - 3^3$

5. $\left[(2 \times 10^0) \div \frac{1}{3}\right] + 8$

Set C pages 19–24

A variable represents an unknown quantity that can change.

The expression $24 + n$ means "the sum of 24 and a number." The unknown number is a variable that is expressed by a letter, n.

Operation Terms

Addition → Sum

Subtraction → Difference

Multiplication → Product

Division → Quotient

Remember that you can use any letter as a variable to represent an unknown value.

Write an algebraic expression to represent each situation.

1. 22 less than 5 times a number f

2. 48 times a number of game markers, g

3. a number of eggs, e, divided by 12

4. 3 times the sum of m and 7

Set D pages 25–30

Each part of an expression that is separated by a plus or a minus sign is called a term.

$$4x + 9 - \frac{x}{2}$$

terms

A coefficient is a number that is multiplied by a variable. In the expression above, 4 is the coefficient of x in the product $4x$.

Remember that terms grouped inside parentheses can also be viewed as a single part of an expression.

In **1** and **2**, write the number of terms in each expression and identify any coefficients.

1. $12 + y$

2. $8x + (9 \div 3) - 4.3$

3. Write an expression that has four terms and includes two variables.

Set E pages 31–36

What is the value of $8a \div b + 2c - d^2$, when $a = 3$, $b = 4$, $c = \frac{1}{2}$, and $d = 2$?

Evaluate the expression.

$8a \div b + 2c - d^2 =$

$8(3) \div 4 + 2(\frac{1}{2}) - 2^2 = 3$

Use substitution to replace each variable with its value.

Remember that using *substitution* means to replace the variables with the given values.

Evaluate each expression for $n = 7$, $x = 4$, $y = 8$, and $z = 1$.

1. $12x - 7$

2. $x^2 \div y$

3. $5z + 3n - z^3$

4. $y^2 \div 2x + 3n - z$

Set F pages 37–42

Equivalent expressions are expressions that have the same value. You can use the properties of operations to write the expression $4(2x + 9)$ as an equivalent expression.

$4(2x + 9) = 4(2x) + 4(9)$ ← Distributive Property

$= (4 \cdot 2)x + 36$ ← Associative Property of Multiplication

$= 8x + 36$

So $8x + 36$ is equivalent to $4(2x + 9)$.

Remember that you may need to use more than one property to write an equivalent expression.

Use properties of operations to complete the equivalent expressions.

1. $2(x + 4)$ and ____ x + ____

2. $5x - 45$ and 5(____ − ____)

3. $3(x + 7)$ and ____ x + ____

© Pearson Education, Inc. 6

Name ______________________

TOPIC 1

Reteaching
Continued

Set G pages 43–48

Simplify the expression $3x + 7 + 6x$.

$3x + 7 + 6x$	Identify the like terms, $3x$ and $6x$.
$= 3x + 6x + 7$	Commutative Property of Addition
$= 9x + 7$	Simplify.

Remember that only like terms can be combined.

Simplify each expression.

1. $9y + 4 - 6y$
2. $3x + 5 + 7x$
3. $2y + 8 - y$
4. $8x + 13 - 3x + 9$
5. $y^2 + 3y^2$
6. $4x + 15 - 3x + 10$
7. $20y - 15 - 6y$
8. $10x + 2x - 12x$

Set H pages 49–54

For algebraic expressions to be equivalent, each expression must name the same value no matter what value is substituted for the variable.

x	$5x + 20$	$5(x + 4)$	$x + 4$
1	25	25	5
2	30	30	6
3	35	35	7

You can use properties of operations to determine whether expressions are equivalent.

Use the Distributive Property to write $5x + 20$ as $5(x + 4)$.

$$5x + 20 = 5 \cdot x + 5 \cdot 4$$
$$= 5(x + 4)$$

Properties of operations cannot be used to write $5x + 20$ or $5(x + 4)$ as $x + 4$.
$5x + 20$ and $5(x + 4)$ are equivalent expressions.

Remember that equivalent algebraic expressions must name the same number regardless of the value of the variable.

Complete the table. Then circle the expressions that are equivalent.

1.

y	$5(2.2y + 1) - 3$	$11y + 5 - y$	$11y + 2$
1			
2			
3			

Write Yes or No to indicate whether the expressions are equivalent.

2. $10x - 3 + 2x - 5$ and $4(3x - 2)$
3. $3y + 3$ and $9\left(y + \frac{1}{3}\right)$
4. $6(3x + 1)$ and $9x + 6 + 9x$

Set I pages 55–60

A formula is a rule that uses symbols to relate two or more quantities.

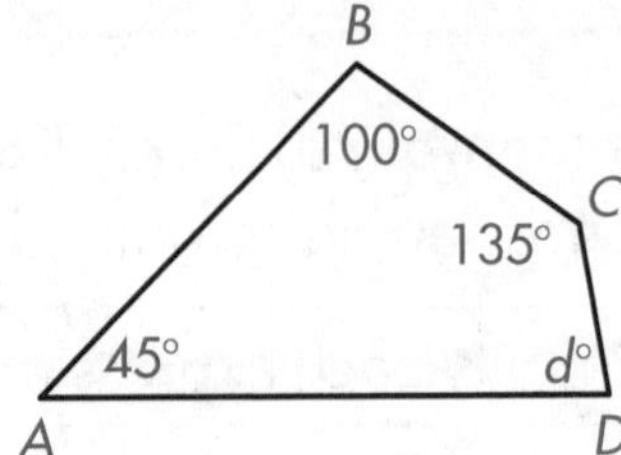

Find the missing angle measure of the quadrilateral by using the formula $d = 360° - (a + b + c)$, where a, b, c, and d are the angle measures of the quadrilateral.

Identify the values in the formula. Then substitute the values in the formula and evaluate.

$$d = 360° - (a + b + c)$$
$$d = 360° - (45° + 100° + 135°)$$
$$d = 360° - 280°$$
$$d = 80°$$

The measure of angle D is 80°.

Remember that you may need to use the order of operations to evaluate formulas.

1. The formula $F = 1.8 \times (K - 273) + 32$ can be used to convert temperature in degrees Fahrenheit, F, to degrees Kelvin, K. Use the formula to convert a temperature of 323 Kelvin to degrees Fahrenheit.
2. Yolanda's bank offers a simple interest loan with a rate of 4%, or 0.04. She plans to borrow $4,000. Use the formula $I = prt$ to find the amount of interest she will pay if she pays off the loan in 5 years.
3. A formula to find the perimeter of a rectangle is $P = 2\ell + 2w$. What is the perimeter of a picture frame with a length of 6.5 centimeters and a width of 5.5 centimeters?

Set J pages 61–66

Think about these questions to help you **look for and make use of structure.**

Thinking Habits

- What patterns can I see and describe?
- How can I use the patterns to solve the problem?
- Can I see expressions and objects in different ways?
- What equivalent expressions can I use?

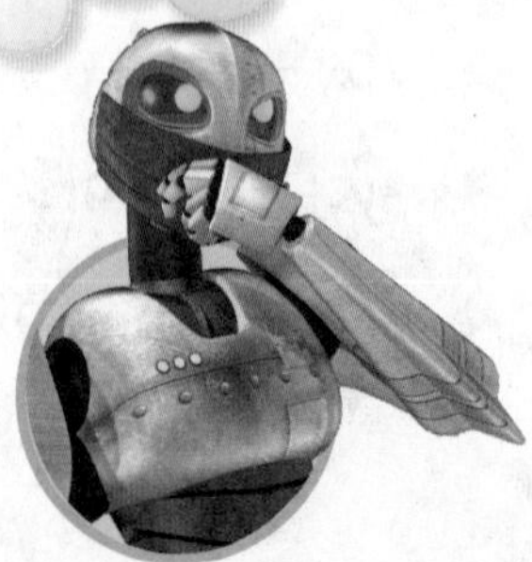

Remember to use the structure of an algebraic expression to write equivalent expressions.

Each week, Michael practices his drums for 5 hours and his cello for 3 hours. To double the amount of practice time, he uses the expression $2(5x + 3x)$ to represent the total hours he will practice over x weeks.

1. Describe what the quantities $5x$ and $3x$ represent in the situation.
2. How can Michael use structure to write an equivalent expression?

© Pearson Education, Inc. 6

Name ___

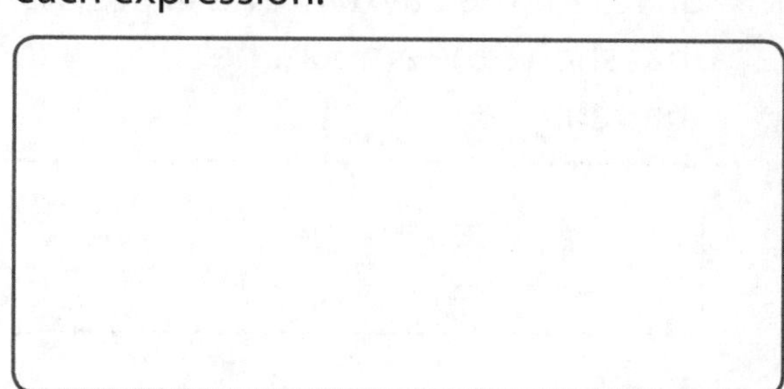

1. Evaluate the expression below.

   $(4.5 + 7.6) - 8 \div 2.5$

2. Large balloons are sold in packages of 12. Select the expressions that can represent the total number of balloons in *p* packages of large balloons.

   - ☐ $12 - p$
   - ☐ $12 \times p$
   - ☐ $p + 12$
   - ☐ $p \div 12$
   - ☐ $12p$

In **3** and **4**, use the expression $5h + 8$.

3. List the terms in the expression.

4. What is the coefficient in the expression?

5. The same digits are used for the expressions 3^4 and 4^3. Explain how to compare the value of each expression.

6. For questions 6a–6d, choose Yes or No to tell if the expressions are equivalent.

   6a. $6.5 \times 4 - 7.8$ and $26 - 7.8$ ○ Yes ○ No

   6b. $10.3 + (8.7 - 4.2)$ and $19 - 4.2$ ○ Yes ○ No

   6c. $(5^2 + 3.4) \div 6.8$ and $13.4 \div 6.8$ ○ Yes ○ No

   6d. $6.5 \times (12.6 - 9.3)$ and 6.5×3.3 ○ Yes ○ No

7. Barb sells necklaces for \$3 each. She spent \$15 on supplies. Write an expression to show how much she earns if she sells *n* necklaces.

8. Mr. Parker wants to rent a cargo van for a day. It will cost the daily fee of \$50 plus \$0.35 per mile driven.

Part A

Let m = the number of miles Mr. Parker drives for the day. Write an expression that shows the amount he will pay for the van.

Part B

Evaluate the expression you wrote to find how much Mr. Parker will pay if he drives 80 miles.

9. Darnell's truck can travel 18 miles on 1 gallon of gasoline.

How many gallons of gasoline will Darnell need to travel 315 miles?

Use the formula $\frac{d}{m} = g$, where m represents miles per gallon, d is distance traveled, and g is the number of gallons of gasoline used.

Ⓐ 11 gallons

Ⓑ 14.5 gallons

Ⓒ 17.5 gallons

Ⓓ 19 gallons

10. For questions 10a–10d, choose Yes or No to tell if the expressions are equivalent.

10a. $4(5c + 3)$ and $9c + 7$ ○ Yes ○ No

10b. $10f - 10$ and $2(8f - 5)$ ○ Yes ○ No

10c. $12g + 21$ and $3(4g + 7)$ ○ Yes ○ No

10d. $6(4j - 6)$ and $24 - 36j$ ○ Yes ○ No

11. Draw lines to match each property on the left to its corresponding pair of equivalent expressions on the right.

Distributive Property	$(6 + 9) + 11 = 6 + (9 + 11)$
Associative Property	$16k - 24 = 8(2k - 3)$
Commutative Property	$12 \times 4 \times 5 = 4 \times 5 \times 12$

12. Choose all of the expressions that are equal to 243.

☐ 3^5

☐ 5^3

☐ $5 \times 5 \times 5$

☐ $3 \times 3 \times 3 \times 3 \times 3$

☐ $3 \times 3 \times 3 \times 5 \times 5$

© Pearson Education, Inc. 6

Name ____________________

13. On a trip, Morgan drives at an average speed of 65 miles per hour. The equation $d = 65t$ can be used to find the distance, d, she travels, where t is the time in hours.

Fill in the table below to find the distances at different times.

Time, t	Distance, d
3	195
4	
6	390
7	
10	

14. Which expression is equivalent to $5b + 13 - 2b - 7$?

Ⓐ $3b + 6$

Ⓑ $7b + 6$

Ⓒ $9b$

Ⓓ $3b + 20$

15. Select the expressions that are equivalent to $12n - 8$.

☐ $3n + 4 + 3n + 4 + 4n$

☐ $11n + 4 + n - 12$

☐ $6(6n - 2)$

☐ $4(3n - 2)$

☐ $4n + 2^2 - 12 + 8n$

16. Use the diagram below.

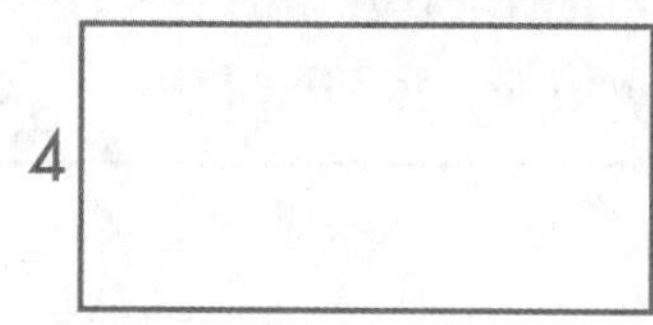

Part A

Write an algebraic expression for the perimeter of the rectangle.

Part B

Write an expression equivalent to the expression you wrote for Part A.

Part C

Find the perimeter of the rectangle if $w = 8$.

17. Quinn says that the expressions $10x - 4x + 6$ and $3(2x + 2)$ are not equivalent because one expression has a term that is subtracted and the other does not. Do you agree? Explain.

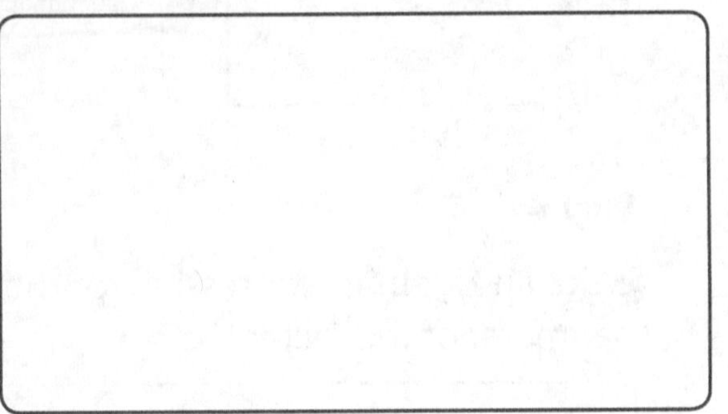

18. Two expressions are shown below.

$3(3x - 5)$

$6x - 15$

Part A

Use the Distributive Property to write an expression that is equivalent to $3(3x - 5)$.

Part B

Use the Distributive Property to write an expression that is equivalent to $6x - 15$.

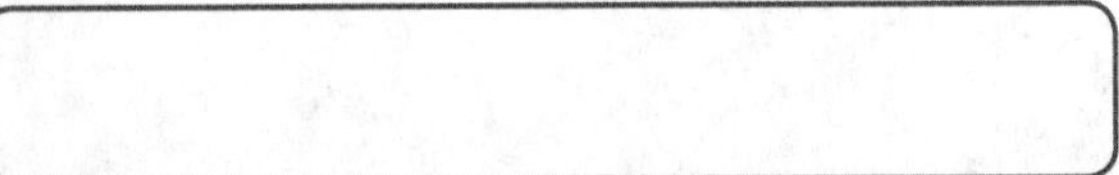

Part C

Explain whether the expressions are equivalent.

19. Use the formula $V = s^3$, where V is the volume and s is the length of each side. Which is the volume of the cube below?

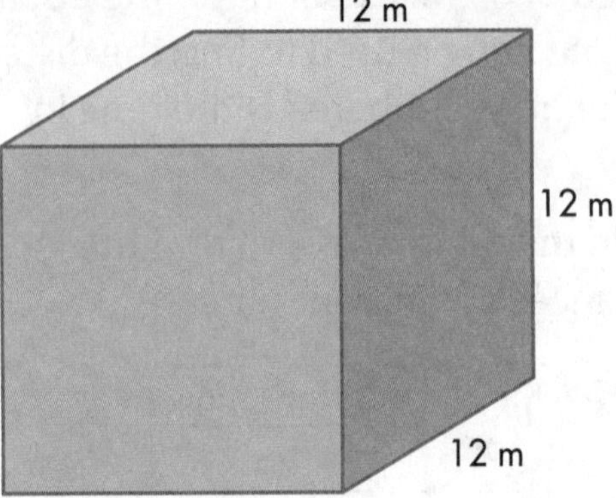

Ⓐ 36 m^3

Ⓑ 288 m^3

Ⓒ $1{,}152 \text{ m}^3$

Ⓓ $1{,}728 \text{ m}^3$

20. Write two algebraic expressions equivalent to $3(14x + 23 + 5x)$.

© Pearson Education, Inc. 6

Name ______________________________

Exercise Classes

Danny teaches an exercise class at the local community center.
He distributed a flyer with the information below to advertise the class.

Danny's Exercise Class	
Registration (includes exercise bands)	$5
Each class	$8

1. Danny wants to know how much his exercise classes cost for each person based on the number of classes taken.

Part A

Use the table above to answer the question.

Let $c =$ the number of exercise classes a person takes. Write an expression that shows the amount a person will pay to take exercise classes.

Part B

Use your expression from Part A to fill in the table below.

Fill in the table below to find the amount a person will pay for taking c exercise classes.

Number of Exercise Classes, c	
1	13
3	
5	45
8	
10	

Part C

Use the table above to answer the question.

Suppose Danny drops the registration fee and increases each class by $1. Write an expression that shows the new amount a person will pay to take exercise classes.

Part D

Use your expression from Part C to fill in the table below.

Fill in the table below to find the amount a person will pay for taking *c* exercise classes.

Number of Exercise Classes, *c*	
1	9
3	
5	45
8	
10	

Part E

Use your tables from Part B and Part D to answer the question.

Will it cost more or less to attend 3 exercise classes after Danny changes the registration fee? 5 exercise classes? 10 exercise classes?

2. If you were running Danny's exercise class, would you prefer the plan before or after Danny changes the registration fee? Explain.

© Pearson Education, Inc. 6

Algebra: Solve Equations and Inequalities

Essential Question: What procedures can be used to solve equations and inequalities?

Do you know that recycled materials can be used to make houses?

Some places recycle as much of their trash as possible, and what's left over, they turn into fuel.

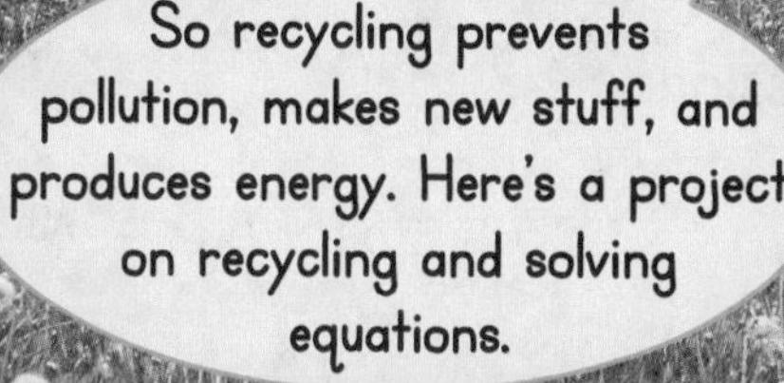

So recycling prevents pollution, makes new stuff, and produces energy. Here's a project on recycling and solving equations.

Math and Science Project: Reduce, Reuse, Recycle

Do Research Use the Internet or other sources to learn about what goes into landfills. How much of the waste stream could be recycled? Think about the stuff you throw out. What would happen if you recycled just one type of waste, such as cloth, food, paper, plastic, or metal?

Journal: Write a Report Include what you found. Also in your report:

- Outline a plan for reducing and recycling waste.
- Write and solve an equation to find how many weeks it would take the average family of four to recycle 1,000 pounds of one type of waste.

Name ________________________________

Review What You Know

Vocabulary

Choose the best term from the box. Write it on the blank.

- algebraic expression
- coefficient
- evaluate
- variable

1. In $6x$, x is a(n) __________.
2. $x + 5$ is an example of a(n) __________________.
3. _________ an expression to find its value.

Equality

Tell whether the equation is true or false.

4. $6 + 2 = 2 + 6$
5. $2.5 - 1 = 1 - 2.5$
6. $\frac{1}{2} \times 3 = 3 \times \frac{1}{2}$
7. $\frac{3}{4} \div 5 = \frac{3}{4} \times \frac{1}{5}$
8. $5 \div \frac{1}{3} = \frac{5}{3}$
9. $\frac{2}{3} \times 5 = \frac{10}{15}$

Expressions

Evaluate each expression.

10. $x - 2$ for $x = 8$
11. $2b$ for $b = 9$
12. $3\frac{3}{4} + y$ for $y = \frac{5}{6}$
13. $\frac{15}{x}$ for $x = 3$
14. $5.6t$ for $t = 0.7$
15. $4x$ for $x = \frac{1}{2}$

Order of Operations

16. In which order should you compute the operations in the expression? Then evaluate the expression.

    $[(33 \div 3) + 1] - 2^2$

© Pearson Education, Inc. 6

My Word Cards

Use the examples for each word on the front of the card to help complete the definitions on the back.

A-Z Glossary

equation

$5 + 3 = 16 - 8$

equal values

Addition Property of Equality

$(d - 4) + 4 = (17) + 4$

Subtraction Property of Equality

$(r + 16) - 16 = (21) - 16$

Multiplication Property of Equality

$(w \div 3) \times 3 = 15 \times 3$

Division Property of Equality

$(7s) \div 7 = (42) \div 7$

inverse relationship

$(k + 6) - 6 = (15) - 6$

$k = 9$

Subtracting 6 "undoes" adding 6.

reciprocals

$\frac{2}{3} \quad \frac{3}{2}$

$\frac{2}{3} \times \frac{3}{2} = \frac{6}{6} = 1$

inequality

$x \geq 4$

My Word Cards

Complete each definition. Extend learning by writing your own definitions.

The property that states that the two sides of an equation remain equal when the same amount is added to both sides of the equation is called the

____

________________________.

A mathematical sentence with equal values on either side of an equal sign (=) is called an

________________________.

The property that states that the two sides of an equation remain equal when both sides of the equation are multiplied by the same amount is called the

____

________________________.

The property that states that the two sides of an equation remain equal when the same amount is subtracted from both sides of the equation is called the

____

________________________.

Operations that undo each other have

an ________________________.

The property that states that the two sides of an equation remain equal when both sides of the equation are divided by the same amount is called the

____

________________________.

A mathematical sentence that contains $<$ (less than), $>$ (greater than), $\leq$ (less than or equal to), $\geq$ (greater than or equal to), or $\neq$ (is not equal to) is called

an ____________________.

Two numbers whose product is 1 are

called ________________________.

© Pearson Education, Inc. 6

Name ______________________

Lesson 2-1
Understand Equations and Solutions

I can ...
find a value for a variable that makes an equation true.

Content Standard 6.EE.B.5
Mathematical Practices MP.2, MP.3, MP.4, MP.5, MP.6, MP.7, MP.8

Solve & Share Unit cubes are placed on a pan balance. There are 3 cubes on one pan and 9 cubes on the other pan. What can you do to make the pans balance? ***Solve this problem any way you choose.***

A pan balance can model the relationship between two quantities. You can write an equation with a variable to show this relationship.

Look Back! **MP.7 Use Structure** Suppose that you added 10 cubes to the pan with 3 cubes and then added 4 cubes to the pan with 9 cubes. Would the pans balance? Write an equation to show this relationship.

How Can You Determine Whether a Given Number Makes an Equation True?

A

Jordan received a \$15.00 gift card for phone apps. He has used \$4.50 of the value and wants to buy one more app to use up the balance. Which app could he buy?

A bar diagram, also called a tape diagram, can be a useful tool for writing and solving an equation.

Phone Apps	
All Recipes	\$ 9.50
Headliners Sports	\$10.50
Remote Desktop	\$12.00

\$15.00

\$4.50	x

B An equation is a mathematical sentence that uses an equal sign to show that two expressions are equal.

A solution of an equation is a value for the variable that makes the equation true.

Find the solution of \$4.50 + x = \$15.00.

C Substitute the cost of each app for x and evaluate.

Try x = \$9.50:	\$4.50 + \$9.50 = \$14.00	Not a solution
Try x = \$10.50:	\$4.50 + \$10.50 = \$15.00	Solution
Try x = \$12.00:	\$4.50 + \$12.00 = \$16.50	Not a solution

The solution is \$10.50, so Jordan should buy the *Headliners Sports* app.

Convince Me! **© MP.8 Generalize** Tracy received a \$21.00 gift card for phone apps. She has used \$9.00 of the value and wants to buy one more app to use up the balance. Use the equation \$21.00 = x + \$9.00 to determine which app she should buy.

© Pearson Education, Inc. 6

Name ______________________________

Practice Buddy Tools Assessment

Guided Practice*

Do You Understand?

1. When is an equation true?

2. **MP.2 Reasoning** Ben says that $n = 5$ is the solution of the equation $7n = 45$. How can you check whether he is correct?

3. There are 3 cubes on one pan and 11 cubes on the other pan. Lucy thinks she should add 7, 8, 9, or 10 cubes to make the pans balance. How can you use the equation $3 + c = 11$ to find the number of cubes Lucy should add?

Do You Know How?

In **4–7**, substitute each value of the variable to find the solution of each equation.

4. $d + 9 = 35$ $d = 16, 22, 26, 36$

5. $13.4 - g = 8.1$ $g = 4.3, 5.3, 5.5, 6.5$

6. $4 = 36 \div m$ $m = 4, 6, 8, 9$

7. $c - 17 = 3.4$ $c = 13.4, 14.6, 18.4, 21.4$

In **8** and **9**, tell if each equation is true or false for $n = 8$.

8. $n = 54 - 36$

9. $5n = 40$

Independent Practice

In **10–15**, tell which value of the variable is the solution of the equation.

10. $t - 2.1 = 0$ $t = 2.1, 2.4, 2.6, 2.8$

11. $49 = 7r$ $r = 3, 6, 7, 9$

12. $24 \div h = 6$ $h = 1, 3, 6, 8$

13. $8.9 + a = 9.7$ $a = 0.7, 0.8, 0.9, 1.2$

14. $u + \$8.44 = \$12.00$ $u = \$2.56, \$2.66, \$3.46, \$3.56$

15. $\$4.10 = \$16.25 - y$ $y = \$12.15, \$12.95, \$13.05, \$13.15$

*For another example, see Set A on page 133.

Math Practices and Problem Solving

16. There are 27 pennies on one pan of a pan balance and 18 pennies on the other. To make the pans balance, Hillary thinks 5 pennies should be added to the higher pan, Sean thinks 8 pennies should be added, and Rachel thinks 9 pennies should be added. Use the equation $27 = 18 + p$ to determine who is correct.

17. **MP.3 Construct Arguments** Gerard spent $5.12 for a drink and a sandwich. His drink cost $1.30. Did he have a ham sandwich for $3.54, a tuna sandwich for $3.82, or a turkey sandwich for $3.92? Use the equation $s + 1.30 = 5.12$ to justify your answer.

18. **Higher Order Thinking** Write an equation that has 12 for a solution. Show how you know that 12 is the solution.

The variable in an equation can be represented with any letter you choose.

19. Gina's family is driving 255 miles to visit Sacramento. After driving for a while, they pass a sign that says "Sacramento: 124 miles." Substitute the values $m = 111$, 121, 131, and 141 in the equation $255 - m = 124$ to find the number of miles the family has already driven.

20. **Algebra** Alisa is making a quilt that uses a pattern of triangles like the one shown. Write an equation that represents the missing side length if the perimeter is 19 centimeters.

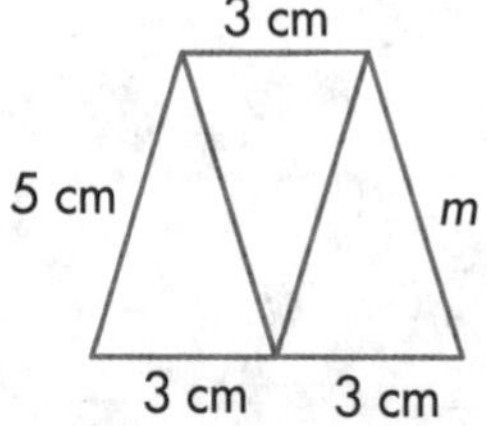

Common Core Assessment

21. Trish has $26.00 to spend at a craft store. She buys fabric that costs $18.62. She also wants to buy knitting needles for $7.32, silk flowers for $7.38, or oil paints for $8.48.

Use the equation $\$18.62 + c = \$26.00$, where c is the item cost, to find the most expensive item she can buy. Explain how you found the answer.

© Pearson Education, Inc. 6

Name ____________________

Homework & Practice 2-1

Understand Equations and Solutions

Another Look!

Anton walked 8.9 miles of his 13.5-mile goal for this week. Which path should Anton walk so he meets his goal for the week?

Path Lengths	
Meadow Path	3.2 miles
Circle Path	4.2 miles
Oak Tree Path	4.6 miles

13.5	
m	8.9

Find the solution of $m + 8.9 = 13.5$
Substitute the different values for the variable, m.

Try $m = 3.2$: $3.2 + 8.9$ miles $= 12.1$ miles Not a solution
Try $m = 4.2$: $4.2 + 8.9$ miles $= 13.1$ miles Not a solution
Try $m = 4.6$: $4.6 + 8.9$ miles $= 13.5$ miles Solution

Since the solution to the equation is 4.6 miles, Anton should walk the Oak Tree Path to complete his 13.5-mile goal for the week.

In **1–12**, tell which value of the variable is the solution of the equation.

1. $5.6 = l + 4.09$ $l = 0.7, 0.97, 1.51, 9.69$

2. $5k = 65$ $k = 11, 12, 13, 14$

3. $t - \$5.60 = \$1.04$ $t = \$6.00, \$6.10, \$6.64, \$7.00$

4. $133 \div y = 19$ $y = 6, 7, 8, 9$

5. $14 = \frac{u}{6}$ $u = 78, 81, 84, 90$

6. $9 + a = 46$ $a = 37, 39, 41, 55$

7. $6.8 = 2.89 + m$ $m = 3.9, 3.91, 4, 4.11$

8. $8c = 64$ $c = 6, 7, 8, 9$

9. $0.06 = n - 4.4$ $n = 4.406, 4.46, 4.64, 5$

10. $\frac{176}{g} = 16$ $g = 10, 11, 12, 13$

11. $25.54 = 83.1 - b$ $b = 57, 57.47, 57.56, 57.65$

12. $\$19.25p = \$115.50$ $p = \$5.25, \$6.00, \$6.50, \$7.00$

In **13** and **14**, use the table.

13. Higher Order Thinking James bought a movie ticket and popcorn for \$12.20. The movie ticket cost \$8.45. Use the equation $c + \$8.45 = \$12.20$ to find which size popcorn James bought. How much change did he get back if he paid with a \$20 bill?

Cost of Popcorn	
Small	\$2.85
Medium	\$3.75
Large	\$4.75
Extra Large	\$4.85

14. MP.2 Reasoning Kyle bought a movie ticket for \$8.45 and a drink for \$1.80. He only had enough money to buy the large popcorn. How much money did Kyle have to start with? Write an equation to show your reasoning.

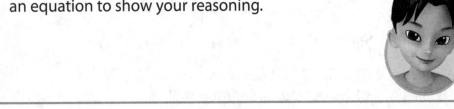

Be precise when you write an equation. Remember to define the variable in the equation.

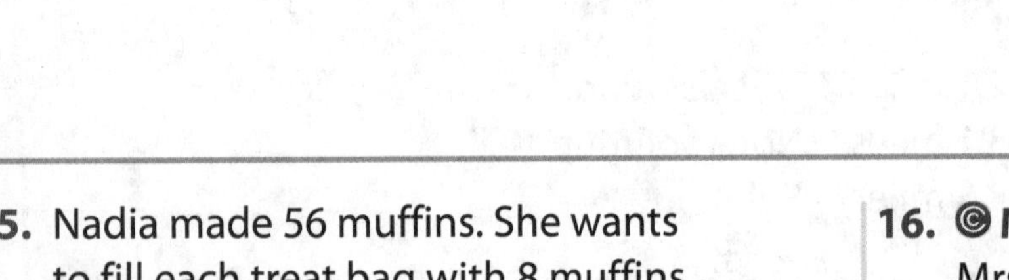

15. Nadia made 56 muffins. She wants to fill each treat bag with 8 muffins. Nadia bought 7 bags. Use the equation $56 \div b = 8$ to explain whether Nadia bought enough bags.

16. MP.7 Use Structure The students in Mrs. Johnson's class are running a race. Let g represent the number of girl runners and b represent the number of boy runners. Write an algebraic expression that describes the total number of students in the race.

Common Core Assessment

17. Jerry built a table with a square top. The perimeter of the tabletop is 18 feet. He knows that each side of the table is 3, $3\frac{1}{2}$, 4, or $4\frac{1}{2}$ feet long. Use the equation $18 = 4s$, where s is the side length of the table, to determine which is the length of the tabletop.

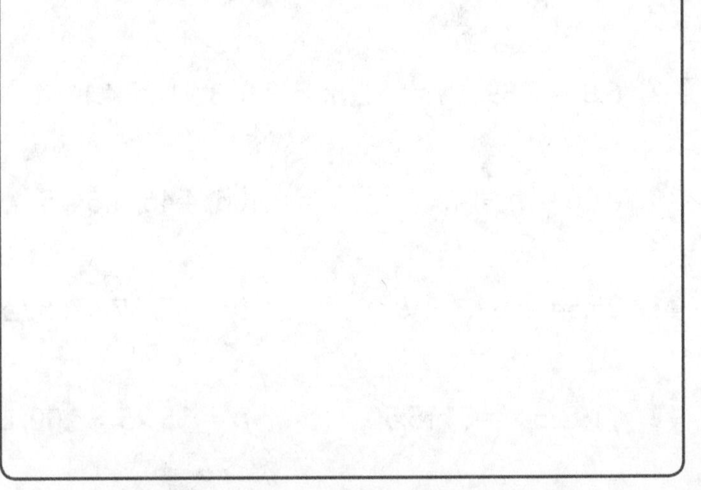

© Pearson Education, Inc. 6

Name ____________________

Solve

Lesson 2-2
Properties of Equality

I can …
use the properties of equality to write equivalent equations.

Content Standards 6.EE.A.4, 6.EE.B.7
Mathematical Practices MP.2, MP.3, MP.4, MP.7

Solve & Share

Start with the equation $4 + 8 = 12$ and complete each computation listed on the poster below. Do each computation individually. You may use the table below to record your results.

Which of the computations keeps the equation true? Tell how you know.

You can use reasoning to determine if an equation is true.

Start	Computation To Do	Result
$4 + 8 = 12$	Add 5 to both sides of the equation.	
$4 + 8 = 12$	Add 3 to the left side of the equation. Add 5 to the right side of the equation.	
$4 + 8 = 12$	Divide the left side of the equation by 2. Multiply the right side of the equation by 2.	
$4 + 8 = 12$	Subtract 4 from both sides of the equation.	

Look Back! **MP.7 Use Structure** Complete the equation $7 + \square = 10 - \square$ by filling in the missing numbers. Describe at least two other operations with numbers that you can do to each side of the equation to keep it balanced.

How Can You Write Equivalent Equations?

A

Recall that an equation uses an equal sign to show that two expressions have the same value.

$$5 + 3 = 8$$

The Addition Property of Equality states that the two sides of an equation stay equal when the same amount is added to both sides of the equation.

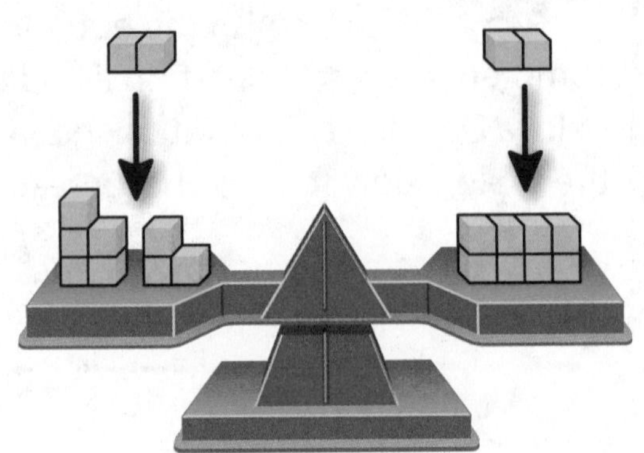

$(5 + 3) + 2 = 8 + 2$

An equation is like a balance. To keep the equation balanced, you must do the same thing to both sides.

B The Subtraction Property of Equality states that when you subtract the same amount from both sides of an equation the two sides of the equation stay equal.

$$5 + 3 = 8$$

$$(5 + 3) - 2 = 8 - 2$$

C The Multiplication Property of Equality states that when you multiply both sides of an equation by the same amount the two sides of the equation stay equal.

$$5 + 3 = 8$$

$$(5 + 3) \times 2 = 8 \times 2$$

You can use the properties of equality to keep both sides of an equation equal.

D The Division Property of Equality states that when you divide both sides of an equation by the same non-zero amount the two sides of the equation stay equal.

$$5 + 3 = 8$$

$$(5 + 3) \div 2 = 8 \div 2$$

Convince Me! **MP.7 Use Structure** If $5y = 25$, which property of equality was used to keep the equation $5y - 7 = 25 - 7$ balanced?

© Pearson Education, Inc. 6

Name ______________________________

Practice Buddy Tools Assessment

Another Example

Addition Property of Equality

If $y - 12 = 30$, does $y - 12 + 12 = 30 + 12$?

Why or why not?

Yes; the same number, 12, was added to both sides of the equation.

Division Property of Equality

If $4y = 20$, does $4y \div 4 = 20 \div 5$?

Why or why not?

No; both sides of the equation are divided by different numbers, not by the same amount.

Guided Practice*

Do You Understand?

1. **MP.2 Reasoning** A pan balance shows $7 + 5 = 12$. If 4 units are removed from one side, what needs to be done to the other side to keep the pans balanced?

2. **MP.2 Reasoning** If one side of the equation $23 + 43 = 66$ is multiplied by 3, what needs to be done to the other side of the equation to keep the sides equal?

Do You Know How?

In **3–5**, answer yes or no and explain why or why not.

3. If $23 + 37 = 60$, does $23 + 37 + 9 = 60 + 9$?

4. If $7m = 63$, does $7m - 9 = 63 - 9$?

5. If $35 - 7 = 28$, does $(35 - 7) \div 7 = 28 \div 4$?

Independent Practice

In **6–9**, tell which property of equality was used.

6. $5m + 4 = 19$
$5m + 4 - 3 = 19 - 3$

7. $3t = 20$
$3t \div 2 = 20 \div 2$

8. $\frac{n}{6} = 9$
$\left(\frac{n}{6}\right) \times 5 = 9 \times 5$

9. $5b - 6 = 14$
$(5b - 6) + 2 = 14 + 2$

*For another example, see Set B on page 133.

Math Practices and Problem Solving

10. Bobbie wrote $y + 6 = 15$. Then she wrote $(y + 6) \div 3 = 15$. Explain why the second equation is not equivalent to the first. What can Bobbie do to make the two equations equivalent?

11. **MP.2 Reasoning** Rolanda is planning a sleep-over. It will start at 7:30 P.M. and end at 11:15 A.M. the next morning. How long will the sleep-over last?

12. **MP.3 Construct Arguments** Scientists often use a pan balance to measure mass when doing experiments. The equation $4 + 3 - 1 = 7 - 1$ represents when a scientist takes one unit of mass from each side of a pan balance. Construct an argument to explain how the scientist knows that the pans are still in balance.

13. **Higher Order Thinking** Emil has \$1 and a quarter in his pile. Jade has 5 quarters in her pile. If Emil gives Jade \$1 and Jade gives Emil 4 quarters, will the two piles still be equal in value? Explain.

14. **A-Z Vocabulary** If $7w = 49$, which property of equality was used to find the equivalent equation $7w \div 7 = 49 \div 7$?

15. **MP.3 Construct Arguments** John wrote that $5 + 5 = 10$. Then he wrote that $5 + 5 + n = 10 + n$. Are the equations John wrote equivalent? Explain.

Common Core Assessment

16. Which equation is equivalent to $n + 4 = 11$?

    Ⓐ $(n + 4) \times 2 = 11$

    Ⓑ $(n + 4) \times 2 = 11 \div 2$

    Ⓒ $(n + 4) \times 2 = 11 \times 4$

    Ⓓ $(n + 4) \times 2 = 11 \times 2$

17. Which of the equations is **NOT** equivalent to $8p = 12$?

    Ⓐ $8p \div 8 = 12 \div 8$

    Ⓑ $8p \div 8 = 12 \div 12$

    Ⓒ $8p + 4 = 12 + 4$

    Ⓓ $8p - 2 = 12 - 2$

© Pearson Education, Inc. 6

Name ____________________

Homework & Practice 2-2

Properties of Equality

Another Look!

You can use the properties of equality to write equivalent equations.

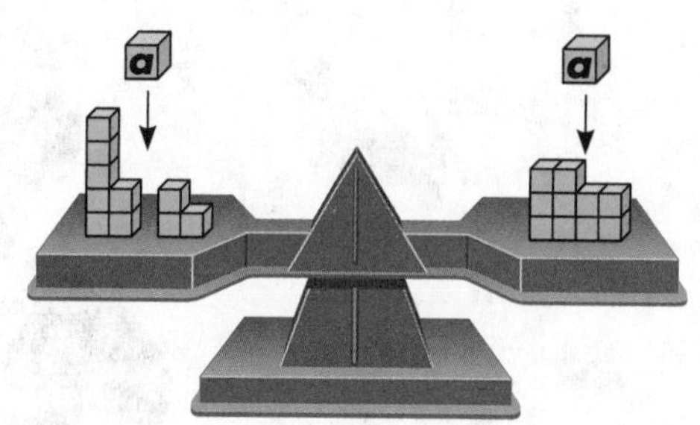

How can you use the properties of equality and a to write four equations that are equivalent to $7 + 3 = 10$?

Add the same number to each side. $7 + 3 = 10$, so $(7 + 3) + a = 10 + a$

Subtract the same number from each side. $7 + 3 = 10$, so $(7 + 3) - a = 10 - a$

Multiply each side by the same number. $7 + 3 = 10$, so $(7 + 3) \times a = 10 \times a$

Divide each side by the same number. $7 + 3 = 10$, so $(7 + 3) \div a = 10 \div a$

In **1–4**, tell which property of equality was used.

1. $49 = \frac{245}{v}$
$49 \times 65 = \left(\frac{245}{v}\right) \times 65$

2. $14 + s = 28$
$(14 + s) - 2 = 28 - 2$

3. $4y = 48$
$4y \div 4 = 48 \div 4$

4. $88 = 33 + 5x$
$88 - 33 = (33 + 5x) - 33$

In **5–8**, answer yes or no and explain why or why not.

5. If $10 \times 3 = 30$, does $10 \times 3 + 4 = 30 + 5$?

6. If $8n = 180$, does $8n \div 8 = 180 \div 8$?

7. If $d \div 3 = 10$, does $d \div 3 + 3 = 10 + 3$?

8. If $12 - 2 = 10$, does $12 - 2 - 3 = 10 - 2$?

9. **MP.4 Model with Math** Wayne has 6 times the number of songs on an MP3 player as his mom. If Wayne has 1,800 songs, what equation could you write to find the number of songs, *s*, his mom has on her MP3 player?

Remember, the expressions on each side of an equation are equal, or equivalent.

10. **MP.3 Construct Arguments** Maggie said she could add 8 to both sides of any equation and the expressions on both sides of the equation would still be equal. Do you agree? Explain why or why not.

11. James multiplies one side of the equation $56 + 124 = 180$ by a number n. What does he need to do to balance the equation?

12. **Number Sense** Write the next three numbers in this pattern. Then describe the pattern.

6, 10, 8, 12, 10, 14, 12, 16, 14

13. **Higher Order Thinking** A store sells 3 pens in a package. There are 12 packages of pens in a box. Write an equation to model the number of pens in a box. Use the equation to write another equation that uses the Subtraction Property of Equality. Explain how the equation is balanced.

An equation is balanced when the same number is subtracted from each side.

Common Core Assessment

14. Which equation is **NOT** equivalent to $5 + n = 10$?

Ⓐ $5 + n - n = 10 - n$

Ⓑ $5 + n - 5 = 10 - 10$

Ⓒ $5 + n - 5 = 10 - 5$

Ⓓ $5 + n + 3 = 10 + 3$

15. Which equation is equivalent to $5 = 95 \div x$?

Ⓐ $5 = (95 \div x) + 6$

Ⓑ $5 + 6 = (95 \div x) + 6$

Ⓒ $5 + 6 = (95 \div x) \times 6$

Ⓓ $5 \div 6 = (95 \div x) + 6$

© Pearson Education, Inc. 6

Name ______________________

Lesson 2-3
Solve Addition and Subtraction Equations

Solve & Share A group of students were on a school bus. At the last stop, the bus picked up 16 more students. The bus arrived at school with a total of 25 students. How many students were on the bus before the last stop? ***Solve this problem any way you choose.***

I can ...
solve an addition or subtraction equation.

Content Standards 6.EE.B.6, 6.EE.B.7
Mathematical Practices MP.2, MP.3, MP.4, MP.5

You can use appropriate tools to help you solve for the unknown.

Look Back! **MP.2 Reasoning** How does using cubes on the pan balance demonstrate the addition and subtraction properties of equality?

Essential Question

How Can You Solve an Addition Equation?

A

George had some plastic figures. After he bought 7 more figures, he had 25. How many plastic figures did George have before he bought more?

Let n represent the number of plastic figures George had before he bought more.

Solve the equation $n + 7 = 25$ to find the answer.

George bought 7 more figures.

To solve the equation, you need to find the value of *n*.

B

You can find the value of *n* by getting it alone on one side of the equation.

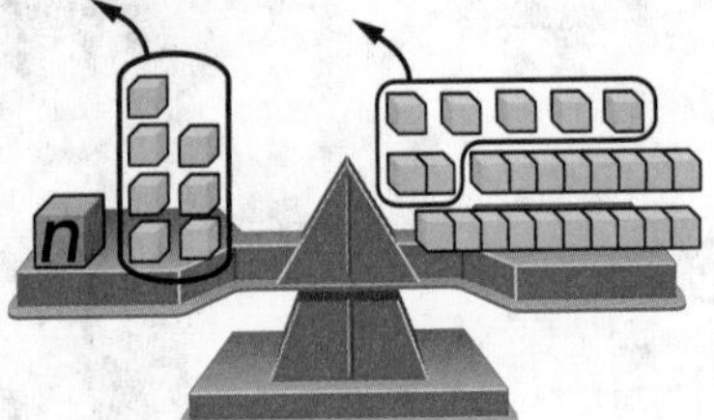

Take 7 away from each side. That will leave the *n* alone.

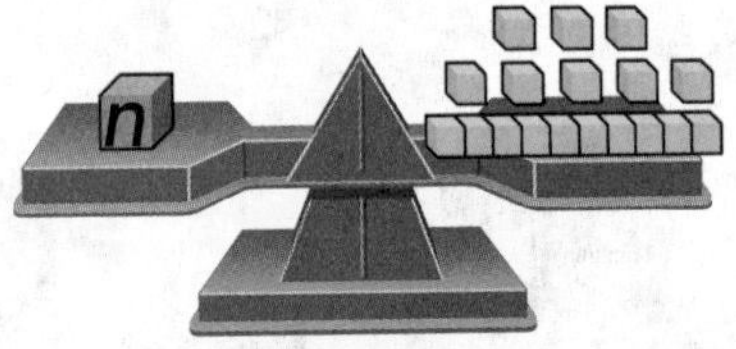

n is 18.

Operations that undo each other have an inverse relationship.

Subtracting 7 is the inverse of adding 7.

C

Solve the addition equation.

$$n + 7 = 25$$

$$n + 7 - 7 = 25 - 7$$

$$n = 18$$

To check, substitute 18 for *n*.

$$n + 7 = 25$$

$$18 + 7 = 25$$

$$25 = 25$$ It checks.

George started with 18 figures.

Convince Me! **MP.3 Construct Arguments** Explain which property of equality was used to solve the addition equation $n + 7 = 25$ and why it was used.

© Pearson Education, Inc. 6

Name

Practice Buddy　Tools　Assessment

Another Example

Solve $n - 19 = 34$.

You can get n alone on one side of the equation $n - 19 = 34$ by adding 19 to both sides.

Adding 19 is the inverse of subtracting 19. So, adding 19 will undo subtracting 19.

$n - 19 = 34$

$n - 19 + 19 = 34 + 19$

$n = 53$

To check, substitute 53 for n.

$n - 19 = 34$

$53 - 19 = 34$

$34 = 34$ It checks.

Guided Practice*

Do You Understand?

1. Explain how you use the inverse relationship of addition and subtraction to solve the equation $n + 7 = 25$.

2. **MP.4 Model with Math** Clare had t books. After she bought 8 more books, she had 24 books. Write and solve an equation to find the number of books Clare started with.

Do You Know How?

In **3–6**, solve each equation and show your work.

3. $24 + m = 49$

4. $t - 40 = 3$

5. $12 = y - 11$

6. $22 = 13 + a$

Independent Practice

Leveled Practice In **7–12**, solve each equation.

7. $y - 12 = 89$
$y - 12 + \square = 89 + 12$
$y = \square$

8. $80 + r = 160$
$80 + r - \square = 160 - \square$
$r = \square$

9. $60 = x - 16$
$60 + \square = x - 16 + \square$
$\square = x$

10. $20 = y + 12$

11. $x + 2 = 19$

12. $z - 313 = 176$

*For another example, see Set A on page 133.

Math Practices and Problem Solving

13. **MP.2 Reasoning** Jeremy bought lunch at school. He had a sandwich and a drink that cost him \$7. His drink cost \$1.75. Solve the equation $7 = s + 1.75$ to find the cost of Jeremy's sandwich, s.

14. **MP.4 Model with Math** Joy added 26 new contacts to her phone list. She had to delete 15 old contacts before she could add any more. Joy now has a total of 100 contacts. Let c represent how many contacts she had on her phone list before she updated it. Write an equation and then solve for c.

15. A triathlon is about 51 kilometers. One participant completed two of the three legs of the race and has traveled 42 kilometers. Solve the equation $42 + d = 51$ for the distance, d, of the third leg of the race.

16. Eve's allowance is \$25 per week. She is saving money to buy a bike for \$109, a helmet for \$14, and a pair of shoes for \$47. How many weeks does Eve have to save her entire allowance to have enough money for everything she would like to buy?

17. **Higher Order Thinking** In the equation $6 + 3y = 4y + 2$ the variable y represents the same value. Is $y = 2, 3, 4,$ or 5 the solution of this equation? Explain how you know.

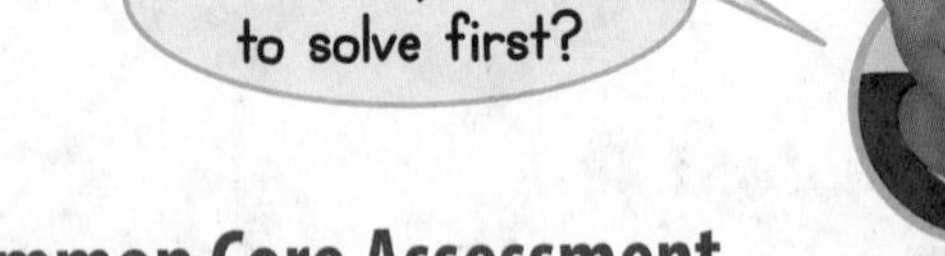
What do you need
to solve first?

18. When ten is subtracted from four times a number the result is six. Write an equation that represents this sentence. Use any letter variable you choose.

Common Core Assessment

19. Select all the equations that have $g = 6$ as the solution.

- ☐ $g + 2 = 10$
- ☐ $g - 1 = 10$
- ☐ $g - 2 = 4$
- ☐ $58 + g = 60$

20. Select all the equations that have $x = 4$ as the solution.

- ☐ $42 = 38 + x$
- ☐ $x + 15 = 19$
- ☐ $18 = x - 2$
- ☐ $36 = x + 32$

© Pearson Education, Inc. 6

Name ______________________

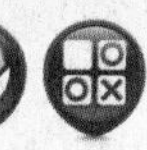

Help Practice Buddy Tools Games

Homework & Practice 2-3

Solve Addition and Subtraction Equations

Another Look!

You can use inverse relationships and the properties of equality to get the variable alone to solve an equation.

Remember, you need to do the same thing to both sides of the equation to keep it balanced.

Addition Equation

Let c represent the unknown.

Solve the equation $5 + c = 15$.

To get c alone, undo adding 5 by subtracting 5 from both sides.

$$5 + c = 15$$
$$5 + c - 5 = 15 - 5$$
$$c = 10$$

Check your solution by substituting 10 for c in the equation.

$$5 + c = 15$$
$$5 + 10 = 15$$
$$15 = 15$$ It checks.

Subtraction Equation

Let m represent the unknown.

Solve the equation $m - 20 = 16$.

To get m alone, undo subtracting 20 by adding 20 to both sides.

$$m - 20 = 16$$
$$m - 20 + 20 = 16 + 20$$
$$m = 36$$

Check your solution by substituting 36 for m in the equation.

$$m - 20 = 16$$
$$36 - 20 = 16$$
$$16 = 16$$ It checks.

In **1** and **2**, write an equation and solve for the variable.

1. 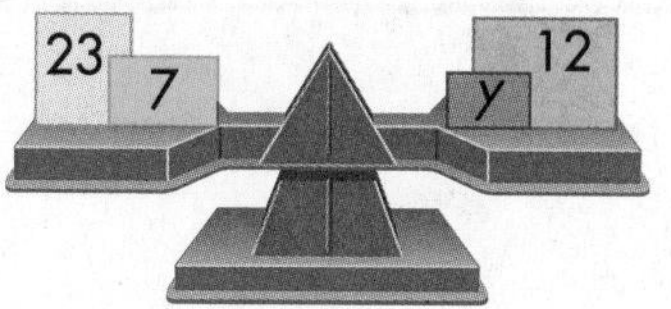

2. 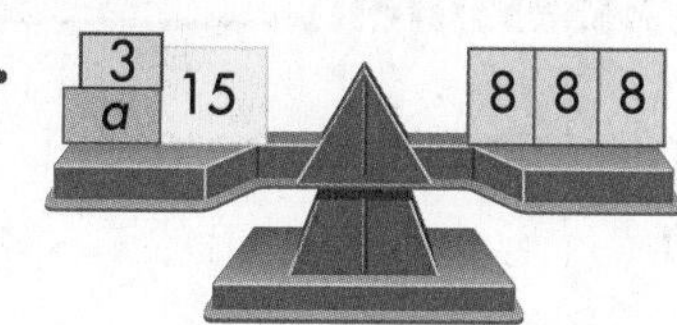

In **3–8**, solve each equation and check your answer.

3. $g - 8 = 25$

4. $25 + y = 42$

5. $r + 82 = 97$

6. $30 = m - 18$

7. $150 = e + 42$

8. $a - 51 = 12$

9. Let a equal the measure of angle A. The equation $360° = a + 90° + 135° + 75°$ represents the sum of the angles in the quadrilateral. Find the missing angle measure by solving the equation.

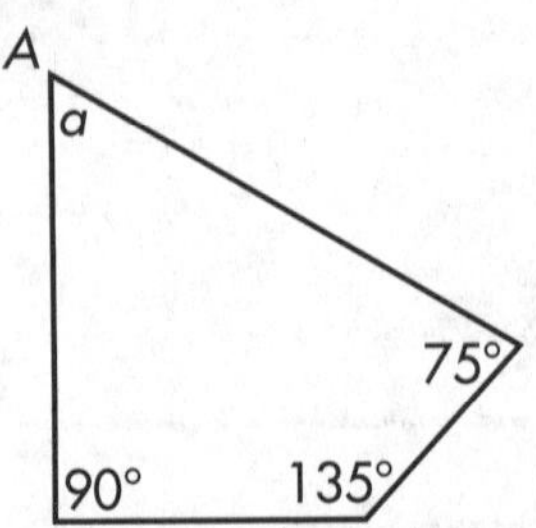

10. **Higher Order Thinking** In the equation $8x - 1 = 3x + 4$ the variable x represents the same value. Which value of x is the solution of the equation; $x = 0, 1, 2,$ or 3? Explain how you know the solution.

The value of a variable remains the same throughout the equation.

11. Cameron has a dog-walking service. He just added 2 more dogs to the 14 dogs he walks each week. Now 10 of the dogs are small dogs. What fraction describes the number of small dogs Cameron walks?

12. **MP.4 Model with Math** Jorge hiked 15.4 miles on Monday. He hiked 20.6 miles on Tuesday, and the rest of the 50-mile trail on Wednesday. If m represents the miles Jorge hiked on Wednesday, write an equation to show the total number of miles Jorge hiked and solve for m.

13. **Vocabulary** If $8t = 72$, which property was used to write $8t \div 8 = 72 \div 8$?

14. **MP.3 Construct Arguments** Explain how to find n in the equation $n + 25 = 233$.

Common Core Assessment

15. Select all the equations that represent the bar diagram.

951	
h	447

- ☐ $951 - h = 447$
- ☐ $447 + h = 951$
- ☐ $h - 447 = 951$
- ☐ $447h = 951$

16. Select all the equations that have $x = 49$ as the solution.

- ☐ $42 = 38 + x$
- ☐ $x + 15 = 19$
- ☐ $18 = x - 2$
- ☐ $36 = x + 32$

© Pearson Education, Inc. 6

Name ______________________________

Solve

Lesson 2-4

Solve Multiplication and Division Equations

I can ...

solve multiplication and division equations.

Content Standards 6.EE.B.6, 6.EE.B.7
Mathematical Practices MP.1, MP.4, MP.6, MP.7, MP.8

Solve & Share David has twice as many colored pencils as Linda. If David has 18 colored pencils, what equation can you write to show how many colored pencils Linda has?

Remember to be precise and define the variable you use to write the equation.

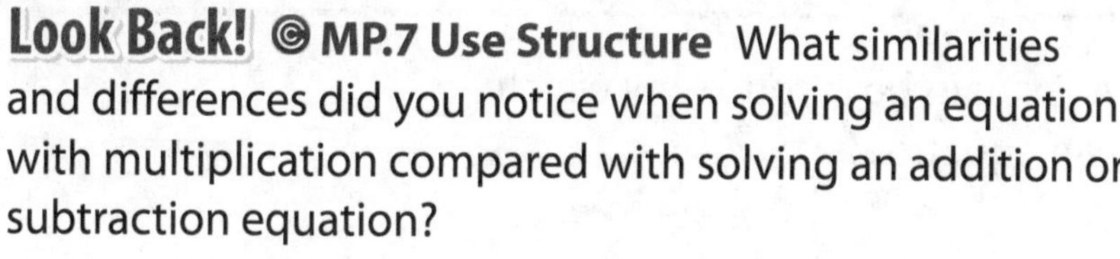

Look Back! **MP.7 Use Structure** What similarities and differences did you notice when solving an equation with multiplication compared with solving an addition or subtraction equation?

Learn Glossary

Essential Question How Can You Solve a Multiplication Equation?

A

Juan charged the same amount for each painting. How much did he charge for each painting?

Let x = the amount Juan charged for each painting.

Solve the equation 3x = 45 to find the answer.

Define the variable before you write and solve an equation.

3 paintings sold for $45.

B

How can you find the value of x that makes the equation true?

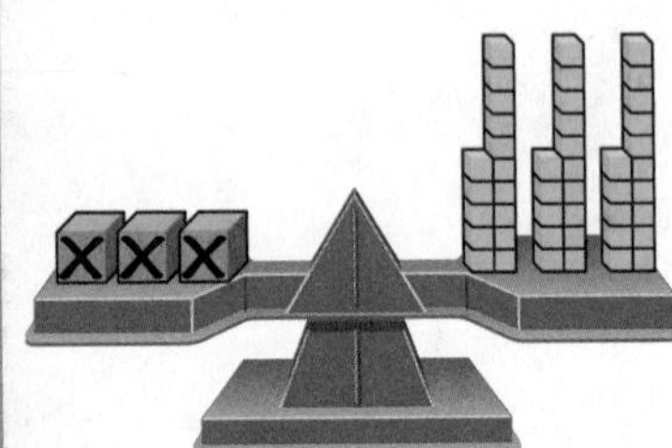

Divide both sides into 3 equal groups.

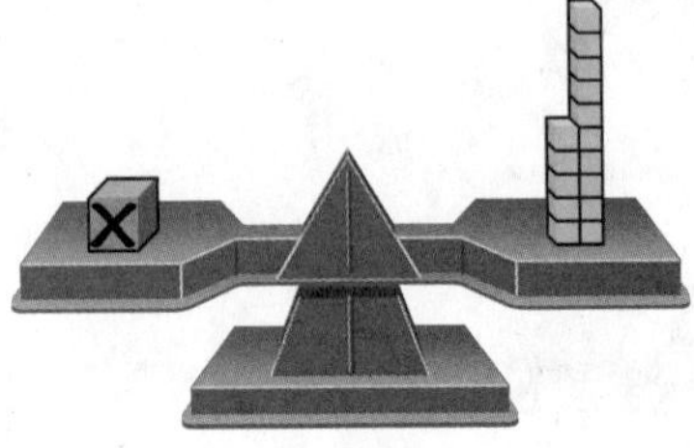

x is 15.

Dividing by 3 is the inverse of multiplying by 3.

C

Use inverse operations to solve.

$$3x = 45$$

$$3x \div 3 = 45 \div 3$$

$$x = 15$$

To check, substitute 15 for x.

$$3x = 45$$

$$3(15) = 45$$

$$45 = 45 \quad \text{It checks.}$$

Juan charged $15 for each painting.

Convince Me! **MP.8 Generalize** Explain how you know which property of equality to use to solve an equation.

© Pearson Education, Inc. 6

Name ______________________________

Practice Buddy   Tools   Assessment

Another Example

Solve $n \div 2 = 40$.

$$n \div 2 = 40$$
$$n \div 2 \times 2 = 40 \times 2$$
$$n = 80$$

To check, substitute 80 for n.

$$n \div 2 = 40$$
$$80 \div 2 = 40$$
$$40 = 40$$ It checks.

So, multiplying by 2 on both sides will undo dividing by 2.

Multiplying by 2 on both sides is the inverse of dividing by 2.

Guided Practice*

Do You Understand?

1. Which property of equality would you use to solve the equation $8n = 16$?

2. How can you check that your answer is correct?

3. Which property of equality would you use to solve the equation $a \div 9 = 2$?

Do You Know How?

In **4** and **5**, explain how to solve each equation.

4. $18m = 36$

5. $t \div 3 = 10$

In **6** and **7**, solve the equation.

6. $2y = 12$

7. $a \div 5 = 22$

Independent Practice

Leveled Practice In **8–11**, explain how to get the variable alone in each equation.

8. $8y = 56$

9. $t \div 15 = 3$

10. $u \div 8 = 12$

11. $31y = 310$

In **12–15**, solve each equation.

12. $d \div 2 = 108$

13. $7{,}200 = 800s$

14. $x \div 3 = 294$

15. $99 = 3x$

*For another example, see Set C on page 133.

Math Practices and Problem Solving

In **16** and **17**, use the triangle.

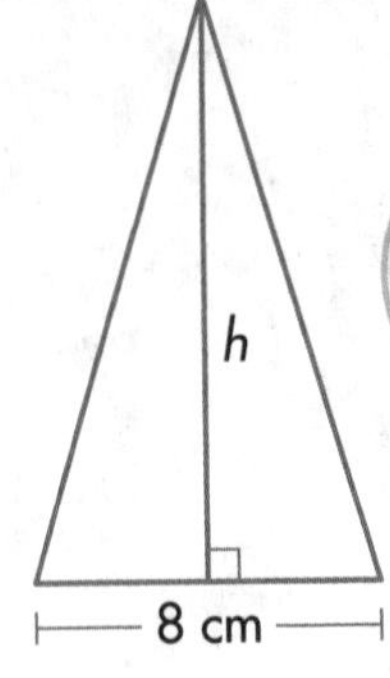

Remember, an isosceles triangle has at least two equal sides. Be precise when you define the variable in your equation.

16. The area of the isosceles triangle is 44 square centimeters. Use the equation $\left(\frac{1}{2}\right)8h = 44$ to find the height of the triangle.

17. Higher Order Thinking If the perimeter of the triangle is 32 centimeters, what is the length of each of the two sides? Write an equation to solve.

---

18. MP.1 Make Sense and Persevere The equation $5x + 10 = 5(x + 2)$ uses the Distributive Property. Substitute the value $x = 4$ to check whether this equation is balanced.

19. MP.4 Model with Math The cost to send a package using a mail service is \$4.95. Write an expression to find the cost to mail p packages.

---

20. Algebra Solve the equation $1.2^2 = x$.

21. Number Sense What are two ways you can represent the number 64 using the number 8?

Common Core Assessment

22. Veronica traveled 562 miles. She drove 85 miles every day. On the last day of her trip she only drove 52 miles.

Write and solve an equation to find the number of days Veronica traveled. Explain each step of your problem solving strategy.

© Pearson Education, Inc. 6

Name ____________________

Help | Practice Buddy | Tools | Games

Homework & Practice 2-4

Solve Multiplication and Division Equations

Another Look!

You can multiply or divide both sides of an equation by the same number and it will remain balanced.

Remember, inverse operations undo each other.

Multiplication Equation

Let m represent the unknown.

Solve the equation $9m = 54$.

To get m alone, divide both sides by 9.

$$9m = 54$$
$$9m \div 9 = 54 \div 9$$
$$m = 6$$

Check your solution by substituting 6 for m in the equation.

$$9m = 54$$
$$9(6) = 54$$
$$54 = 54$$ It checks.

Division Equation

Let p represent the unknown.

Solve the equation $p \div 8 = 7$.

To get p alone, multiply both sides by 8.

$$p \div 8 = 7$$
$$p \div 8 \times 8 = 7 \times 8$$
$$p = 56$$

Check your solution by substituting 56 for p in the equation.

$$p \div 8 = 7$$
$$56 \div 8 = 7$$
$$7 = 7$$ It checks.

In **1–4**, explain how to solve each equation.

1. $81 = \frac{m}{9}$

2. $h \div 3 = 12$

3. $4r = 20$

4. $34 = 17b$

In **5–12**, solve each equation. Check your answers.

5. $\frac{t}{35} = 42$

6. $1 = \frac{u}{2}$

7. $7s = 245$

8. $600a = 2{,}400$

9. $936 = 78p$

10. $29 = k \div 5$

11. $16d = 2{,}864$

12. $180 = \frac{g}{12}$

13. ◎ **MP.4 Model with Math** Teddy is seven times older than Bella. If Teddy is 42 years old, how old is Bella? Write an equation to solve for Bella's age.

14. A cheese farmer distributes 672 ounces of cheese each day. The cheese is packaged in 16-ounce containers. Find the number of containers of cheese distributed each day by solving the equation $16c = 672$.

15. ◎ **MP.1 Make Sense and Persevere** Kris left the library at 4:30 P.M. She had been studying at the library for 45 minutes. It takes her 12 minutes to walk to the library from her home. At what time did Kris leave home to walk to the library?

16. **Math and Science** In Science class, Krissy labeled 26 vertebrae bones on a diagram of an adult human. Doug labeled 1 bone in the throat and 6 bones of the inner ear for both ears. Most adult humans have 206 bones. Write an equation to solve for the number of bones left in the diagram that need to be labeled.

17. **Higher Order Thinking** Stanley bought 108 feet of fencing to put around his backyard. The backyard is a perfect square. Write an equation to find the dimensions of his backyard. Is the area big enough for a pool that is 800 $feet^2$?

How do you find the perimeter of a perfect square?

◎ Common Core Assessment

18. Maggie brought $188.50 to spend on her 7-day vacation. After 4 days of her vacation, she had spent $107.50. The last 3 days, she spent the remaining money in the same amount each day.

Write an equation to find how much money Maggie spent each of the remaining 3 days of her vacation.

© Pearson Education, Inc. 6

Name ____________________

Lesson 2-5
Solve Equations with Fractions

I can ...
solve equations that include fractions.

Content Standards 6.EE.B.6, 6.EE.B.7
Mathematical Practices MP.1, MP.2, MP.4, MP.6, MP.7, MP.8

Solve & Share

A rain gauge showed that $\frac{3}{8}$ inch of rain fell in the morning. The gauge below shows the total amount of rain that fell the entire day. How much rain fell during the afternoon and evening? ***Solve this problem any way you choose.***

You can use reasoning to solve an equation with fractions in the same way you solve an equation with whole numbers.

2

1

0

Look Back! **MP.2 Reasoning** Write an equation that includes fractions and has a solution of 1.

How Can You Solve Equations Involving Fractions and Mixed Numbers?

A

A 6-foot piece of fruit snack is cut into two pieces. What is the length of the shorter piece of fruit snack?

You can use a bar diagram to show how the quantities are related and to write an equation.

$3\frac{3}{4}$ feet

B Use a bar diagram and write an equation.

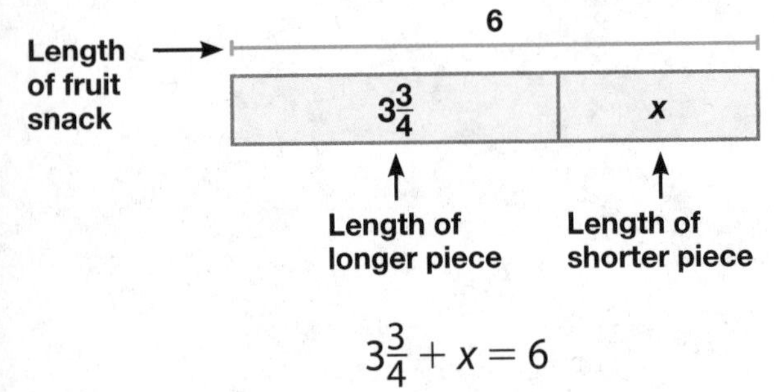

$3\frac{3}{4} + x = 6$

C Solve $3\frac{3}{4} + x = 6$.

Use inverse relationships and properties of equality.

$3\frac{3}{4} + x = 6$

$3\frac{3}{4} + x - 3\frac{3}{4} = 6 - 3\frac{3}{4}$

$x = 5\frac{4}{4} - 3\frac{3}{4}$

$x = 2\frac{1}{4}$

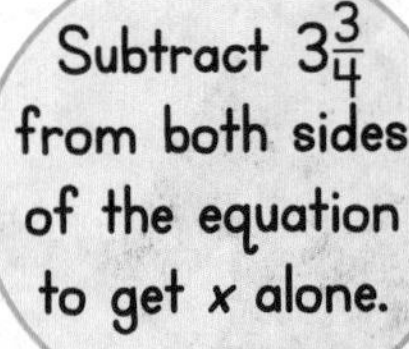

Subtract $3\frac{3}{4}$ from both sides of the equation to get x alone.

The shorter piece is $2\frac{1}{4}$ feet long.

Convince Me! © **MP.4 Model with Math** Suppose you cut the shorter piece of fruit snack from the example above into two pieces. The longer of the two pieces is $1\frac{3}{8}$ feet long. Draw a strip diagram to model the equation. Then find the length of the shorter piece.

© Pearson Education, Inc. 6

Name ______________________

Practice Buddy Tools Assessment

Another Example

Subtraction Equation

Solve: $y - \frac{4}{9} = 5\frac{1}{3}$

$y - \frac{4}{9} + \frac{4}{9} = 5\frac{1}{3} + \frac{4}{9}$

$y = 5\frac{7}{9}$

Multiplication Equation

Solve: $\frac{3}{8}n = 15$

Two numbers whose product is 1 are called reciprocals.

$\left(\frac{8}{3}\right)\frac{3}{8}n = \left(\frac{8}{3}\right)15$

$n = \frac{8}{3} \times \frac{15}{1}$

$n = 40$

Division Equation

Solve: $\frac{p}{5} = 8$

To solve for p, multiply by the reciprocal of $\frac{1}{5}$, or $\frac{5}{1}$.

$\frac{(5)}{1} \cdot \frac{1}{5}p = \frac{(5)}{1} \cdot 8$

$p = 5 \cdot 8$

$p = 40$

I got it! Multiplying by $\frac{8}{3}$ is the same as dividing by $\frac{3}{8}$.

Guided Practice*

Do You Understand?

1. MP.8 Generalize When solving an equation involving a mixed number, such as $y + \frac{3}{4} = 4\frac{1}{2}$, what do you need to do to the mixed number?

Do You Know How?

In **2–5**, solve each equation.

2. $t - \frac{2}{3} = 25\frac{3}{4}$

3. $v + \frac{5}{8} = 9\frac{1}{3}$

4. $\frac{1}{8}k = 2$

5. $\frac{2}{3}r = 6$

Independent Practice

For **6–13**, solve each equation.

6. $6s = \frac{4}{5}$

7. $16 = n + \frac{3}{4}$

8. $3\frac{1}{6} + f = 7\frac{5}{6}$

9. $p - 6 = 2\frac{7}{12}$

10. $7\frac{1}{9} = 2\frac{4}{5} + m$

11. $a + 3\frac{1}{4} = 5\frac{2}{9}$

12. $\frac{1}{8} \cdot y = 4$

13. $k - 6\frac{3}{8} = 4\frac{6}{7}$

*For another example, see Set D on page 134.

Math Practices and Problem Solving

14. ⓒ **MP.7 Use Structure** A fraction, *f*, multiplied by 5 equals $\frac{1}{8}$. Write an algebraic sentence to show the equation. Then solve the equation and explain how you solved it.

15. Yelena needs to swim a total of 8 miles this week. So far, she swam $5\frac{3}{8}$ miles. Use the equation $5\frac{3}{8} + m = 8$ to find how many more miles she needs to swim.

16. **Higher Order Thinking** Is the solution of $b \times \frac{5}{6} = 25$ greater than or less than 25? How can you tell before computing?

17. What is the width of a rectangle with a length of $\frac{3}{7}$ feet and an area of 2 feet^2? Write an equation to show your work.

18. ⓒ **MP.1 Make Sense and Persevere** About how many gallons of fuel does it take to move the space shuttle 3 miles from its hangar to the Vehicle Assembly Building?

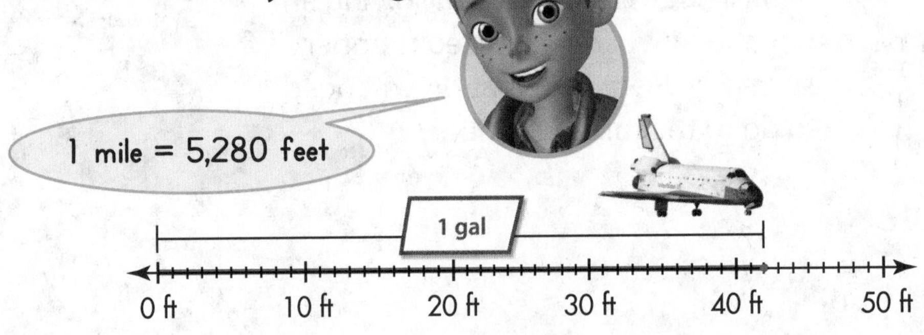

ⓒ Common Core Assessment

19. Dale put up $8\frac{3}{4}$ feet of fence around his triangular-shaped garden. The front of his garden is $1\frac{3}{4}$ feet wide. The other two sides are the same length.

Which equation does **NOT** model how to find the length of the other two sides of Dale's garden?

Ⓐ $8\frac{3}{4} - 2s = 1\frac{3}{4}$

Ⓑ $1\frac{3}{4} + 2s = 8\frac{3}{4}$

Ⓒ $2s = 8\frac{3}{4} - 1\frac{3}{4}$

Ⓓ $2s - 1\frac{3}{4} = 8\frac{3}{4}$

© Pearson Education, Inc. 6

Name ______________________________

Help Practice Buddy Tools Games

Homework & Practice 2-5

Solve Equations with Fractions

Another Look!

Solve each equation below.

Remember, inverse operations undo each other. Properties of Equality say you can do the same thing to both sides and the equation will remain equal.

Addition Equation	Subtraction Equation	Multiplication Equation	Division Equation
$h + \frac{3}{5} = \frac{2}{3}$	$y - \frac{2}{3} = \frac{4}{9}$	$\frac{3}{4}t = 9$	$\frac{r}{5} = 14$
$h + \frac{3}{5} - \frac{3}{5} = \frac{2}{3} - \frac{3}{5}$	$y - \frac{2}{3} + \frac{2}{3} = \frac{4}{9} + \frac{2}{3}$	$\frac{(4)}{3} \bullet \frac{3}{4}t = \frac{(4)}{3} \bullet \frac{9}{1}$	$\frac{(5)}{1} \bullet \frac{1}{5}r = \frac{(5)}{1} \bullet \frac{14}{1}$
$h = \frac{1}{15}$	$y = 1\frac{1}{9}$	$t = 12$	$r = 70$

For **1–12**, solve each equation.

1. $s + \frac{1}{4} = 12\frac{1}{2}$

2. $2\frac{2}{3} + y = 4\frac{1}{4}$

3. $a - 4\frac{3}{8} = 2\frac{1}{2}$

4. $\frac{2}{7}q = 3$

5. $14\frac{1}{6} = d + 12\frac{3}{4}$

6. $7f = \frac{1}{12}$

7. $\frac{t}{3} = 6\frac{1}{2}$

8. $u + 2\frac{7}{8} = 6\frac{1}{6}$

9. $7\frac{1}{5} = m - \frac{2}{3}$

10. $\frac{8}{9} = 13p$

11. $9\frac{1}{12} = \frac{k}{9}$

12. $x + \frac{1}{3} = \frac{2}{5}$

13. $n - 5\frac{3}{8} = \frac{1}{5}$

14. $\frac{3}{5} = 12g$

15. $h + \frac{11}{12} = 120\frac{1}{2}$

For **16–18**, use the information given in the recipe.

16. **MP.6 Be Precise** Sam needs a bowl to mix her punch. She has a 2-cup bowl, 4-cup bowl, and a 6-cup bowl. What is the smallest bowl she can use to make her punch? Explain.

Sam's Fruit Party Punch

$\frac{2}{3}$ cup	pineapple juice
$\frac{1}{2}$ cup	orange juice
$\frac{3}{4}$ cup	lemon/lime juice
$\frac{1}{3}$ cup	ginger ale

17. The recipe makes 1 serving of punch. If Sam used 2 cups of pineapple juice to make her punch, how many servings did she make? Use the equation $\frac{2}{3}m = 2$ to find the number of servings.

18. **Algebra** Sam needs $7\frac{1}{2}$ cups of orange juice to make punch for a group of her friends. She only has $5\frac{1}{3}$ cups. Write an equation to represent how many more cups of orange juice Sam needs. Then solve.

19. There are 6 people seated equally along a counter. If each person has $1\frac{7}{8}$ feet of counter space, how long is the counter? Tell how you can check that your answer is reasonable.

20. **Higher Order Thinking** A bus left New York City and arrived in Philadelphia after $2\frac{1}{3}$ hours. From there, it took $1\frac{3}{4}$ hours to travel to Baltimore. It took another $\frac{5}{6}$ hour to go from Baltimore to Washington. If the bus arrived in Washington at 10:05 P.M., what time did it leave New York City? Tell how you know.

Common Core Assessment

21. Abigail participated in an 18-mile race. She ran $6\frac{3}{4}$ miles, climbed a $\frac{1}{4}$-mile trail on a mountain, and then swam and biked an equal number of miles to complete the race.

Which equation models how to find the number of miles Abigail swam and biked in the race?

Ⓐ $18 = \frac{1}{2}r$

Ⓑ $2r = 11$

Ⓒ $\frac{r}{2} = 11$

Ⓓ $r + 7 = 18$

© Pearson Education, Inc. 6

Name ______________________

Lesson 2-6
Write Inequalities

I can . . .
write an inequality to describe a real-world situation.

Content Standards 6.EE.B.5, 6.EE.B.8
Mathematical Practices MP.2, MP.3, MP.4, MP.6, MP.8

Solve & Share

The record time for the girls' 50-meter free style swimming competition is 24.49 seconds. Camilla has been training and wants to swim the 50-meter free style in less time. What are some possible times Camilla would have to swim to break the current record? ***Solve this problem any way you choose.***

You can use reasoning to write a math sentence using the symbols <, >, ≤, or ≥ to show the relationship between quantities.

50-METER FREE STYLE	
Swimmer A	26.56
Swimmer B	25.14
Swimmer C	24.49
Swimmer D	25.32

Look Back! **MP.6 Be Precise** Fran won a blue ribbon for growing the heaviest pumpkin. It weighed 217 pounds. Write an inequality that describes the weights of pumpkins that are heavier than Fran's pumpkin. Write an inequality that describes the weights of pumpkins that weigh the same as or are heavier than Fran's pumpkin.

How Can You Write an Inequality to Describe a Situation?

A

An inequality is a mathematical sentence that contains < (less than), > (greater than), ≤ (less than or equal to), or ≥ (greater than or equal to).

How can you write an inequality to describe the ages of the children who must be accompanied by an adult at the sledding hill?

It is easier to use an inequality to represent many values rather than making a list.

Morgan Park Sledding Hill

NOTICE: Children under the age of 8 must be accompanied by an adult.

B What are some ages of children who must be accompanied by an adult?

You can show some of the ages on a number line.

0 1 2 3 4 5 6 7 8

C Let a represent the ages of children who must be accompanied by an adult. Use the *less than* symbol (<) to write the inequality.

$$a < 8$$

This inequality is read as "a is less than 8."

Must children who are 8 years old be accompanied by an adult?

Convince Me! **MP.4 Model with Math** Show some of the ages of people who do not need to be accompanied by an adult on a number line. Let n = the ages of people who do not need to be accompanied by an adult and write an inequality to represent the ages.

© Pearson Education, Inc. 6

Name ________________________________

Another Example

The table shows inequalities for given situations.

Situation	Inequality
The length of a piece of wire, ℓ, is longer than 20 feet.	$\ell > 20$
The cost of the pizza, c, will cost at least $8.	$c \geq 8$
Henry's height, h, is less than 60 inches.	$h < 60$
The number of students, s, is at most 30.	$s \leq 30$
Zoe's age, z, is not 11 years old.	$z \neq 11$

The *not equal to* symbol ($\neq$) tells you that the values on the two sides of the inequality are not equal, but it does not tell you which quantity is greater.

Guided Practice*

Do You Understand?

1. MP.8 Generalize What is the difference between an equation with a variable and an inequality with a variable?

Do You Know How?

In **2** and **3**, write an inequality for each situation.

2. A number, n, is greater than 22.

3. The value, v, does not equal 2.

Independent Practice

In **4–7**, write an inequality for each situation.

4. Up to 12 people, p, can ride in the van.

5. A number of days, d, of sunshine is not 28.

6. The distance of the race, r, is farther than 6.2 miles.

7. The value, v, of the bracelet is less than $85.

*For another example, see Set E on page 134.

Math Practices and Problem Solving

8. The record for the city's greatest 1-day snowfall is 19.7 inches. Write an inequality to represent a snowfall that would beat this record.

9. **Algebra** The first bookshelf in the literature section of a library can hold 2,492 books. The bookshelf has 7 shelves. Each shelf can hold the same number of books. How many books can each shelf hold? Write an equation to help you solve.

10. **Higher Order Thinking** Bryan said he is 9 inches shorter than the top of a 6-foot ladder. Allen said he is taller than Bryan because he is 63 inches tall. Is Allen correct? Explain why or why not.

11. **MP.3 Construct Arguments** To ride a certain roller coaster, a rider must be more than 42 inches tall. To represent this situation, Elias wrote $h \geq 42$ and Nina wrote $h > 42$. Who is correct? Explain your thinking.

Common Core Assessment

12. Miguel earns extra money working two weekends with his dad. He is saving to buy a new bike that costs $140.

Heather says that Miguel needs to earn more than $6 each hour he works to have enough money to buy the bike. Her work is shown below. Explain why she is incorrect.

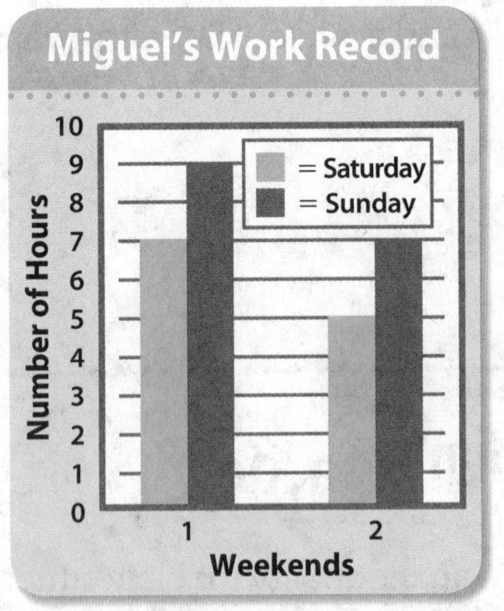

Heather's Solution

Weekend 1: 16 hours
Weekend 2: + 7 hours
23 hours

$140 ÷ 23 hours ≥ $6.00 per hour

Miguel has to earn more than $6.00 per hour.

© Pearson Education, Inc. 6

Name ____________________

Help | Practice Buddy | Tools | Games

Homework & Practice 2-6

Write Inequalities

Another Look!

How can you write an inequality to show there were more than 50 people at a picnic? What about 50 or more people?

Inequality Symbols

Symbol	Meaning
$<$	is less than
$\leq$	is less than or equal to
$>$	is greater than
$\geq$	is greater than or equal to
$\neq$	is not equal to

What are some numbers of people that might have been at the picnic? 52, 67, 102, 115

If there were more than 50 people at the picnic, every possible number will be greater than 50. $p > 50$

If there were 50 or more people at the picnic, 50 must be included as a possible answer. $p \geq 50$

In **1–10**, write an inequality for each situation.

1. The number of students the bus holds, *s*, is less than 40.

2. The weight limit, *w*, on the bridge is 12 tons.

3. The distance, *d*, is at least 110 miles.

4. The depth of the swimming pool, *d*, cannot be deeper than $3\frac{1}{2}$ feet.

5. The least amount of water, *w*, that hikers must bring is 30 ounces.

6. The least number of minutes, *m*, that a player must practice per day is 45 minutes.

7. Tim's age, *t*, is not 21 years old.

8. The cost, *c*, is less than $45.

9. The length of the driveway, *d*, is longer than $\frac{1}{5}$ mile.

10. The height of the sunflower, *s*, is not $45\frac{5}{6}$ inches tall.

11. **MP.6 Be Precise** A test has 50 questions, with 25 questions worth 1 point each and 25 questions worth 3 points each. Julia had no more than 20 points subtracted from the total possible points. Write an inequality that shows the possible points, p, that Julia earned.

12. Lorraine practices piano for 1 hour every week and dances for h hours 3 times every week. Evaluate $3h + 1$ for $h = 2, 5,$ and 9 to see how many hours Lorraine could spend practicing piano and dancing each week.

13. **Higher Order Thinking** In 4th grade, Richard read 37 books. In 5th grade, he read 9 more books than the year before. This year in 6th grade, Richard plans to read at least 12 more books than the total number of books read in both 4th and 5th grades. Richard writes the inequality $b \geq 180$ to show the total number of books he will have read in 4th, 5th, and 6th grade. Is his inequality correct? Why or why not?

14. **Math and Science** The waste-to-energy process generates energy in the form of electricity, heat, or fuel from the incineration of waste. Converting non-recyclable waste materials into electricity, heat, or fuel generates a renewable energy source. The 86 facilities in the United States have the capacity to produce 2,720 megawatts of power per year by processing more than 28 million tons of waste per year. Write an inequality to show the possible power, p, the waste-to-energy facilities in the United States are capable of producing.

Common Core Assessment

15. The Cruz family shares a family cell phone plan. The plan is for 3,200 cell phone minutes each month. The father has used 1,200 minutes. The mother has used at least 600 minutes. The two children have used 675 minutes each.

Write an inequality that shows the number of minutes the Cruz family has used. Explain your reasoning.

© Pearson Education, Inc. 6

Name ____________________

Solve

Lesson 2-7

Solve Inequalities

I can ...
write and represent solutions of inequalities.

Content Standards 6.EE.B.5, 6.EE.B.8
Mathematical Practices MP.2, MP.4, MP.5, MP.7

Solve & Share Henry is thinking of a number that is less than 17. What numbers make the statement $q < 17$ true? ***Solve this problem any way you choose.***

You can use appropriate tools. How can you use a number line to show all the numbers less than 17?

Look Back! **MP.2 Reasoning** Could Henry be thinking of the number 17? Explain.

Learn Glossary

Essential Question How Can You Solve an Inequality?

A

An inequality uses >, <, ≥, or ≤ to compare two expressions. One solution to the inequality x > 5 is x = 7 because 7 > 5. Inequalities have infinitely many solutions. Graph all of the solutions of x > 5.

0 1 2 3 4 5 6 7 8 9 10

Inequalities have infinitely many solutions. This means that there are an unlimited number of solutions.

B

Step 1

To graph $x > 5$, draw an open circle at 5 on a number line. The open circle shows that 5 is NOT a solution.

0 1 2 3 4 5 6 7 8 9 10

C

Step 2

Find some solutions and plot those on a number line. 7 and 9 are solutions because $7 > 5$ and $9 > 5$.

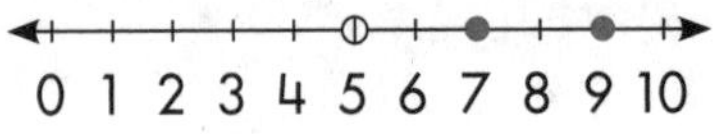

D

Step 3

Start at the open circle and shade the solutions you found. Draw an arrow to show that the solutions go on forever.

0 1 2 3 4 5 6 7 8 9 10

Convince Me! **MP.2 Reasoning** How many solutions does the inequality $x > 5$ have? Explain.

© Pearson Education, Inc. 6

Name ______

Another Example

The inequality $j \geq 18$ describes the length of a jump that qualifies for the finals. Which athletes qualify for the finals?

Long Jump Results	
Amir	$22\frac{1}{3}$ ft
Jake	16 ft
Tyrell	$18\frac{1}{2}$ ft
Ryan	$20\frac{1}{2}$ ft

One Way

Substitute each of the values for j.

Amir: $22\frac{1}{3} \geq 18$

Jake: $16 < 18$

Tyrell: $18\frac{1}{2} \geq 18$

Ryan: $20\frac{1}{2} \geq 18$

Another Way

Graph the inequality. Draw a closed circle at 18, to indicate that 18 can be a solution, and an arrow from the closed circle to the right. Check which points are on the graph.

15 16 17 18 19 20 21 22 23

Amir, Tyrell and Ryan qualify for the finals because $22\frac{1}{3}$, $18\frac{1}{2}$, and $20\frac{1}{2}$ are solutions.

Guided Practice*

Do You Understand?

1. In the problem on the previous page, explain why 9 is a solution to $x > 5$.

2. Explain why 2 is **NOT** a solution to $x > 5$.

Do You Know How?

In **3**, complete the inequality that the graph represents.

3. z ◯ ____

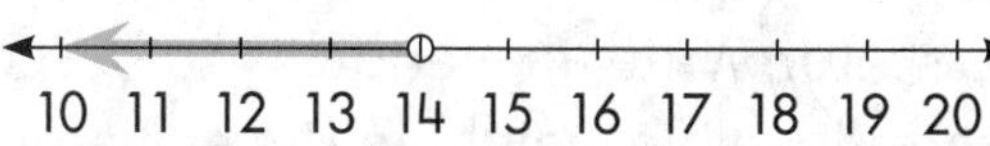

Independent Practice

In **4–7**, write the inequality that each graph represents.

4. 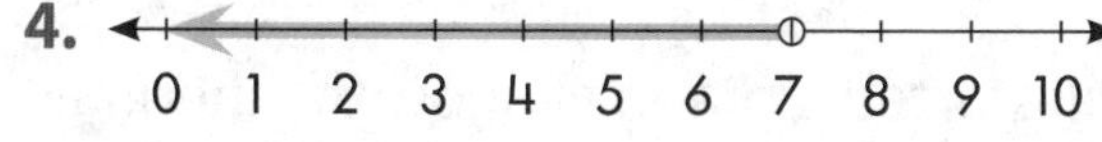

5. 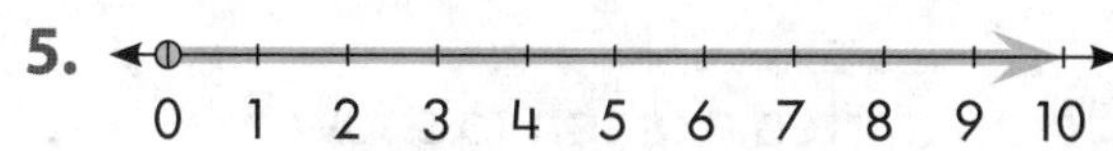

6. 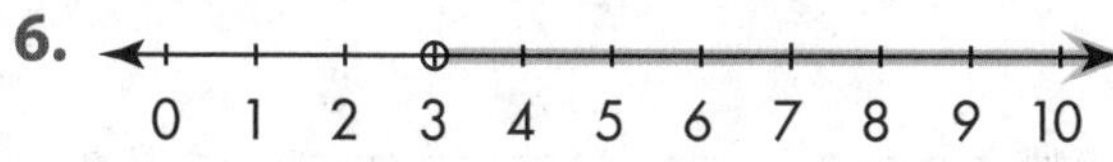

7. 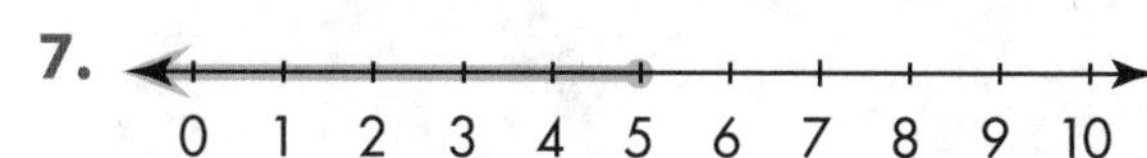

*For another example, see Set E on page 134.

Math Practices and Problem Solving

8. The number line below represents the solutions of the inequality $x > 7$. Is 7.1 a solution? Is 7.01 a solution? Explain how you can tell.

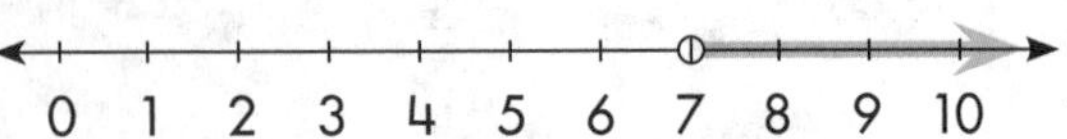

9. **MP.4 Model with Math** Death Valley is the hottest place in the United States. The highest temperature ever recorded there was 134°F. The lowest temperature recorded there was 15°F. Write two inequalities that would describe the temperature, in °F, in Death Valley at any time since temperatures have been recorded.

10. **Higher Order Thinking** Francine received a gift card to buy cell phone apps. She says the card's value is enough to buy any of the apps shown at the right. Let v be the dollar value of the gift card. Write an inequality that best describes the value of the gift card.

Phone Apps	
All Recipes	\$ 9.50
Headliners Sports	\$10.50
Remote Desktop	\$12.00

11. The maximum load in a freight elevator is 1,500 pounds. Let $w =$ the weight in the elevator. Write an inequality to describe the allowable weight in the elevator.

12. **Algebra** A chessboard is made up of 64 square places. Let $s =$ the side length of each square on a chessboard. Evaluate the expression $64s^2$ to find the area of a chessboard for which $s = 1\frac{1}{2}$ inches.

Common Core Assessment

13. Tania started a graph to show the inequality $y < 3.7$. Finish labeling the number line and draw the graph.

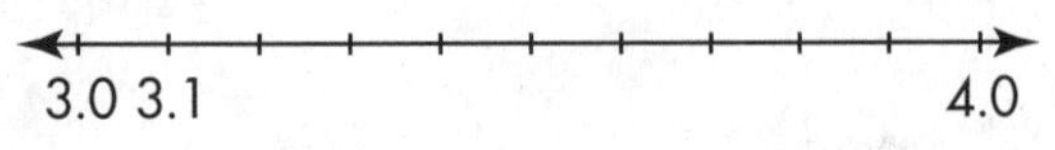

14. Bill started a graph to show the inequality $x \leq 25$. Finish labeling the number line and draw the graph.

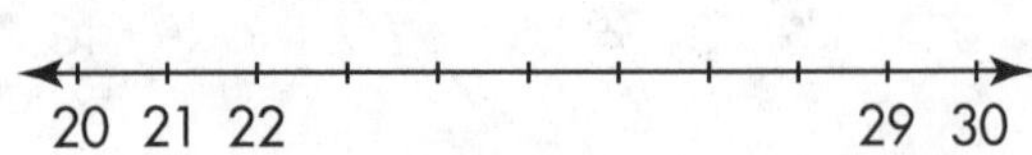

© Pearson Education, Inc. 6

Name ________________________

Help | Practice Buddy | Tools | Games

Homework & Practice 2-7

Solve Inequalities

Another Look!

Graph the solutions of the inequalities $x < 3$ and $x \geq 5$.

Draw an open circle at 3. The values of x are less than 3, so shade to the left on the number line.

$x < 3$

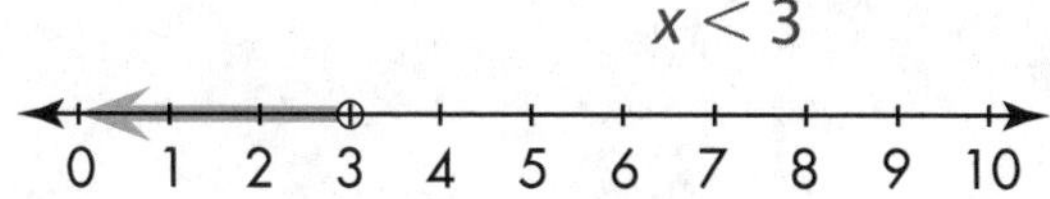

An inequality uses <, >, ≤, and ≥, to compare two expressions.

Draw a closed circle at 5. The values of y are greater than 5, so shade to the right on the number line.

$y \geq 5$

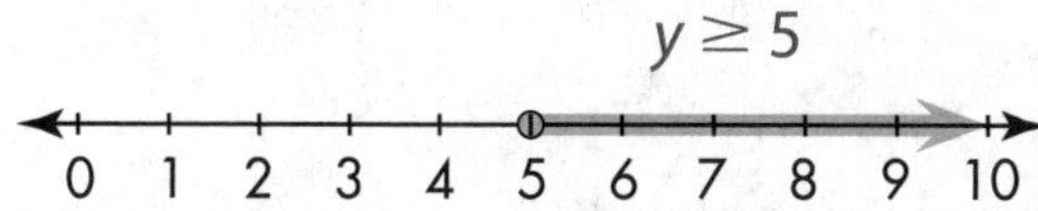

In **1–4**, write the inequality that each graph represents.

1. 5 6 7 8 9 10 11 12 13 14 15

2.

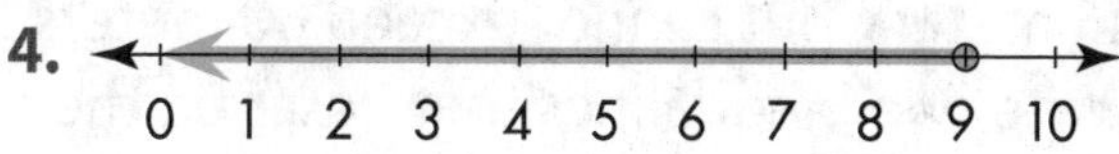

3. 0 1 2 3 4 5 6 7 8 9 10

4. 0 1 2 3 4 5 6 7 8 9 10

In **5** and **6**, graph each inequality on a number line.

5. $x < 7$

0 1 2 3 4 5 6 7 8 9 10

6. $x \geq 7$

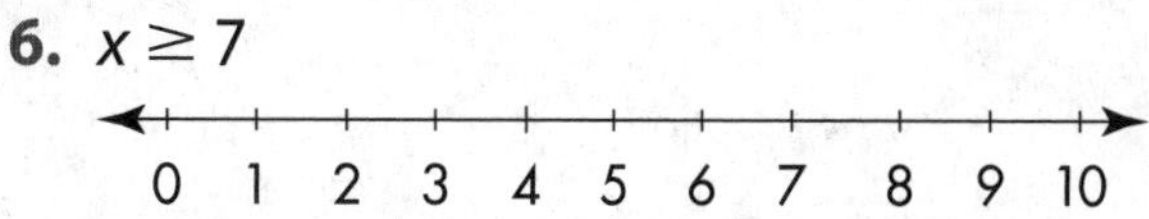

In **7–14**, name three solutions of each inequality.

7. $x < 9$

8. $x < 6$

9. $y > 2$

10. $y \geq 100$

11. $z < 8$

12. $x \geq 77$

13. $u > 10.9$

14. $u \leq 13.99$

15. **MP.7 Use Structure** The number line below represents the solutions of the inequality $y < 6$. How many solutions are there? Write three of the solutions that are greater than 5.

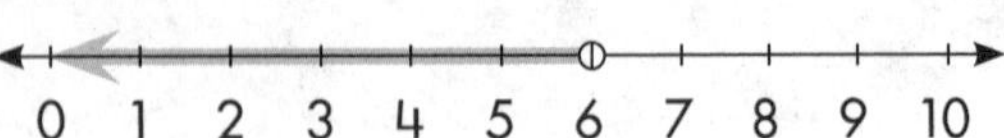

16. **MP.4 Model with Math** In 1992, the women's world record in the pole vault was officially recognized as 4.05 meters. The most recent world record, set in 2009, is 5.06 meters. What inequality can you write that would describe a new world record in the women's pole vault?

17. At the right is a portion of the menu at a diner. The inequality $m < 5$ represents the amount of money, m, that Elizabeth has to spend on lunch at the diner. Which items can she choose for lunch?

Diner	
Turkey Sandwich	$3.99
Tuna Sandwich with Fruit	$5.45
Italian Beef Sandwich	$4.75
Slice of Cheese Pizza	$2.25
Grilled Chicken Sandwich	$6.00

18. **Higher Order Thinking** The width of a youth soccer field must be at least 45 meters, but cannot exceed 60 meters. Write two inequalities that describe the width, w, of a youth soccer field. Then write two integers that are solutions of the inequalities.

19. **MP.2 Reasoning** Two friends split the cost of 1 medium pizza equally. Each friend's share of the cost was $5.60. If 4 friends split the cost of 2 medium pizzas equally, how much would each friend's share of the cost be? Explain how you know without calculating.

Common Core Assessment

20. Andy started a graph to show the inequality $z > 0.4$. Finish labeling the number line and draw the graph.

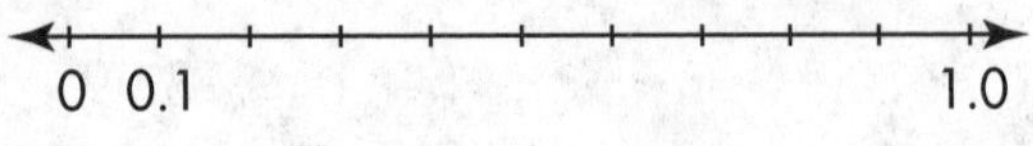

21. Tricia started a graph to show the inequality $x \geq 12$. Finish labeling the number line and draw the graph.

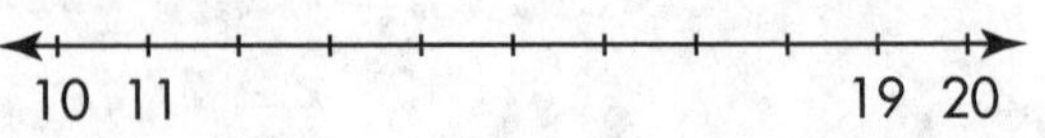

© Pearson Education, Inc. 6

Name ______________________

Solve & Share

Barb is three times as old as her twin nieces Allie and Sam. The sum of their three ages is 55. How old is each person now?

Math Practices and Problem Solving

Lesson 2-8

Make Sense and Persevere

I can ...
make sense of problems and keep working if I get stuck.

Mathematical Practices MP.1 Also MP.2, MP.4, MP.6, MP.8
Content Standards 6.EE.B.6, 6.EE.B.7

Thinking Habits

Think about these questions to help you make sense of problems and persevere in solving them.

- What do I need to find?
- What do I know?
- What's my plan for solving the problem?
- What else can I try if I get stuck?
- How can I check that my solution makes sense?

Look Back! **MP.1 Make Sense and Persevere** What information in the problem tells you that Barb is older than her nieces?

Essential Question

How Can You Make Sense of Problems and Persevere in Solving Them?

A

John drew the isosceles triangle ABC. Side lengths AB and AC are equal. Side length BC is half as long as each of the other two sides. What are the side lengths of the triangle?

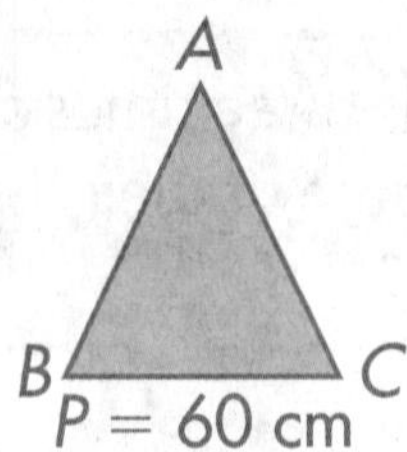

What do I need to do?

I need to make sense of the problem before I can solve it.
If I get stuck, I need to persevere until I find the side lengths of the triangle.

B

How can I make sense of and solve this problem?

I can

- identify what I know and what I need to find.
- make a plan for solving the problem.
- try other strategies if I get stuck.
- check that my solution makes sense.

To persevere you can check your strategy and your work.

C

Here's my thinking...

I can draw a picture and write an equation to show what I know.

Let x = the lengths AB and AC.
Then $\frac{1}{2}x$ = length BC.

$P = x + x + \frac{1}{2}x$

$60 = x + x + \frac{1}{2}x$

$60 = \frac{5}{2}x$

$\frac{2}{5} \cdot \frac{60}{1} = \frac{5}{2}x \cdot \frac{2}{5}$

$24 = x$

$AB = 24$ cm

$AC = 24$ cm

$BC = \frac{1}{2}(24) = 12$ cm

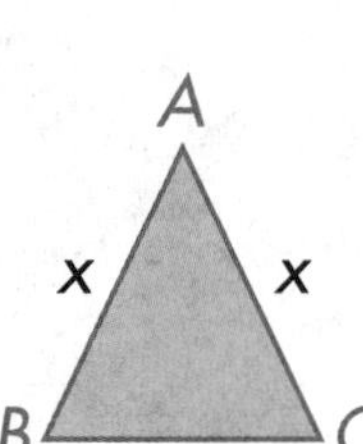

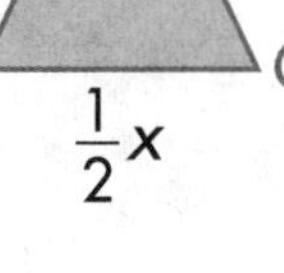

Convince Me! **MP.1 Make Sense and Persevere**

Rectangle $GHJK$ is shown at the right. Its length is 4 times its width. What is the length and the width of rectangle $GHJK$?

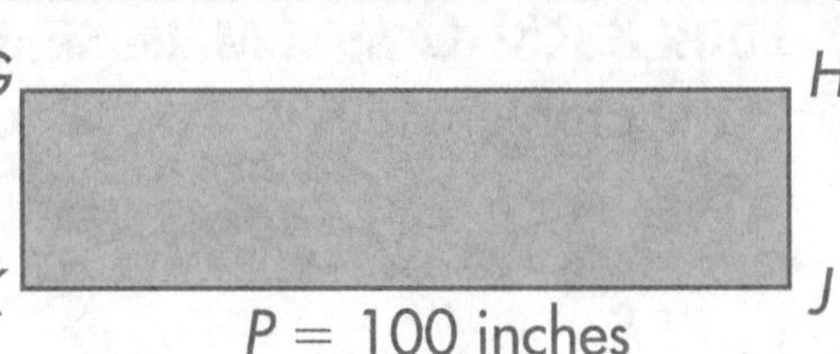

© Pearson Education, Inc. 6

Name ___

Guided Practice*

MP.1 Make Sense and Persevere

Trapezoid *GHJK* has a perimeter of 66 cm. Side lengths *GK* and *HJ* are equal. Side *GH* is $1\frac{1}{2}$ times as long as *GK*. Side *KJ* is twice as long as *GK*. What are the lengths of each of the sides?

1. How are the measurements given in the problem related?

2. Describe a strategy you can use. Then solve the problem.

You persevere when you try different strategies until you find one that helps you solve the problem.

Independent Practice

MP.1 Make Sense and Persevere

Bo kept track of how far he walked in May and June with his pedometer. He walked 3 times as far in June as he did in May. He walked 152 miles during the two months. How far did Bo walk in May and in June?

152

June ___	May ___

3. What information in the problem tells you that Bo walked farther in June than in May?

4. How can you use the bar diagram to help you solve the problem?

5. Find a solution to the problem. Then describe how you can check your answer.

*For another example, see Set F on page 134.

Math Practices and Problem Solving

Common Core Performance Assessment

Berry Smoothie

A berry smoothie recipe is made with 24 pieces of fruit. There are 4 times as many strawberries as blackberries, and twice as many banana slices as blackberries. There is the same number of blueberries as blackberries. How many of each fruit are used to make this berry smoothie?

6. **MP.1 Make Sense and Persevere** What do you know? How is the known information related?

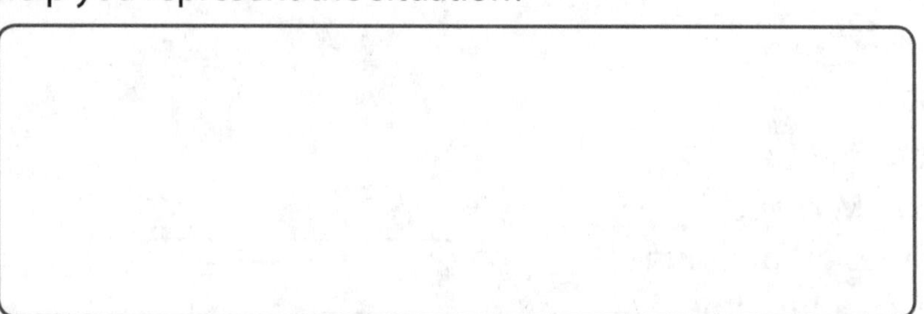

7. **MP.4 Model with Math** How can you use a variable to help you represent the situation?

8. **MP.2 Reasoning** Ben says that you need 2 blueberries, 2 blackberries, 4 banana slices, and 12 strawberries to make the berry smoothie. Describe how you know that Ben's answer is incorrect.

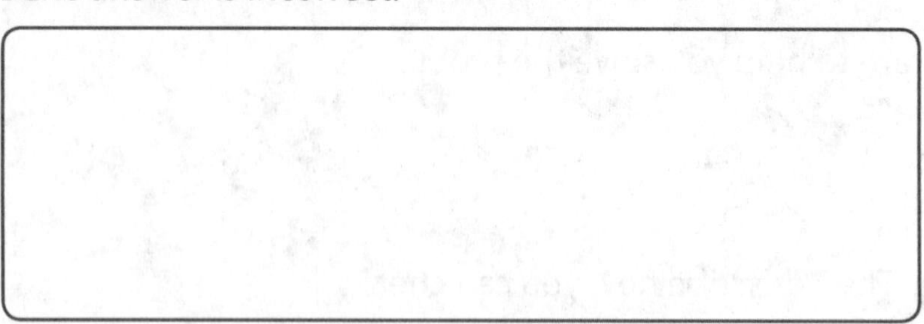

To make sense of a problem, identify what you know and look for relationships.

9. **MP.6 Use Precision** Solve the problem. Explain how you can check your answer.

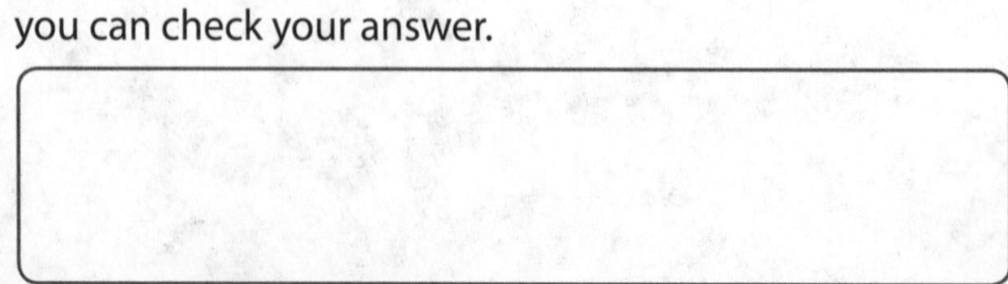

© Pearson Education, Inc. 6

Name ______________________________

Homework & Practice 2-8

Make Sense and Persevere

Another Look!

Harold downloads a song, a movie, and a game onto his tablet. The game uses 5 times as many megabytes of storage as the song. The movie takes up 100 times the storage space as the game. The total storage needed for all 3 downloads is 4,048 MB. How many megabytes of storage are needed for each download?

Make sense of the problem and then make a plan to solve it.

Make Sense of the Problem	Plan	Solve
What You Know Harold uses 4,048 MB of storage on downloads. game = 5 times the song movie = 100 times the game **What You Need to Find** The storage amount needed for each download	Define a variable and then use the relationships between the quantities to write an equation. x = song storage $5x$ = game storage $100(5x) = 500x$ = movie storage	$x + 5x + 500x = 4{,}048$ $506x = 4{,}048$ $506x \div 506 = 4{,}048 \div 506$ $x = 8$ $5x = 5 \cdot 8 = 40$ $500x = 500 \cdot 8 = 4{,}000$ The song uses 8 MB, the game uses 40 MB, and the movie uses 4,000 MB of storage space.

MP.1 Make Sense and Persevere

Vi walks five days each week. She walks the same distance on the first two days. On days three and four, Vi walks twice as long as on each of the first two days. On day five, she walks half as far as on day one. If Vi walks 13 miles each week, how far does she walk each day?

1. Write expressions to represent the distance Vi walks each day. Then write an equation to represent how far she walks each week.

2. Solve the problem.

Common Core Performance Assessment

Zoo Keeper

A local zoo budgets $750,000 for salaries and benefits of all of its employees. The salaries are estimated at $35,000 per employee and benefits at $15,000 per employee. What is the greatest number of employees the zoo can have without going over budget?

3. **MP.2 Reasoning** Can the zoo have 10 employees? Explain how you know.

4. **MP.4 Model with Math** Model the problem situation. You can use a bar model, drawing, or equation.

5. **MP.1 Make Sense and Persevere** Find the greatest number of employees the zoo could have without going over budget. Show two ways you know your answer is correct.

6. **MP.8 Repeated Reasoning** Suppose the zoo received a budget increase to $1,000,000. How many additional employees could the zoo hire? Explain your reasoning.

There are many ways to model with math. Choose a model that helps you visualize the problem situation.

© Pearson Education, Inc. 6

Name ____________________

Shade a path from **START** to **FINISH**. Follow products in which the digit in the hundreds place is greater than the digit in the tens place. You can only move up, down, right, or left.

TOPIC 2

Fluency Practice Activity

I can ...
multiply multi-digit whole numbers.

Content Standard 5.NBT.B.5

Start

593 × 56	57 × 26	746 × 421	2,951 × 17	91 × 15
44 × 12	1,599 × 31	453 × 367	276 × 252	37 × 21
75 × 39	41 × 23	5,201 × 43	277 × 58	806 × 264
214 × 21	114 × 76	85 × 52	247 × 111	6,250 × 18
576 × 136	1,822 × 67	142 × 99	853 × 28	3,049 × 60

Finish

TOPIC 2
Vocabulary Review

Word List

- Addition Property of Equality
- Division Property of Equality
- equation
- inequality
- inverse relationship
- Multiplication Property of Equality
- reciprocal
- Subtraction Property of Equality

Understand Vocabulary

Choose the best term from the Word List. Write it on the blank.

1. A(n) ____________________ compares two quantities using an equal sign.

2. The ____________________ of 4 is $\frac{1}{4}$.

3. Addition and subtraction have a(n) ____________________.

Draw a line from each equation in Column A to the property of equality it illustrates in Column B.

Column A	Column B
4. $(6 + 3) - 3 = 9 - 3$	Addition Property of Equality
5. $(6 + 3) \times 3 = 9 \times 3$	Division Property of Equality
6. $(6 + 3) + 3 = 9 + 3$	Multiplication Property of Equality
7. $(6 + 3) \div 3 = 9 \div 3$	Subtraction Property of Equality

What mathematical operation has an *inverse relationship* to the operation shown in each equation? Write *addition, subtraction, multiplication,* or *division.*

8. $k + 6 = 13$ ____________

9. $c \div 6 = 42$ ____________

10. $5n = 30$ ____________

11. $p - 7 = 15$ ____________

Use Vocabulary in Writing

12. Describe how to solve $\frac{3}{7}n = 27$. Use at least 3 words from the Word List in your explanation.

© Pearson Education, Inc. 6

Name ____________________

Reteaching

Set A pages 83–88, 95–100

Which value of x is the solution of the equation?

$x + 4.8 = 19$ $\quad$ $x = 13, 14.2, 15.8$

Try $x = 13$: $\quad 13 + 4.8 = 17.8$ ✗
Try $x = 14.2$: $\quad 14.2 + 4.8 = 19$ ✓
Try $x = 15.8$: $\quad 15.8 + 4.8 = 20.6$ ✗

You can also use properties to solve.

$$x + 4.8 - 4.8 = 19 - 4.8$$
$$x = 14.2$$

Remember the solution of an equation makes the equation true.

Tell which value of the variable is the solution of the equation.

1. $d + 9 = 25$ $\quad d = 6, 14, 16, 21$

2. $c - 8 = 25$ $\quad c = 17, 28, 33, 35$

Solve for x.

3. $x + 2 = 11$ $\qquad$ **4.** $x - 17 = 13$

Set B pages 89–94

The properties of equality are illustrated in the table.

Properties of Equality	
Addition Property of Equality	$4 + 3 = 7$ So, $4 + 3 + 2 = 7 + 2$
Subtraction Property of Equality	$9 + 8 = 17$ So, $9 + 8 - 5 = 17 - 5$
Multiplication Property of Equality	$3 \times 5 = 15$ So, $3 \times 5 \times 2 = 15 \times 2$
Division Property of Equality	$16 + 2 = 18$ So, $(16 + 2) \div 2 = 18 \div 2$

Remember that the properties of equality allow you to apply the same operation with the same amount to both sides of an equation.

1. If $6 + 2 = 8$, does $6 + 2 + 3 = 8 + 3$? Why or why not?

2. If $8 - 1 = 7$, does $8 - 1 - 2 = 7 - 3$? Why or why not?

Set C pages 101–106

Solve $9x = 18$.

Dividing by 9 is the inverse of multiplying by 9.

$9x = 18$ ← Solve the equation.

$9x \div 9 = 18 \div 9$ ← Use the Division Property of Equality.

$x = 2$ ← Simplify.

Remember that multiplication and division have an inverse relationship. To check, substitute your answer back into the original equation.

Solve for x.

1. $8x = 64$ $\qquad$ **2.** $x \div 20 = 120$

3. $x \div 12 = 2$ $\qquad$ **4.** $7x = 77$

5. $26 = 13x$ $\qquad$ **6.** $242 = x \div 22$

Set D pages 107–112

Find $w + 4\frac{1}{3} = 7$.

Subtract $4\frac{1}{3}$ from both sides.

$w + 4\frac{1}{3} - 4\frac{1}{3} = 7 - 4\frac{1}{3}$

$w = 2\frac{2}{3}$

Remember that you can use inverse relationships and properties of equality to solve each equation.

1. $g + 3\frac{5}{8} = 7\frac{1}{4}$
2. $b \div 15 = 8\frac{1}{3}$

Set E pages 113–118, 119–124

Molly is less than 15 years old is represented by the inequality $x < 15$.

To graph the inequality on a number line, draw an open circle at 15 and shade any solutions that you found. Draw an arrow to show all numbers less than 15.

10 11 12 13 14 15 16 17 18 19 20

Remember you use an open circle for $<$ or $>$ and a closed circle for $\leq$ or $\geq$.

Write the inequality that each graph represents.

1. 5 6 7 8 9 10 11 12 13 14 15
2. 0 1 2 3 4 5 6 7 8 9 10

Set F pages 125–130

Think about these questions to help you **make sense of problems and persevere** in solving them.

Thinking Habits

- What do I need to find?
- What do I know?
- What is my plan for solving the problem?
- What else can I try if I get stuck?
- How can I check that my solution makes sense?

Remember you can try different strategies to solve a problem. Then check that your solution makes sense.

Lee is thinking of two numbers. One number is 12 less than the other number. The sum of the two numbers is 208. What two numbers is Lee thinking of?

1. Explain how you can use what you know to decide how to solve the problem.

2. Solve the problem.

© Pearson Education, Inc. 6

Name ______________________________

TOPIC 2

Assessment

1. The local animal shelter has 3 times as many cats as dogs. There are 27 cats at the shelter. Let x = the number of dogs at the shelter. Solve the equation $3x = 27$ to find the number of dogs at the shelter.

Ⓐ $x = 81$

Ⓑ $x = 30$

Ⓒ $x = 24$

Ⓓ $x = 9$

2. Solve each equation. Then write the equation in the appropriate box below.

$8x = 56$ $\quad x + 5\frac{3}{4} = 8\frac{3}{4}$ $\quad \frac{x}{2} = 3.5$

$2\frac{1}{4} + x = 9\frac{1}{8}$ $\quad x - 2.56 = 0.44$

Equations with solution $x = 3$	Equations with solution $x = 7$	Neither

3. Ed's birthday is less than 16 days away. Ann writes the inequality $d \leq 16$, where d equals the number of days, to represent this. Is Ann correct? Explain.

4. Choose all the equations that are true if $x = 9$.

☐ $32.54 - 23.54 = x$

☐ $x \div 27 = 4$

☐ $\frac{3}{8}x = 3\frac{3}{8}$

☐ $8.7 + x = 17$

☐ $5x = 45$

5. The library carries a total of 750 biography, mystery, fantasy, and science fiction books. There are 3 times as many science fiction books as fantasy books, twice as many mystery books as fantasy books, and four times as many biographies as fantasy books.

Write an equation that describes the number of each type of book in the library.

How many of each genre is there in the library?

Biography ☐ books

Fantasy ☐ books

Mystery ☐ books

Science Fiction ☐ books

6. Write an algebraic equation that represents the total weight (W) of five boxes of blueberries, if b equals the weight of one box of blueberries.

7. Which graph represents the solutions of the inequality $p \geq 10$?

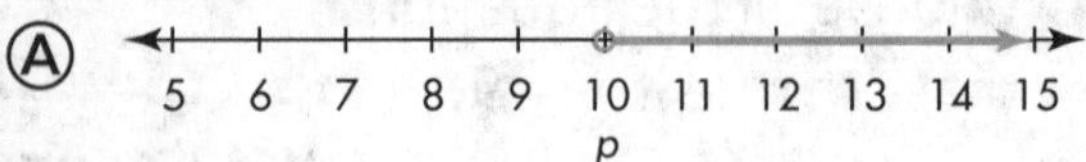

Ⓐ number line from 5 to 15, p

Ⓑ number line from 5 to 15, p

Ⓒ number line from 5 to 15, p

Ⓓ number line from 5 to 15, p

8. Read each of the following problem situations. Draw lines to match each equation to the situation it represents.

$8 + r = 24$

Lee will work 8 hours today. He will have worked 24 hours at the end of the week. How many hours did Lee work the rest of the week?

$8x = 24$

A polygon has a perimeter of 24 centimeters. Each side is 8 centimeters long. How many sides does the polygon have?

9. The choir had 50 members after 3 students joined. The equation $x + 3 = 50$ can be used to find the membership, x, before the students joined. What step should be taken to get x alone on one side of the equation?

Ⓐ Multiply each side of the equation by 3.

Ⓑ Add 3 to each side of the equation.

Ⓒ Subtract 3 from each side of the equation.

Ⓓ Divide each side of the equation by 3.

10. Noah wrote that $6 + 6 = 12$. Then he wrote that $6 + 6 - n = 12 - n$. Are his equations balanced? Explain.

11. Mr. Daniels is organizing a class trip on a budget of $900. The bus rental costs $600. Mr. Daniels will also buy tickets that cost $9.50 per student.

Write an inequality to represent the number of students, y, that Mr. Daniels can bring on the trip.

© Pearson Education, Inc. 6

Name ______________________________

The Gadget Factory

The Gadget Factory makes all kinds of electronic gadgets. The sales managers at the Gadget Factory keep track of the items and their prices in the chart below.

Items at the Gadget Factory

Item	Number of items per box	Number of boxes per carton	Number of items per carton	Cost per item	Cost per box	Cost per carton
Key Chain	4	8	32	$0.32	$1.28	$10.24
Batteries	6	10	60	$0.53	$3.18	$31.80
Mini Alarm Clock	10	14	140	$3.73	$37.30	$522.20

1. Janie buys some cartons of key chains. She spends $51.20.

Part A

Write an algebraic equation to represent the total number of cartons of key chains, x, that Janie buys.

Part B

Solve for x. How many cartons does Janie buy?

2. Sam owns a clock store and wants to buy some boxes of mini alarm clocks from The Gadget Factory. He has a budget of $200. Write an inequality to represent the number of boxes of alarm clocks, a, Sam can buy. What is the greatest number of boxes of alarm clocks Sam can buy?

3. The Gadget Factory just received a shipment.

Part A

Complete the chart.

Item	Number of items per box	Number of boxes per carton	Number of items per carton	Cost per item	Cost per box	Cost per carton
Magnet	25		300		$66.25	$795.00
Binoculars	16	19	304	$17.68		$5,374.72
Flash Drive		18	540	$14.99	$449.70	

Part B

Write and solve the equation you used to find the missing number of flash drives in each box. Let $n =$ the number of flash drives.

4. Mo wrote and solved the equation below to find the cost per magnet.

$$66.25w = 795$$
$$w = 12$$

Is Mo correct? Explain.

© Pearson Education, Inc. 6

TOPIC 3 Rational Numbers

Essential Questions: What are integers and rational numbers? How can you compare and order rational numbers?

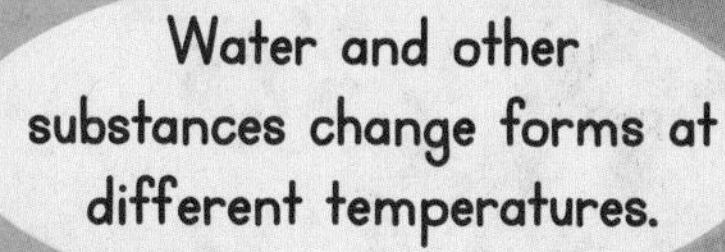

Water and other substances change forms at different temperatures.

Elevation affects the boiling point at which liquid water changes to a gas.

That explains high-altitude cooking directions for food! Here's a project on boiling points and rational numbers.

Math and Science Project: Elevation and Boiling Point

Do Research Use the Internet or other sources to learn about the highest and lowest elevations in the United States and the highest and lowest elevations recorded on Earth. Then, find information about the boiling point of water at sea level and at the different elevations on land that you found.

Journal: Write a Report Include what you found. Also in your report:

- Identify the elevations using positive and negative numbers.
- Present the boiling points of water in degrees Fahrenheit and in degrees Celsius.
- Compare the boiling points based on elevation.
- What generalization can you make about elevation and the boiling point of water?

Name ____________________

Review What You Know

Vocabulary

Choose the best term from the box. Write it on the blank.

- decimal
- fraction
- denominator
- numerator

1. A __________ names part of a whole, part of a set, or a location on a number line.

2. The number above the fraction bar that represents the part of the whole is the __________.

3. The number below the fraction bar that represents the total number of equal parts in one whole is the __________.

Fractions and Decimals

Write each fraction as a decimal.

4. $\frac{2}{5}$

5. $\frac{3}{4}$

6. $\frac{10}{4}$

7. $\frac{12}{5}$

8. $\frac{3}{5}$

9. $\frac{15}{3}$

Division

Divide.

10. $1.25 \div 0.5$

11. $13 \div 0.65$

12. $12.2 \div 0.4$

13. $21.6 \div 5.4$

14. $26.35 \div 4.25$

15. $28.71 \div 8.7$

Explain

16. Les said that the quotient of $3.9 \div 0.75$ is 0.52. Explain how you know Les is incorrect without completing the division.

© Pearson Education, Inc. 6

My Word Cards

Use the examples for each word on the front of the card to help complete the definitions on the back.

integers

. . . , − 3, − 2, − 1, 0, 1, 2, 3, . . .

opposites

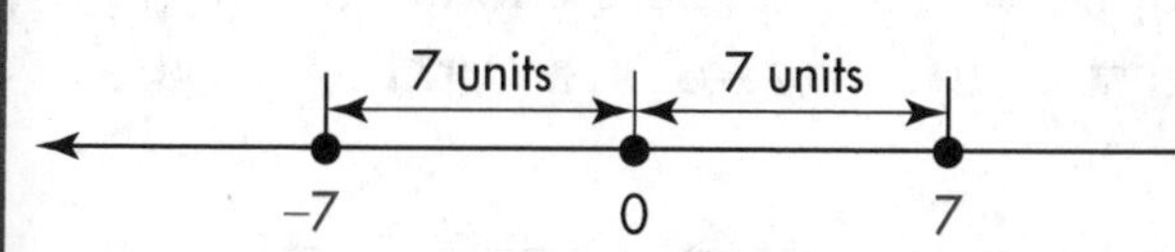

−7 and 7 are opposite integers.

rational number

$-\frac{1}{4}$ **3.25** **9** **− 0.7** $\frac{2}{3}$ **− 52**

absolute value

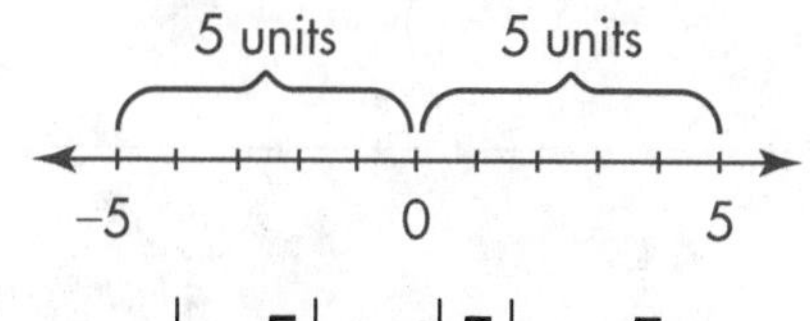

$|-5| = |5| = 5$

My Word Cards

Complete each definition. Extend learning by writing your own definitions.

Numbers that are located on the opposite sides of zero and are the same distance from zero on a number line are

______________________.

The counting numbers, their opposites, and zero are

______________________.

The distance a number is from zero on a number line is its

______________________.

Any number that can be written as the quotient $\frac{a}{b}$, where a and b are integers and b does not equal zero, is a

______________________.

© Pearson Education, Inc. 6

Name ________________________

Lesson 3-1
Understand Integers

I can ...
use positive and negative integers.

Content Standards 6.NS.C.5, 6.NS.C.6a, 6.NS.C.6c
Mathematical Practices MP.2, MP.5, MP.8

Solve & Share Make a blue mark on the thermometer at 10°C and 4°C. Make a black mark at 0°C. Make a red mark at −4°C and −10°C. Tell how you decided where to place each mark.

20
10
0
−10
−20
°C

You can use appropriate tools. A thermometer is like a vertical number line.

Look Back! **MP.2 Reasoning** 0°C is the temperature at which water freezes. Which is colder, 10°C or −10°C?

What Are Integers?

A

The counting numbers, their opposites, and zero are integers. Numbers that are located on opposite sides of 0 and are the same distance from 0 on a number line are opposites. What integer is the opposite of 6?

You can extend a number line to include negative numbers.

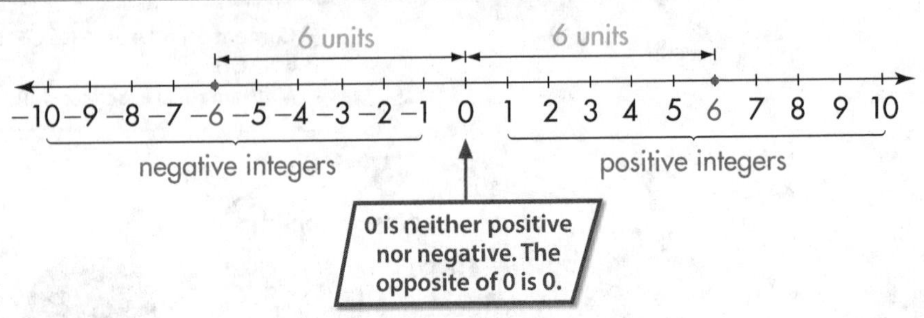

B

One Way

A thermometer is like a vertical number line that uses integers to show temperatures measured in degrees.

0 represents 0°C.
6°C is 6°C warmer than 0°C.
−6°C is 6°C colder than 0°C.

The integer −6 is the opposite of 6.

6°C
−6°C
20
10
0
−10
−20
°C

C

Another Way

The opposite of the opposite of a number is the number itself.

For example, the opposite of the number 6 is −6, and the opposite of −6 is 6.

Convince Me! ⊚ **MP.2 Reasoning** What is the value of $-(-9)$? Explain.

© Pearson Education, Inc. 6

Name ____________________

Practice Buddy Tools Assessment

Guided Practice*

Do You Understand?

1. What do you know about two different integers that are opposites?

2. How do you read −17?

3. MP.8 Generalize Which integers are **NOT** used for counting?

Do You Know How?

In **4–9**, write the opposite of each integer.

4. 1 5. −1 6. −11

7. 30 8. 0 9. −16

Independent Practice

In **10–15**, use the number line. Write the integer value that each point represents, then write its opposite.

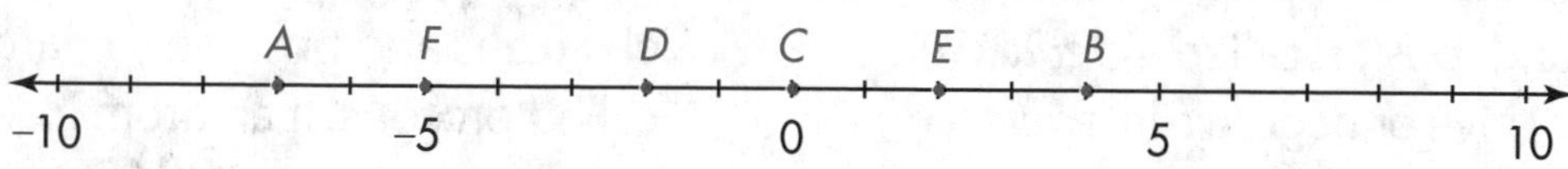

10. *A* 11. *B* 12. *C* 13. *D* 14. *E* 15. *F*

In **16–21**, plot each point on the number line below.

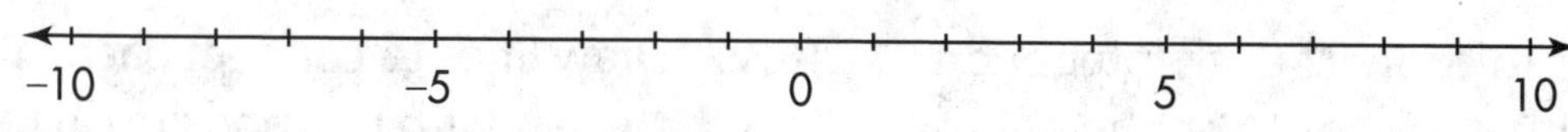

16. *G* (−10) 17. *H* (8) 18. *I* (−1) 19. *J* (9) 20. *K* (6) 21. *L* (−3)

In **22–27**, write the opposite of each integer.

22. 5 23. −13 24. −(−22) 25. −31 26. −50 27. −(−66)

*For another example, see Set A on page 175.

Math Practices and Problem Solving

In **28–31**, use the pictures at the right.

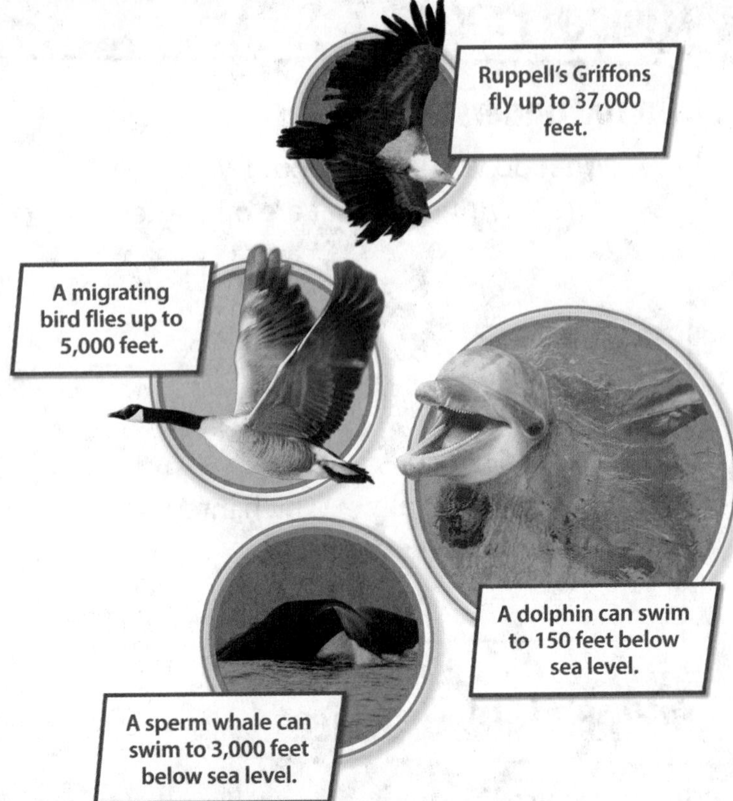

Ruppell's Griffons fly up to 37,000 feet.
A migrating bird flies up to 5,000 feet.
A dolphin can swim to 150 feet below sea level.
A sperm whale can swim to 3,000 feet below sea level.

28. **MP.8 Generalize** Which integer represents sea level? Explain.

29. Use a negative integer to represent the depth to which a dolphin may swim.

30. Which of these animals can travel at the greatest distance from sea level?

31. **Number Sense** How many times deeper can a sperm whale swim than a dolphin?

32. **Higher Order Thinking** In a bank account, a paid-out expense is called a *debit*, and a deposit is called a *credit*. Would you use positive or negative integers to represent credits? Debits? Explain.

33. **Math and Science** Atoms have negatively charged particles called electrons and positively charged particles called protons. If an atom loses an electron, it has a positive electric charge. If it gains an electron, it has a negative electric charge. Which integer would represent the electric charge of an atom that has an equal number of electrons and protons?

Common Core Assessment

34. Draw lines to connect each integer on the left with its opposite on the right.

-24

19

24

-8

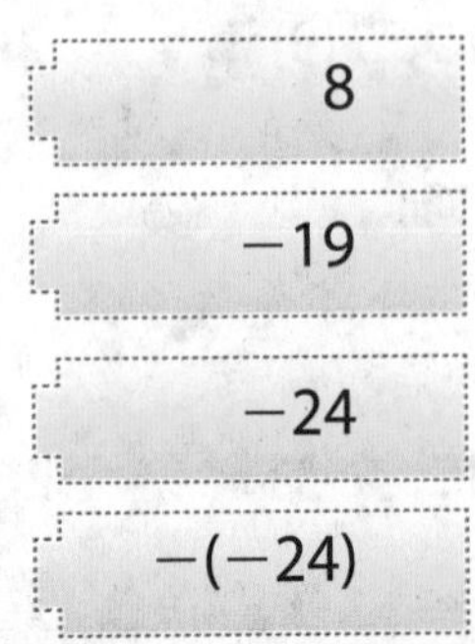

35. Draw lines to connect each integer on the left with its opposite on the right.

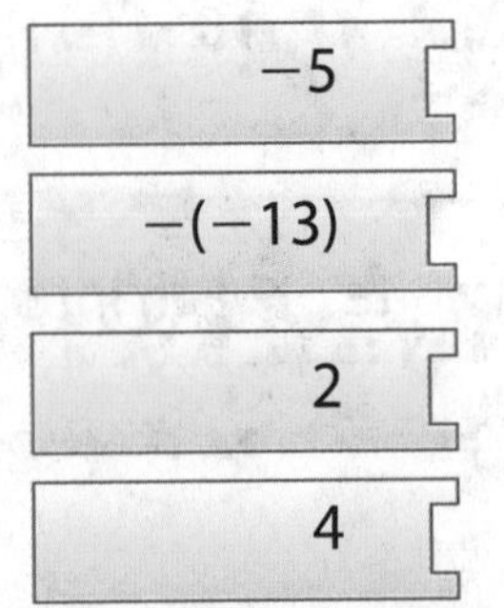

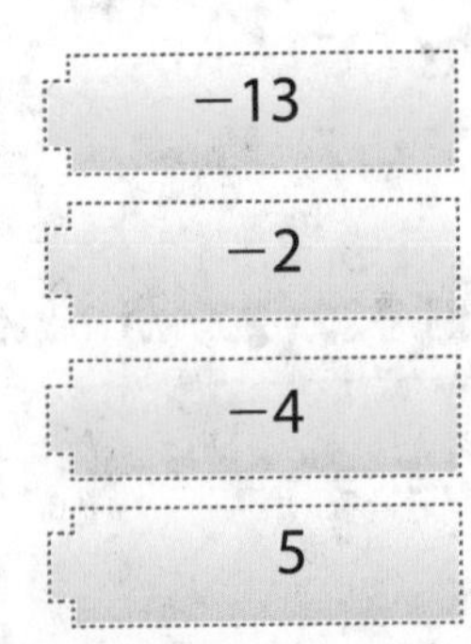

© Pearson Education, Inc. 6

Name ____________________

Help | Practice Buddy | Tools | Games

Homework & Practice 3-1

Understand Integers

Another Look!

What is the opposite of -7?

You can extend a number line to show both positive and negative numbers.

Integers are all of the counting numbers, their opposites, and 0.
Opposites are integers that are the same distance from 0 and on opposite sides of 0 on a number line.

The integers -7 and 7 are opposites.

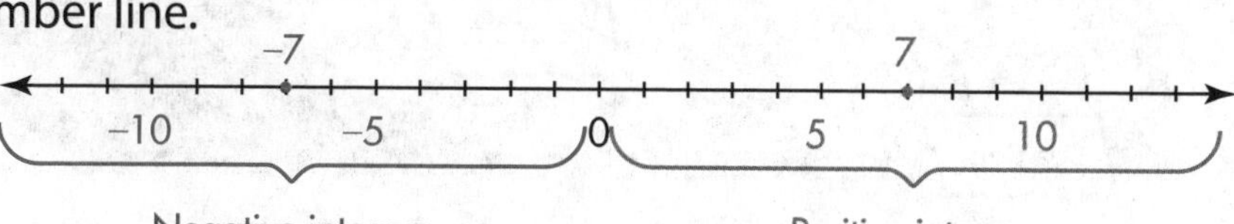

In **1–5**, use the number line below. Write the integer value that each point represents, then write its opposite.

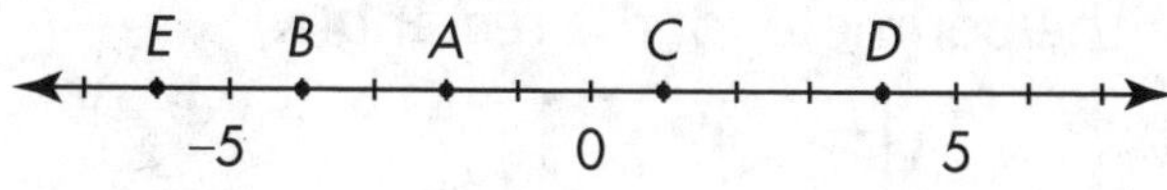

You only need to write the negative sign for negative integers.

1. *A* **2.** *B* **3.** *C* **4.** *D* **5.** *E*

In **6–10**, plot each point on the number line below.

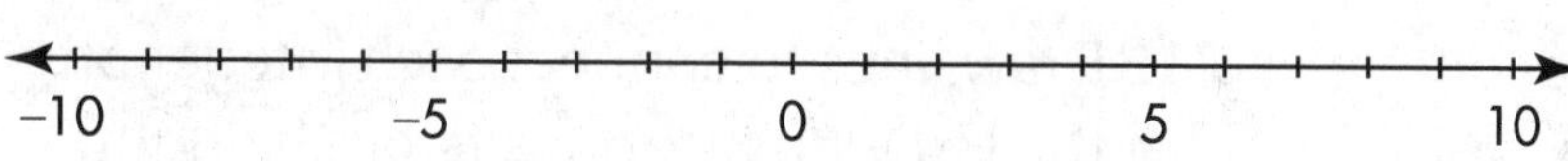

6. *L* (−8) **7.** *M* (3) **8.** *N* (−4) **9.** *O* (2) **10.** *P* (−1)

In **11–15**, write the opposite of each integer.

11. −12 **12.** 63 **13.** −(−10) **14.** 33 **15.** −101

Mauna Loa, in Hawaii, is the largest above-sea-level volcano. In **16–17**, use the diagram of Mauna Loa.

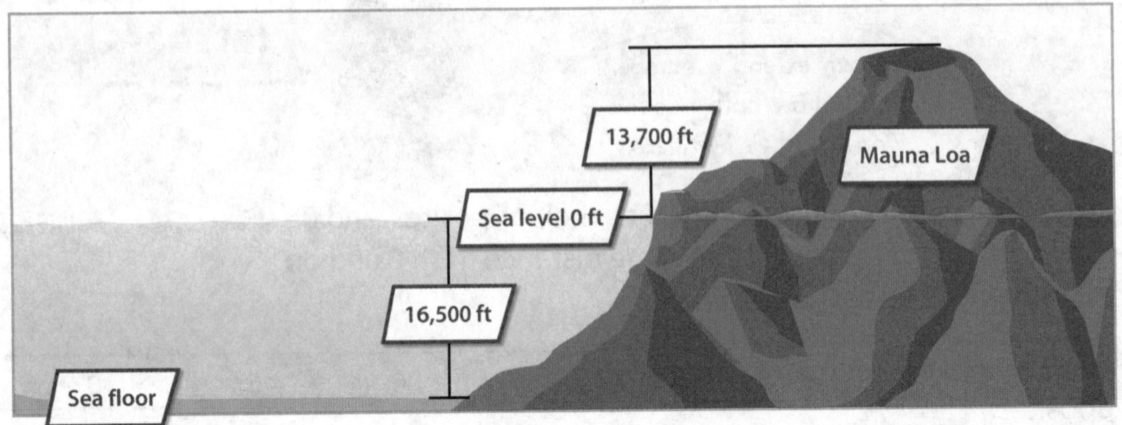

16. **MP.2 Reasoning** Use a negative integer to represent the depth, in feet, of the sea floor.

17. Mauna Loa depresses the sea floor, resulting in 26,400 more feet added to its height. What is the total height of Mauna Loa?

18. **Higher Order Thinking** In math, a letter such as p can be assigned as a variable to represent an unknown value. Give an example of a value for p that results in $-p$ being a positive integer. Explain your reasoning.

19. Evaluate the expression $2\ell + 2w$ to find the perimeter of the rectangle.

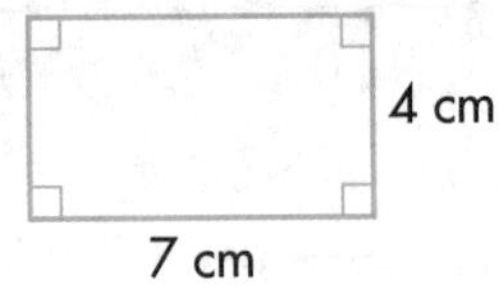

Common Core Assessment

20. Draw lines to connect each integer on the left with its opposite on the right.

−4
40
−40
4

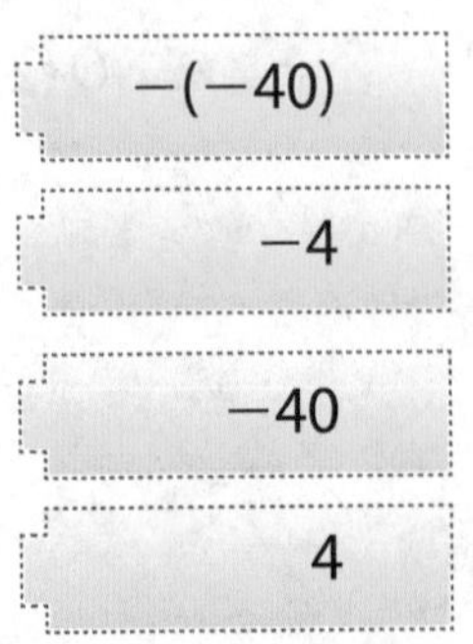

21. Draw lines to connect each integer on the left with its opposite on the right.

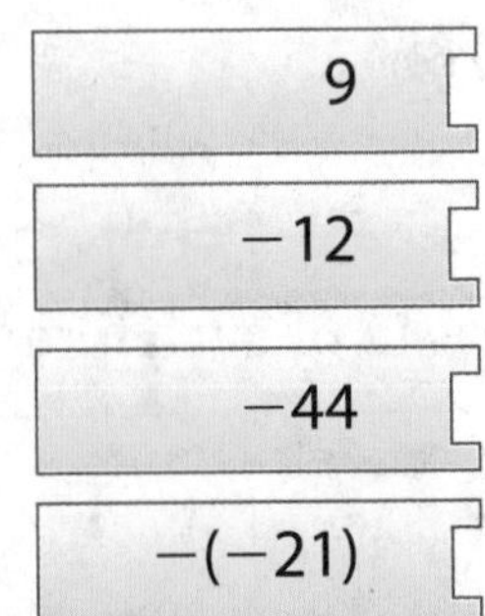

44
−9
−21
12

© Pearson Education, Inc. 6

Name ____________________

Lesson 3-2

Rational Numbers on a Number Line

I can ...
find and position rational numbers on a number line.

Content Standard 6.NS.C.6c
Mathematical Practices MP.2, MP.3, MP.6, MP.8

Solve & Share

Plot $-\frac{3}{4}$ on a vertical number line. Explain how you did it. ***Solve this problem any way you choose.***

Use reasoning. How can you use what you know about plotting integers and positive fractions to help you?

Look Back! **MP.8 Generalize** Plot $-\frac{3}{4}$ on a horizontal number line. How is plotting negative fractions like plotting positive fractions? How is it different?

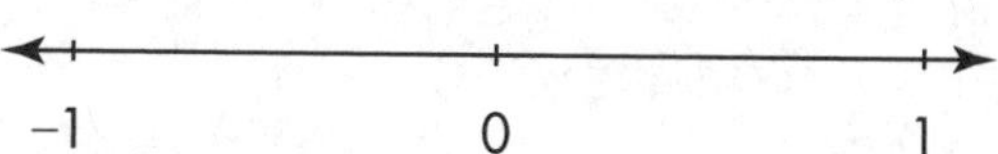

How Can You Plot Rational Numbers on a Number Line?

A

Any number that can be written as the quotient of two integers is called a rational number. A rational number can be written in the form $\frac{a}{b}$ or $-\frac{a}{b}$, where a and b are integers and b $\neq$ 0.

A rational number can be a whole number, fraction, or decimal.

Find and position $-\frac{4}{3}$ and -1.5 on the number lines.

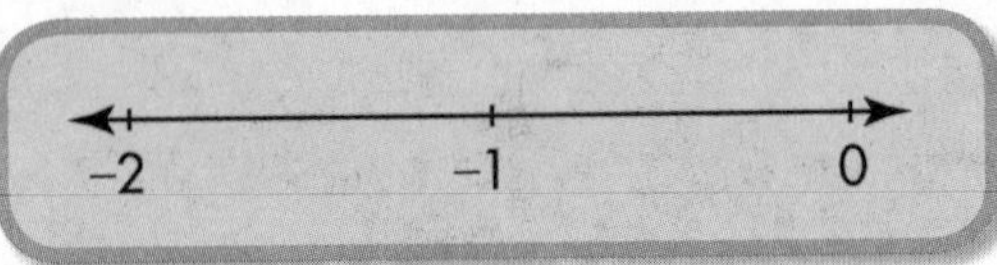

You can plot numbers on horizontal or vertical number lines.

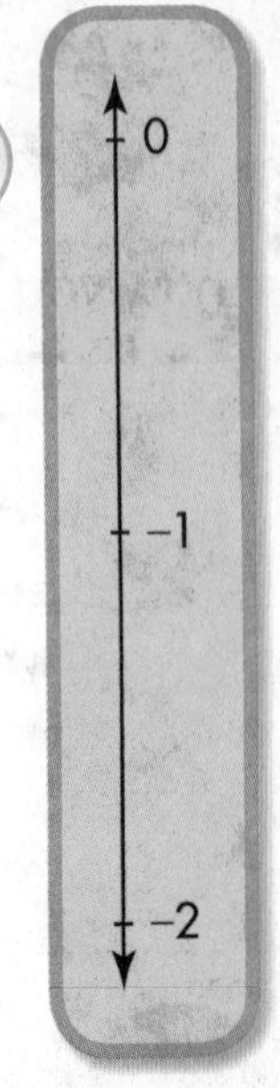

B

One Way

Use a horizontal number line to plot $-\frac{4}{3}$.

You can think of $-\frac{4}{3}$ as a mixed number.

$$-\frac{4}{3} = -1\frac{1}{3}$$

Divide the units on the number line into thirds and find one and one-third to the left of 0.

Plot the point $-\frac{4}{3}$.

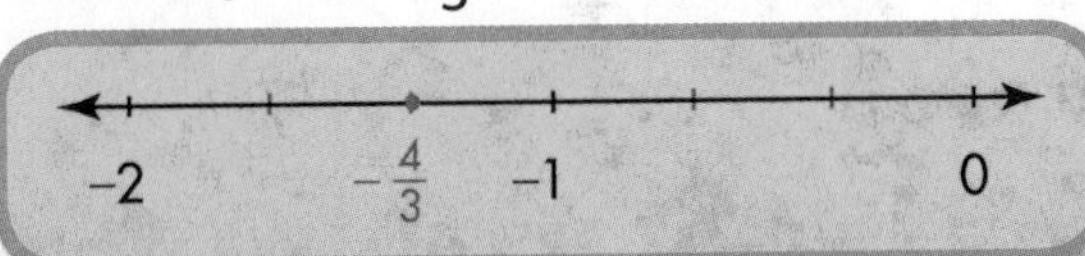

C

Another Way

Use a vertical number line to plot -1.5. You can think of -1.5 as a mixed number.

$$-1.5 = -1\frac{5}{10}$$
$$= -1\frac{1}{2}$$

Divide the units on the number line into halves and find one and one-half below 0. Plot the point -1.5.

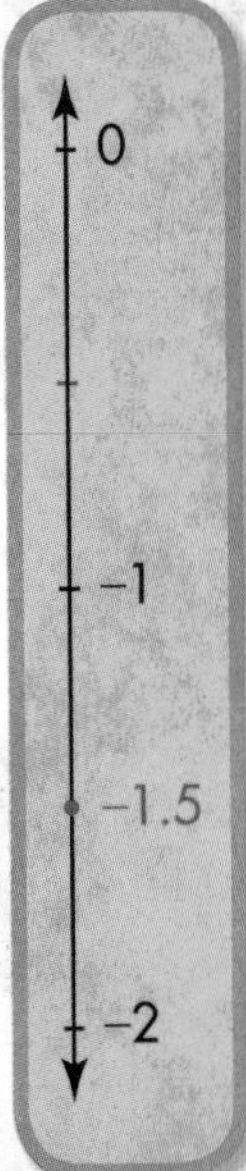

Convince Me! **MP.2 Reasoning** Why is thinking of $-\frac{4}{3}$ and -1.5 as mixed numbers helpful when plotting these points on number lines?

© Pearson Education, Inc. 6

Name ____________________

Guided Practice*

Practice Buddy Tools Assessment

Do You Understand?

1. MP.8 Generalize Why are decimals rational numbers? Use −1.5 as an example.

2. Vocabulary Why are integers rational numbers? Give an example.

3. MP.6 Be Precise In Another Way on the previous page, why does the point plotted represent −1.5 instead of −2.5?

Do You Know How?

In **4–6**, write the number positioned at each point.

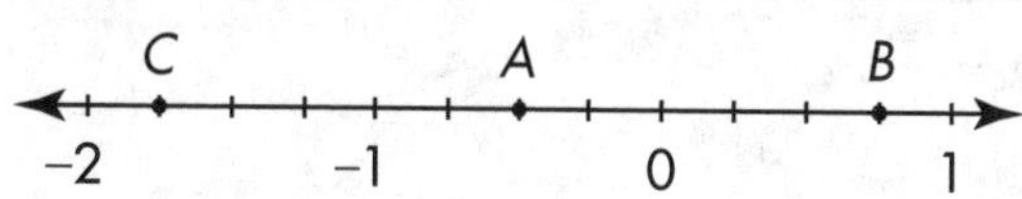

4. *A* 5. *B* 6. *C*

7. Plot a point *P* at $-1\frac{1}{4}$ on the number line above.

Remember, $\frac{a}{b} = a \div b$.

Independent Practice

In **8–13**, write the number positioned at each point.

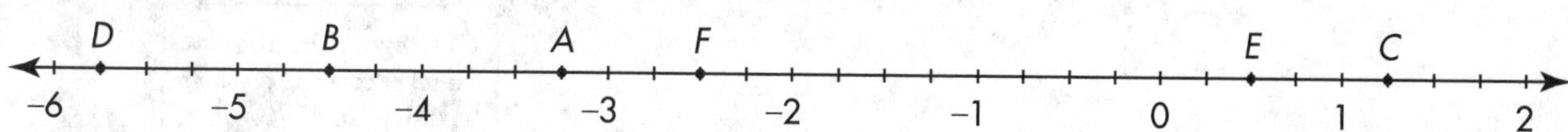

8. *A* 9. *B* 10. *C*

11. *D* 12. *E* 13. *F*

14. Plot −6.3 on the number line below.

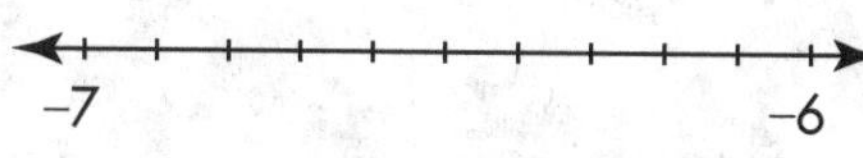

15. Draw a number line and plot $-\frac{7}{5}$.

*For another example, see Set B on page 175.

Math Practices and Problem Solving

16. **MP.2 Reasoning** Suppose you plot the locations of the sea animals on a number line. Which animal would be represented by the point farthest from zero on the number line? Explain.

DATA

Animal	Possible Locations Relative to Ocean's Surface
Bloodbelly comb jelly	−0.8 km
Deep sea anglerfish	$-\frac{2}{3}$ km
Fanfin anglerfish	$-2\frac{1}{4}$ km
Gulper eel	−1.1 km
Pacific blackdragon	$-\frac{3}{10}$ km
Slender snipe eel	−0.6 km

17. Which animal is closest to a depth of −0.7 km?

18. Evaluate the expression for $x = 3$.

$$3x^2 + (2x - 1) - 4$$

19. The change in the value of a stock is represented by the rational number −5.90. Describe, in words, what this means.

20. **Higher Order Thinking** What is the least number of points you must plot in order to have examples of all four sets of numbers, including at least one positive and one negative integer? Explain.

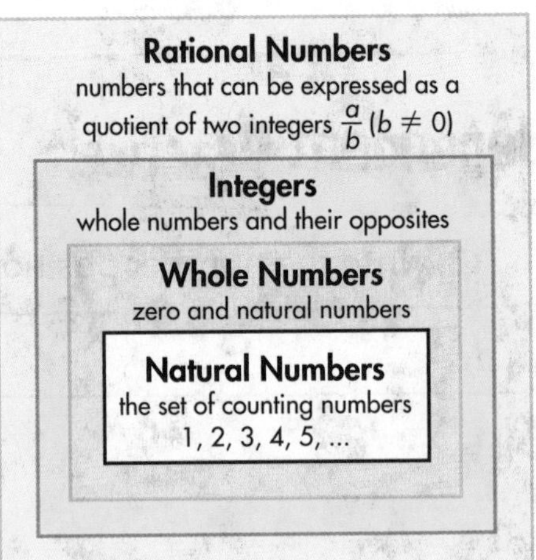

Rational Numbers
numbers that can be expressed as a quotient of two integers $\frac{a}{b}$ $(b \neq 0)$
Integers
whole numbers and their opposites
Whole Numbers
zero and natural numbers
Natural Numbers
the set of counting numbers
1, 2, 3, 4, 5, ...

Common Core Assessment

21. Plot and label points $A\left(-5\frac{1}{2}\right)$, B (0.25), and C (−3.5) on the number line below.

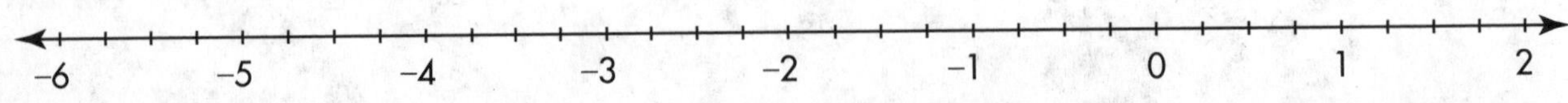

© Pearson Education, Inc. 6

Name ____________________

Help Practice Buddy Tools Games

Homework & Practice 3-2

Rational Numbers on a Number Line

Another Look!

A **rational number** can be expressed as a fraction in the form $\frac{a}{b}$ or $-\frac{a}{b}$, where a and b are integers and b is not 0. Integers and decimals are rational numbers. On a horizontal number line, negative rational numbers are to the left of 0. On a vertical number line, negative rational numbers are below 0.

Find and position $-\frac{1}{2}$ on the number line.

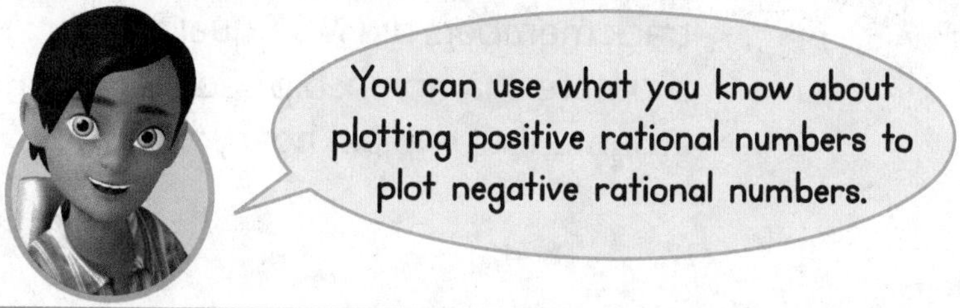
You can use what you know about plotting positive rational numbers to plot negative rational numbers.

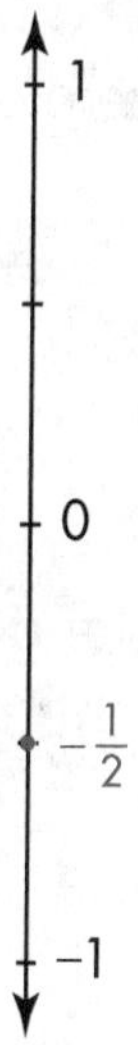
1
0
$-\frac{1}{2}$
−1

In **1–8**, write the number positioned at each point on the number line at the right.

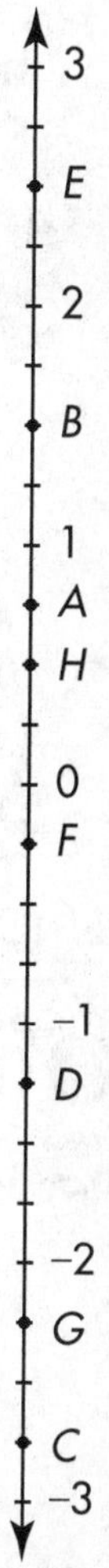
3
E
2
B
1
A
H
0
F
−1
D
−2
G
C
−3

1. *A* **2.** *B* **3.** *C* **4.** *D*

5. *E* **6.** *F* **7.** *G* **8.** *H*

In **9–16**, plot each point on the number line at the right.

9. $S(2.75)$ **10.** $T\left(\frac{1}{4}\right)$ **11.** $U\left(-2\frac{1}{2}\right)$ **12.** $V(2.25)$

13. $W\left(1\frac{3}{4}\right)$ **14.** $X(-0.75)$ **15.** $Y -1.75$ **16.** $Z\left(-\frac{3}{1}\right)$

17. Plot −8.7 on the number line below.

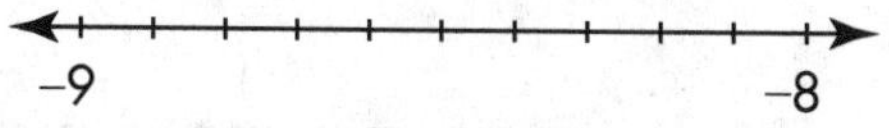
−9
−8

18. Draw a number line and plot $-\frac{5}{3}$.

19. **MP.2 Reasoning** Suppose you plot the lengths in the table on a number line. Which track member's long jump length would be represented by the point closest, but not equal to, zero on the number line? Explain.

DATA

Track Members	Long Jump Length Relative to State Qualifying Distance
Theresa	−5.625 in.
Ann	2 in.
Shirley	−3 in.
Delia	0 in.

20. Delia's relative long jump length was recorded as 0. What does this mean?

21. **MP.3 Construct Arguments** Which track members did **NOT** qualify for the state championship? Construct an argument to explain how you know.

22. **MP.2 Reasoning** Find a number that has exactly 7 different prime factors. Explain how you found it.

You can use what you know about prime numbers and factors to find a number.

23. **Higher Order Thinking** Tom is thinking of a number. He says that the opposite of the opposite of the number is −12.4. Write the number Tom is thinking of as a mixed number. Explain.

Common Core Assessment

24. Plot and label points $X\left(-4\frac{1}{4}\right)$, $Y(-2.75)$, and $Z\left(1\frac{1}{2}\right)$ on the number line below.

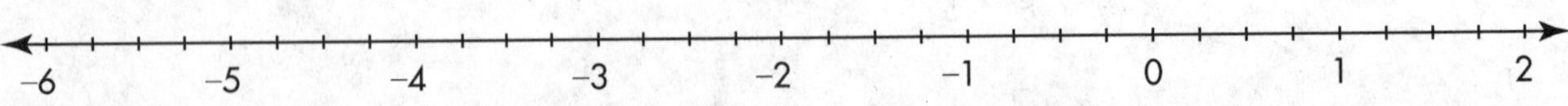

© Pearson Education, Inc. 6

Name ______________________ Solve

Solve & Share Four tiles from a number game are shown below. Order the number tiles from greatest to least. ***Solve this problem any way you choose.***

$-\frac{2}{3}$ -1 $\frac{1}{4}$ -0.5

Lesson 3-3
Compare and Order Rational Numbers

I can ...
compare and order rational numbers.

Content Standards 6.NS.C.7a, 6.NS.C.7b
Mathematical Practices MP.1, MP.2, MP.3, MP.4, MP.5, MP.8

How can you use appropriate tools, like a number line, to help you solve the problem?

Look Back! **MP.4 Model with Math** Write an inequality to compare the two middle values among the four tiles that you ordered above. Explain how the inequality relates to the position of the two numbers on a number line.

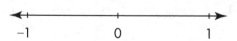

−1 0 1

How Can You Compare and Order Rational Numbers?

A

You can use number lines to help you compare and order rational numbers. Use <, >, or = to compare $\frac{2}{3}$, 1.75, and − 0.75. Then order these numbers from least to greatest.

You can use number sense and a number line to order rational numbers.

B

One Way

Think!

- −0.75 is a negative number, so it will be farthest to the left on the number line.
- $\frac{2}{3}$ is between 0 and 1.
- 1.75 is between 1 and 2.

Place the numbers on a number line.

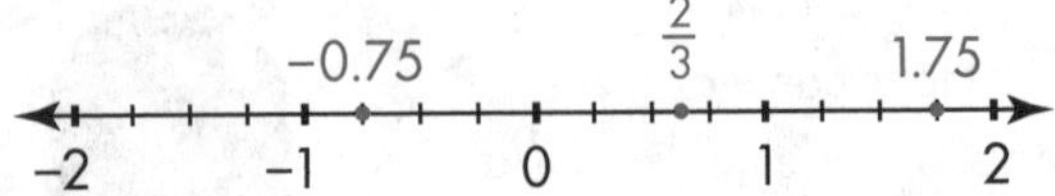

So, $-0.75 < \frac{2}{3} < 1.75$, and their order from least to greatest is −0.75, $\frac{2}{3}$, 1.75.

C

Another Way

Write the numbers in a common form to order rational numbers.

Write $\frac{2}{3}$ as a decimal.

$\frac{2}{3} = 0.\overline{6}$

Remember, $\frac{a}{b} = a \div b$.

Use a number line to compare and order the decimals $0.\overline{6}$, 1.75, −0.75.

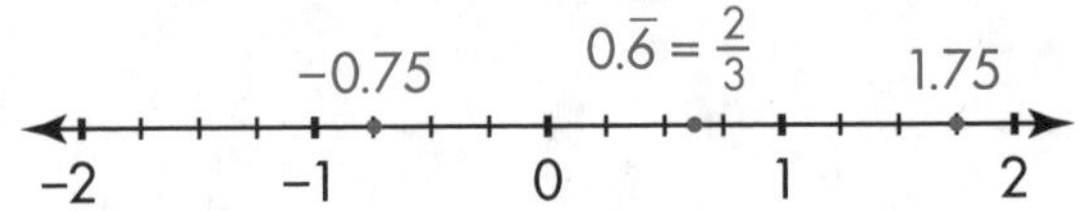

So, $-0.75 < \frac{2}{3} < 1.75$, and their order from least to greatest is −0.75, $\frac{2}{3}$, 1.75.

Convince Me! **MP.8 Generalize** If the number $\frac{1}{4}$ is ordered within the list of numbers in the example above, between which two numbers would it be placed?

© Pearson Education, Inc. 6

Name ______________________

Practice Buddy Tools Assessment

Another Example

At 10:00 P.M. one winter night, the temperature was $-3°C$. At midnight, the temperature was $-7°C$. Use $<$, $>$, or $=$ to compare the two temperatures and explain their relationship.

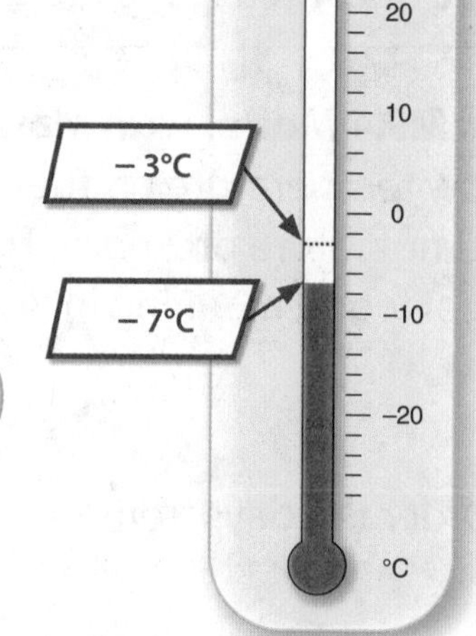

On a thermometer, $-7°C$ is below $-3°C$, so $-7°C < -3°C$.

That means that $-7°C$ is colder than $-3°C$.

You can explain statements of order in real-world contexts.

Guided Practice*

Do You Understand?

1. How can a number line help you to compare and order rational numbers?

2. **MP.2 Reasoning** Explain how the inequality $-3°C > -7°C$ describes how the temperatures are related.

Do You Know How?

3. Use the number line to order the numbers from least to greatest.

$1.3, -\frac{3}{2}, -1.2, 1\frac{1}{2}$

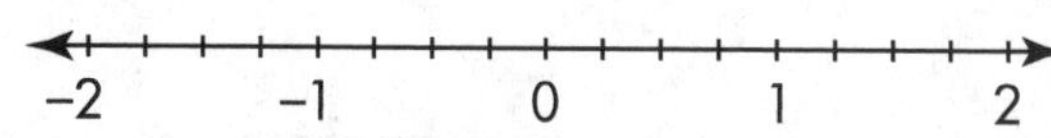

Independent Practice

In **4–6**, use $<$, $>$, or $=$ to compare.

Draw and use number lines to help.

4. $\frac{1}{10}$ ◯ 0.09

5. -1.44 ◯ $-1\frac{1}{4}$

6. $-\frac{2}{3}$ ◯ -0.8

In **7–9**, order the numbers from least to greatest.

7. $-6, 8, -9, 13$

8. $-\frac{4}{5}, -\frac{1}{2}, 0.25, -0.2$

9. $4.75, -2\frac{1}{2}, -\frac{8}{3}, \frac{9}{2}$

*For another example, see Set B on page 175.

Math Practices and Problem Solving

For **10** and **11**, use the table of daily low temperatures.

10. MP.4 Model with Math Compare the low temperature on Tuesday with the low temperature on Friday. Then explain the real-world meaning in words.

DATA

Day	Temperature
Monday	3°C
Tuesday	−6°C
Wednesday	5°C
Thursday	1°C
Friday	−5°C

11. Order the days from warmest to coldest.

12. MP.3 Construct Arguments A classmate ordered these numbers from greatest to least. Is he correct? Construct an argument to justify your answer.

$4.4, 4.2, -4.42, -4.24$

13. MP.1 Make Sense and Persevere Order $-3.25, -3\frac{1}{8}, -3\frac{3}{4}$, and -3.1 from least to greatest. Explain how you decided.

14. The San Francisco–Oakland Bay Bridge, opened in 2013, allows for five traffic lanes totaling 57.5 feet across. Write this width as a fraction.

15. Higher Order Thinking Suppose $\frac{a}{b}$, $\frac{c}{d}$, and $\frac{e}{f}$ represent three rational numbers. If $\frac{a}{b}$ is less than $\frac{c}{d}$, and $\frac{c}{d}$ is less than $\frac{e}{f}$, compare $\frac{a}{b}$ and $\frac{e}{f}$. Explain your reasoning.

Common Core Assessment

16. Which inequality is **NOT** true?

Ⓐ $4\frac{1}{2} > \frac{25}{4}$

Ⓑ $-4\frac{1}{2} > -\frac{25}{4}$

Ⓒ $-6 < -5$

Ⓓ $-\frac{1}{2} < \frac{1}{2}$

17. The numbers below are listed in order from greatest to least. Which could be a value for *n*?

$1.2, 0, n, -\frac{1}{5}$

Ⓐ $-\frac{1}{2}$

Ⓑ $-\frac{1}{3}$

Ⓒ $-\frac{1}{4}$

Ⓓ $-\frac{1}{6}$

© Pearson Education, Inc. 6

Name ______________________

Homework & Practice 3-3
Compare and Order Rational Numbers

Another Look!

Order $\frac{3}{5}$, 1.25, and -1.75 from least to greatest. When ordering rational numbers on a number line, the number that is farthest to the right is greatest. The number farthest to the left is least.

- -1.75 is negative, so it is farthest to the left.
- $\frac{3}{5}$ is between 0 and 1.
- 1.25 is greater than 1.

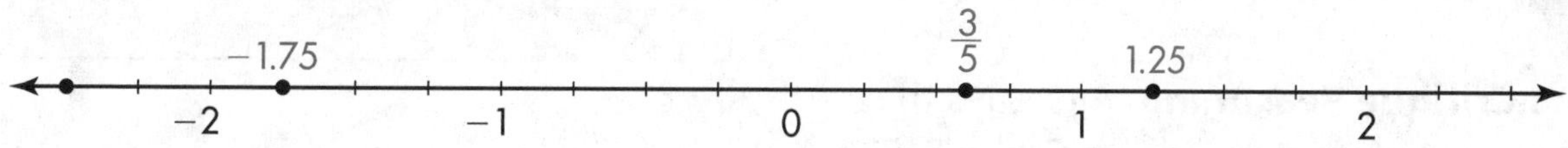

The numbers, in order from least to greatest, are: -1.75, $\frac{3}{5}$, 1.25.

In **1–8**, use <, >, or = to compare.

1. $-12 \bigcirc -15$ **2.** $-\frac{1}{3} \bigcirc -1$ **3.** $-2 \bigcirc -2.1$ **4.** $\frac{1}{5} \bigcirc \frac{1}{4}$

5. $\frac{7}{10} \bigcirc -0.85$ **6.** $-0.66 \bigcirc -\frac{3}{4}$ **7.** $-4\frac{1}{2} \bigcirc -3.9$ **8.** $7\frac{1}{2} \bigcirc 7.75$

In **9–11**, order the numbers from least to greatest.

9. 7, -8, -4, 5 **10.** $-\frac{3}{8}$, $1\frac{1}{2}$, -0.5, -0.9 **11.** -3.05, $-3\frac{1}{2}$, $-\frac{10}{3}$, 3

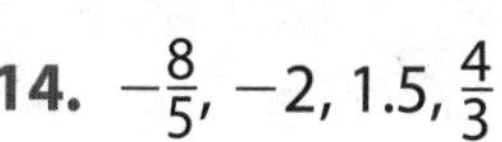

You can write rational numbers in the same form to help you compare and order.

In **12–14**, order the numbers from greatest to least.

12. -14, -25, 7, -1 **13.** -0.33, $-\frac{1}{4}$, 0.35, $\frac{3}{5}$ **14.** $-\frac{8}{5}$, -2, 1.5, $\frac{4}{3}$

In **15–17**, use the map at the right.

15. The map shows how deep archaeologists have dug at several excavation sites. Order the archaeological excavation sites from the least depth to the greatest depth.

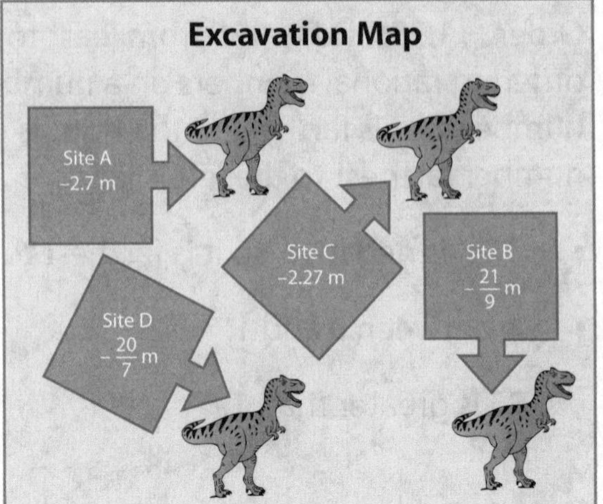

16. Number Sense Archaeologists are excavating a new Site E. On a number line, the depth of Site E is in between the depths of Site A and Site B. What is a possible depth of Site E?

17. MP.3 Critique Reasoning Alex says that the sites should be ordered Site C, Site B, Site A, and Site D because $-2.27 > -\frac{21}{9} > -2.7 > -\frac{20}{7}$.

Explain the error in Alex's reasoning.

18. MP.1 Make Sense and Persevere Order $-6\frac{1}{4}$, -6.35, $-6\frac{1}{5}$, and -6.1 from greatest to least. Explain how you decided.

19. Math and Science Olinquitos are small raccoonlike animals that live in cloud forest habitats in the Andes Mountains, at altitudes of between about 1,500 meters and 2,750 meters. Write two inequalities that describe the altitude, *A*, at which olinquitos can be found.

20. Higher Order Thinking Tyler says there are infinitely many rational numbers between 0 and 1. Do you agree? Explain.

Common Core Assessment

21. Which inequality is true?

Ⓐ $6.5 > \frac{25}{4}$

Ⓑ $-6.5 > -\frac{25}{4}$

Ⓒ $-6 > -5$

Ⓓ $5 > \frac{25}{4}$

22. The numbers below are listed in order from least to greatest. Which could be a value for *m*?

$-0.75, m, -\frac{1}{2}, 0$

Ⓐ $\frac{2}{3}$

Ⓑ $\frac{1}{3}$

Ⓒ $-\frac{2}{3}$

Ⓓ $-\frac{1}{3}$

© Pearson Education, Inc. 6

Name ______________________________

Solve

Lesson 3-4
Absolute Value

I can ...
interpret absolute value in mathematics and real-world situations.

Content Standards 6.NS.C.7c, 6.NS.C.7d
Mathematical Practices MP.1, MP.2, MP.3, MP.8

Solve & Share Credit cards may be used to purchase items on credit and pay for them later. A portion of a credit card account statement is shown below. How would you interpret the value of the ending balance? Explain your reasoning. ***Solve this problem any way you choose.***

Use reasoning. A balance of $0 means that no payment is due.

Credit Card Account	
Ending Balance	– $ 30.00

Look Back! **MP.2 Reasoning** What is an example of a credit card balance that represents an amount owed greater than $40?

How Can You Represent and Interpret Absolute Values?

A

Stock prices rise and fall during the year.

The table shows the overall change in the price of a company's stock from year to year.

During which two years was the overall change in the stock price the greatest?

Year	Change in Price ($)
2015	11
2014	19
2013	– 34
2012	6

It makes sense that positive values show increases and negative values show decreases.

B

The absolute value of a number is its distance from zero on the number line. Distance is always positive.

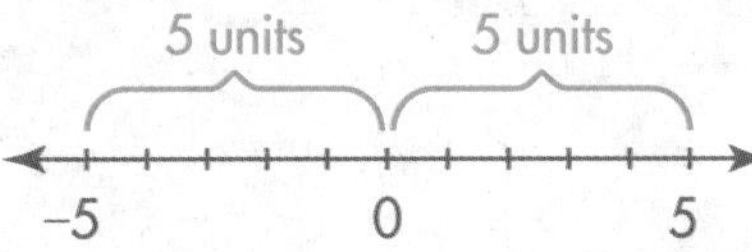

The absolute value of 5 is written $|5|$. The absolute value of -5 is written as $|-5|$.

$|-5| = 5 \quad |5| = 5$

C

To find the two years with the greatest change, use absolute values.

–34 0 6 11 19

The absolute values of the changes in the company's stock price each year are shown below.

2015: $|11| = 11$

2014: $|19| = 19$ ← 2nd greatest change

2013: $|-34| = 34$ ← greatest change

2012: $|6| = 6$

So, the two years in which the change in stock price was the greatest were 2013 and 2014.

Convince Me! **MP.8 Generalize** Write the absolute values of $-7\frac{1}{4}$, 2.2, and -4.38.

© Pearson Education, Inc. 6

Name ________________________________

Practice Buddy Tools Assessment

Another Example

Negative numbers sometimes represent debts. The table shows three account balances that represent debts. Tell which account balance is the least number. Then use absolute value to find which account represents the greatest debt.

Account	Balance ($)
A	−35
B	−50
C	−12

On a number line, −50 is farther from 0 than either −35 or −12 are. So −50 is the least number.

The money owed is the absolute value of each balance.

Account A	**Account B**	**Account C**
$\lvert -35 \rvert = \$35$	$\lvert -50 \rvert = \$50$	$\lvert -12 \rvert = \$12$

$50 is the greatest amount of money owed. So Account B represents the greatest debt.

Guided Practice*

Do You Understand?

1. **MP.3 Construct Arguments** Explain why −7 has a greater absolute value than the absolute value of 6.

2. **MP.2 Reasoning** Give an example of a balance that has a greater integer value than the balance of Account C above but represents a debt of less than $5.

Do You Know How?

In **3–5**, find each absolute value.

3. $\lvert -9 \rvert$ 4. $\lvert 5\frac{3}{4} \rvert$ 5. $\lvert -5.5 \rvert$

In **6** and **7**, use <, >, or = to compare.

6. $\lvert -19 \rvert$ ◯ $\lvert -11 \rvert$ 7. $\lvert -2\frac{1}{2} \rvert$ ◯ $\lvert 2.5 \rvert$

Independent Practice

Leveled Practice In **8–12**, find each absolute value.

8. $\lvert -46 \rvert$ 9. $\lvert 0.7 \rvert$ 10. $\lvert -\frac{2}{3} \rvert$ 11. $\lvert -7.35 \rvert$ 12. $\lvert -4\frac{3}{4} \rvert$

In **13–16**, use <, >, or = to compare.

13. $\lvert 14 \rvert$ ◯ $\lvert -21 \rvert$ 14. $\lvert -11.5 \rvert$ ◯ $\lvert 11\frac{3}{4} \rvert$ 15. $\lvert -6.3 \rvert$ ◯ $\lvert 5.2 \rvert$ 16. $\lvert 3.75 \rvert$ ◯ $\lvert -3\frac{3}{4} \rvert$

17. Order $\lvert -6 \rvert$, $\lvert -4 \rvert$, $\lvert 11 \rvert$, $\lvert 0 \rvert$ from greatest to least.

18. Order $\lvert 4 \rvert$, $\lvert -3 \rvert$, $\lvert -18 \rvert$, $\lvert -3.18 \rvert$ from least to greatest.

For another example, see Set C on page 176.

Math Practices and Problem Solving

Alberto and Rebecca toss horseshoes at a stake that is 12 feet away from where they are standing. Whoever is closer to the stake wins a point. Use the picture at the right to help answer **19** and **20**.

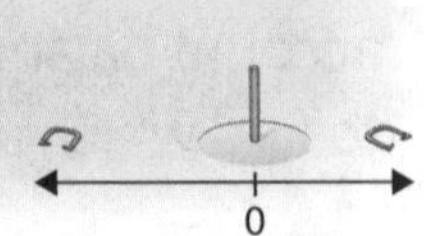

19. **MP.2 Reasoning** Alberto's horseshoe lands 3 feet in front of the stake and Rebecca's lands 2 feet past the stake. Which integer best describes the location of Alberto's horseshoe in relation to the stake? Which best describes Rebecca's horseshoe?

20. **MP.3 Critique Reasoning** Alberto says that -3 is less than 2, so he wins a point. Is Alberto correct? Explain.

21. **Higher Order Thinking** Let $a =$ any rational number. Is the absolute value of a different if a is a positive number or a negative number? Explain.

22. **Algebra** Solve the equation for x.

$$x + 9.5 = 18.48$$

Common Core Assessment

23. The table below shows the scores at the end of the first round of a golf tournament. The scores are relative to and record the number of strokes greater or lesser than par needed to finish the hole.

DATA

Golfer	Score
Kate	-6
Sam	5
Lisa	2
Carlos	-3

Part A

Arrange the scores in order from least strokes to greatest strokes in the first round.

Part B

Arrange the absolute values of the scores in order from least to greatest.

© Pearson Education, Inc. 6

Name ______________________

Homework & Practice 3-4

Absolute Value

Another Look!

The **absolute value** of a number is its distance from 0 on a number line. Distance is always positive. The absolute value of 0 is 0.

Except for 0, absolute values are always positive.

The absolute value of any number, n, is written $|n|$.

Order the absolute values from least to greatest.
$|-4|, |-1|, |3|$

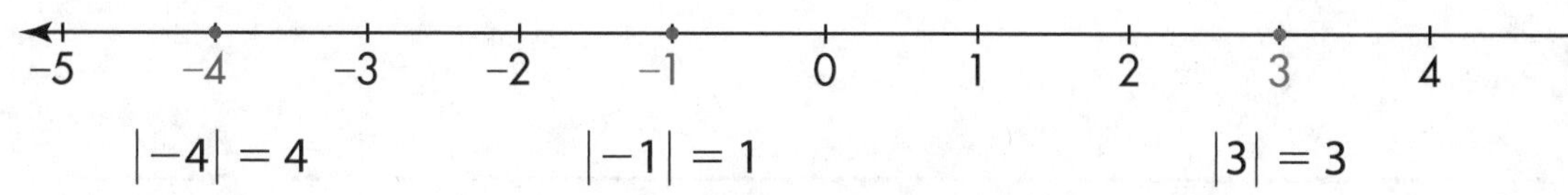

$|-4| = 4$ $|-1| = 1$ $|3| = 3$

The order of the absolute values from least to greatest is $|-1|, |3|, |-4|$.

In **1–5**, find each absolute value.

1. $|-21|$ **2.** $|7|$ **3.** $|-\frac{3}{5}|$ **4.** $|-5.5|$ **5.** $|8\frac{3}{4}|$

In **6–11**, use <, >, or = to compare.

6. $|-22|$ ◯ $|-12|$ **7.** $|45|$ ◯ $|-46|$ **8.** $|13|$ ◯ $|-2|$

9. $|48|$ ◯ $|-39|$ **10.** $|-55.5|$ ◯ $|55|$ **11.** $|21\frac{1}{3}|$ ◯ $|-21\frac{1}{2}|$

12. Order $|-20|, |16|, |-2|, |37|$ from greatest to least.

13. Order $|\frac{1}{4}|, |-\frac{1}{3}|, |-\frac{1}{8}|, |0|$ from least to greatest.

14. Which account balance represents a debt greater than $50?

Account	Balance ($)
A	–60
B	–25
C	–35

You can use absolute values to compare the account balances.

15. The table at the right shows the changes in the number of items answered correctly from a first math test to a second math test for five students. Order the students based on the least change to the greatest change.

Student	Change in Number of Correct Answers
Antoine	4
Lauren	−6
Micah	3
Beth	0
Pat	−5

16. Higher Order Thinking Is it possible that Lauren answered more questions correctly on the second math test than Antoine did? Explain your reasoning.

17. A-Z **Vocabulary** Write an inequality using the *absolute values* of −.3 and $\frac{1}{4}$. Explain how you know the inequality is correct.

18. Algebra Evaluate the expression $\frac{1}{5}(3x + 4)$ for $x = 2$.

Common Core Assessment

19. The table below shows the daily low temperatures for four days.

Day	Low Temperature
Monday	3°F
Tuesday	−4°F
Wednesday	−1°F
Thursday	2°F

Part A

Arrange the temperatures in order from coldest to warmest.

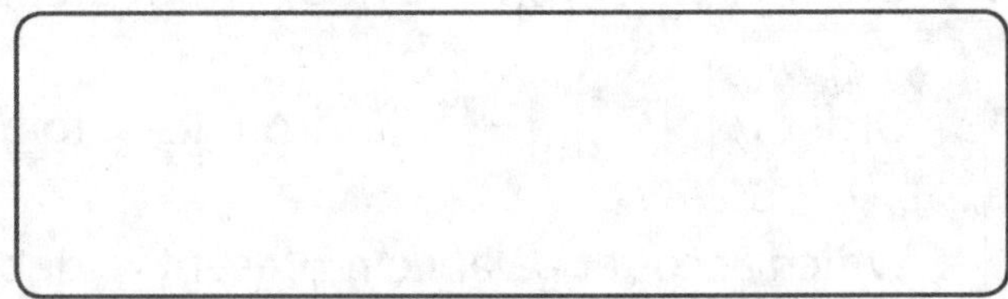

Part B

Arrange the absolute values of the temperatures in order from least to greatest.

© Pearson Education, Inc. 6

Name ___

Math Practices and Problem Solving

Lesson 3-5

Reasoning

I can ...
make sense of quantities and relationships in problem situations.

Mathematical Practices MP.2, MP.1, MP.4, MP.6
Content Standards 6.NS.C.5, 6.NS.C.6

Solve & Share

A football team has four chances, called downs, to move the football 10 yards toward their goal. A team loses 6 yards on the first down, gains 2 yards on the second down, loses 2 yards on the third down, and gains 14 yards on the fourth down. Did the team move the football 10 yards toward their goal?

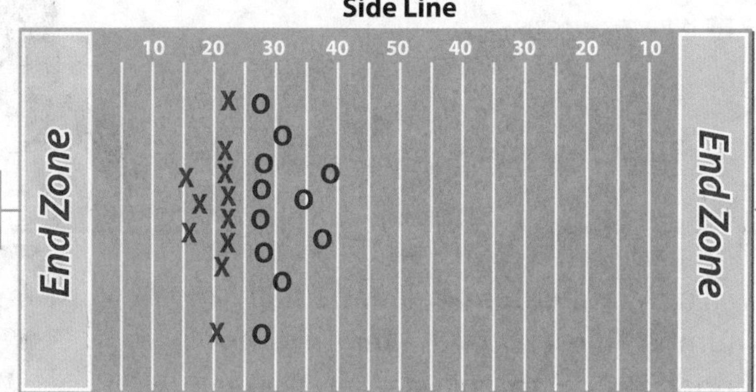

Thinking Habits

Be a good thinker!
These questions can help you.

- What do the numbers and symbols in the problem mean?
- How are the numbers or quantities related?
- How can I represent a word problem using pictures, numbers, or equations?

Look Back! **MP.2 Reasoning** The line of scrimmage is the vertical line that separates the two teams in the diagram. The team represented by the red circles has the ball. The team gains 8 yards, loses 3 yards, and gains 0 yards in its three downs. How many yards must they gain on the next down to score a touchdown? Explain how you know.

How Can You Use Reasoning to Solve Problems?

A

One summer night between 8 P.M. and 10 P.M., the temperature dropped 17°F. The next day, the temperature had increased 6°F by 10 A.M. and another 12°F from 10 A.M. to noon. The temperature was 92°F at noon. What was the temperature at 8 P.M. the previous night?

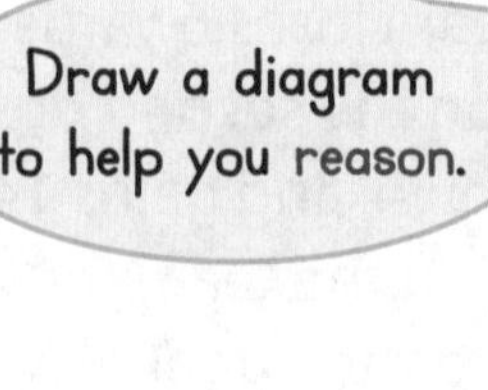

What do I need to do to solve this problem?

I need to use what I know about integers and use reasoning to find the temperature at 8 P.M. the previous day.

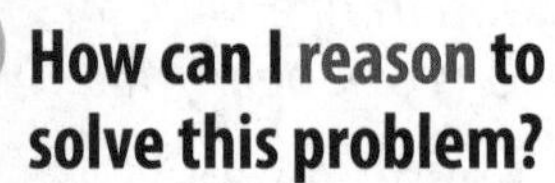

B

How can I reason to solve this problem?

I can

- identify the quantities I know.
- draw a diagram to show relationships.
- apply what I know about integers.

C

I will draw a thermometer and use it like a number line. I know the temperature at noon is 92°F, so I will start at 92°F and use opposite integers to work backward to find the temperature at 8 P.M. the previous night.

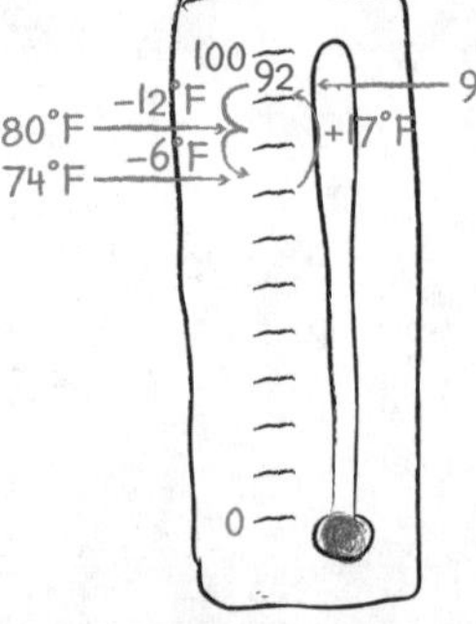

$92 - 12 = 80$
$80 - 6 = 74$
$74 + 17 = 91$

The temperature was 91°F at 8 P.M. the previous night.

Convince Me! © **MP. 2 Reasoning** The temperature change between noon and 8 A.M. the next morning is represented by the integer −40. What is the temperature at 8 A.M. the next morning?

© Pearson Education, Inc. 6

Name ______________________________

Practice Buddy Tools Assessment

Guided Practice*

MP.2 Reasoning

A scuba diver steps off a dive platform that is 2 feet above sea level and descends to 12.5 feet below sea level. The diver descends an additional 11.75 feet before ascending 10 feet. What is the diver's altitude at this point during the dive?

You use reasoning when you represent a problem graphically.

1. Which integers would you use to represent the depths described in the situation?

2. Draw a number line to represent the situation and solve the problem.

Independent Practice

MP.2 Reasoning

Enrique was asked to order this set of numbers from least to greatest.

$$-5, 2, -5\frac{1}{2}, -6, 2\frac{1}{4}, 1, 3$$

How could he order these numbers using a number line?

3. The set of numbers includes fractions. What scale should Enrique use for a number line? Explain your reasoning.

4. What are the greatest and least numbers Enrique needs to show on the number line? How does knowing this help him draw a number line?

5. Plot and label points for each number in the set in a number line.

*For another example, see Set D on page 176.

Math Practices and Problem Solving

Common Core Performance Assessment

Stock Market

The value of company stocks can rise and fall each day. The table below shows how five companies' stock prices increased or decreased compared to the previous day's closing value.

Stock	Company A	Company B	Company C	Company D	Company E
Rise or Fall in Price ($)	−1.25	2.5	0.75	−1.25	−2.5

6. **MP.2 Reasoning** How can you represent the change in stock prices for the five companies on a horizontal number line?

7. **MP.4 Model with Math** Draw a number line and plot each price change. Explain how you determined the units and intervals to use for your number line.

To make sense of the problem, think about verbal descriptions. *Positive numbers* are used to represent an *increase* in price.

8. **MP.2 Reasoning** The stock prices of all 5 companies were the same at the end of the day. Which company had the greatest stock price at the beginning of the day? Explain your reasoning.

© Pearson Education, Inc. 6

Name ______________________________

Homework & Practice 3-5
Reasoning

Another Look!

Two hikers climb a mountain that begins at sea level and rises to an altitude of 4,010 feet. They stop at 2,540 feet for a break and then continue climbing until they reach the peak. They descend 3,085 feet before stopping for another break. What is their altitude when they stop for the second break?

You use reasoning when you determine how to model a problem situation.

Use reasoning to describe the hikers' locations and plot them on a number line.

- The mountain begins at sea level. So the base of the mountain can be represented by 0.
- They stop for a break at an altitude of 2,540 feet, so the integer 2,540 represents their location during their first break.
- The peak is 4,010 feet high, so the integer 4,010 represents their location when they reach the peak.
- They stop for another break after descending 3,085 feet, so the integer −3,085 represents the decrease in altitude before their second break.

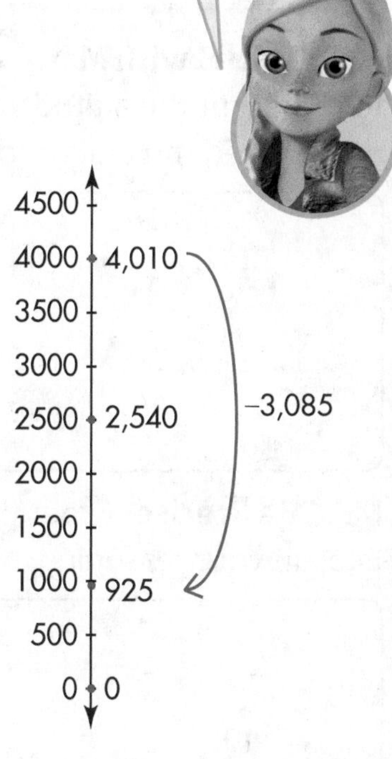

The hiker's altitude at their second break is 925 feet above sea level.

MP.2 Reasoning

The Lopez family is on a road trip to visit an amusement park. They entered the highway at mile marker 27. The amusement park is at mile marker 216. They stop at mile marker 146 for gas. How could you use a number line to represent their trip?

To represent a situation graphically, remember to consider the meaning of the given values.

1. What information from the problem can you use to describe the Lopez's locations?

2. Draw a number line and plot the points for the Lopez's locations.

Common Core Performance Assessment

Water Animals

Fish and other aquatic animals sometimes jump out of or dive under the water to avoid predators or to capture prey. The altitude, or height, of five sea animals in relation to sea level are recorded in the table below.

Animal	Dolphin (D)	Albatross (A)	Shark (S)	Tuna (T)	Marlin (M)
Altitude (yd)	1.5	−1.25	$-1\frac{1}{2}$	−1	$1\frac{3}{4}$

3. **MP.4 Model with Math** Use the number line at the right to represent the altitude of each animal. Explain how you determined the units and intervals to use for your number line.

4. **MP.6 Be Precise** Order the animals' altitudes from least to greatest. Explain your reasoning.

5. **MP.2 Reasoning** Which animal is farthest from the ocean's surface? Which animal is nearest to the ocean surface? Explain.

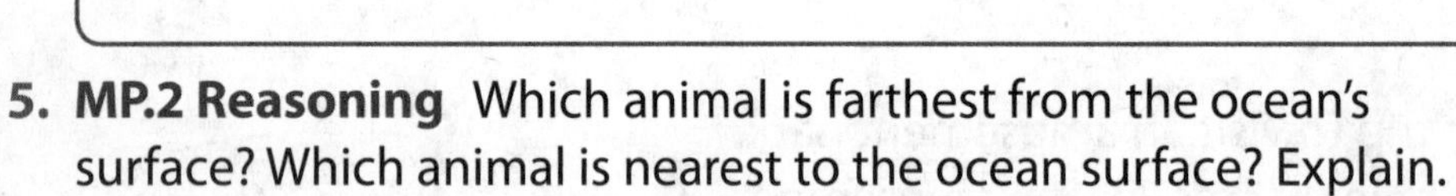

6. **MP.1 Make Sense and Persevere** Dalton saw a loon dive 1.5 yards below sea level to catch a fish. What is the difference between how far the loon and the albatross dove? How do you know?

© Pearson Education, Inc. 6

Name ____________________

Fluency Practice Activity

Find a partner. Get paper and a pencil. Each partner chooses a different color: light blue or dark blue.

Partner 1 and Partner 2 each point to a black number at the same time. Both partners multiply those numbers.

If the answer is on your color, you get a tally mark. Work until one partner has twelve tally marks.

I can ...
multiply multi-digit whole numbers.

Content Standard 5.NBT.B.5

Partner 1

18
27
24
15
21

504	315	432
729	180	252
576	648	567
324	288	270
216	486	378
360	405	441

Partner 2

21
12
18
27
24

Tally Marks for Partner 1	Tally Marks for Partner 2

TOPIC 3

Vocabulary Review

Glossary

Word List

- absolute value
- greater than (>)
- integers
- less than (<)
- opposites
- rational number

Understand Vocabulary

Choose the best term from the Word List. Write it on the blank.

1. The ________________ of a positive integer is a negative integer.

2. The value of the absolute value of −5 is ________________ 0.

3. A(n) ________________ is any number that can be written as the quotient of two integers.

4. Cross out the numbers below that are NOT *integers*.

−3 61 −1.5 0 98.6 −102 75

5. Write the *opposite* of each number.

-13 ____ $|52|$ ____ 26 ____ $|-1|$ ____

Write *always*, *sometimes*, or *never* for each statement.

6. *Absolute value* can be negative. ________________

7. A *rational number* is __?__ an *integer*. ________________

8. An *integer* is __?__ a *rational number*. ________________

9. The *opposite* of a number is __?__ negative. ________________

Use Vocabulary in Writing

10. Explain how you completed the statement in Problem 9. Provide examples and counter-examples. Include at least 2 terms from the Word List in your explanation.

© Pearson Education, Inc. 6

Name ______________________________

Set A pages 143–148

Integers are all of the counting numbers, their opposites, and 0. Opposites are integers located on opposite sides of 0 and are the same distance from 0 on a number line.

For each point on the number line, write the integer and its opposite.

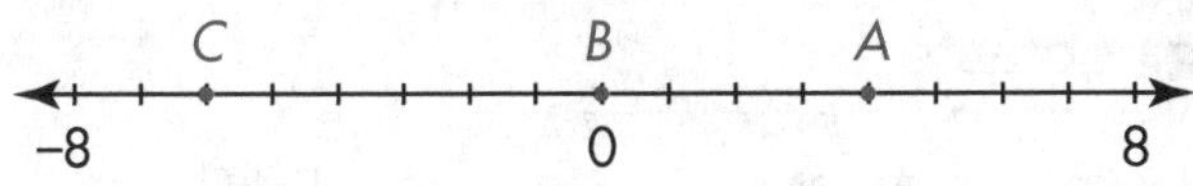

A: 4, −4

B: 0, 0

C: −6, 6

Remember that the opposite of the opposite of a number is the number itself.

Reteaching

For each point on the number line, write the integer and its opposite.

D B A C

–7 0 7

1. *A* 2. *B* 3. *C* 4. *D*

Set B pages 149–154, 155–160

Rational numbers are numbers that can be written as a quotient $\frac{a}{b}$, where *a* and *b* are integers and *b* does not equal 0.

Compare and order the numbers −0.1, 0.75, and $-\frac{1}{4}$ from least to greatest.

Place the numbers on a number line.

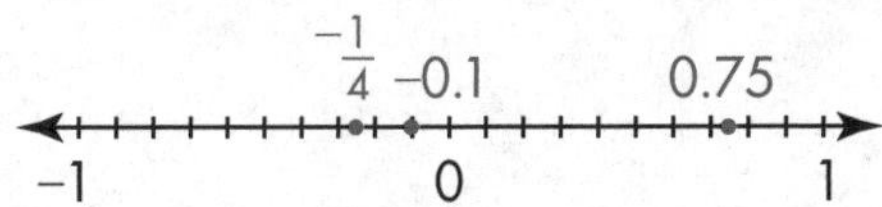

So $-\frac{1}{4} < -0.1 < 0.75$, and their order from least to greatest is $-\frac{1}{4}$, −0.1, 0.75.

Remember that all positive decimals, mixed numbers, and fractions have opposites that are located to the left of the zero on the number line.

In **1–3**, graph each rational number on the same number line.

1. $\frac{3}{4}$ 2. $-\frac{2}{5}$ 3. 0.5

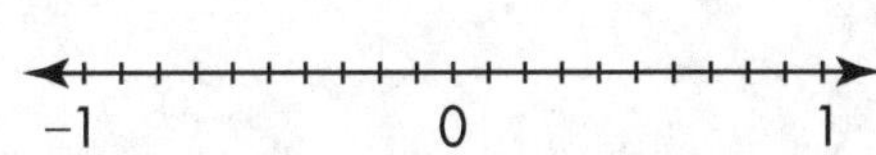

In **4–7**, use <, >, or = to compare.

4. 0.25 ◯ $\frac{1}{4}$

5. $1\frac{5}{8}$ ◯ 1.6

6. 3.65 ◯ $3\frac{3}{4}$

7. $-\frac{2}{3}$ ◯ $-\frac{3}{4}$

Set C pages 161–166

The absolute value of a number is its distance from zero on the number line. Distance is always positive.

Find the absolute values and order $|3|, |4|, |-2|, |-5|$ from *least* to *greatest*.

$|-5| = 5$
$|-2| = 2$
$|3| = 3$
$|4| = 4$

Ordered from least to greatest:

$|-2|, |3|, |4|, |-5|$

Remember that absolute values are always positive.

In **1–4**, find each value.

1. $|-9|$

2. $|-2|$

3. $|4|$

4. $-|-10|$

In **5–7**, order the values from least to greatest.

5. $|-3|, |-2|, |10|$

6. $|-7|, |0|, |-5|$

Set D pages 167–172

Think about these questions to help you **reason abstractly and quantitatively.**

Thinking Habits

- What do the numbers and symbols in the problem mean?
- How are the numbers or quantities related?
- How can I represent a word problem using pictures, numbers, or equations?

Remember to use reasoning and what you know about rational numbers to solve problems.

Sarah spent \$15.75 at the movies on a ticket and snacks. Then she earned \$40 babysitting, and bought a book for \$9.50. Sarah has \$34.75 left. How much money did she start with?

1. Which integers would you use to represent the dollar amounts described in the situation?

2. Draw a number line to represent the situation and solve the problem.

© Pearson Education, Inc. 6

Name ______________________________

Tracking Stocks

Groups of students in Ms. Kim's 6th-grade class chose 5 stocks to track for a class project. The share price of a stock can go up or down each day as the result of trading on the stock market. A student in each group tracked the change in share price of one stock for a week.

Closing Stock Prices (Day 1)

Stock	Closing Price $	Change $
Trends 'n' Threadz (TRDZ)	45.34	+3
U.S. Toy Maker (USTY)	52.27	−2
Cupcakes & More (CCML)	44.17	+5
Ling Ling Purses (LLPC)	48.87	−3
Whirly Tech (WHRL)	177.26	−7

1. Bonita is tracking the stock that had the least change in share price after 1 day. What stock is she tracking and what integer represents its change in price?

2. **Part A**

   Sidney made a number line to compare the changes in price of the stocks after Day 1. Use the following list of acronyms to name and plot each stock on the number line.

   TRDZ USTY CCML LLPC WHRL

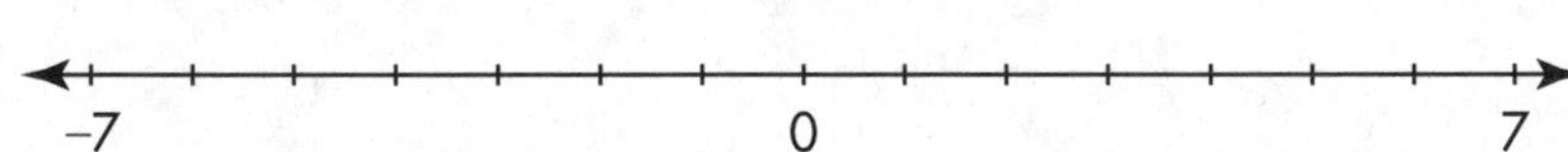

   Part B

   Jalen and Kyra are tracking stocks whose price changes after Day 1 are opposites. Which two stocks are they tracking and what are the integers that represent the price change for each stock?

3. Monroe is tracking the stock whose share price changed the least after 1 week. Yu is tracking the stock whose share price changed the most after 1 week.

DATA

Closing Stock Prices (Week)

Stock	Closing Price $	Change $
Trends 'n' Threadz (TRDZ)	44.84	+2.5
U.S. Toy Maker (USTY)	55.77	+1.5
Cupcakes & More (CCML)	37.92	−1.25
Ling Ling Purses (LLPC)	48.62	−3.25
Whirly Tech (WHRL)	188.51	+4.25

Part A

Which stock is Monroe tracking? Write the decimal number and the mixed number that represent its overall change in share price after 1 week.

Part B

Which stock is Yu tracking? Plot the mixed numbers representing the change for Yu's stock and Monroe's stock on the number line.

Then explain how the number line can help you order the price changes for each of the 5 stocks from least change to greatest change after 1 week.

5

0

–5

© Pearson Education, Inc. 6

TOPIC 4

Algebra: Coordinate Geometry

Essential Question: How are points graphed on a coordinate plane?

The seismic activity of a region refers to the type, frequency, and size of earthquakes that occur in that area over a certain time period.

By looking at the history of seismic activity in a region, we can plan and prepare for possible future earthquakes.

Alaska

Others

Let's be prepared! We may not be able to predict precisely, but we can plan ahead. Here's a project on seismic activity and graphing.

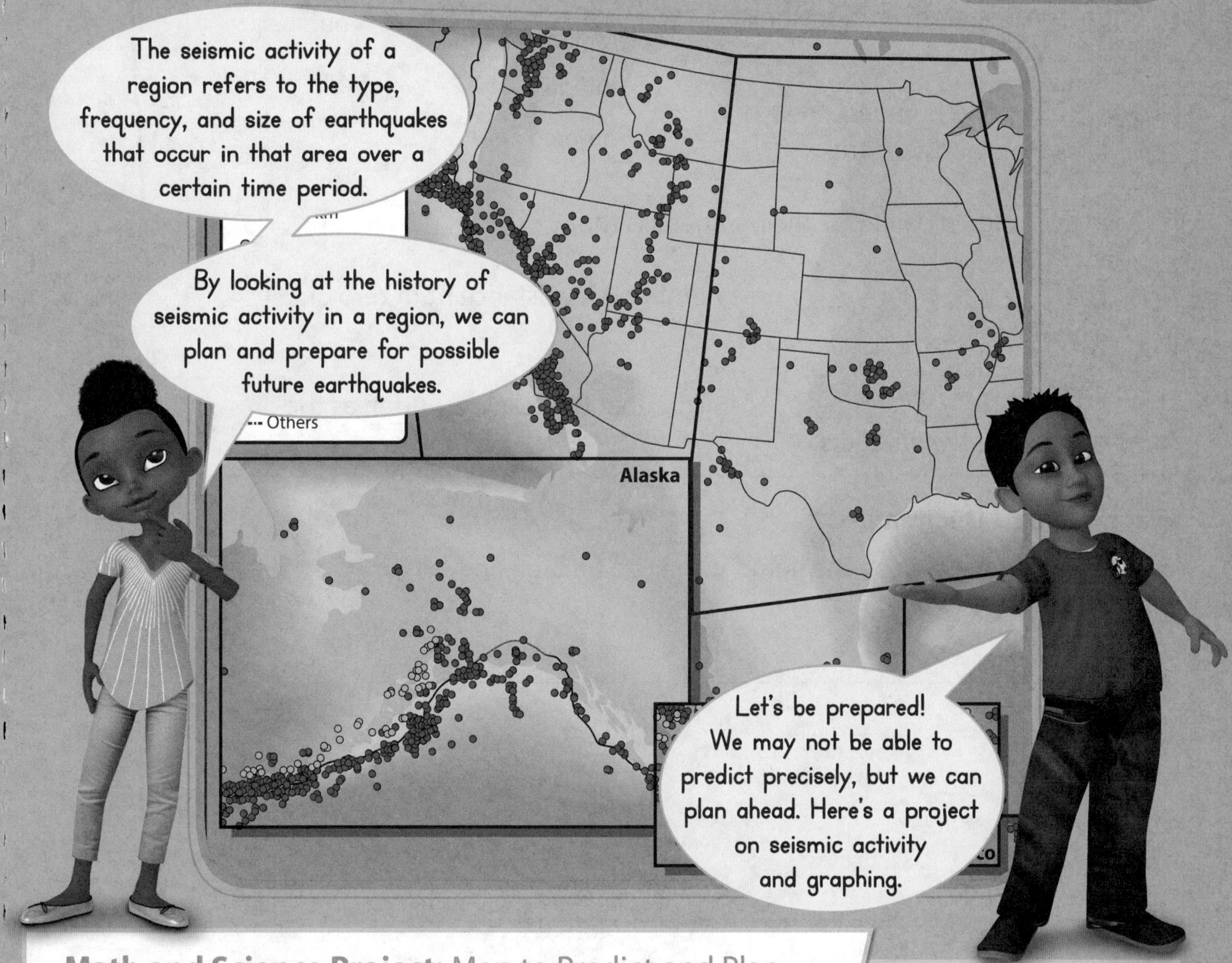

Math and Science Project: Map to Predict and Plan

Do Research Use the Internet or other sources to learn more about seismic activity in the United States. Pick a state that has had 10 or more earthquakes.

Journal: Write a Report Include what you found. Also in your report:

- On a coordinate plane, draw a map of recent seismic activity in your chosen state. Plot the state's capital at the origin (0, 0).
- Plot up to 10 recent earthquakes based on their location relative to the state capital.

Name ______________________

Review What You Know

Vocabulary

Choose the best term from the box. Write it on the blank.

- absolute value
- coordinate grid
- integers
- ordered pair
- rational number
- *x*-coordinate
- *y*-coordinate

1. The counting numbers, their opposites, and zero are __________.

2. In the ordered pair (6, 2), the number 2 is the ______________.

3. The ______________ of a number is its distance from zero on a number line.

4. A(n) ______________ is any number that can be written as the quotient of two integers.

Fractions and Decimals

Write each point shown on the number line as a fraction and as a decimal.

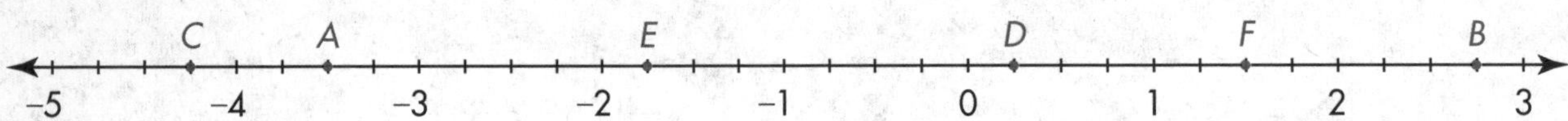

5. *A**6.** *B**7.** *C*

8. *D**9.** *E**10.** *F*

Ordered Pairs

Write the ordered pair for each point shown on the graph.

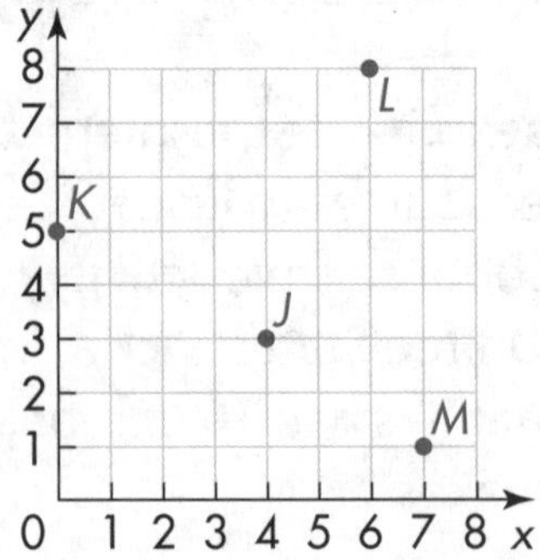

11. *J**12.** *K*

13. *L**14.** *M*

Plot each point on the coordinate grid.

15. *A* (6, 2)

16. *B* (1, 3)

17. *C* (5, 7)

18. *D* (3, 4)

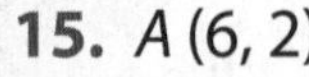

© Pearson Education, Inc. 6

My Word Cards

Use the examples for each word on the front of the card to help complete the definitions on the back.

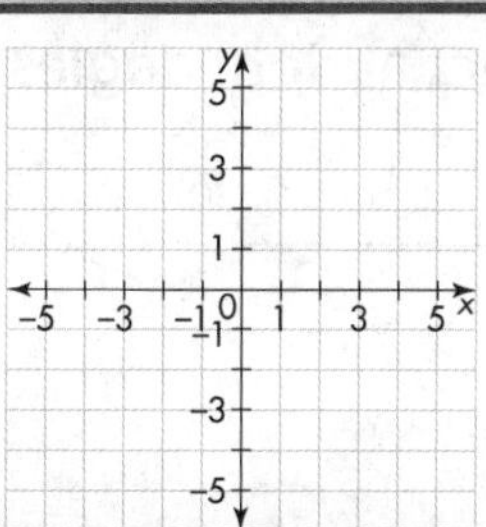

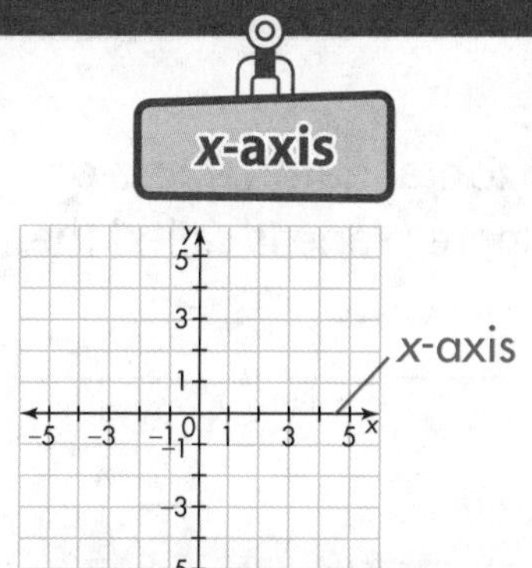

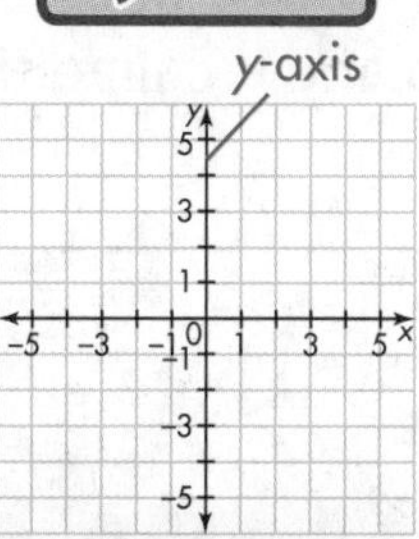

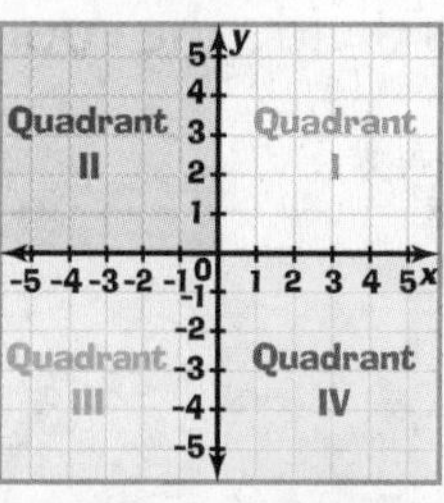

ordered pair

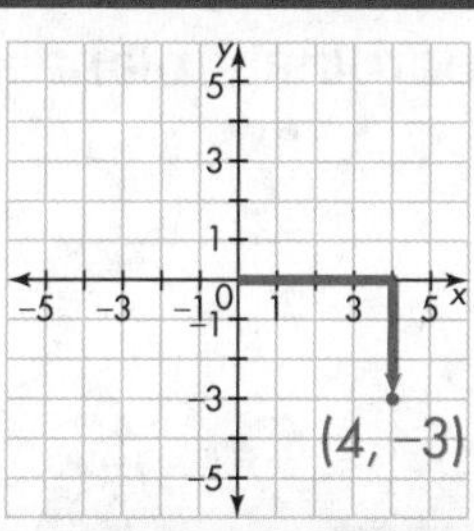

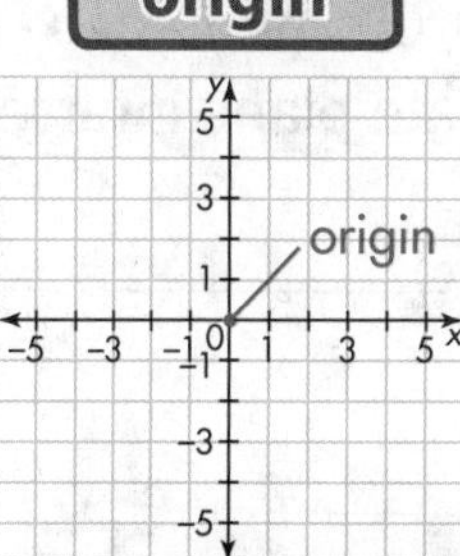

My Word Cards

Complete each definition. Extend learning by writing your own definitions.

The horizontal number line on a coordinate plane is called the

____________________________.

A grid containing two number lines that intersect at right angles is called a

____________________________.

One of the four regions in which the *x*- and *y*-axes divide the coordinate plane

is called a ____________________.

The vertical number line on a coordinate plane is called the

____________________________.

The point (0, 0) where the *x*-axis and *y*-axis of a coordinate plane intersect is called

the ____________________________.

A pair of numbers (*x*, *y*) used to locate a point on a coordinate plane is called an

____________________________.

© Pearson Education, Inc. 6

Name ______________________________

Lesson 4-1

Integers on the Coordinate Plane

I can ...
graph points on a coordinate plane.

Content Standards 6.NS.C.6b, 6.NS.C.6c
Mathematical Practices MP.1, MP.7, MP.8

Solve & Share Point B has the same x-coordinate as point A below, but its y-coordinate is the opposite of the y-coordinate of point A. Plot point B and write the ordered pair of coordinates for point B. ***Solve this problem any way you choose.***

You can make sense and persevere by using what you know about integers and graphing points on a coordinate plane to plot point B.

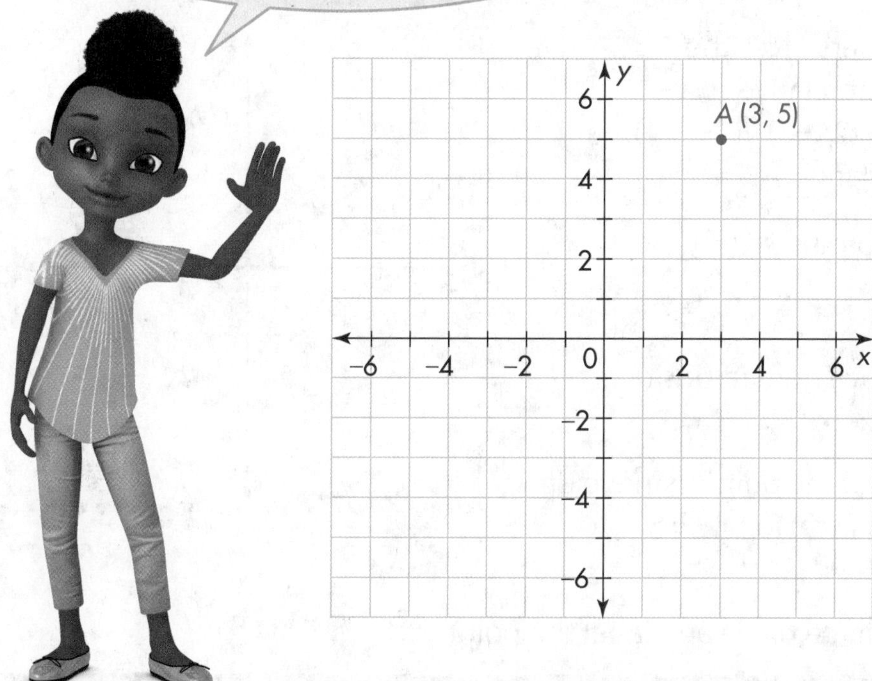

Look Back! **MP.8 Generalize** Two points have the same x-coordinate but opposite y-coordinates. Across which axis do they form mirror images of each other?

How Can You Graph a Point on a Coordinate Plane?

A

Extend what you know about grids to the coordinate plane.

A coordinate plane is a grid containing two number lines that intersect in a right angle at zero. The number lines, called the x- and y-axes, divide the plane into four quadrants. How can you graph and label points on a coordinate plane?

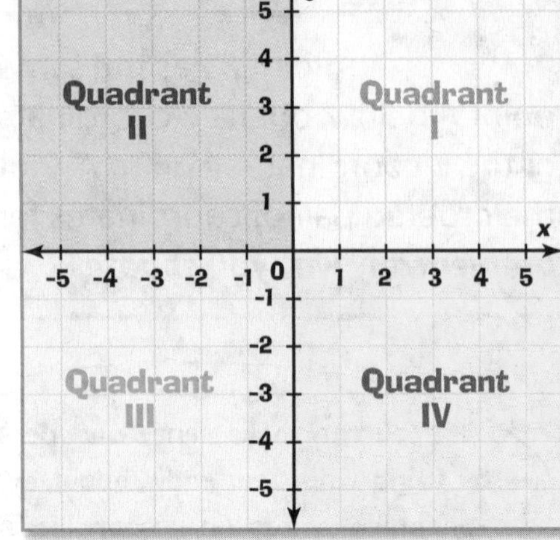

B An ordered pair (x, y) of numbers gives the coordinates that locate a point relative to each axis. Graph the points $Q\ (2, -3)$, $R\ (-1, 1)$, and $S\ (0, 2)$ on a coordinate plane.

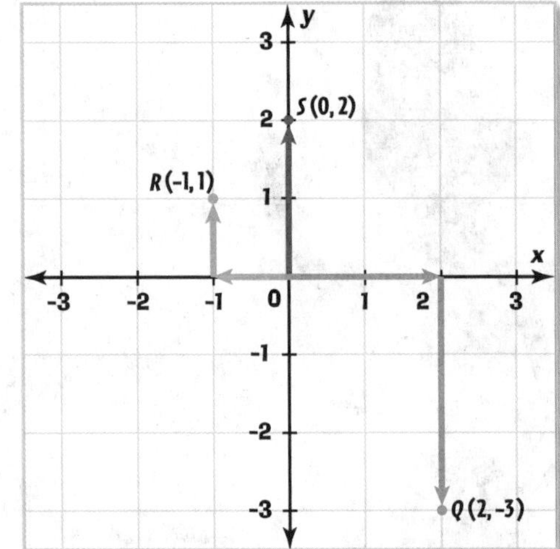

To graph any point P with coordinates (x, y):

- Start at the origin, (0, 0).
- Use the x-coordinate to move right (if positive) or left (if negative) along the x-axis.
- Then use the y-coordinate of the point to move up (if positive) or down (if negative) following the y-axis.
- Draw a point on the coordinate plane and label the point.

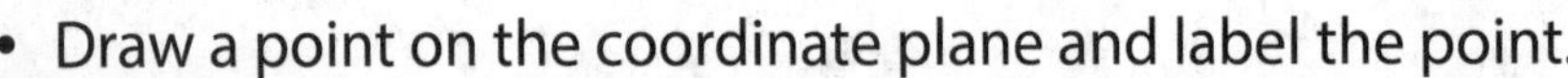

Convince Me! **MP.7 Look for Relationships** Both coordinates of an ordered pair are negative numbers. In which quadrant is that point always located?

© Pearson Education, Inc. 6

Name ______________________________

Practice Buddy   Tools   Assessment

Another Example

How are points $N(-3, 2)$, $P(3, -2)$, and $Q(-3, -2)$ related to point $M(3, 2)$?

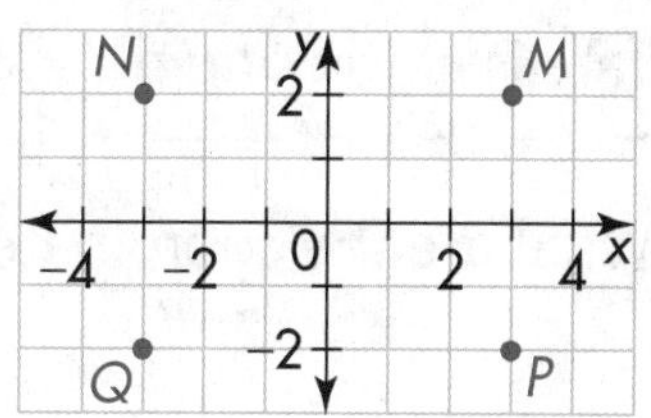

Point $N(-3, 2)$ and point $M(3, 2)$ differ only in the sign of the *x*-coordinate. They are reflections of each other across the *y*-axis.

Point $P(3, -2)$ and point $M(3, 2)$ differ only in the sign of the *y*-coordinate. They are reflections of each other across the *x*-axis.

Point $Q(-3, -2)$ and point $M(3, 2)$ differ in the signs of the *x*-coordinate and *y*-coordinate. They are reflections of each other across both axes.

A *reflection* is a mirror image across a line.

Guided Practice*

Do You Understand?

1. What is the *y*-coordinate of any point that lies on the *x*-axis?

2. MP.7 **Look for Relationships** How are the points (4, 5) and (−4, 5) related?

Do You Know How?

In **3–5**, graph and label each point on the coordinate plane.

3. $A(-4, 1)$

4. $B(4, 3)$

5. $C(0, -2)$

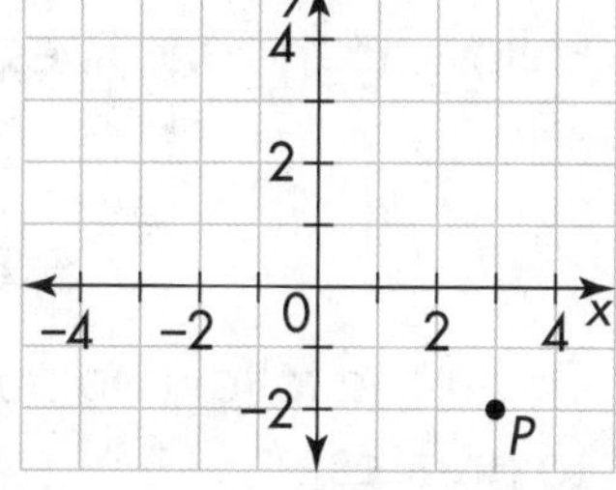

6. What ordered pair gives the coordinates of point *P* above?

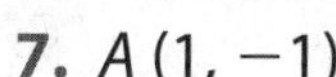

Independent Practice

In **7–10**, graph and label each point.
In **11–14**, write the ordered pair for each point.

7. $A(1, -1)$

8. $B(4, 3)$

9. $C(-4, 5)$

10. $D(5, -2)$

11. *P*

12. *Q*

13. *R*

14. *S*

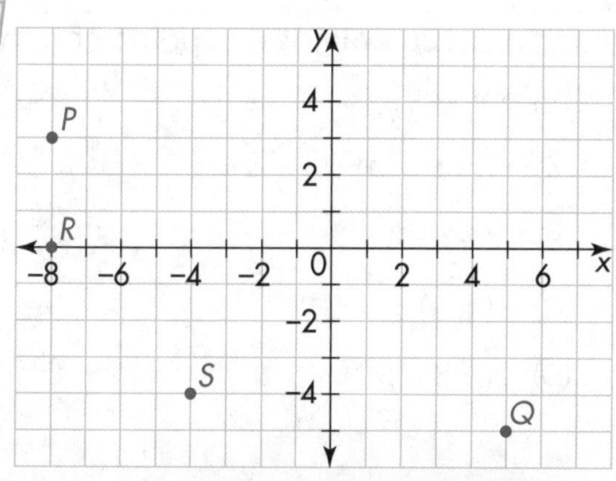

*For another example, see Set A on page 217.

Math Practices and Problem Solving

In **15–19**, use the map at the right. The Market Square is at the origin.

15. What are the coordinates of the Library?

16. Which building is located in Quadrant III?

17. Which two places have the same x-coordinate?

18. **MP.7 Use Structure** The city council wants the location of the entrance to a new city park to be determined by the reflection of the school entrance across the y-axis. What are the coordinates of the entrance to the new city park on this map?

19. Higher Order Thinking You are at the Market Square and want to get to the Doctor's Office. Following the grid lines, what is the shortest route?

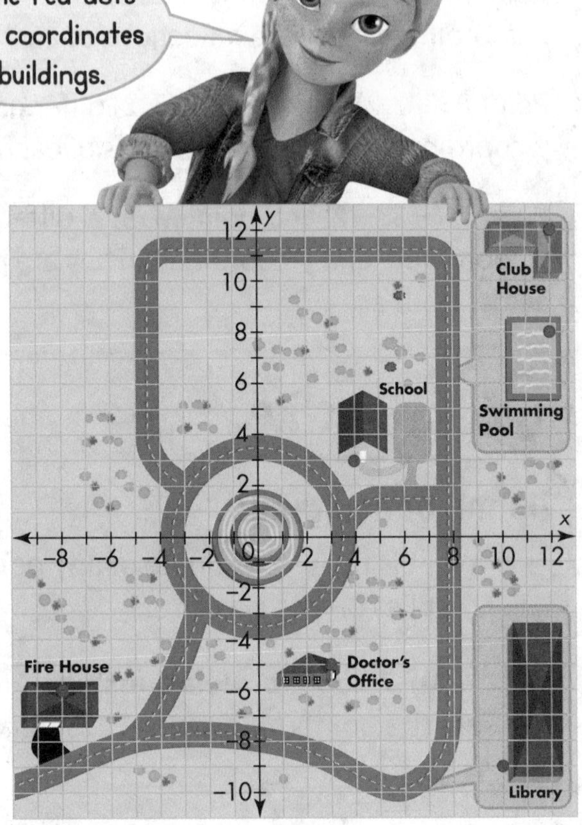

20. Order the following numbers from least to greatest.

$\frac{1}{2}, -\frac{2}{3}, |-2|, -\frac{3}{4}, -0.5$

21. Number Sense The number of points a basketball team scored has 3, 4, and 5 as factors. What is the least number of points the team could have scored?

Common Core Assessment

22. Which ordered pair locates point P on the coordinate plane?

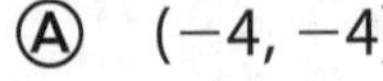

Ⓐ (−4, −4)

Ⓑ (−4, 4)

Ⓒ (4, 3)

Ⓓ (−3, 4)

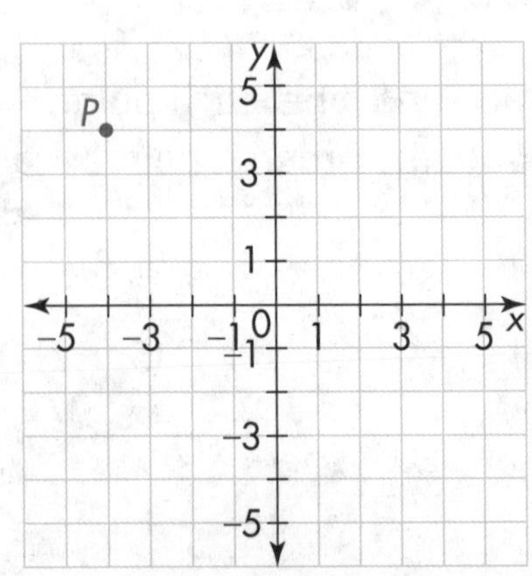

© Pearson Education, Inc. 6

Name ______________________________

Homework & Practice 4-1

Integers on the Coordinate Plane

Another Look!

A **coordinate plane** is a grid that contains number lines that intersect at right angles and divide the plane into four **quadrants**. The horizontal number line is called the ***x*-axis** and the vertical number line is called the ***y*-axis**.

The location of a point on a coordinate plane is written as an **ordered pair** (x, y).

Graph and label the point $K(4, -3)$ on the coordinate plane at the right.

To locate point (4, −3), start at the origin. Move to 4 on the *x*-axis. Then move to −3 by following the *y*-axis.

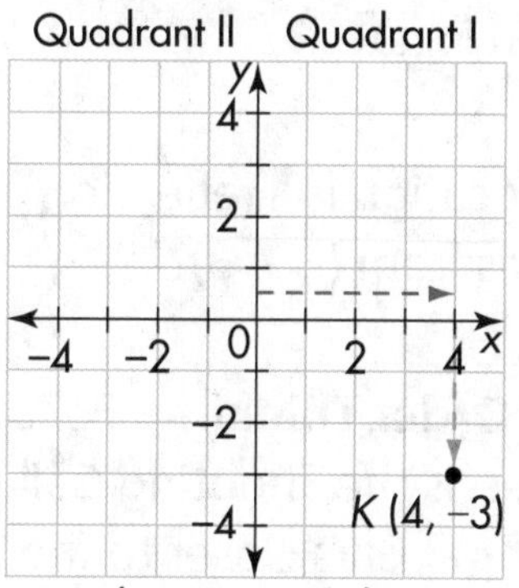

In **1–10**, write the ordered pair for each point.
In **11–16**, graph and label each point.

1. *A* **2.** *B*

3. *C* **4.** *D*

5. *E* **6.** *F*

7. *G* **8.** *H*

9. *I* **10.** *J*

11. $U(-5, -3)$ **12.** $V(-9, 3)$

13. $W(3, 8)$ **14.** $X(8, 3)$

15. $Y(6, -6)$ **16.** $Z(-5, 0)$

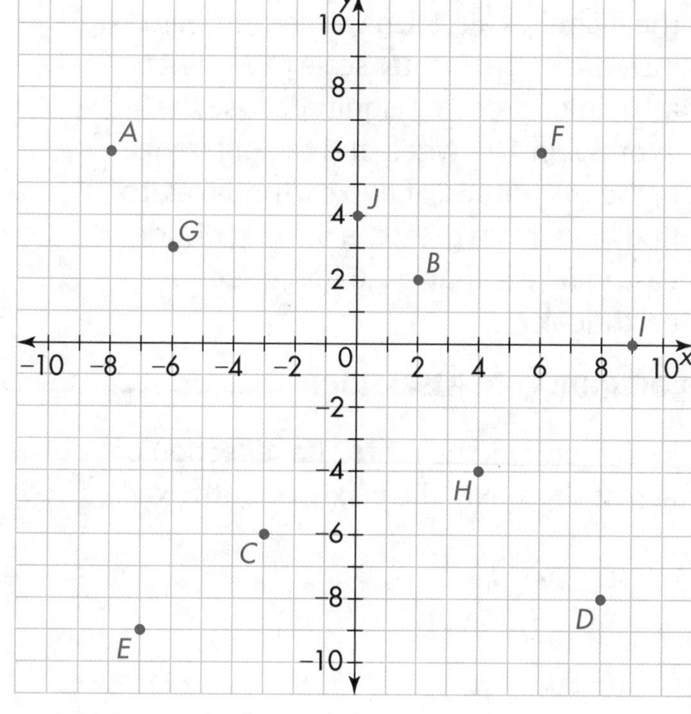

In **17–20**, use the map at the right.

Use the red dots to locate the coordinates of places in the fun park.

17. What are the coordinates of the Roller Coaster?

18. In which quadrant is the Drinking Fountain located?

19. Which location is a reflection across the *y*-axis from $(-7, 3)$?

20. Higher Order Thinking Follow the grid lines. Is the Shooting Gallery or the Bumper Cars closer to the Hot Dog Stand? Explain.

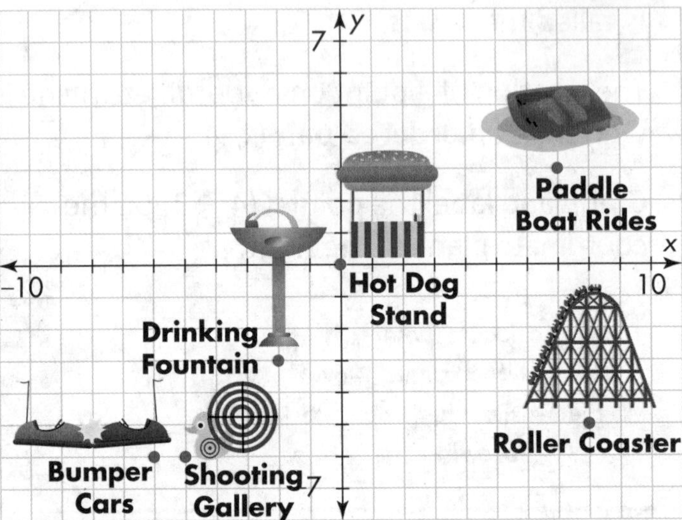

21. Math and Science The magnitude of an earthquake is frequently expressed using the Richter scale. Each whole-number increase in the Richter scale represents a 10 times greater magnitude. Use the expression 10^a, where a is the difference in the magnitude of two earthquakes, to find how much greater a 5.6 magnitude earthquake is than a 2.6 magnitude earthquake.

22. A-Z **Vocabulary** Write four examples of ordered pairs, each located in a different quadrant of the coordinate plane.

Common Core Assessment

23. Which ordered pair is **NOT** a reflection of point *P* across the *x*-axis, the *y*-axis, or both axes?

Ⓐ (2, 4)

Ⓑ (2, −4)

Ⓒ (−2, 4)

Ⓓ (−2, −4)

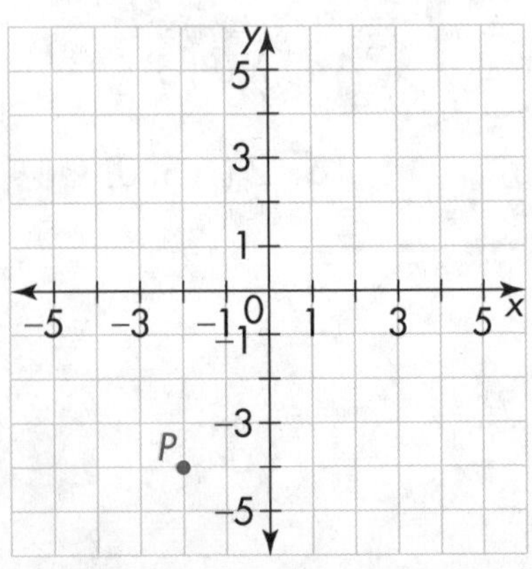

© Pearson Education, Inc. 6

Name ____________________

Solve

Lesson 4-2

Rational Numbers on the Coordinate Plane

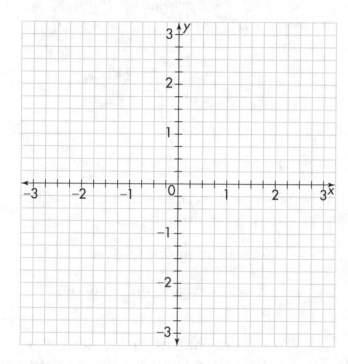

I can ...
graph rational numbers on a coordinate plane.

Content Standards 6.NS.C.6b, 6.NS.C.6c
Mathematical Practices MP.3, MP.5, MP.6, MP.7

Solve & Share

The x-coordinate of point B is $-1\frac{3}{4}$. The y-coordinate is $2\frac{1}{2}$. Graph and label point B on the coordinate plane.

How can you use appropriate tools? How can grid paper help you plot ordered pairs of rational numbers?

Look Back! **MP.6 Be Precise** Point R is a reflection, or mirror image, of point B across the x-axis. Graph and label point R.

How Can You Describe Points That Have Rational Numbers as Coordinates?

A

A grid map of Washington, D.C., is shown at the right. What are the coordinates of the location of the Jefferson Memorial?

You can use structure to describe the exact location.

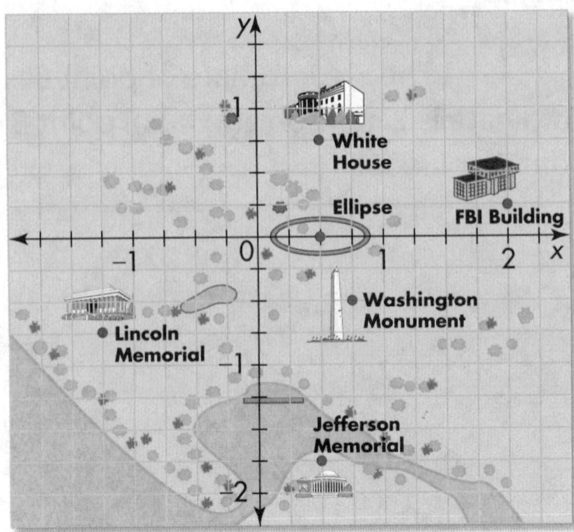

B

Use decimals.

Find the Jefferson Memorial on the map.

- Follow the grid lines directly to the x-axis to find the x-coordinate, 0.5.
- Follow the grid lines directly to the y-axis to find the y-coordinate, -1.75.

The coordinates of the location of the Jefferson Memorial are $(0.5, -1.75)$.

You can write rational numbers as decimals and as fractions.

C

Use fractions.

Change the values of the coordinates from decimals to fractions.

- $0.5 = \frac{1}{2}$, so the x-coordinate is $\frac{1}{2}$.
- $-1.75 = -1\frac{3}{4}$, so the y-coordinate is $-1\frac{3}{4}$.

The coordinates of the location of the Jefferson Memorial can also be written as $\left(\frac{1}{2}, -1\frac{3}{4}\right)$.

Convince Me! **MP.6 Be Precise** Write the coordinates of the location of the FBI Building using decimals and using fractions.

© Pearson Education, Inc. 6

Name ______________________________

Guided Practice*

Do You Understand?

1. MP.3 Construct Arguments On a larger map, the coordinates for the location of another D.C. landmark are (8, −10). In which quadrant of the map is this landmark located? Explain how you can tell from the coordinates.

2. What are the coordinates of the point that is a reflection of the point at the Jefferson Memorial across the *y*-axis?

Do You Know How?

In **3** and **4**, use the map on the previous page and write the ordered pair of each location.

3. White House

4. Lincoln Memorial

In **5** and **6**, use the map on the previous page and write the landmark located at each ordered pair.

5. (0.5, 0)

6. $\left(\frac{3}{4}, -\frac{1}{2}\right)$

Independent Practice

In **7–14**, graph and label each point.
In **15–18**, write the ordered pair for each point.

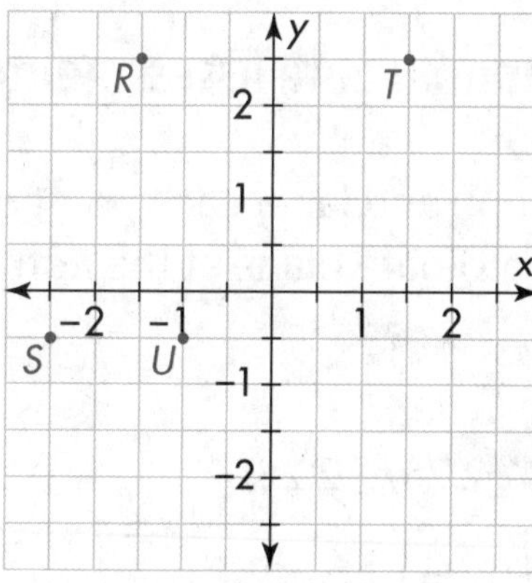

7. $A(-2.5, 1.5)$

8. $B(2, 1.5)$

9. $C\left(-2, -1\frac{1}{2}\right)$

10. $D\left(1\frac{1}{2}, -1\right)$

11. $E(-0.5, 1.5)$

12. $F(2.5, -2)$

13. $G\left(0, -1\frac{1}{2}\right)$

14. $H\left(-1, -2\frac{1}{2}\right)$

15. *R*

16. *S*

17. *T*

18. *U*

*For another example, see Set A on page 217.

Math Practices and Problem Solving

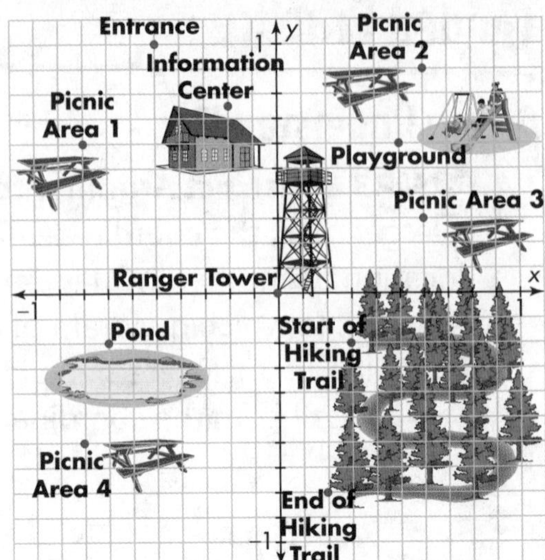

19. What is located at (−0.7, −0.2)?

20. What is located at $\left(\frac{3}{10}, -\frac{1}{5}\right)$?

21. Write the ordered pair to locate The End of Hiking Trail in two different ways.

22. Higher Order Thinking What are the coordinates of the Information Center? Explain how you determined the *y*-coordinate.

23. MP.7 Use Structure Which picnic areas are located at points that are reflections of each other across one of the axes of the coordinate plane?

24. Number Sense Avi wrote the equation shown below. Insert parentheses, if needed, to make the equation true. If no parentheses are needed, write, "parentheses not needed."

$$6 + 2 \times 2^3 = 64$$

Remember to use the order of operations to evaluate the expression.

Common Core Assessment

25. Graph and label each point on the coordinate plane at the right.

$A\left(\frac{3}{4}, -1\frac{1}{2}\right)$

$B(-2.75, -2.25)$

$C\left(0, 2\frac{1}{4}\right)$

$D(-1.75, 2)$

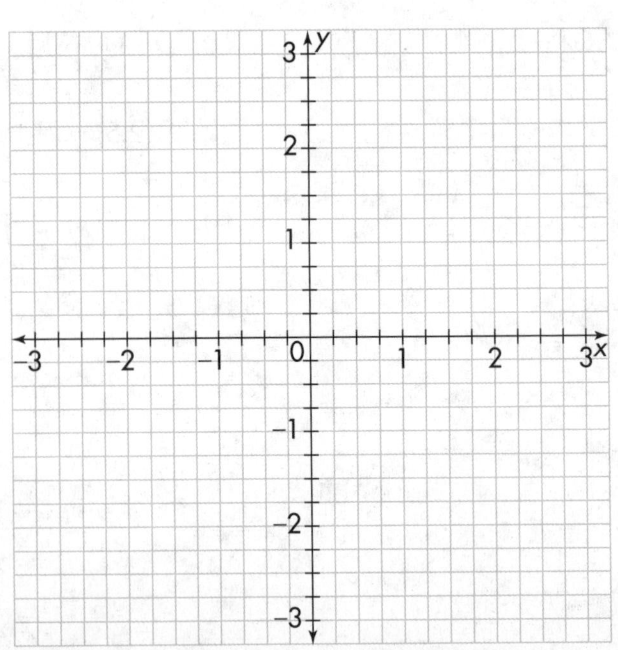

© Pearson Education, Inc. 6

Name ______________________________

Help Practice Buddy Tools Games

Homework & Practice 4-2

Rational Numbers on the Coordinate Plane

Another Look!

The coordinate plane has two units between each integer value. So the length of each unit is $\frac{1}{2}$. Graph and label the point $\left(-2, -1\frac{1}{2}\right)$.

To locate point $\left(-2, -1\frac{1}{2}\right)$, start at the origin. Move 2 units to the left on the x-axis. Then move down $1\frac{1}{2}$ units on the y-axis.

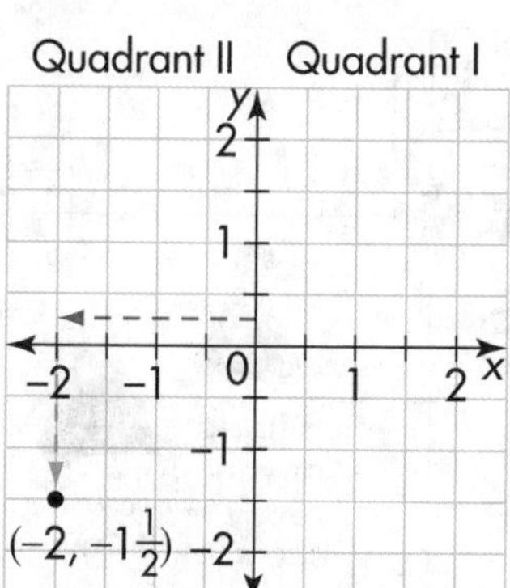

Ordered pairs of rational numbers can be graphed just like ordered pairs of integers.

In **1–10**, write the ordered pair for each point.
In **11–16**, plot and label each point.

1. A

2. B

3. C

4. D

5. E

6. F

7. G

8. H

9. I

10. J

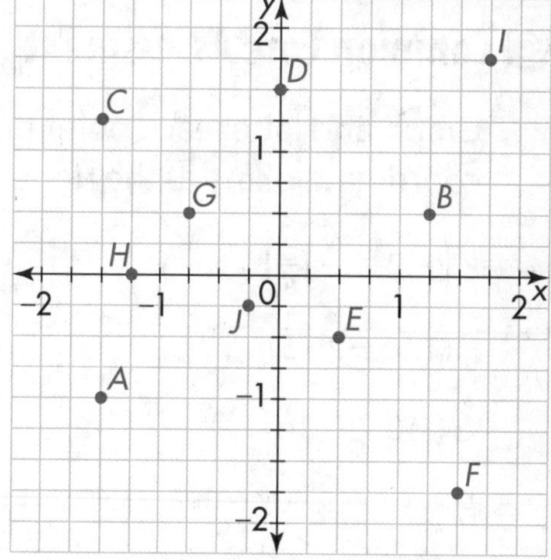

11. $U(1, -1.5)$

12. $V\left(-\frac{1}{2}, 1\right)$

13. $W\left(-1\frac{3}{4}, -1\frac{3}{4}\right)$

14. $X(1.75, -0.75)$

15. $Y\left(0, -1\frac{3}{4}\right)$

16. $Z\left(\frac{3}{4}, 1\right)$

17. What is located at (0.5, −0.5)?

18. What is located at $\left(-\frac{1}{2}, \frac{2}{5}\right)$?

19. Write the ordered pair to locate Brown Bat Cave.

20. **Higher Order Thinking** Suppose ✠ marks the spot where the treasure is buried. Explain the shortest route, using grid lines as units, from Pirate's Cove to the treasure.

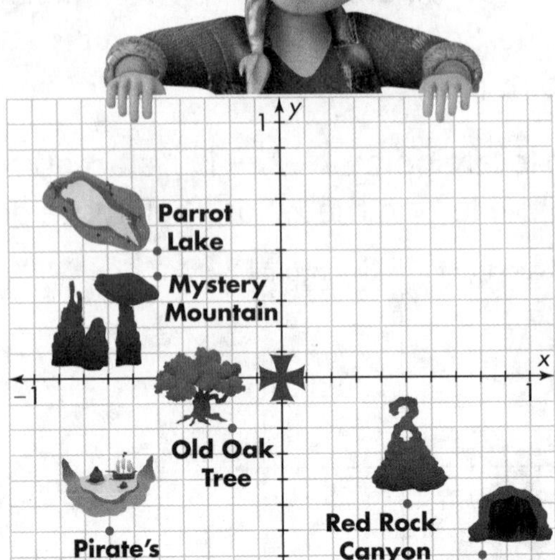

21. Which two locations are reflections of each other across one or both of the axes of the coordinate plane?

22. **Number Sense** Maria wrote the equation shown below. Insert parentheses, if needed, to make the equation true. If no parentheses are needed, write, "parentheses not needed."

$$3^3 - 2^2 \times 5 = 7$$

Common Core Assessment

23. Graph and label each point on the coordinate plane at the right.

$E\left(-2\frac{1}{4}, -1\frac{3}{4}\right)$

F (1.5, −2.75)

G (−0.75, 0)

H (3, 1.5)

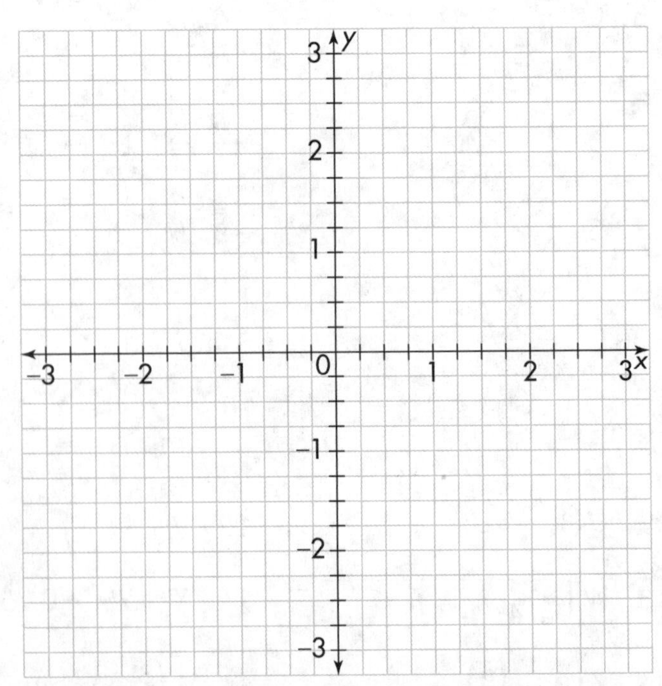

© Pearson Education, Inc. 6

Name ____________________

Lesson 4-3
Distance on the Coordinate Plane

Solve & Share What is the distance between point *A* and point *B*? What is the distance between point *A* and point *C*? ***Solve this problem any way you choose.***

I can …
use absolute value to find distance on a coordinate plane.

Content Standard 6.NS.C.8
Mathematical Practices MP.1, MP.2, MP.3, MP.7

You can use structure. How can the grid lines on the coordinate plane help you find distance?

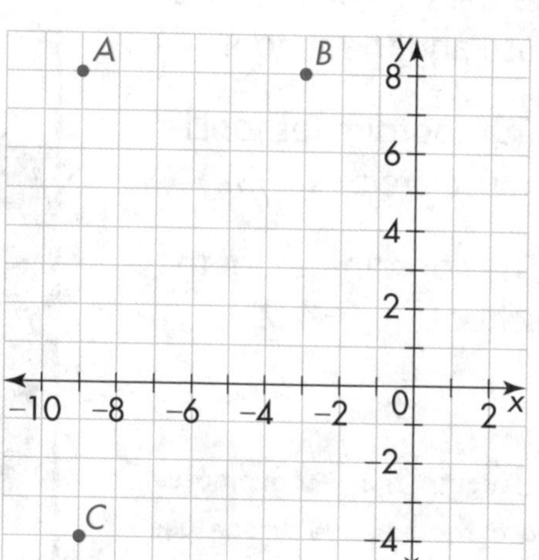

Look Back! **MP.3 Construct Arguments** Explain how you could use the absolute values of the coordinates of points *A*, *B*, and *C* to find the distances between points *A* and *B* and between points *A* and *C*.

How Can You Find the Distance Between Two Points on a Coordinate Plane?

A

Tammy drew a map of her neighborhood. How far is it from Li's house to school?

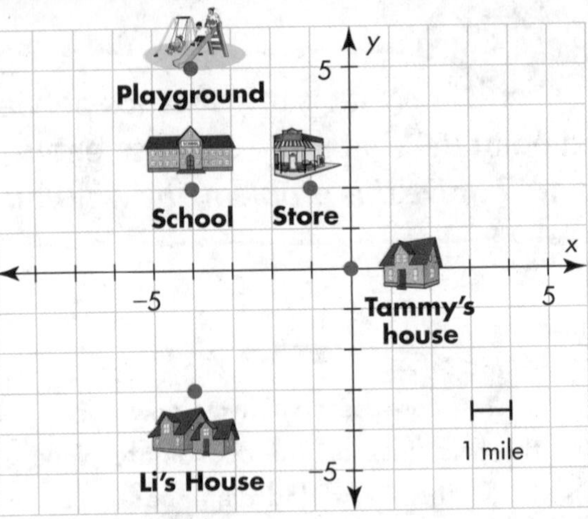

You can use what you know about absolute value to find distances.

B Find the coordinates of Li's house and the school.

- The coordinates for Li's house are (−4, −3).
- The coordinates for the school are (−4, 2).

Because the x-coordinates are the same, you can use the y-coordinates to find the distance between Li's house and the school.

C The absolute values of the y-coordinates tell you the distance between each point and the x-axis.

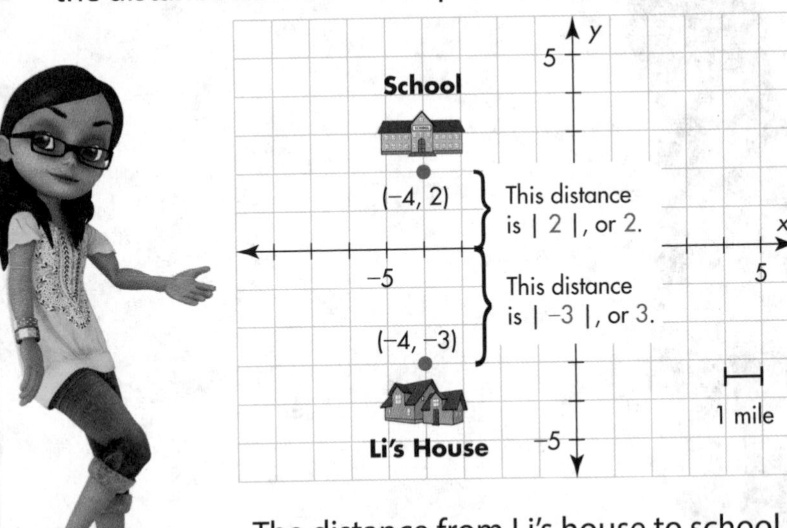

The distance from Li's house to school is $|2| + |-3| = 2 + 3 = 5$ miles.

Convince Me! **MP.7 Use Structure** To find the distance between the school and the playground, would you add or subtract the absolute values of the y-coordinates? Explain.

© Pearson Education, Inc. 6

Name ____________________

Guided Practice*

Do You Understand?

1. MP.7 Use Structure How would you use absolute values to find the distance between the school and the store?

2. MP.7 Look for Relationships To find the distance between two points using their coordinates, when do you add their absolute values and when do you subtract them?

Do You Know How?

In **3–8**, find the distance between each pair of points.

3. $(-5, 2)$ and $(-5, 6)$

4. $(-3, -1)$ and $(2, -1)$

5. $(4.5, -3.3)$ and $(4.5, 5.5)$

6. $(-1.6, -1)$ and $(0.6, -1)$

7. $\left(5\frac{1}{2}, -7\frac{1}{2}\right)$ and $\left(5\frac{1}{2}, -1\frac{1}{2}\right)$

8. $\left(-2\frac{1}{4}, -8\right)$ and $\left(7\frac{3}{4}, -8\right)$

Independent Practice

Leveled Practice In **9–14**, find the distance between each pair of points.

9. $(-2, 8)$ and $(7, 8)$
$|\square| + |\square|$
$= \_\_ + \_\_$
$= \_\_\_\_$ units

10. $(-6.1, -8.4)$ and $(-6.1, -4.2)$
$|\square| - |\square|$
$= \_\_\_\_ - \_\_\_\_$
$= \_\_\_\_$ units

11. $\left(12\frac{1}{2}, 3\frac{3}{4}\right)$ and $\left(-4\frac{1}{2}, 3\frac{3}{4}\right)$
$|\square| + |\square|$
$= \_\_\_\_ + \_\_\_\_$
$= \_\_\_\_$ units

12. $(-5, -3)$ and $(-5, -6)$

13. $(-5.4, 4.7)$ and $(0.6, 4.7)$

14. $\left(7\frac{1}{2}, -5\frac{3}{4}\right)$ and $\left(7\frac{1}{2}, -1\frac{1}{4}\right)$

*For another example, see Set B on page 217.

Math Practices and Problem Solving

In **15–18**, use the map at the right.

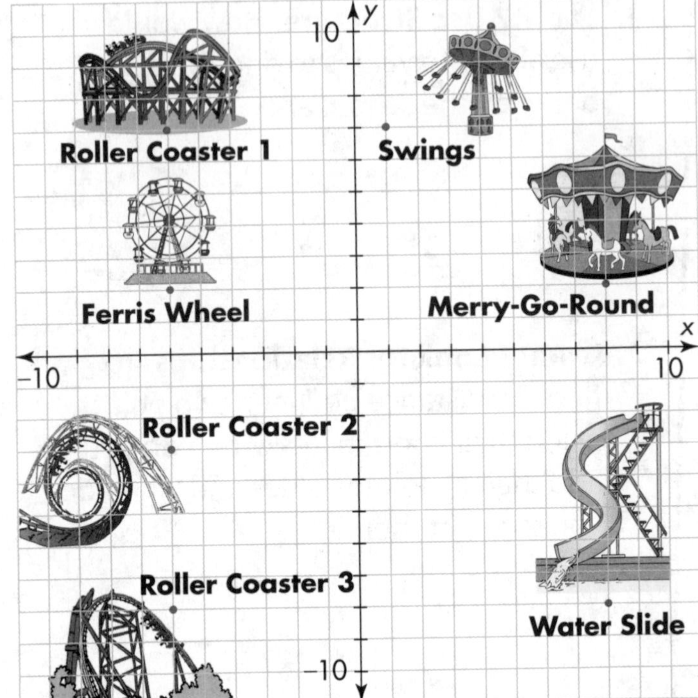

15. Find the distance from Roller Coaster 1 to the Swings.

16. Find the distance from the Ferris Wheel to Roller Coaster 3.

17. Find the total distance from Roller Coaster 2 to Roller Coaster 3 and then to the Water Slide.

18. Higher Order Thinking Is the distance from the Merry-Go-Round to the Water Slide the same as the distance from the Water Slide to the Merry-Go-Round? Explain.

19. MP.7 Use Structure Suppose a, b, and c are all negative numbers. How do you find the distance between points (a, b) and (a, c)?

20. Math and Science A scientist graphed the locations of the epicenter of an earthquake and all of the places where people reported feeling the earthquake. She positioned the epicenter at $(-1, 8)$ and the farthest location reported to have felt the quake was positioned at $(85, 8)$. If each unit on the graph represents 1 mile, how far from its epicenter was the earthquake felt?

Common Core Assessment

21. Find the two ordered pairs that are 4.5 units apart. Then write those ordered pairs in the second row of the chart.

Distance = 4.5 units
(5.5, −1) (−1.5, 3) (−3, 3) (5.5, 2.5) (−1.5, −1.5)

© Pearson Education, Inc. 6

Name ______________________________

Homework & Practice 4-3

Distance on the Coordinate Plane

Another Look!

What is the distance between the dentist and the museum? Between the park and the gym?

You can use absolute values to find distances.

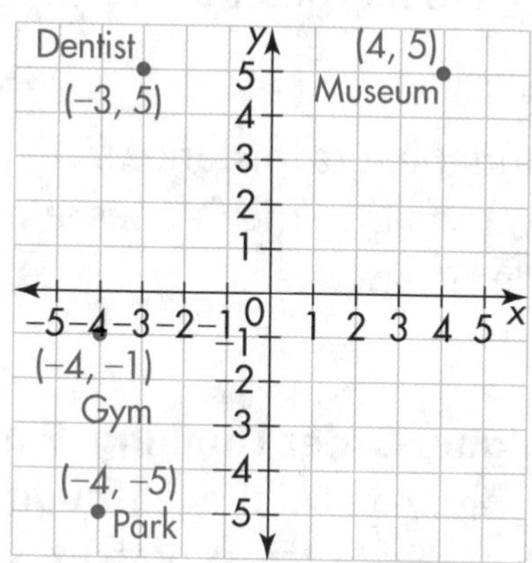

Dentist to Museum: (−3, 5) to (4, 5)
The *y*-coordinates are the same so use the *x*-coordinates. Since the points are in different quadrants, add the absolute values: $|-3| + |4| = 3 + 4 = 7$ units.

Park to Gym: (−4, −5) to (−4, −1)
The *x*-coordinates are the same so use the *y*-coordinates. Since the points are in the same quadrants, subtract the absolute values: $|-5| - |-1| = 5 - 1 = 4$ units.

In **1–9**, find the distance between each pair of points.

1. (5, −6) and (2, −6)
$|\square| + |\square|$
= ___ − ___
= ___ units

2. (−6, −4.7) and (−6, 4.1)
$|\square| + |\square|$
= ___ + ___
= ___ units

3. $\left(-2\frac{1}{2}, 1\frac{3}{4}\right)$ and $\left(-1\frac{1}{4}, 1\frac{3}{4}\right)$
$|\square| - |\square|$
= ___ − ___
= ___ units

4. (−7, −4) and (−7, 9)

5. (2.4, 1.8) and (−0.6, 1.8)

6. $\left(7\frac{1}{2}, -6\right)$ and $\left(7\frac{1}{2}, -2\frac{1}{2}\right)$

7. (0, −6) and (−10, −6)

8. (−3, 8.5) and (−3, 7.7)

9. $\left(\frac{1}{2}, 3\frac{3}{4}\right)$ and $\left(\frac{1}{2}, -1\frac{1}{4}\right)$

10. On a map, a museum is located at (15, −2). A library is located at (15, −17). If each unit on the map is a city block, how many city blocks is the museum from the library?

When subtracting absolute values to find distance, always subtract the lesser value.

In **11–14**, use the map at the right.

11. Find the distance from the Fishing area to the Canoes.

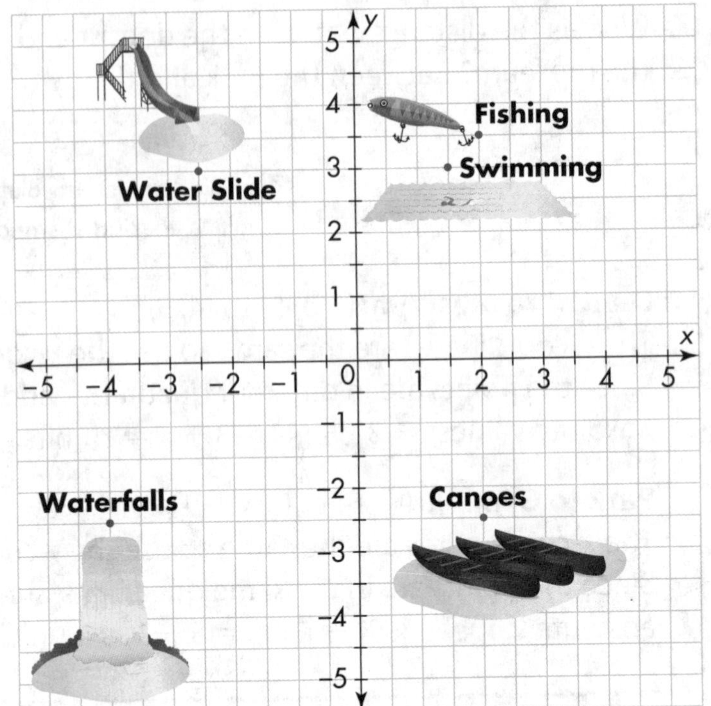

12. What is the distance from the Swimming area to the Water Slide?

13. Find the total distance from the Waterfalls to the Canoes and then to the Fishing area.

14. **Higher Order Thinking** What are the coordinates of the reflection of the Water Slide across both axes?

15. **MP.2 Reasoning** On a map, Jorge is standing at (11, −11). His friend Leslie is standing at (1, −11). If Jorge walks 10 units to the right, will he be standing with Leslie? Explain.

16. **MP.1 Make Sense and Persevere** Helena is thinking of a number. That number raised to the third power is 100 greater than when it is raised to the second power. What number is Helena thinking about?

Common Core Assessment

17. Find the two ordered pairs that are $3\frac{1}{2}$ units apart. Then write those ordered pairs in the second row of the chart.

Distance = 3.5 units

$\left(4\frac{1}{2}, -1\right)$ $\left(-1\frac{1}{4}, 2\frac{1}{2}\right)$ $\left(2\frac{1}{4}, 2\frac{1}{2}\right)$ $\left(5\frac{1}{2}, 1\frac{1}{2}\right)$ $\left(5\frac{1}{2}, -2\frac{1}{2}\right)$

© Pearson Education, Inc. 6

Name ___

Lesson 4-4

Polygons on the Coordinate Plane

I can …
find side lengths of polygons on a coordinate plane.

Content Standards 6.NS.C.8, 6.G.A.3
Mathematical Practices MP.2, MP.3, MP.7, MP.8

Solve & Share Draw a polygon with vertices at A (−1, 6), B (−7, 6), C (−7, −3), and D (−1, −3). Then find the perimeter of the polygon. ***Solve this problem any way you choose.***

You can use the structure of the coordinate plane to draw the polygon and find its perimeter.

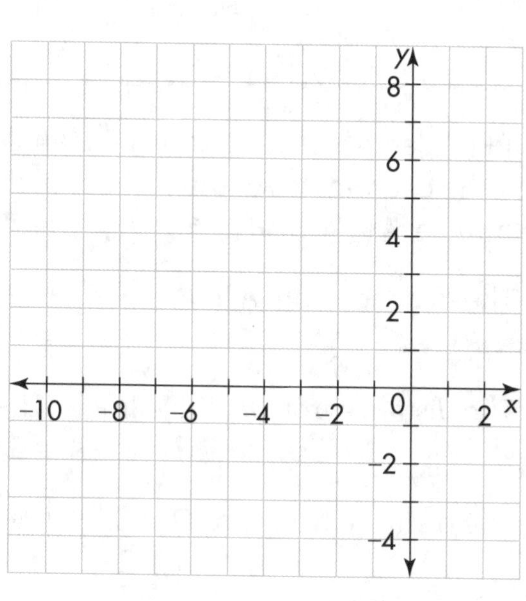

Look Back! **MP.3 Construct Arguments** What type of polygon did you draw? Use a definition to justify your answer.

How Can You Find the Perimeter of a Polygon on a Coordinate Plane?

A

An archaeologist used a coordinate plane to map a dig site. She marked the corners of a building with flags as shown. How much rope does she need to go around the building?

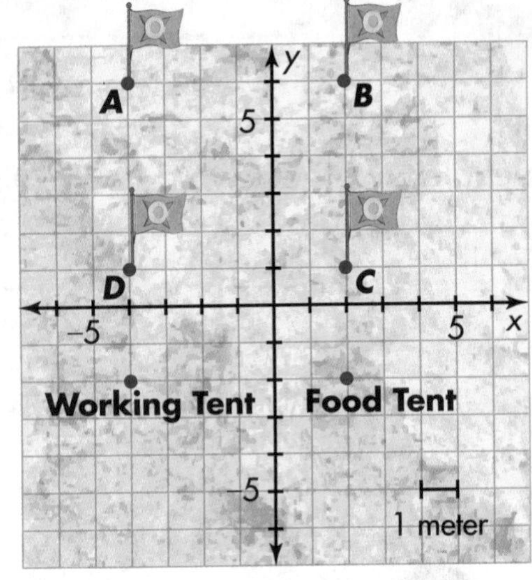

You can use what you know about finding distances to find the perimeter of the building.

B Find the length of each side of rectangle *ABCD*. Use the coordinates of the vertices of the rectangle; $A(-4, 6)$, $B(2, 6)$, $C(2, 1)$, and $D(-4, 1)$.

- The distance from A to $B = |-4| + |2|$
  $= 4 + 2 = 6$ m
- The distance from B to $C = |6| - |1|$
  $= 6 - 1 = 5$ m
- The distance from C to $D = |2| + |-4|$
  $= 2 + 4 = 6$ m
- The distance from A to $D = |6| - |1|$
  $= 6 - 1 = 5$ m

C Add the side lengths to find the perimeter of rectangle *ABCD*.

Perimeter $= 6\text{ m} + 5\text{ m} + 6\text{ m} + 5\text{ m}$
$= 22$ meters

The archaeologist needs 22 meters of rope.

Convince Me! **MP.8 Generalize** How could you use what you know about the formula for perimeter of a rectangle to find the perimeter using two of the distances?

© Pearson Education, Inc. 6

Name ______________________________

Practice Buddy Tools Assessment

Guided Practice*

Do You Understand?

1. **MP.2 Reasoning** In the problem on the previous page, why do you add absolute values to find the distance from A to B, but subtract absolute values to find the distance from B to C?

2. **MP.3 Construct Arguments** Could you use the method of adding or subtracting the absolute values of coordinates to find the length of the diagonal AC of rectangle $ABCD$? Explain.

Do You Know How?

3. Use the map of the archaeological dig site on the previous page. What is the perimeter of the rectangle with vertices at point D, point C, the food tent, and the working tent?

4. Find the perimeter of rectangle $MNOP$ with vertices $M(-2, 5)$, $N(-2, -4)$, $O(3, -4)$, and $P(3, 5)$.

Independent Practice

Leveled Practice In **5** and **6**, find the perimeter of each rectangle.

5. Rectangle $JKLM$: $J(-3, 8)$, $K(-3, -1)$, $L(4, -1)$, $M(4, 8)$

$JK = |\square| + |\square|$

$= \_ + \_ = \_$

$KL = |\square| + |\square|$

$= \_ + \_ = \_$

Perimeter $= JK + KL + LM + MJ$

$= \_ + \_ + \_ + \_ = \_$ units

6. Rectangle $WXYZ$: $W(-3, -2)$, $X(4, -2)$, $Y(4, -5)$, $Z(-3, -5)$

$WX = |\square| + |\square|$

$= \_ + \_ = \_$

$XY = |\square| - |\square|$

$= \_ - \_ = \_$

Perimeter $= WX + XY + YZ + ZW$

$= \_ + \_ + \_ + \_ = \_$ units

7. Rectangle $EFGH$ has vertices $E(-9, 10)$, $F(-9, 2)$, $G(6, 2)$, and $H(6, 10)$. What is the perimeter of rectangle $EFGH$?

*For another example, see Set B on page 217.

Math Practices and Problem Solving

8. Mike used a coordinate plane to design the patio shown at the right. Each unit on the grid represents 1 yard. To buy materials to build the patio, he needs to know its perimeter. What is the perimeter of the patio?

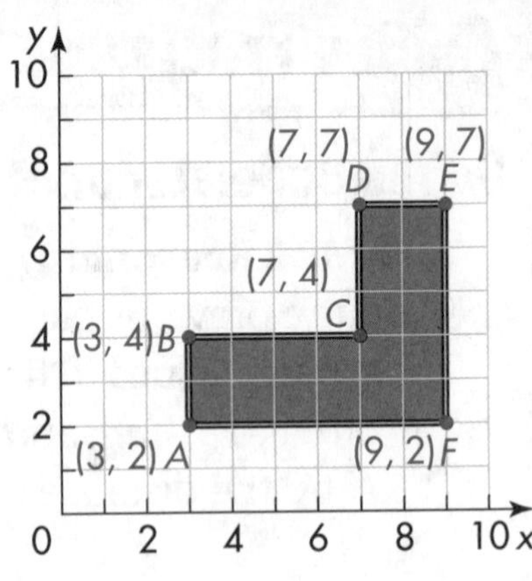

9. **Higher Order Thinking** A square on a coordinate plane has one vertex at (−0.5, −2) and a perimeter of 10 units. If all of the vertices are located in Quadrant III, what are the coordinates of the other 3 vertices?

10. **MP.7 Use Structure** Ana drew a plan for a rectangular piece of material that she will use for a quilt. Three of the vertices are (−1.2, −3.5), (−1.2, 4.4), and (5.5, 4.4). What are the coordinates of the fourth vertex?

11. **Vocabulary** Why is absolute value used to find distances on a coordinate plane?

12. **Number Sense** Suzanne is dividing 439 prizes among 14 booths set up for a fair. She wants to share the prizes equally. About how many prizes will each booth get?

Common Core Assessment

13. The coordinates of triangle ABC are $A\left(-1\frac{1}{2}, -\frac{1}{2}\right)$, $B\left(-1\frac{1}{2}, -3\right)$, and $C\ (4, -3)$.

Part A

What is the distance between points A and B?

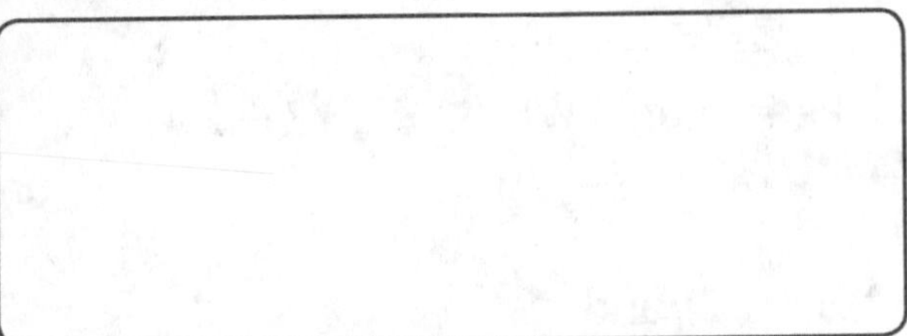

Part B

Give the coordinates for two points that are 8 units from point C.

© Pearson Education, Inc. 6

Name ____________________

Homework & Practice 4-4
Polygons on the Coordinate Plane

Another Look!

Remember, perimeter is the distance around a figure.

Find the perimeter of rectangle $ABCD$. Add or subtract absolute values to find the length of each side.

AB: $|-3| + |2| = 3 + 2 = 5$ units

BC: $|4| - |2| = 4 - 2 = 2$ units

CD: $|-3| + |2| = 3 + 2 = 5$ units

DA: $|4| - |2| = 4 - 2 = 2$ units

The perimeter is $5 + 2 + 5 + 2 = 14$ units.

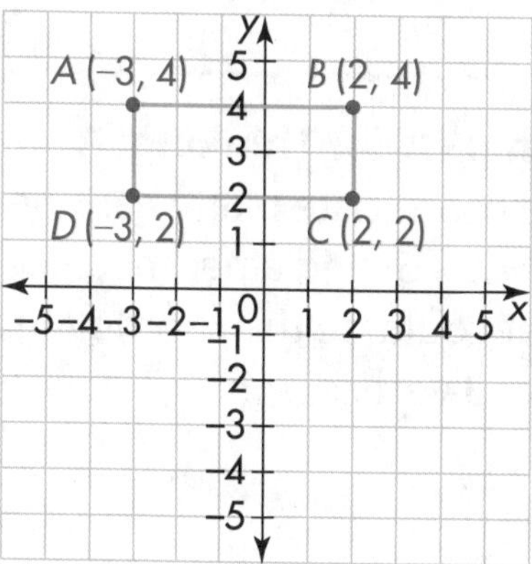

In **1** and **2**, use the coordinate plane below.

1. What is the perimeter of rectangle $ABCD$?

2. What is the perimeter of square $EFGH$?

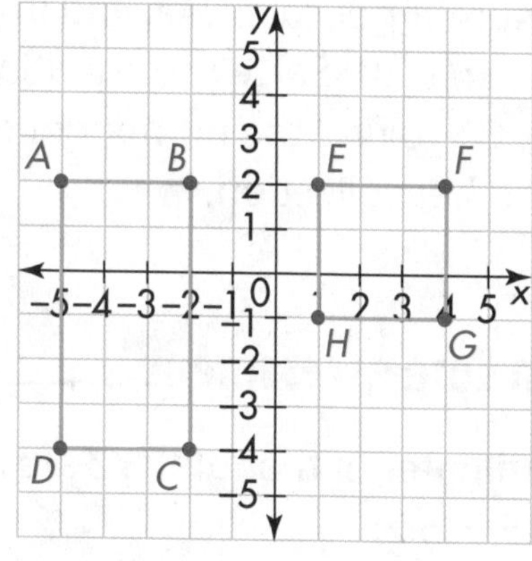

3. Rectangle $QRST$ has vertices $Q\left(4\frac{1}{2}, 2\right)$, $R\left(8\frac{1}{2}, 2\right)$, $S\left(8\frac{1}{2}, -3\frac{1}{2}\right)$, $T\left(4\frac{1}{2}, -3\frac{1}{2}\right)$. What is the perimeter of rectangle $QRST$?

You can draw a picture to show the rectangle.

4. Madison used a coordinate plane to map out an herb garden, shown at the right. To buy a fence for the garden, she needs to know its perimeter. What is the perimeter of the garden?

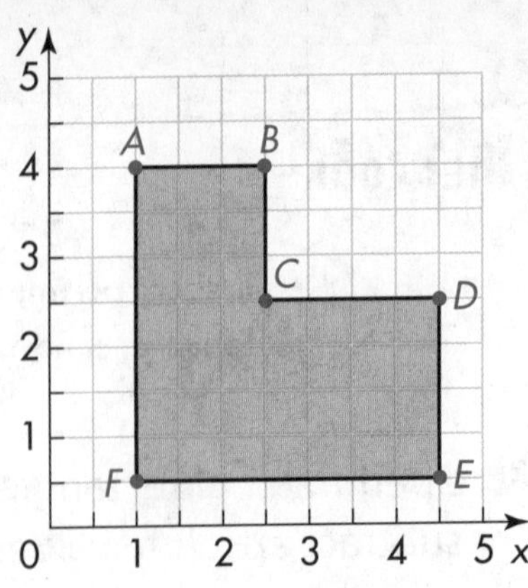

5. **Higher Order Thinking** A rectangle on a coordinate plane has one vertex at $(-5, -6)$ and a perimeter of 30 units. What could be the coordinates of the other 3 vertices?

6. **MP.7 Use Structure** Mr. Wells drew a plan for a rectangular dog run. Three of the vertices are $\left(2\frac{1}{3}, 7\frac{1}{2}\right)$, $\left(12, 7\frac{1}{2}\right)$, and $(12, 1)$. What are the coordinates of the fourth vertex?

7. **Algebra** Mai gave half of the coins in her coin collection to her younger brother. Then, she sold 18 coins to a friend. Now Mai has 35 coins left in her collection. Let $c =$ the number of coins Mai had in her collection to start. Solve the equation $\frac{1}{2}c - 18 = 35$ to find the number of coins Mai had in her collection.

8. Joaquín has 513 stamps in his collection. He organizes them in a 26-page album. About how many stamps will be on each page?

Common Core Assessment

9. The coordinates of triangle XYZ are $X(-3, 3.3)$, $Y(-3, -5.2)$, and $Z(4.5, -5.2)$.

Part A

What is the distance between points X and Y?

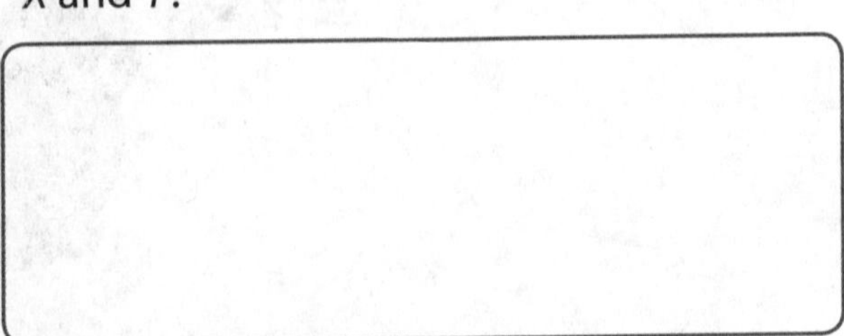

Part B

Give the coordinates for two points that are 5 units from point Z.

© Pearson Education, Inc. 6

Name ___________________________

Solve

Math Practices and Problem Solving

Lesson 4-5

Construct Arguments

I can ...
construct arguments using what I know about finding distances on the coordinate plane.

Mathematical Practices MP.3, MP.1, MP.4, MP.6
Content Standards 6.NS.C.8, 6.G.A.3

Solve & Share

Nathan uses a coordinate plane to draw a plan for his new garden. For one section, he draws a square with one vertex at (−4, 3). Show one way that Nathan could draw the square.

Construct an argument that explains how you know that the figure is a square.

(−4, 3)

Thinking Habits

Be a good thinker! These questions can help you.

- How can I use numbers, objects, drawings, or actions to justify my argument?
- Am I using numbers and symbols correctly?
- Is my explanation clear and complete?
- Can I use a counterexample in my argument?

Look Back! **MP.3 Construct Arguments** Suppose that Nathan plotted another vertex of the garden area at (0, 3). Could this represent the corner of a square section of the garden? Construct an argument to justify your answer.

How Can You Construct Arguments to Justify Your Answers?

A

A polygon on a coordinate plane has vertices A (−3, 2), B (9, 2), C (9, −10), and D (−3, −10). Is polygon ABCD a square? Construct an argument to justify your answer.

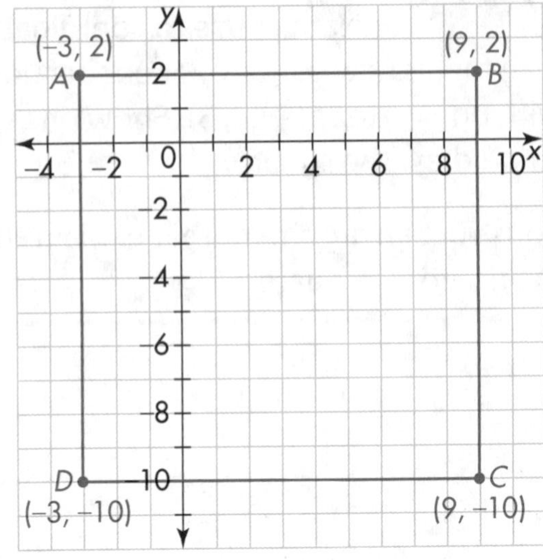

What do I need to do to solve the problem?

I need to use what I know about polygons and finding distances on a coordinate plane. Then I need to state my conclusion by writing a good argument to justify it.

B

How can I construct an argument?

I can

- use math to explain my reasoning.
- use the correct words and symbols.
- give a complete explanation.

C

Here's my thinking...

All four angles are right angles because the sides follow the grid lines.

Find the side lengths.

$AB = |-3| + |9| = 3 + 9 = 12$ units
$BC = |2| + |-10| = 2 + 10 = 12$ units
$CD = |9| + |-3| = 9 + 3 = 12$ units
$DA = |-10| + |2| = 10 + 2 = 12$ units

Polygon *ABCD* has four right angles and four sides of equal length. Polygon *ABCD* is a square.

Convince Me! ◎ **MP.3 Construct Arguments** Construct an argument to justify that the perimeter of square *ABCD* above is 48 units.

© Pearson Education, Inc. 6

Name ______________________

Practice Buddy Tools Assessment

Guided Practice*

MP.3 Construct Arguments

Charlie used a coordinate plane to draw a map of a campground. He placed the corners of the floor of his cabin at $J(-9, 8)$, $K(-1, 8)$, $L(-1, 1)$, and $M(-9, 1)$. Charlie claims that polygon $JKLM$ is a rectangle. Construct an argument to justify his claim.

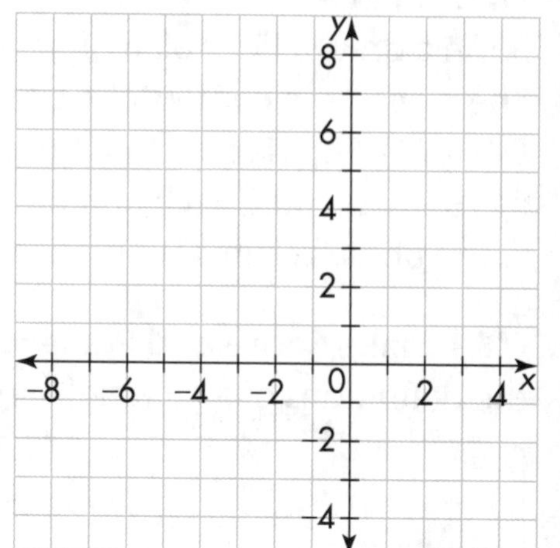

1. Describe how you can use the definition of a rectangle to justify Charlie's claim.

2. Draw polygon $JKLM$ on the coordinate plane. How does the graph help you construct an argument?

You can use definitions, graphs, calculations, and math words to construct arguments.

Independent Practice

MP.3 Construct Arguments

Vic drew a polygon with vertices $P(2, -4)$, $Q(2, 1)$, $R(7, 1)$, and $S(7, -4)$. Is Vic's polygon a square? Construct an argument to justify your answer.

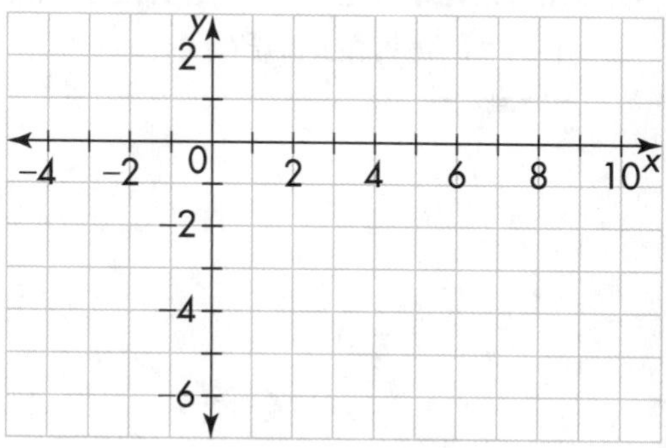

3. How can you use the definition of a square to construct an argument about Vic's polygon?

4. Graph the polygon on the coordinate plane and find its side lengths.

5. Construct an argument to justify whether Vic's polygon is a square.

*For another example, see Set C on page 218.

Math Practices and Problem Solving

Common Core Performance Assessment

Floor Plan

Sophia drew a floor plan of her classroom on a coordinate plane. She placed the corners of a closet floor at $A(-4, 4)$, $B(2, 4)$, $C(2, 1)$, and $D(-4, 1)$. Sophia says that the closet floor is a rectangle with an area of 18 square feet. Each unit on the grid represents 1 foot. Do you agree with Sophia's claims? Construct an argument to justify your answer.

6. MP.1 Make Sense and Persevere What do you need to know about the definitions of a rectangle and area to check Sophia's claim?

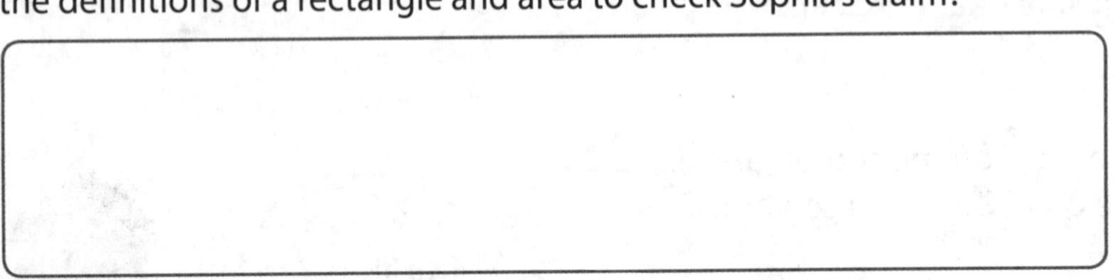

7. MP.4 Model with Math Graph and label the polygon that represents the closet floor on the coordinate plane. What do you know about the angles of polygon *ABCD*?

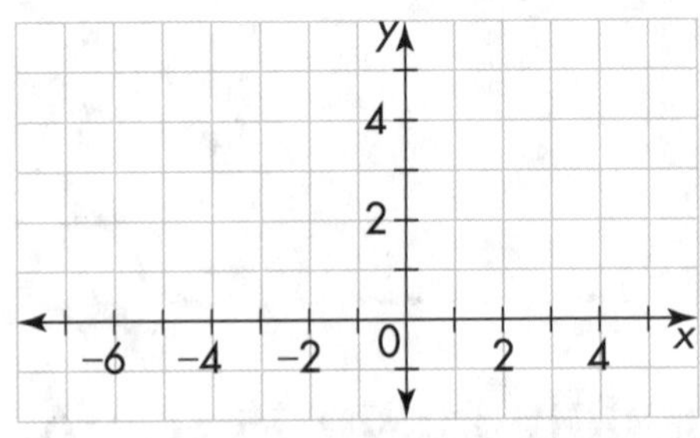

8. MP.6 Be Precise Find the side lengths and the area of polygon *ABCD*.

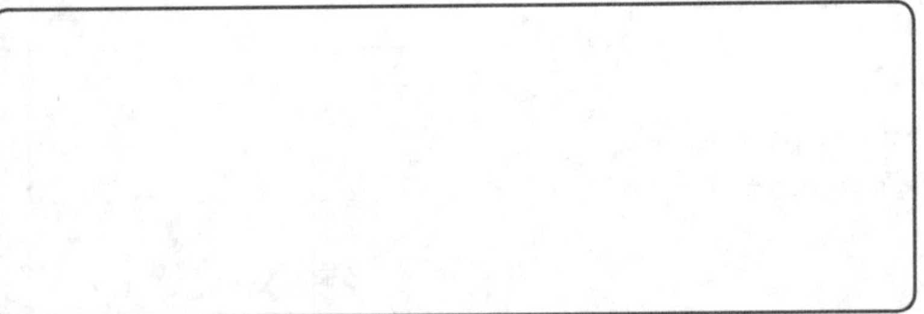

9. MP.3 Construct Arguments Do you agree with Sophia's claims? Construct an argument to justify your answer.

When you are precise, you use math words and symbols to explain your thinking and show your work.

© Pearson Education, Inc. 6

Name ______________________

Help | Practice Buddy | Tools | Games

Homework & Practice 4-5
Construct Arguments

Another Look!

The vertices of triangle *RST* are *R* (−6, 8), *S* (−6, 1), and *T* (1, 1). Is triangle *RST* an isosceles right triangle?

How can you construct an argument to justify your answer?

I can Draw

triangle *RST* on a coordinate plane.

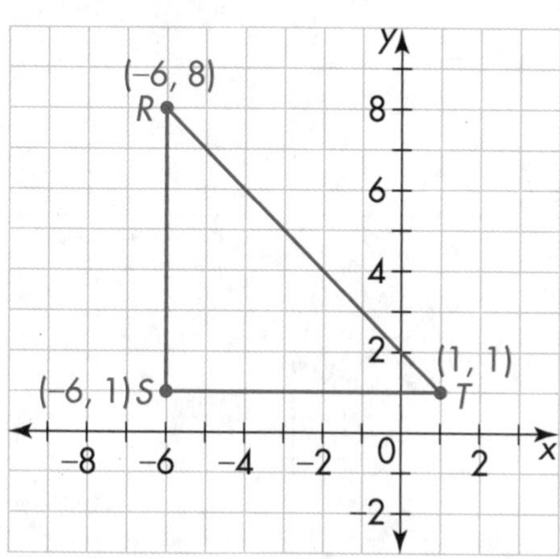

Show that triangle *RST* has a right angle and two sides of equal length.

Angle *S* is a right angle because its sides follow the grid lines.

Find the lengths of the two shorter sides.

$RS = |8| - |1| = 8 - 1 = 7$ units
$ST = |-6| + |1| = 6 + 1 = 7$ units

Triangle *RST* has a right angle and two sides of equal length, so it is an isosceles right triangle.

MP.3 Construct Arguments

Cynthia drew a plan for a triangular pennant on a coordinate plane using vertices *U* (2, −4), *V* (8, −4), and *W* (2, 2). Cynthia claims that the pennant is in the shape of an isosceles right triangle. Is she correct? Construct an argument to justify your answer.

1. Graph triangle *UVW* on the coordinate plane. Is one of the angles a right angle? Explain.

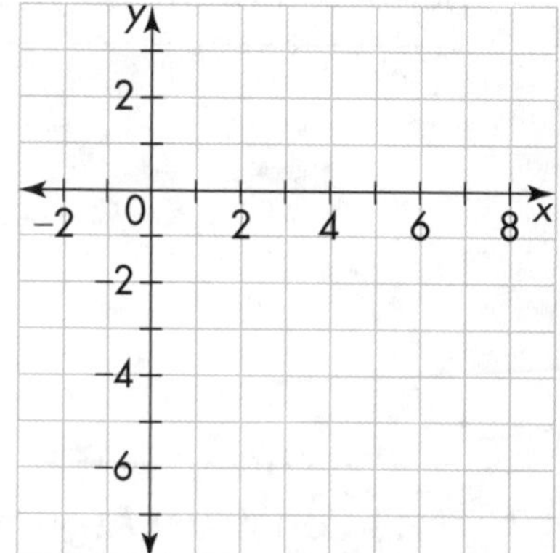

2. Does triangle *UVW* have two sides that are the same length? Explain.

3. Is Cynthia's claim correct? Construct an argument to justify your answer.

Common Core Performance Assessment

Downtown Map

Rolando drew a map of downtown on a coordinate plane. He placed the bank at $B(0, -7)$, City Hall at $C(0, 0)$, the library at $L(5, 0)$, and the post office at $P(5, -7)$. Each unit on the grid represents 5 yards. Rolando claims that the path that joins the landmarks is a rectangle with a perimeter of 120 yards.

Is Rolando's claim correct? Construct an argument to justify your answer.

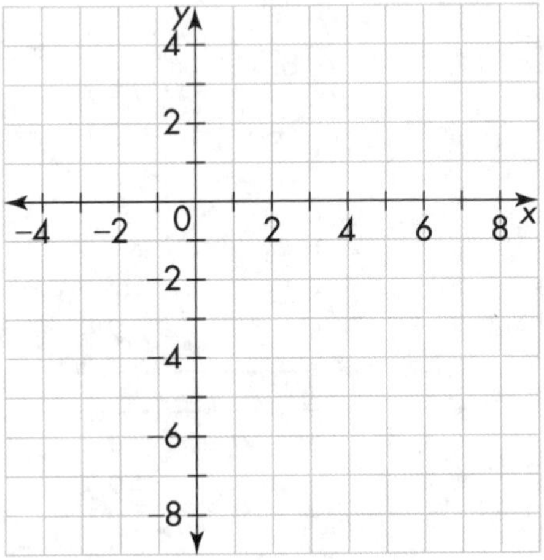

4. **MP.1 Make Sense and Persevere** What do you need to know about the definitions of a rectangle and perimeter to check Rolando's claim?

5. **MP.4 Model with Math** Graph and label the polygon on the coordinate plane. What do you know about the angles of the polygon?

6. **MP.6 Be Precise** Find the side lengths and perimeter of the polygon.

Remember to be precise. Each unit represents 5 yards.

7. **MP.3 Construct Arguments** Is Rolando's claim correct? Construct an argument to justify your answer.

© Pearson Education, Inc. 6

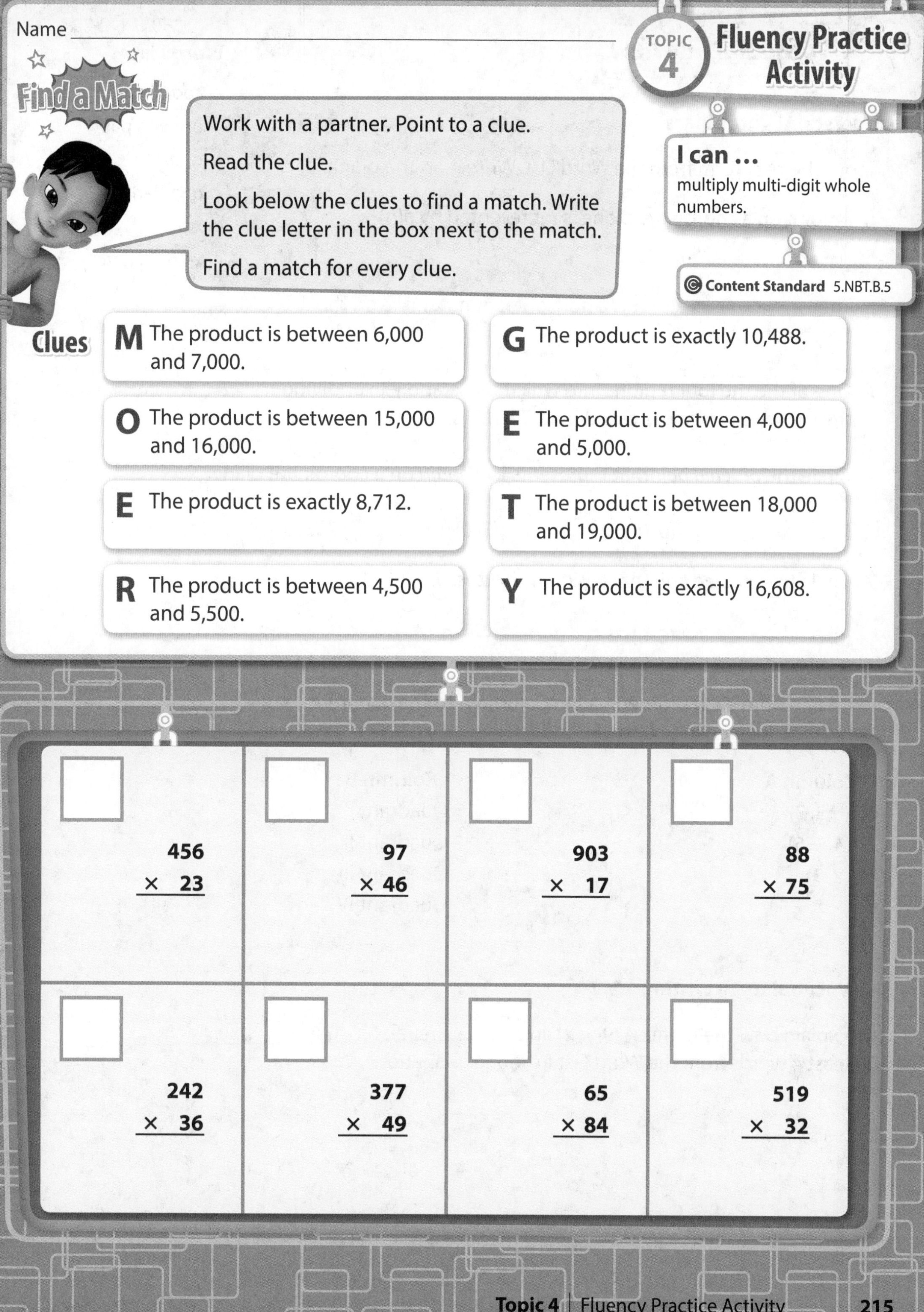

Name ______________________________

Find a Match

TOPIC 4 Fluency Practice Activity

Work with a partner. Point to a clue.

Read the clue.

Look below the clues to find a match. Write the clue letter in the box next to the match.

Find a match for every clue.

I can ...
multiply multi-digit whole numbers.

Content Standard 5.NBT.B.5

Clues

M The product is between 6,000 and 7,000.

O The product is between 15,000 and 16,000.

E The product is exactly 8,712.

R The product is between 4,500 and 5,500.

G The product is exactly 10,488.

E The product is between 4,000 and 5,000.

T The product is between 18,000 and 19,000.

Y The product is exactly 16,608.

☐ 456×23	☐ 97×46	☐ 903×17	☐ 88×75
☐ 242×36	☐ 377×49	☐ 65×84	☐ 519×32

TOPIC 4

Vocabulary Review

Word List

- coordinate plane
- ordered pair
- origin
- quadrant
- *x*-axis
- *x*-coordinate
- *y*-axis
- *y*-coordinate

Understand Vocabulary

Choose the best term from the Word List. Write it on the blank.

1. A point on a coordinate plane is represented by a(n) ______________.

2. The ______________ is a horizontal number line on the coordinate plane.

3. One of the the four regions into which the *x*- and *y*-axes divide the coordinate plane is called a ______________.

4. Circle the *ordered pair* that represents the *origin* on a coordinate plane.

(0, 3)   (0, 0)   (3, 0)   (3, 3)

5. Circle the *ordered pair* that lies on the *y-axis*.

(0, 6)   (6, 0)   (−6, 6)   (6, −6)

Draw a line from each ordered pair in Column A to the *quadrant* in which it is located in Column B.

Column A	Column B
6. (−3, 7)	Quadrant I
7. (4, −6)	Quadrant II
8. (2, 9)	Quadrant III
9. (−7, −1)	Quadrant IV

Use Vocabulary in Writing

10. Explain how the points *A* (9, −2) and *B* (9, 2) are related. Use at least 4 words from the Word List in your explanation.

© Pearson Education, Inc. 6

Name ________________________________

Reteaching

Set A pages 185–190, 191–196

An ordered pair (x, y) of numbers gives the coordinates that locate a point on a coordinate plane.

To graph any point P with coordinates (x, y):

- Start at the origin, (0, 0).
- Use the x-coordinate to move right (if positive) or left (if negative) along the x-axis.
- Then use the y-coordinate of the point to move up (if positive) or down (if negative) following the y-axis.
- Draw and label the point on the coordinate plane.

To give the location of a point on a coordinate plane, follow the grid line from the point to the x-axis to name the x-coordinate, and follow the grid line from the point to the y-axis to name the y-coordinate.

Remember that coordinates can be whole numbers, fractions, mixed numbers, or decimals.

In **1–6**, give the ordered pair for each point.

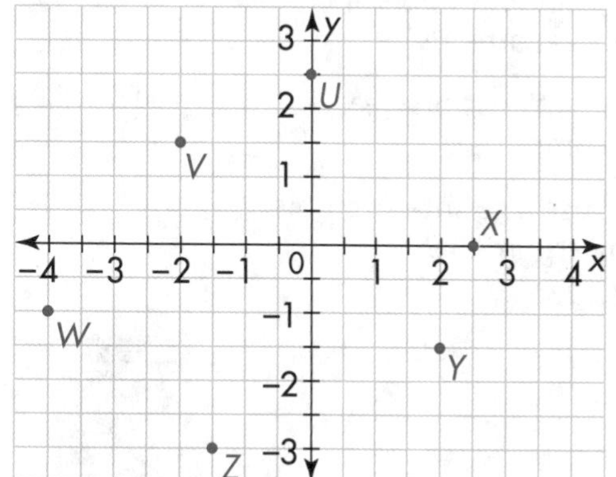

1. *U*

2. *V*

3. *W*

4. *X*

5. *Y*

6. *Z*

Set B pages 197–202, 203–208

Find the the length of side *AB*.

You can use what you know about finding the distance between two points to find the lengths of the sides of a polygon on a coordinate plane.

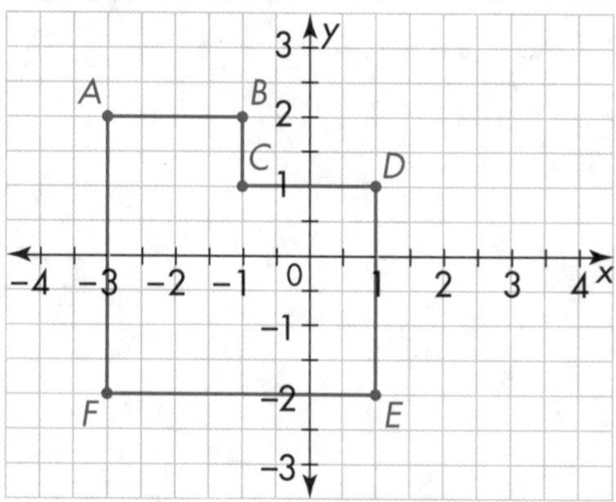

Find the distance from $A(-3, 2)$ to $B(-1, 2)$.

$$|-3| - |-1| = 3 - 1 = 2 \text{ units}$$

Remember to use absolute value to find the distance between two points that share the same x- or y-coordinate.

In **1–6**, find the remaining side lengths of polygon *ABCDEF*. Then find its perimeter.

1. Length of *BC*

2. Length of *CD*

3. Length of *DE*

4. Length of *EF*

5. Length of *FA*

6. Perimeter of *ABCDEF*

7. Find the perimeter of rectangle *WXYZ* with vertices $W(-2, 8)$, $X(2.5, 8)$, $Y(2.5, -2)$, and $Z(-2, -2)$.

Set C pages 209–214

Think about these questions to help you **construct arguments.**

Thinking Habits

- How can I use numbers, objects, drawings, or actions to justify my argument?
- Am I using numbers and symbols correctly?
- Is my explanation clear and complete?
- Can I use a counterexample in my argument?

Remember that you can use definitions, reasoning, and math words to make a good argument.

Elise draws a polygon on a coordinate plane. It has vertices $Q(-4, -1)$, $R(-4, 5)$, $S(2, 5)$, and $T(2, -1)$. Is polygon *QRST* a square? Construct a math argument to justify your answer.

1. How can you use the definition of a square to determine whether the polygon *QRST* is a square?

2. Draw and label polygon *QRST* on the coordinate plane.

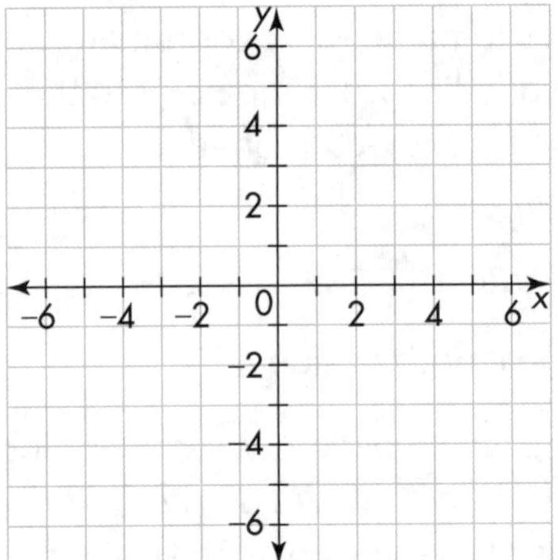

3. Construct an argument to justify whether polygon *QRST* is a square.

© Pearson Education, Inc. 6

Name ____________________

1. Which ordered pair locates point P on the coordinate plane below?

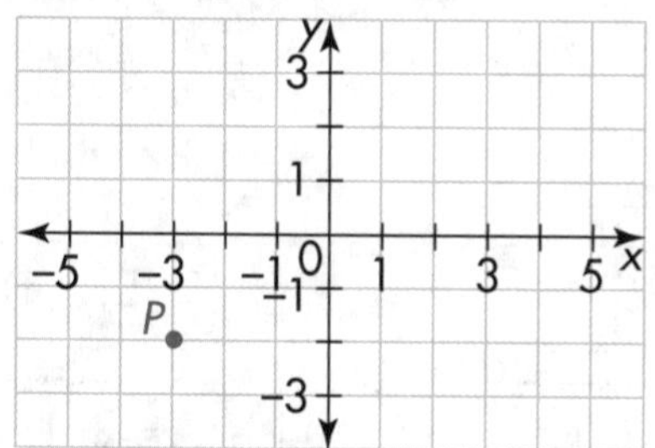

Ⓐ $(-3, -2)$ Ⓑ $(-3, 2)$

Ⓒ $(-2, -3)$ Ⓓ $(-3, -3)$

2. Write the ordered pair that locates point Q on the coordinate plane.

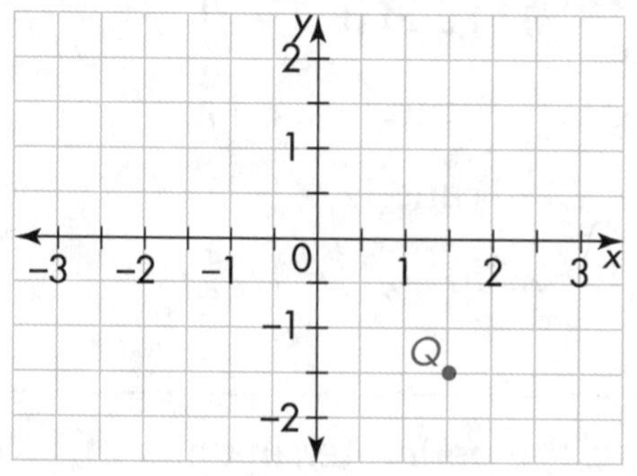

3. For questions 3a–3d, choose Yes or No to tell if the statement is correct.

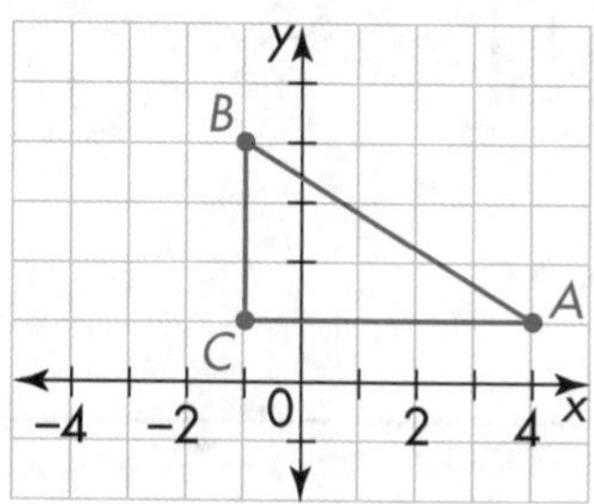

3a. BC is 2 units long. ○ Yes ○ No

3b. CA is 5 units long. ○ Yes ○ No

3c. BC is shorter than BA. ○ Yes ○ No

3d. AC is 2 units longer than BC. ○ Yes ○ No

4. What is the distance from point $P(-4, 4)$ to point $R(-4, -3)$?

5. Carlos drew a plan for his garden on a coordinate plane. Rose bushes are located at $A(-5, 4)$, $B(3, 4)$, and $C(3, -5)$.

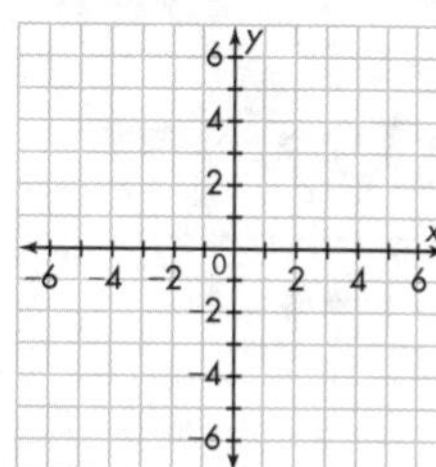

Part A

Graph and label the points to show the locations of the rose bushes.

Part B

Where should Carlos place a fourth rose bush if he wants to have the bushes form a rectangle? Explain.

6. Choose all of the ordered pairs that are 3 units apart.

- ☐ (2, 2) and (−2, 1)
- ☐ (2, −1) and (2, −4)
- ☐ (2, 2) and (2, 5)
- ☐ (−1, 2) and (2, 2)

7. Liana graphs a point *B* in Quadrant II on the coordinate plane below, so that point *B* is $2\frac{1}{2}$ units away from point *A*.

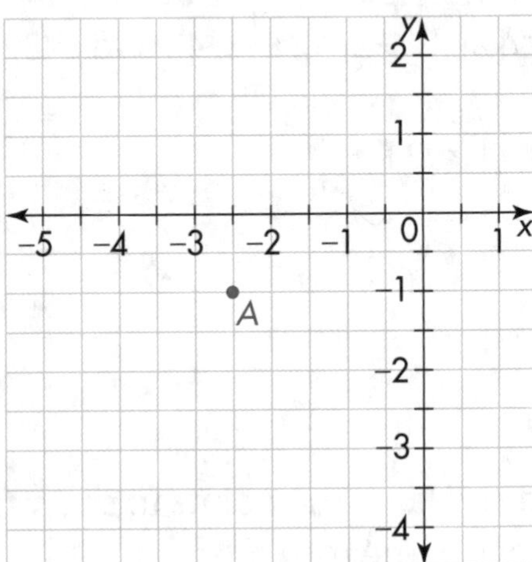

Part A

What are the coordinates of point *B*? Graph and label the point on the coordinate plane.

Part B

Are there other points on the coordinate plane that are $2\frac{1}{2}$ units from point *A*? If so, graph them on the coordinate plane and write their coordinates.

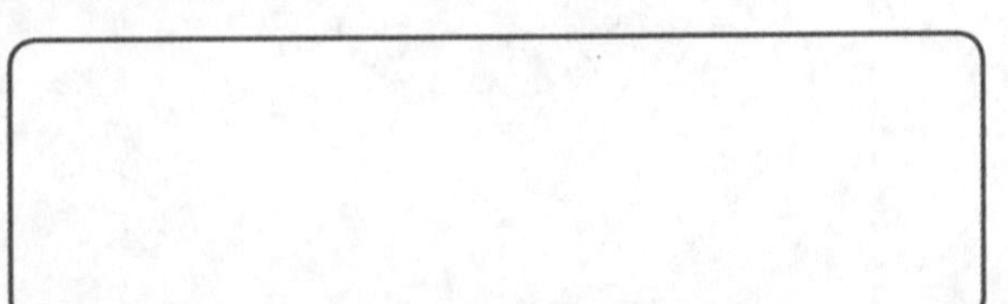

8. Draw lines to match the coordinates of each point with the coordinates of that point's reflection across the *y*-axis.

(5, −1)	(−1, −5)
(2, 1)	(2, −1)
(1, −5)	(−5, −1)
(−2, −1)	(−2, 1)

9. Choose all of the points that are reflections of each other across both axes.

- ☐ $\left(-4\frac{1}{2}, 1\right)$ and $\left(-1, 4\frac{1}{2}\right)$
- ☐ (2.5, −1) and $\left(-2\frac{1}{2}, 1\right)$
- ☐ (4.2, −1) and (2.4, −1)
- ☐ (1, −2.25) and $\left(-1, 2\frac{1}{4}\right)$

10. What is the perimeter, in units, of polygon *PQRSTU*?

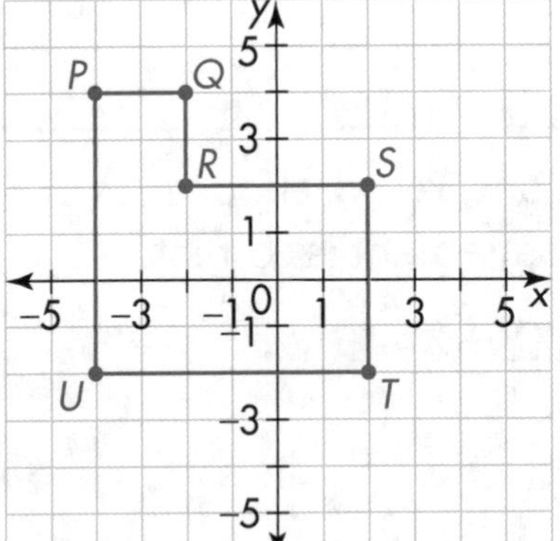

© Pearson Education, Inc. 6

Name ______________________________

TOPIC 4

Performance Assessment

Find the Treasure

Michael and Melita are making a treasure map on a coordinate plane. Answer the questions to help them complete the treasure map.

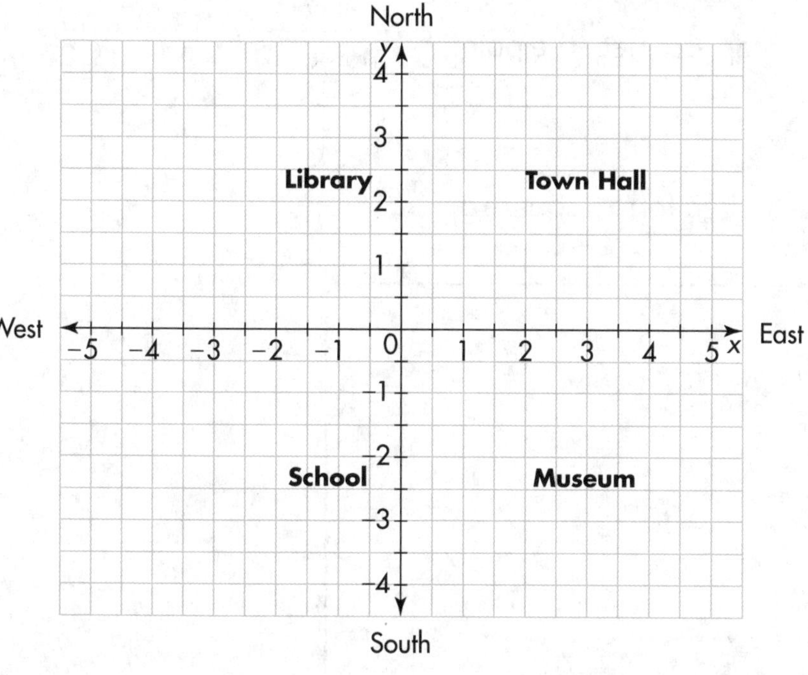

1. A tall palm tree is located at $\left(-2\frac{1}{2}, 2\right)$. Graph and label the tree point T on the map.

2. West Park is L-shaped. Its 6 corners are located at $\left(-4\frac{1}{2}, 1\frac{1}{2}\right)$, $\left(-4\frac{1}{2}, -1\frac{1}{2}\right)$, $\left(-2, -1\frac{1}{2}\right)$, $\left(-2, -\frac{1}{2}\right)$, $\left(-3\frac{1}{2}, -\frac{1}{2}\right)$, and $\left(-3\frac{1}{2}, 1\frac{1}{2}\right)$.

Part A

Graph the 6 corners and connect the points to show the borders.

Part B

What is the perimeter of West Park?

3. Michael and Melita searched for more information about the treasure map. They visited the sites shown in the table.

Site	Location
Library	(−1, 2)
Museum	(3, −2)
School	(−1, −2)
Town Hall	(3, 2)

Part A

Graph and label the points on the map. Connect the points to form a quadrilateral.

Part B

Melita says that the locations they visited form a square on the map. Is Melita correct? Explain.

4. The treasure is located 6 units east of the far southeast corner of West Park. Graph and label the treasure point *X*.

5. The perimeter of West Park is 44 kilometers. Show how Michael can use the perimeter of the park to determine the distance represented by one unit on the map.

© Pearson Education, Inc. 6

TOPIC 5

Algebra: Patterns and Equations

Essential Questions: How can equations be written? What patterns can be found in tables of values? How are equations that can relate real-world quantities graphed?

The ocean plays an important role in weather and climates.

Earth's main source of energy is the sun, and ocean currents help distribute its energy.

That's not surprising considering most of our planet is covered by water! Here's a project about ocean currents and patterns and equations.

Math and Science Project: Ocean Currents and Weather Patterns

Do Research Use the Internet or other sources to learn more about how ocean currents affect weather patterns. How does an ocean current cool or warm a city? Compare weather data for two cities, one coastal and one far inland, which are at the same latitude.

Journal: Write a Report Include what you found. Also in your report:

- Find and record each city's average monthly daytime temperature for all twelve months of a year in a data table.
- For each month, write an equation that shows the difference between the two cities' monthly average temperatures.

Name ____________________

Review What You Know

Vocabulary

Choose the best term from the box. Write it on the blank.

• equation	• variable
• ordered pair	• x-axis
• solution	• y-axis

1. The horizontal number line on the coordinate plane is called the ________.

2. The value of the variable that makes an equation true is the ________.

3. A(n) ____________ contains the coordinates of a point located on the coordinate plane.

4. The expressions on each side of the equal sign in a(n) __________ are equal.

Using Variables

Solve each equation by finding the value of the variable.

5. $52 - x = 17$ $x =$ ☐

6. $61 = g + 13$ $g =$ ☐

7. $8 = t \div 9$ $t =$ ☐

8. $m - 3.7 = 8.6$ $m =$ ☐

9. $12n = 84$ $n =$ ☐

10. $54 \div c = 9$ $c =$ ☐

Equations

Solve each equation.

11. $y \div 20 = 3$

12. $52 = 4a$

13. $z - 67 = 141$

14. $489 = b + 313$

15. $s \div 8 = 11$

16. $15d = 45$

Graphing in the Coordinate Plane

17. Describe how to plot point $A\ (-6, 2)$ on a coordinate plane.

© Pearson Education, Inc. 6

My Word Cards

Use the examples for each word on the front of the card to help complete the definitions on the back.

A-Z Glossary

dependent variable

Tia paid *m* dollars for 6 video games. Each video game cost *v* dollars.

The total amount, ***m***, Tia paid **depends** on the price of one video game, *v*. So ***m*** is the **dependent variable**.

independent variable

Alek can read one page in 2 minutes. He has to read *p* pages for homework and wants to calculate his total time, *t*.

The total time, *t*, Alek needs to read changes based on the number of pages, ***p***, he has to read. So ***p*** is the **independent variable**.

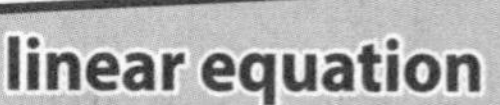

$y = x - 4$

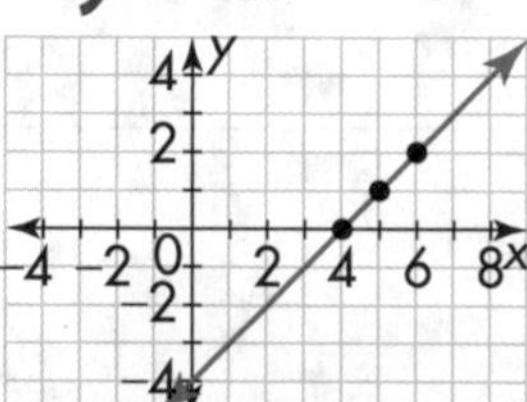

My Word Cards

Complete each definition. Extend learning by writing your own definitions.

A variable that causes another variable to change is called an

______________________________.

A variable that changes in response to another variable is called a

______________________________.

An equation whose graph is a straight line is a

______________________________.

© Pearson Education, Inc. 6

Name ____________________

Solve & Share

Think inside and outside the box. Write three things that determine the weight of the box. Then write three things about the box that do not relate to its weight. ***Solve this problem any way you choose.***

Lesson 5-1
Dependent and Independent Variables

I can …
identify dependent and independent variables.

Content Standard 6.EE.C.9
Mathematical Practices MP.2, MP.3, MP.6, MP.7

You can use reasoning to describe the box and what could be inside. Then ask yourself if that relates to its weight.

Look Back! **MP.7 Look for Relationships** Explain how the box's size and its contents may affect the weight.

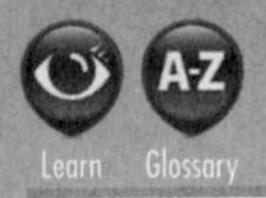

What Does It Mean for One Quantity to Be Dependent on Another Quantity?

A

An orchard sells apples by the pound. Each day, p pounds of apples are sold and the amount of money taken in, m, is recorded. Which variable, p or m, depends on the other variable?

When you think about how total cost is dependent on the amount and price of items sold, you are reasoning quantitatively.

B

A dependent variable changes in response to another variable.

For the apple orchard, the amount of money, m, taken in depends on the number of pounds, p, of apples sold.

The more pounds sold, the more money taken in. You can call m, the amount of money taken in, the dependent variable.

C

An independent variable causes the dependent variable to change.

The number of pounds of apples sold, p, is the independent variable.

When the orchard sells 50 pounds of apples for a certain price, it will take in less than when it sells 65 pounds of the same apples. This is because the dependent variable, m, changes in response to the independent variable, p.

Convince Me! **MP.2 Reasoning** A baker used a certain number of cups of batter, b, to make p medium pancakes. Which variable, p or b, is the dependent variable? Explain.

© Pearson Education, Inc. 6

Name

Practice Buddy Tools Assessment

Guided Practice*

Do You Understand?

1. **MP.3 Critique Reasoning** Jake and Viola keep track of the number of miles, *m*, they bike to help measure the number of calories, *c*, they burn in an hour. Viola says the number of calories, *c*, they burn is the dependent variable. Do you agree?

2. **MP.2 Reasoning** In the biking problem above, identify at least one other independent variable that could affect the dependent variable.

Do You Know How?

In **3–5**, identify the independent variable and the dependent variable.

3. The amount of money, *m*, earned if *t* raffle tickets are sold

4. The number of hours, *h*, worked and the amount of money, *m*, earned

5. The number of shelves, *s*, in a bookcase and the number of books, *b*, the bookcase can hold.

Independent Practice

In **6–9**, identify the independent variable and the dependent variable.

6. The pages, *p*, in a book and the weight, *w*, of the book

7. The number of hamburgers, *h*, sold and the dollar amount of sales, *s*, taken in

8. The pounds, *p*, of flour you buy and the number of bread loaves, *l*, you want to make

9. The temperature, *t*, of water and the number of minutes, *m*, the water is in the freezer

10. Write your own situation. Identify the independent and dependent variables.

*For another example, see Set A on page 265.

Math Practices and Problem Solving

Family Vacation	
Day	**Distance**
1	480 mi
2	260 mi
3	40 mi
4	150 mi
5	100 mi
6	320 mi

11. The table records distances driven by the Williams family each day of their vacation. What is an independent variable that would affect the total distance they drove each day?

12. **MP.7 Look for Relationships** The Williams family drove 50 miles each hour on Day 6. How many hours did they drive to equal the distance shown?

13. **MP.6 Be Precise** On Monday, Jill bought $3\frac{2}{3}$ feet of ribbon for her art project. On Tuesday, she bought another $1\frac{1}{6}$ feet of ribbon. How many inches of ribbon did she buy in all?

14. **MP.2 Reasoning** Name something that could result in a change in a person's heart rate. Is this a dependent or an independent variable?

15. **MP.7 Use Structure** Darryl put 8 boxes of apples on a cart. Each box contains 6 rows of 5 apples. Use the Associative Property of Multiplication to show two different ways to find the number of apples in all.

16. **Higher Order Thinking** Lidia said that time, *t*, could be either an independent or dependent variable. Write a situation where time, *t*, is an independent variable. Then write a situation where time, *t*, is a dependent variable.

Common Core Assessment

17. The dependent variable *g* represents the growth of a plant. Which of the variables described below can represent an independent variable in this situation?

- ☐ The height of the plant, *h*, when placed in the ground
- ☐ The amount of sunlight, *s*
- ☐ How many leaves, *m*, the plant has
- ☐ The amount of water, *w*, it receives

© Pearson Education, Inc. 6

Name ______________________________

Homework & Practice 5-1

Dependent and Independent Variables

Another Look!

A bicycle shop rents bicycles by the hour. Each day, *b* bicycles are rented. The shop collects *d* dollars per day in total rental fees. Identify which variable is the independent variable and which is the dependent variable.

Think about whether a variable causes change or changes in response to other variables.

A **dependent variable** changes in response to another variable, called an independent variable.

An **independent variable** causes the change in a dependent variable. It is *independent* because its value is not affected by other variables and can be used to find the value of the dependent variable.

The number of bikes *b*, that are rented each day affects the total rental fees collected each day, *d*.

So, the number of bikes rented, *b*, is the independent variable that causes the dependent variable, *d*, the total rental fees, to change.

In **1–8**, underline the independent variable and circle the dependent variable in each situation.

1. The number of hours, *h*, spent studying and the score, *s*, on a test

2. The length, *l*, of a pencil and the number of times, *t*, it has been sharpened

3. The length of a story in pages, *p*, and the number of words, *w*, in a story

4. The number of students, *s*, ahead of you in the lunch line and the time, *t*, it takes you to get lunch

5. The amount of time, *t*, to finish a race and the number of laps, *l*, around a track

6. Tickets, *t*, sold for a race and the amount of money, *m*, collected

7. The length, *l*, of a fence and the amount of wood, *w*, to make the fence

8. The height, *h*, of a fence and the time, *t*, it takes to climb the fence

9. Write your own situation where speed, *s*, is an independent variable.

10. **MP.2 Reasoning** Two friends hiked the Appalachian Trail from Georgia to Maine. List at least two independent variables that could affect the number of days they took to hike the trail.

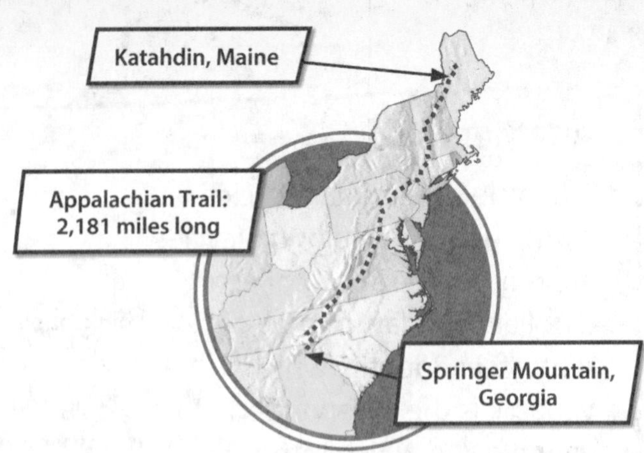

11. **Algebra** Steve had 21 songs on his MP3 player. He bought some new songs. Now he has 30 songs on his player. Write an equation to show how many new songs he put on his player. Let *s* stand for the number of new songs. Solve for s and show your work.

12. **MP.3 Construct Arguments** A baseball team gets 3 outs for each inning it comes up to bat. So far this season, Silvio's team has batted in 45 innings, *n*, and has made 135 outs, *t*. What is the dependent variable? Explain your reasoning.

13. **Vocabulary** Underline the *independent variable* and circle the *dependent variable* in the situation below.

    The number of laps you swim, *s*, and the time, *t*, you spend swimming.

14. **Higher Order Thinking** Ivan says that length, *l*, can be used as an independent variable and as a dependent variable. Give an example of a case where length, *l*, is a dependent variable. Then describe another situation where it is an independent variable.

Common Core Assessment

15. The cost, *c*, of a hamburger at a restaurant depends on other factors at the restaurant. Which of the variables described below can represent an independent variable in this situation?

- ☐ The number of hamburgers, *h*, typically sold at the restaurant
- ☐ The distance, *d*, the owner lives from the restaurant
- ☐ The cost, *c*, to maintain the restaurant
- ☐ The color of the table cloths, *t*

 © Pearson Education, Inc. 6

Name ______________________________

Solve & Share

The table below shows how many candles are in different numbers of boxes. Find a pattern that explains the relationship between the values of c and b. Use words and numbers to describe the pattern. How many candles will there be in 10 boxes? ***Solve this problem any way you choose.***

Lesson 5-2

Patterns and Equations

I can …
use patterns to write equations with variables.

Content Standard 6.EE.C.9
Mathematical Practices MP.1, MP.2, MP.7

Look for relationships in the table that help you get from each value in the left column to its matching value in the right column.

Number of candles, c	Number of boxes, b
8	2
12	3
16	4

Look Back! **MP.7 Use Structure** Write a rule that explains how you get from the values in the right column of the table above to the values in the left column.

How Can You Find a Pattern to Write and Solve an Equation?

A

The table shows the cost of weekend tickets to the Slide and Splash Water Park. Find a pattern between the number of tickets, n, and the cost, c, of the tickets. Write a rule and an equation that represents the pattern. How much would 6 tickets cost?

Number, n	Cost, c
3	$16.50
4	$22.00
5	$27.50
6	

To help make sense of the problem, find the price of one ticket. 3 tickets cost $16.50.

B Find the price of one ticket, p, when 3 tickets cost $16.50.

$3p = \$16.50$

$p = \frac{\$16.50}{3}$

$p = \$5.50$

C One ticket costs $5.50. Check the cost for 4 and 5 tickets.

$4 \times \$5.50 = \$22.00$

$5 \times \$5.50 = \$27.50$

$5.50 checks for 4 and 5 tickets.

D State the rule:
The total cost, c, is $5.50 times the number of tickets, n.

Write an equation:
$c = 5.50 \times n$, or $c = 5.5n$

Find the cost of 6 tickets.

$c = 5.5(6)$

$c = 33$

The cost of 6 tickets is $33.00.

Convince Me! **MP.2 Reasoning** Make a table of values for the equation $12.2s = y$, where s is the number of seconds, and y is the number of yards someone bikes. Complete the table for different values of s and their matching y values.

 © Pearson Education, Inc. 6

Name ______________________________

Practice Buddy | Tools | Assessment

Guided Practice*

Do You Understand?

1. MP.7 Use Structure How can you find a pattern in a table? How can you use the pattern to write a rule and an equation?

2. In the example on the previous page, how much will 12 tickets cost?

3. MP.1 Make Sense and Persevere What should be done if the pattern does not check for other values in the table?

Do You Know How?

4. The table shows Brenda's age, b, when Talia's age, t, is 7, 9, and 10. Write a rule and an equation that represents the pattern. Then find Brenda's age when Talia is 12.

Talia's age, t	Brenda's age, b
7	2
9	4
10	5
12	b

Independent Practice

In **5** and **6**, write a rule and an equation to fit a pattern in each table.

5.

x	1	2	3	4	5
y	33	34	35	36	37

6.

m	0	1	2	3	4
n	0	3	6	9	12

In **7** and **8**, write a rule and an equation to fit a pattern in each table. Then use the rule to complete the table.

7.

g	32	37	42	47	52
k	17	22	27		

8.

x	0	9	18	27	36
y	0	1	2		

*For another example, see Set B on page 265.

Math Practices and Problem Solving

9. Algebra To celebrate their 125th anniversary, a company produced 125 very expensive teddy bears. The bears, known as the "125 Karat Teddy Bears," are made of mohair, silk, and gold thread. They have diamonds and sapphires for eyes. The chart at the right shows the approximate cost of different numbers of these bears. Write an equation that can be used to find c, the cost of n bears.

Cost of "125 Karat Teddy Bears"	
Number, n	Cost, c
4	\$188,000
7	\$329,000
11	\$517,000
15	\$705,000

In **10** and **11**, write an equation that best describes the pattern in each table.

10.

w	2	4	6	8	10
z	0	2	4	6	8

11.

x	0	$\frac{1}{2}$	1	$1\frac{1}{2}$	2	$2\frac{1}{2}$
y	0	2	4	6	8	10

12. Higher Order Thinking Maya wrote the equation $h = d + 22$ to represent the relationship shown in the table. Is this equation correct? Explain.

h	3	5	7	9
d	33	55	77	99

Common Core Assessment

13. The table below shows the total cost, c, for the number of movie tickets purchased, t. Write an equation that can be used to find the cost, c, of 5 movie tickets. Use the equation and complete the table to find the cost of 5 tickets.

Number of Tickets, t	3	5	7	9
Cost, c	\$26.25		\$61.25	\$78.75

© Pearson Education, Inc. 6

Name ____________________

Help Practice Buddy Tools Games

Homework & Practice 5-2

Patterns and Equations

Another Look!

Write a rule and an equation for the pattern in the table.

j	1	4	7	8	9
m	3	12	21	24	27

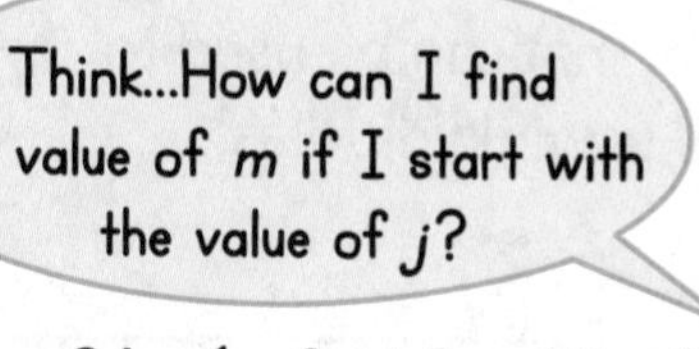

Think...How can I find the value of *m* if I start with the value of *j*?

Think: 3 is 1×3 12 is 4×3

State a theory: It seems that $3j = m$.

Test the other pairs: $7 \times 3 = 21$ ✔ $8 \times 3 = 24$ ✔ $9 \times 3 = 27$ ✔

Write a rule: The value of *m* is the value of *j* times 3.

Write an equation: $m = j \cdot 3$, or $m = 3j$

In **1–4**, write a rule and an equation for the pattern in each table.

1.

x	3	6	11	13	15
y	5	8	13	15	17

2.

x	2	5	6	8	9
y	6	15	18	24	27

3.

x	4	12	20	36	40
y	1	3	5	9	10

4.

x	5	7	9	10	12
y	0	2	4	5	7

5. Complete the table to show a pattern. Then write a rule and an equation for the pattern.

x					
y					

6. Explain how you would find the pattern in this table, and how you would write a rule and an equation for the pattern.

x	4	5	7	10	12
y	0	1	3	6	8

7. MP.2 Reasoning The Gadget Factory sells winkydiddles. The table shows the cost, c, of w winkydiddles. If each winkydiddle costs the same amount, what is the price of each winkydiddle?

Number of Winkydiddles, w	7	12	26	31
Cost, c	$24.50	$42.00	$91.00	$108.50

8. Write an equation that can be used to find c, the cost of w winkydiddles.

For **9** and **10**, write an equation that best describes the pattern in each table.

9.

n	4	6	8	10	12
v	11	13	15	17	19

10.

x	5	6	7	10	11	12
y	2.5	3	3.5	5	5.5	6

11. Write a real-world problem that could be represented in the table below.

x	1	2	3	4
y	2.5	5	7.5	10

12. Higher Order Thinking All the values of x in a table are greater than the corresponding values of y. Write a rule that fits this situation. Then write an equation to go along with the rule.

Common Core Assessment

13. The table below shows the total cost, c, for the number of raffle tickets purchased, t. Write an equation that can be used to find the cost, c, of 10 raffle tickets. Use the equation and complete the table to find the cost of 10 tickets.

Number of Tickets, t	5	8	10	11
Cost, c	$417.50	$668		$918.50

© Pearson Education, Inc. 6

Name ________________________________

Lesson 5-3

More Patterns and Equations

I can ...

use tables, graphs, and equations to show the relationship between independent and dependent variables.

Content Standard 6.EE.C.9
Mathematical Practices MP.2, MP.4, MP.7, MP.8

Solve & Share

The equation $c = 3 + 2g$ represents the cost for bowling when the shoe rental costs $3 and each game costs $2. Make a table to display the costs of 1, 2, 3, and 4 games. Let c equal the cost of bowling and g equal the number of games played. Describe any patterns that you see in the table.

You can use reasoning to decide which is the independent variable and which is the dependent variable.

$c = 3 + 2g$	
g	c

Look Back! **MP.7 Use Structure** Explain how you can use the equation to find the cost for 8 games of bowling and extend the table.

Essential Question: How Can You Use Patterns to Solve an Equation That Has More Than One Operation?

A

Ethan owes his mother \$75. He is repaying her \$5 each week. Write and solve an equation to find how much Ethan will owe after 12 weeks.

You can use a table to organize data.

B Make a table to show the amount Ethan will owe after 0, 1, 2, 3, and 4 weeks.

Week, w	Amount still owed, a
0	\$75
1	\$70
2	\$65
3	\$60

Continue the table.

C Use the pattern you see in the table to write an equation.

Amount still owed		Loan amount		Amount paid after w weeks
a	=	\$75	−	$5w$

You can let a stand for the amount still owed and w for the number of weeks.

D Substitute 12 for w to find how much Ethan still owes after 12 weeks.

$a = 75 - 5w$

$a = 75 - 5(12)$

$a = 75 - 60$

$a = 15$

Ethan still owes \$15 after 12 weeks.

Convince Me! **MP.8 Generalize** If Ethan continues to pay \$5 per week, how long will it take for him to pay the \$75? Explain your answer.

© Pearson Education, Inc. 6

Name ______________________________

Practice Buddy   Tools   Assessment

Guided Practice*

Do You Understand?

1. MP.2 Reasoning In the problem on the previous page, what happens to the value of the dependent variable, a, when the value of the independent variable, w, is increased by 1?

2. MP.7 Look for Relationships Use the pattern in the table below to write an equation.

x	y
1	7
2	12
3	17
4	22

Do You Know How?

In **3** and **4**, use the table below to answer the questions.

3. Use the equation $y = 2x - 7$ to complete the table.

x	4	5	6	7	8
y	1	3	5		

4. State the rule for the pattern in words.

Independent Practice

In **5–8**, use the equation to complete each table.

5. $t = 5d + 5$

d	0	1	2	3	4
t	5	10	15	☐	☐

6. $y = \frac{1}{2}x - 1$

x	2	4	6	8	10
y	0	1	2	☐	☐

7. $y = 2x + 1$

x	0	1	2	3
y	1	3	☐	☐

8. $b = \frac{a}{2} - 2$

a	17	14	11	8	5
b	☐	☐	☐	☐	☐

9. Complete the equation that represents the data in the table.

x	1	2	3	4
y	2	5	8	11

$y = \square x - \square$

*For another example, see Set B on page 265.

Math Practices and Problem Solving

10. **MP.7 Look for Relationships** A county fair charges \$8 for general admission and \$2.50 for each ride. Use the pattern in the table to the find the cost of 5 rides and 8 rides. Then write an equation for the pattern.

Rides, r	Cost, c
3	\$15.50
4	\$18.00
5	
6	\$23.00
8	

11. **MP.8 Generalize** Find the cost, c, for 12 rides.

12. Elizabeth is using 1-inch square tiles to decorate a wall. Use the equation $p = 2t + 2$ to make a table to record the perimeter, p, of t tiles in a single row when t is 1, 2, 3, and 6.

13. **Number Sense** Of the 60 students who take art class, 12 are going to display their art at the local art museum. What fraction of the students are **NOT** going to display their art?

In **14–16,** use the pattern.

14. **MP.7 Look for Relationships** Complete the table and describe any patterns you see.

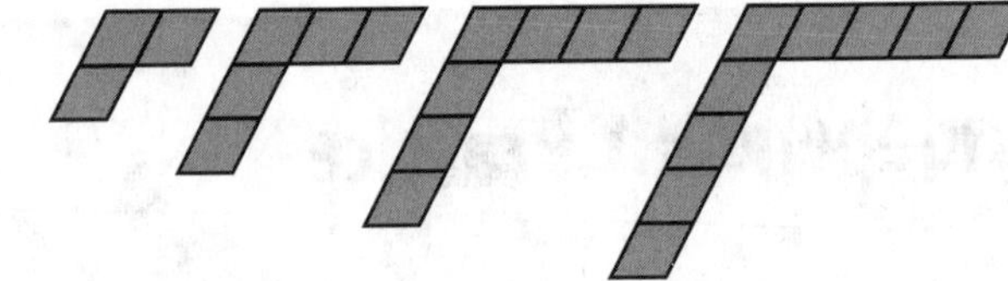

Pattern Number, p	1	2	3	4	5
Number of Blocks, b	3				

15. **Higher Order Thinking** Write an equation for the pattern.

16. How many blocks are needed to make the 10th figure in the pattern?

Common Core Assessment

17. Complete each table below by writing the y-values in the right column. Use the choices in the box to the right.

$y = 4x - 3$

x	y
2	
4	
5	
7	

$y = 3x + 2$

x	y
2	
3	
6	
9	

Possible y Values					
3	5	8	11	13	15
17	20	23	25	29	30

© Pearson Education, Inc. 6

Name ______________________

Help | Practice Buddy | Tools | Games

Homework & Practice 5-3

More Patterns and Equations

Another Look!

The entry fee to a carnival is \$3. Each ride ticket is \$2. The cost, *c*, of going to the carnival equals the entry fee plus two times the number of tickets, *t*, purchased. Find the cost for going on 10 rides.

You can organize these values in a table that shows the total cost based on the number of tickets purchased.

Tickets, t	$3 + 2t$	Cost, c
0	$3 + 2(0)$	\$3
2	$3 + 2(2)$	\$7
4	$3 + 2(4)$	\$11
6	$3 + 2(6)$	\$15

The table shows the costs if you go on 0, 2, 4, and 6 rides.

Use the table rule to write an equation: $c = 3 + 2t$.

You can substitute numbers into the equation to find the total cost when ten ride tickets are purchased.

$c = 3 + 2(10)$
$c = 23$

When you purchase 10 ride tickets, the total cost is \$23.

In **1–4**, use the equation to complete each table.

1. $y = 3x + 7$

x	0	1	2	3
y				

2. $y = 4x - 4$

x	2	4	6	8
y				

3. $y = 2x + 7$

x	1	3	5	7
y				

4. $y = \frac{1}{4}x + 5$

x	0	4	8	12
y				

5. Grace has \$100. She is buying charms for her bracelet that cost \$5 each. Write an equation showing the relationship between the number of charms, *c*, she buys and the amount of money she has left, *m*.

6. Use the equation you wrote for Exercise 5 to find the number of charms Grace can buy before she runs out of money.

7. **MP.7 Look for Relationships** The first ride on a kiddie train at the mall is \$2.50. Each additional ride is \$1.50. Use the equation $c = 2.50 + 1.50(r - 1)$ to complete the table and find the cost of 2, 3, and 6 rides.

Rides, *r*	Cost, *c*
1	\$2.50
2	
3	
4	\$7.00
6	

8. **MP.8 Generalize** Find the cost, *c*, for 9 rides.

In **9** and **10**, the equation $\ell = 3w$ represents that the length, ℓ, of a rectangle is 3 times its width, *w*.

9. **MP.4 Model with Math** Create a table to show the length of the rectangle when its width is 1, 2, 3, 5, and 8 units.

10. **Higher Order Thinking** How could you use the equation $p = 2\ell + 2w$ to find the perimeter, *p*, of the rectangle when the width, *w*, is 15?

11. **MP.7 Use Structure** A triangular pattern has 21 dots in the 6th pattern. Use the equation $\frac{p(p+1)}{2}$, where *p* is the pattern number, to find the number of dots in the 7th pattern.

12. Use the equation from Exercise 11. How many dots will be in the 10th pattern?

Common Core Assessment

13. Complete each table below by writing the *y*-values in the right column. Use the choices in the box to the right.

$y = \frac{1}{2}x + 5$

x	*y*
4	
6	
9	
16	

$y = 3(x - 2)$

x	*y*
3	
6	
8	
11	

Possible *y* Values					
3	4	7	8	9.5	12
13	16	18	22.5	27	32

© Pearson Education, Inc. 6

Name ______________________________

Lesson 5-4
Graph Equations

I can ...
graph algebraic expressions.

Content Standard 6.EE.C.9
Mathematical Practices MP.2, MP.3, MP.4

Solve & Share

Nancy walks 4 blocks to Maria's house. Together, they continue the walk. Graph the equation $n = m + 4$ on a coordinate plane, where n is the number of blocks Nancy walks and m is the number of blocks Maria walks.

How can you use what you know about making tables and plotting points to model the problem on a graph?

$n = m + 4$	
m	n
1	
2	
3	

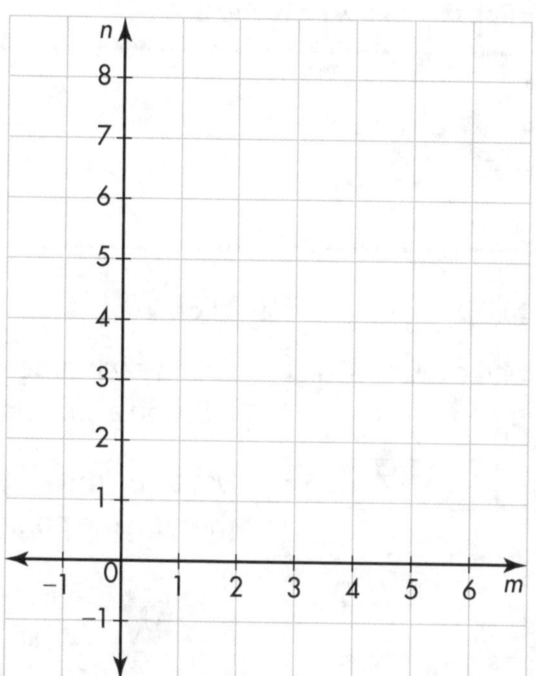
n
8
7
6
5
4
3
2
1
0
−1
−1
1
2
3
4
5
6
m

Look Back! MP.4 Model with Math Draw a line through the points you graphed. What ordered pair on the line includes $m = 5$? Explain what that ordered pair represents.

How Can You Graph a Linear Equation?

A

The booster club members are making school pompoms. Their supplies cost \$4, and they plan to sell the pompoms for \$1 apiece.

Let n = the number of pompoms sold.

Let p = the profit.

Graph the equation p = n − 4 to show the relationship between n and p.

You can use any variables to represent the axes on a coordinate plane.
Each pompom sells for \$1.

B

Step 1

Make a table for $p = n - 4$.

$p = n - 4$	
n	p
4	0
5	1
6	2

C

Step 2

Graph each ordered pair in the table on a coordinate plane.

Use a straight edge to draw a line through the points.

Always choose at least 3 values for the independent variable.

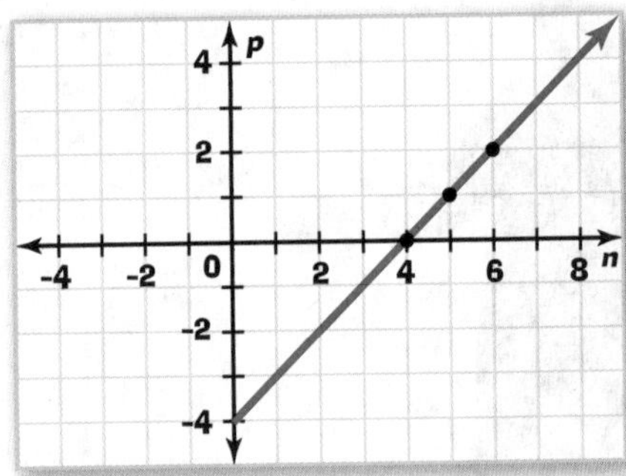

Since the graph of $p = n - 4$ is a straight line, the equation is a linear equation.

Convince Me! **MP.4 Model with Math** How many pompoms must be sold for the club to make a \$4 profit? Explain how graphing the equation helps you find the answer.

© Pearson Education, Inc. 6

Name

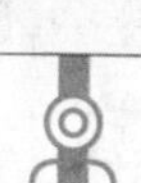

Guided Practice*

Do You Understand?

1. **MP.2 Reasoning** In the problem on the previous page, why is the line for the graph not extended to show negative values for n?

2. **MP.3 Construct Arguments** How can you use the equation $y = x - 4$ to check that the point (9, 5) is on the line that graphs this equation?

Do You Know How?

In **3** and **4**, use the equation $d = 4t$.

3. Complete the table.

d = distance
t = time

$d = 4t$	
t	d
1	
2	
3	

4. Name four ordered pairs found on the line plotted using this equation.

Independent Practice

In **5** and **6**, complete the table and graph for each.

5. A rectangle is $\frac{1}{2}$ inch longer than it is wide.

Let w = width.
Let ℓ = length.
Graph $\ell = w + \frac{1}{2}$.

$\ell = w + \frac{1}{2}$	
w	ℓ
1	
2	

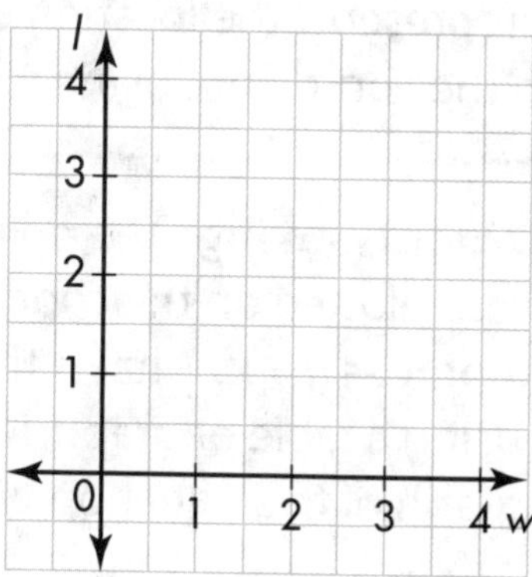

6. The sale price is $5 less than the regular price.

Let s = the sale price.
Let r = the regular price.
Graph $s = r - 5$.

$s = r - 5$	
r	s
10	
20	

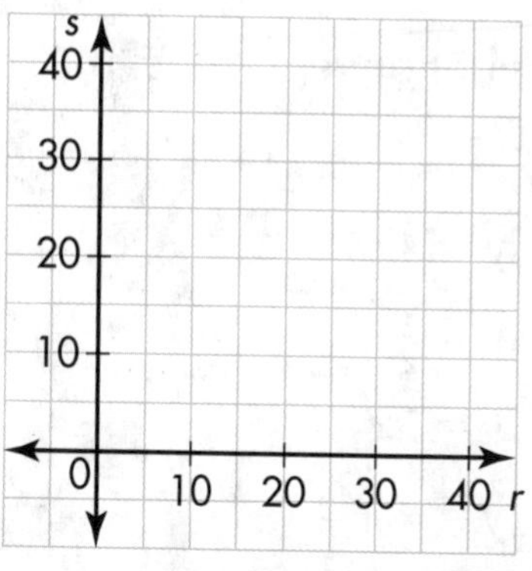

*For another example, see Set C on page 266.

Math Practices and Problem Solving

7. **MP.4 Model with Math** During a movie matinee, the film projector broke. The theater manager refunded the ticket price to everyone attending. Let n represent the number of people watching the movie. Let r represent the total amount of money refunded. Write an equation to represent amount of money refunded.

Movie Price Board	
Adults	\$8.50
Children & Seniors	\$7.00
Matinees: All Ages	\$5.00

8. **MP.2 Reasoning** Complete the table using the equation $r = 7n + 3$.

n	r

9. **Vocabulary** The *origin* of a coordinate grid is located at which point?

10. Jerry and Tim made a map of their home town on grid paper. Jerry's house is located at $(-3, 2)$. Tim's house is located 4 units east and 8 units south of Jerry's house on the map. Name the ordered pair that represents the location of Tim's house on the coordinate plane.

11. **MP.2 Reasoning** Angela wrote the expression $3(12k \div 4) - 10$. She says the value of k is 5. Evaluate the expression.

12. **Higher Order Thinking** The points $(2, 4)$ and $(-2, -4)$ are plotted on the coordinate plane using the equation $y = a \cdot x$. What is the value of a? Without using a table or graph, identify 3 other points a graph of this equation will pass through.

Common Core Assessment

13. Which equation represents the graph on the right?

Ⓐ $y = 4x$

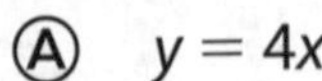

Ⓑ $y = \frac{x}{2}$

Ⓒ $y = 2x$

Ⓓ $y = x + 2$

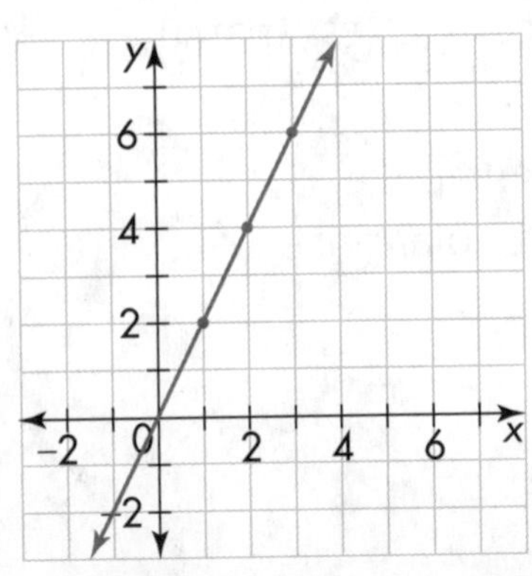

© Pearson Education, Inc. 6

Name ______________________________

Help | Practice Buddy | Tools | Games

Homework & Practice 5-4
Graph Equations

Another Look!

Graph the equation $y = x - 3$.

First make a table. Use at least 3 values for the independent variable, x, in this problem. Find the corresponding values for the dependent variable.

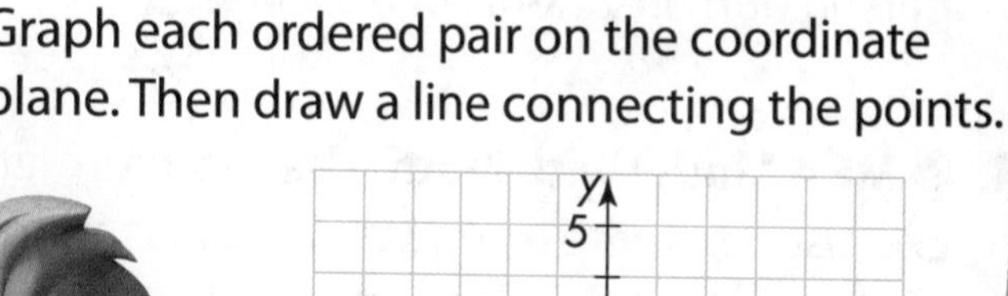

Graph each ordered pair on the coordinate plane. Then draw a line connecting the points.

$y = x - 3$	
x	y
3	0
4	1
5	2

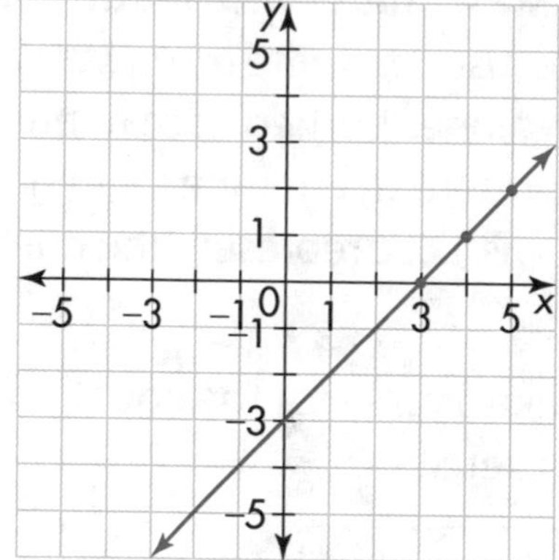

The graph of this equation is a straight line. So it is called a linear equation.

In **1** and **2**, complete the table and graph for each.

1. Bodie drew a triangle. The base of his triangle is $\frac{1}{2}$ the height of the triangle.

Let h = height.
Let b = base.
Graph $b = \frac{h}{2}$.

$b = \frac{h}{2}$	
h	b
1	
2	

2. Eva's mother will add \$5 to all other donations she collects for the school fund drive.

Let a = all other donations.
Let t = total donations.
Graph $t = a + 5$.

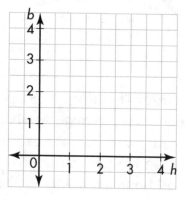

$t = a + 5$	
a	t
10	
20	

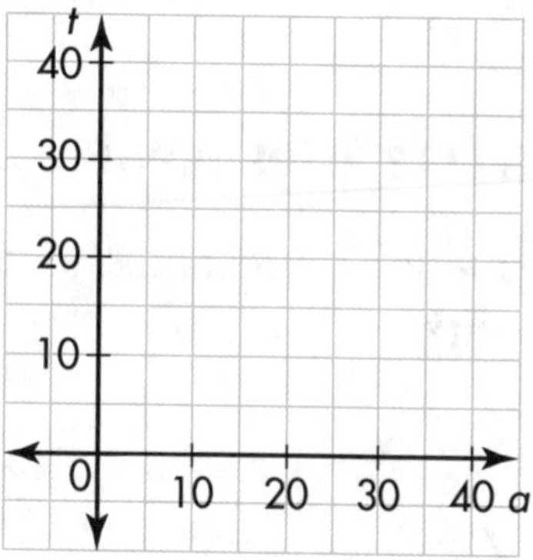

3. **Math and Science** People get energy from the food they eat. This energy is measured in calories. When you exercise, you use up or burn calories. The picture at the right shows about how many calories a 125-pound person burns each minute bowling. How many calories does a 125-pound person burn in 2 hours of bowling?

4. **MP.4 Model with Math** Use the information from Exercise 3 to write an equation representing the number of calories burned each minute while bowling. Let m represent the number of minutes a 125 pound person bowls. Let c represent the number of calories burned.

5. Make a table for the equation you wrote in Exercise 4.

m	c

6. Make a graph using the table data you recorded in Exercise 5.

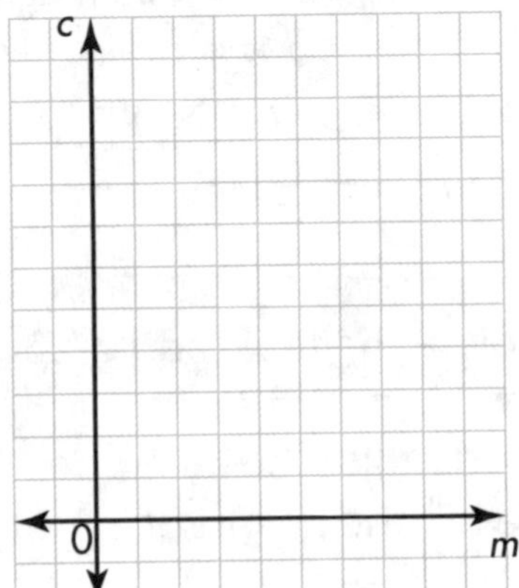

7. **Higher Order Thinking** A 185-pound person burns about 64.5 calories every 15 minutes while bowling. Write an equation to represent how many calories a 185-pound person burns every minute. Will a 185-pound person or a 125-pound person burn more calories in 1 hour of bowling? Explain.

Common Core Assessment

8. Which equation represents the table on the right?

x	y
0	0
2	5
4	10

Ⓐ $y = 2x$

Ⓑ $y = 2.5x$

Ⓒ $y = x + 3$

Ⓓ $y = x + 6$

© Pearson Education, Inc. 6

Name ____________________

Lesson 5-5

Continue to Graph Equations

I can ...

graph algebraic equations with more than one operation.

Content Standard 6.EE.C.9
Mathematical Practices MP.2, MP.3, MP.4, MP.8

Solve & Share

Greg registered to be in a walk-a-thon for his grandmother's charity. His grandmother said that she will contribute \$1 for his participation and \$2 for each mile he walks. Graph the equation $c = 2m + 1$ on a coordinate plane, where c is the contribution his grandmother will make and m is the number of miles Greg walks.

How can you generalize what you know about graphing one-step equations to graph a two-step equation?

$c = 2m + 1$	
m	c
1	
2	
3	

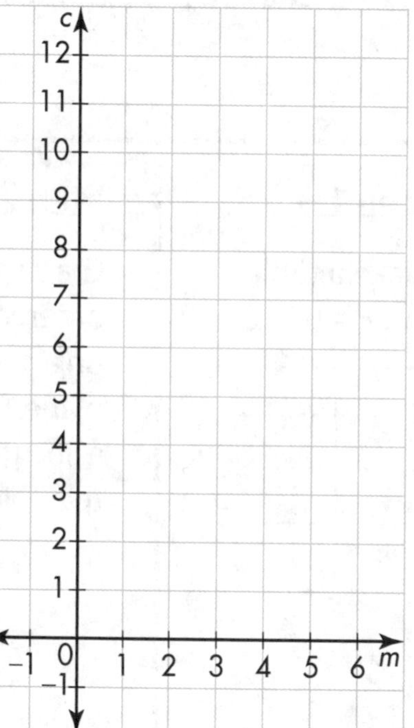

Look Back! **MP.4 Model with Math** Use your graph. How many miles must Greg walk if he wants to raise \$11 for the charity?

How Can You Graph a Linear Equation Involving Two Operations?

A

The temperature was 6°C and increased 2°C each hour for 6 hours.

Let x = the number of hours.

Let y = the temperature in °C.

The equation $y = 6 + 2x$ shows the relationship between the number of hours and the increase in temperature. After how many hours was the temperature 12°C?

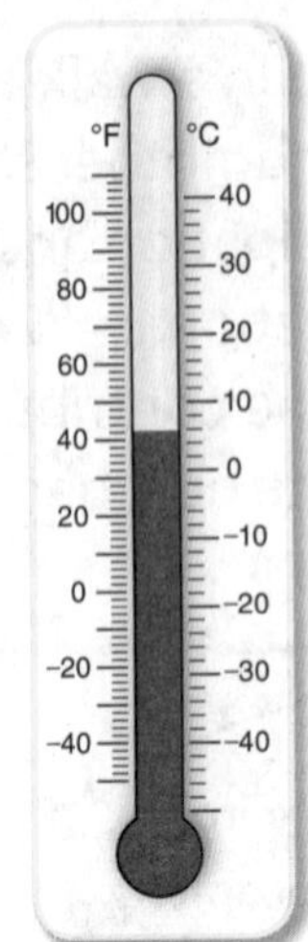

Temperature is the dependent variable. It depends on how much time goes by.

B

Step 1

Make a table for $y = 6 + 2x$.

x	y
0	6
2	10
4	14

C

Step 2

Graph each ordered pair on a coordinate plane. Draw a line through the points.

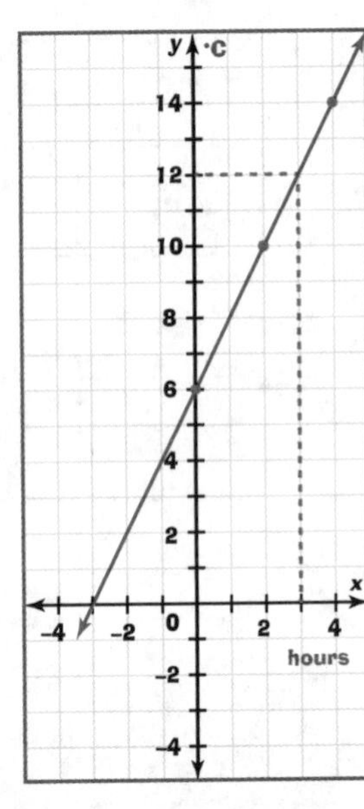

D

Step 3

Use the graph to find the point with a y-value of 12.

The dashed blue segments show that (3, 12) is a point on the line.

The temperature was 12°C after 3 hours.

Convince Me! **MP.2 Reasoning** Suppose it was noon when the temperature was 6°C. What time would it be when the temperature reached 12°C?

© Pearson Education, Inc. 6

Name

Practice Buddy Tools Assessment

Guided Practice*

Do You Understand?

1. MP.3 **Construct Arguments** Is the point (10, 26) on the line of the equation $y = 6 + 2x$? Explain.

2. MP.4 **Model with Math** Suppose the temperature is 6°C and decreases 0.5°C each hour. What equation could you use to graph this relationship if h is the number of hours and t is the temperature?

Do You Know How?

In **3**, complete the table and graph of $d = 5 + 5t$.

3. d = distance
t = time

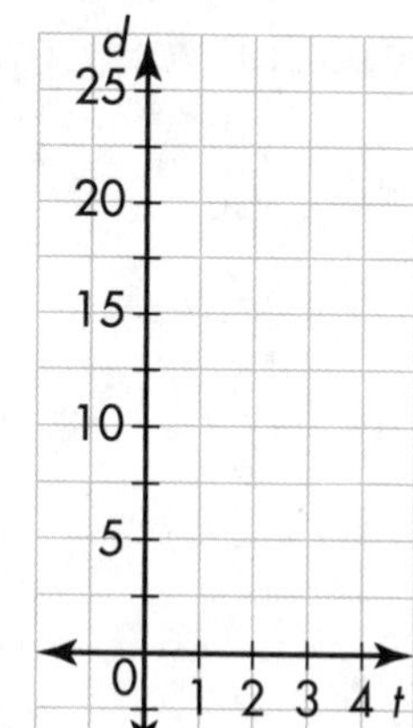

$d = 5 + 5t$	
t	d
0	
2	

Independent Practice

In **4**, write an equation, complete the table and then graph to solve the problem.

4. A puppy weighs 1 pound and gains $\frac{1}{2}$ pound each week. What does the puppy weigh after 4 weeks?

Let x = the number of weeks.
Let y = the weight of the puppy, in pounds.

x	y
0	
2	

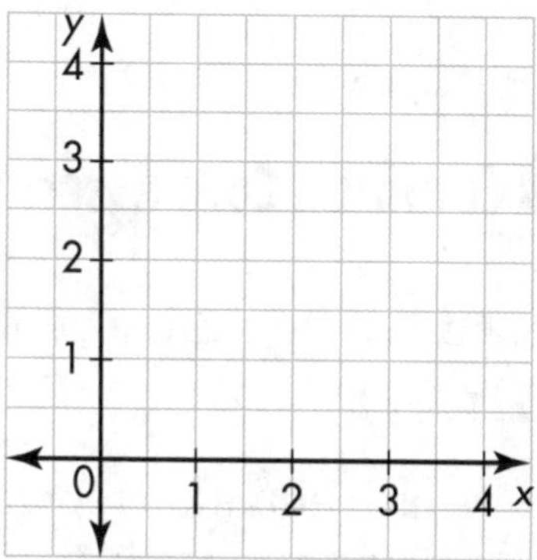

*For another example, see Set C on page 266.

Math Practices and Problem Solving

5. **MP.2 Reasoning** The Jackson family is planning a weekend vacation. They plan to rent a car from the ABC Car Rental Company. Let *m* represent the number of miles the family will drive. Let *c* represent cost for renting a car. Write an equation that shows what the cost for renting a car will be.

6. **MP.4 Model with Math** Make a table and a graph for the equation you wrote in Exercise 5.

m	*c*

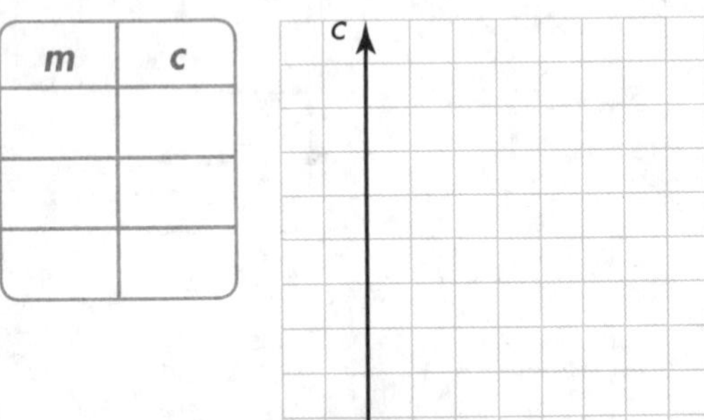

7. **Vocabulary** In which *quadrant* on the coordinate plane is the point $(-40, -100)$ located?

8. **Higher Order Thinking** Write an algebraic equation that matches the values shown in the table at the right. Explain how you solved the problem.

x	*y*
1	8
2	11
3	14
4	17

Common Core Assessment

9. Carl wrote the equations $y = 2x$ and $y = x + 2$.

Part A

Which equation represents the graph on the right?

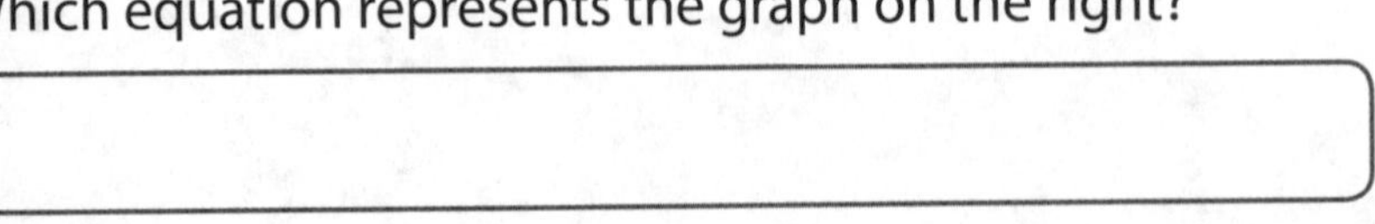

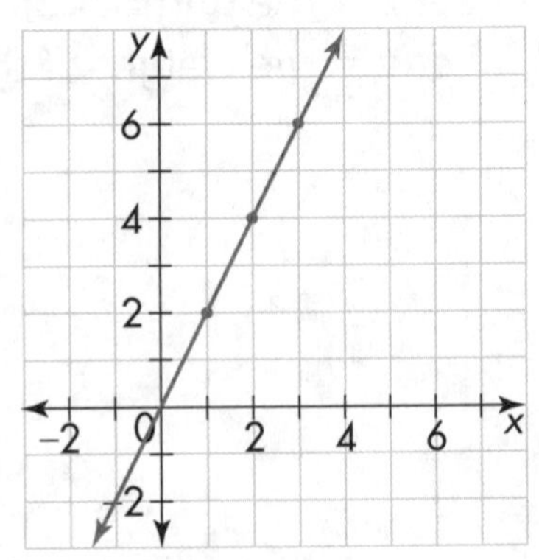

Part B

Identify a point on the line that is not shown on this graph.

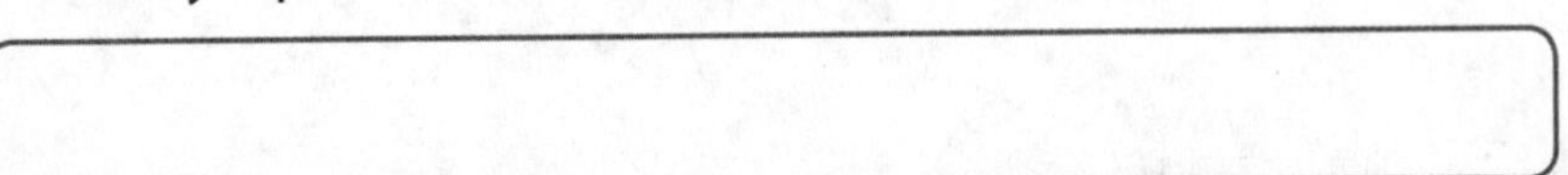

© Pearson Education, Inc. 6

Name ______________________

Help Practice Buddy Tools Games

Homework & Practice 5-5

Continue to Graph Equations

Another Look!

Graph the equation $y = 2x - 4$.

First make a table. Choose at least 3 values for the independent variable, x. Find the corresponding values for the dependent variable, y.

$y = 2x - 4$	
x	y
2	0
3	2
4	4

Use the same steps to graph an equation with more than one operation as you would to graph an equation with only one operation.

Graph each ordered pair on the coordinate plane. Then draw a line to connect the points.

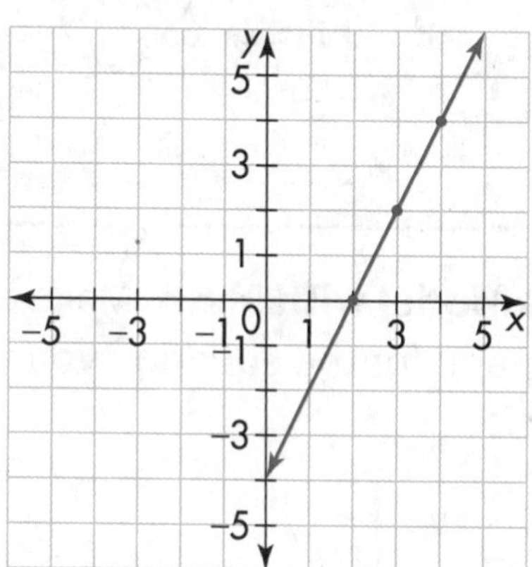

In **1**, write an equation, make a table and then graph to solve the problem.

1. An artist draws a collage of rectangles. The length of each rectangle is 2 units more than half its width. If the artist paints a rectangle that is 6 units wide, what is its length?

Let ℓ = the length of the rectangle.
Let w = the width of the rectangle.

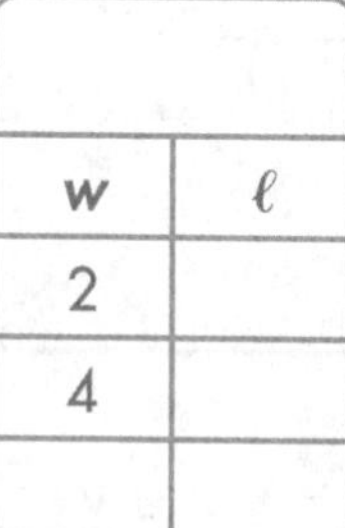

w	ℓ
2	
4	

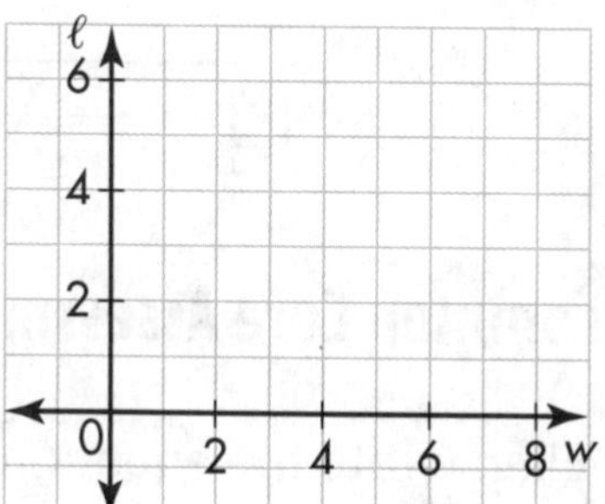

2. **Math and Science** Forensic anthropologists analyze skeletons to help solve crimes. They can use the length of a femur bone to estimate the height of a skeleton. The height of a skeleton is about 30 inches taller than twice the length of the femur bone. Let h represent the height of a skeleton. Let f represent the length of a femur bone. Write an equation to represent the height of a skeleton.

Adult femur bones are often between 15 and 20 inches long.

femur bone

3. **MP.4 Model with Math** Make a table and a graph for the equation you wrote in Exercise 3.

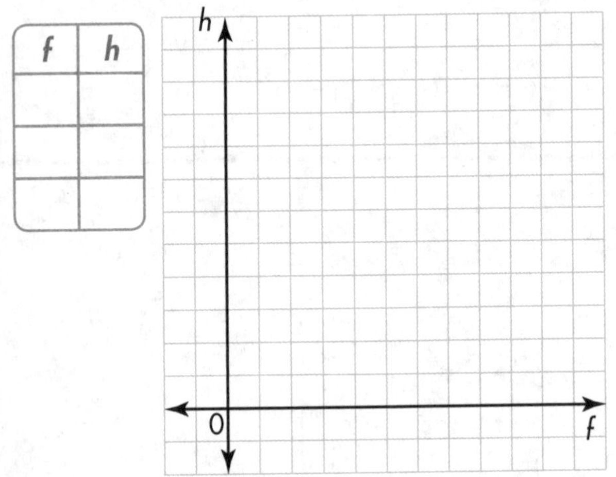

f	h

4. **Higher Order Thinking** Rhonda is 5 feet tall. About how long is her femur? Explain how you know.

Common Core Assessment

5. Ellen wrote the equations $y = 2\frac{1}{2} \cdot x + 1$ and $y = 2\frac{1}{2} \cdot x - 1$.

x	y
2	4
4	9
6	14

Part A

Which equation represents the table on the right?

Part B

If $x = 10$, what is the value of y that would be recorded in the table?

© Pearson Education, Inc. 6

Name ____________________

Math Practices and Problem Solving

Lesson 5-6

Model with Math

Solve & Share The sixth grade class is planning a skating party. What is the total cost if 20 students go to the party? 60 students? 100 students? *n* students?

I can ...
use math models to represent and solve problems.

Mathematical Practices MP.4, Also MP.1, MP.5, MP.6, MP.7
Content Standards 6.EE.C.9, 6.EE.B.5

Thinking Habits

Be a good thinker!
These questions can help you.

- How can I use math I know to help solve this problem?
- How can I use pictures, objects, or an equation to represent the problem?
- How can I use numbers, words, and symbols to solve the problem?

Look Back! **MP.4 Model with Math** How can you use equations to represent and solve this problem? How are each of the equations similar? How are they different?

How Can You Model with Math?

A

Hal has $45 in savings. He earns $25 per week for mowing his neighbor's lawn. Hal wants to buy a smartphone that costs $320. If he saves all of the money he earns, in how many weeks will Hal have enough money to buy the phone?

Hal's Earnings	
Week	**Total $ Earned**
1	$25
2	$50
3	$75
4	$100
5	$125
6	
7	

What do I need to do to solve this problem?

I need to find how long it will take Hal to earn enough money so that he can buy a smartphone.

B

How can I model this problem?

I can

- use a table, words, numbers, and symbols to represent Hal's total savings each week.
- write and solve equations.
- decide if my results make sense and improve my math model if needed.

C

Here's my thinking...

Hal has $45. He needs to earn $320 − $45 = $275.

I can write an equation to find the number of weeks it will take Hal to earn $275.

If w = the number of weeks Hal earns $25, then $25w = 275$.

$$\frac{25w}{25} = \frac{275}{25}$$
$$w = 11$$

Solve the equation by dividing both sides by 25.

It will take Hal 11 weeks to earn enough money to buy a smartphone.

My answer makes sense because $25(11) + 45 = 275 + 45 = 320$.

Convince Me!  **MP.4 Model with Math** Can you solve the problem another way? Explain.

© Pearson Education, Inc. 6

Name ________________________________

Practice Buddy | Tools | Assessment

Guided Practice*

MP.4 Model with Math

Joanne wants to buy a sweater that costs $72. She earns $12 a week and saves half of it. Joanne started the table below to record her savings after each week. How many weeks will it be until Joanne has enough money to buy the sweater?

1. What equation can you use to represent Joanne's savings each week? Complete the table for the first 4 weeks.

Joanne's Savings		
Week	Total Earned	Total Saved
1	12	6
2	24	
3		
4		

2. How can you use math you know to solve the problem? Explain.

You are modeling with math when you use a table or an equation to describe a problem.

Independent Practice

MP.4 Model with Math

Joe has $372 and spends $12 each week. He made a table to record how much money he has. How long will it be until he spends all of his money?

Joe's Spending	
Week	Dollars Remaining
0	372
1	360
2	348
3	336

3. What equation can you use to model the problem? Show how you can use numbers, words, and symbols to represent the given information.

4. How can you use math you know to solve the problem? Explain.

*For another example, see Set D on page 266.

Math Practices and Problem Solving

Common Core Performance Assessment

Soccer Cookie Sale
The soccer team is selling cookies to make money to travel to the state championship. They are hoping to raise $200. Each box of cookies sells for $3.50 and costs the team $1.50. There are 12 boxes of cookies in a carton. How many cartons do they need to sell to meet their goal?

To make sense of a problem, identify what you know and look for relationships.

5. **MP.1 Make Sense and Persevere** What do you know and what do you need to find out?

6. **MP.7 Use Structure** What relationship do you see between the profit made on 1 box of cookies and the number of boxes in a carton? Can this pattern help you solve the problem? Explain.

Number of Cartons Sold	Earnings
1	
2	
3	
4	
5	
6	

7. **MP.4 Model with Math** Explain how you can use a table, a graph, or an equation to represent the problem.

8. **MP.5 Use Appropriate Tools** Complete the table and the graph. Explain how they help you solve the problem.

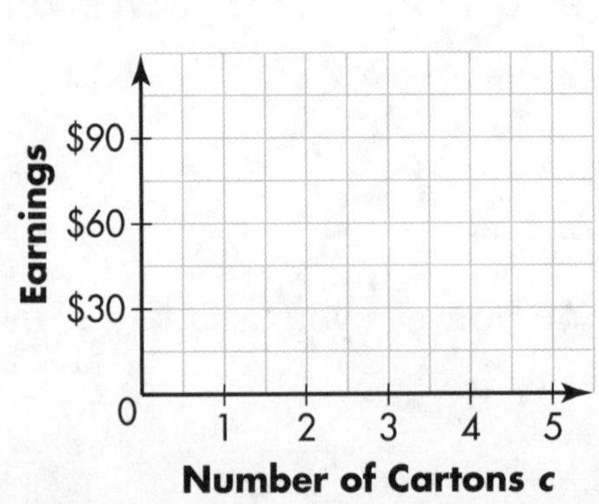

© Pearson Education, Inc. 6

Name ______________________

Homework & Practice 5-6
Model with Math

Another Look!

Dave is training for a 10-kilometer race. In the next two weeks, he plans to run 100 miles. He runs 8.4 miles every day. How long will it take Dave to run at least 100 miles?

Explain how you can model and solve this problem.

- I can use a table or graph to record Dave's daily mileage.
- I can write and solve equations.
- I can represent the problem in different ways to check that my math is correct.

Tables, graphs, and equations are three ways of modeling problems.

Model and solve the problem.

Make a table and write an equation.

Number of Days	Total Miles Run
1	8.4
2	16.8
4	33.6
8	67.2
12	100.8

Let d = the number of days and m = the total number of miles run: $m = 8.4d$.

Solve the equation:

$$100 = 8.4d$$
$$\frac{100}{8.4} = d$$
$$11.9 = d$$

Dave will have run at least 100 miles by the end of the 12th day.

MP.4 Model with Math

Helen's cookie recipe calls for 1.5 packages of chocolate chips for each batch of cookies. She has 1 package of chocolate chips. How many more packages will she need to buy to have enough for 16 batches?

1. How does the table represent the problem? Complete the table.

2. What equation can you write to represent the problem? Use the equation to solve the problem.

Helen's Cookies		
Batches	**Number of Packages**	**Number of Packages Helen Needs**
1	1.5	
2		
3		
4		

Common Core Performance Assessment

Trapezoidal Tables

A cafeteria has trapezoidal tables. There is enough space at one table to seat 5 students. The tables can also be arranged in a row, as shown below. For each table that is added to the row, 3 more students can be seated. How many tables can be assembled in a row to seat 53 students?

3. **MP.1 Make Sense and Persevere** How can you use a table to represent what you know? Complete the table below.

Number of Tables	1	2	3	4	5
Number of Students	5				

4. **MP.4 Model with Math** What equation can you write to represent the number of students, *S*, that can sit around *t* tables?

5. **MP.7 Use Structure** How can patterns help you solve the problem?

6. **MP.6 Be Precise** Use the equation you wrote to solve the problem. How can you check to make sure your calculations are accurate?

You persevere when you try different strategies until you find one that helps you solve the problem.

© Pearson Education, Inc. 6

Name ______________________________

Fluency Practice Activity

Find a partner. Get paper and a pencil. Each partner chooses a different color: light blue or dark blue.

Partner 1 and Partner 2 each point to a black number at the same time. Both partners multiply those numbers. Use mental math if you can.

If the answer is on your color, you get a tally mark. Work until one partner has twelve tally marks.

I can ...

multiply multi-digit whole numbers.

Content Standard 5.NBT.B.5

Partner 1

30

45

40

25

35

1,400	875	1,200
2,025	500	700
1,600	1,800	1,575
900	800	750
600	1,350	1,050
1,000	1,125	1,225

Partner 2

35

20

30

45

40

Tally Marks for Partner 1	Tally Marks for Partner 2

TOPIC 5

Vocabulary Review

Word List

- dependent variable
- independent variable
- linear equation
- ordered pair
- variable

Understand Vocabulary

Choose the best term from the box. Write it on the blank.

1. A quantity that can change or vary is a(n) ____________.

2. A(n) ____________ shows pairs of values (c, h) that are solutions of the equation $c = 2h$.

3. The graph of a(n) ____________ is a straight line.

4. In the equation $y = x + 9$, the variable x is the ____________.

Identify the *independent variable* and the *dependent variable* in each situation. Write **I** if the variable is independent. Write **D** if the variable is dependent.

5. The number of hours a canoe is rented, h, and the cost in dollars to rent the canoe, c h ______ c ______

6. The weight of a box in pounds, w, and the number of oranges in the box, n w ______ n ______

7. The length of a pool, l, and the time it takes to swim the length of the pool, t l ______ t ______

8. Look at each *ordered pair*. Write **Y** if the ordered pair (h, c) represents a point on the line $c = h - 2$. Write **N** if it does not.

(3, 5) ______ (7, 5) ______ (4, 5) ______

Use Vocabulary in Writing

9. Explain how to graph the equation $d = 5t$ on a coordinate plane. Use at least 5 words from the Word List in your explanation.

© Pearson Education, Inc. 6

Name ______________________________

TOPIC 5

Reteaching

Set A pages 227–232

The spirit squad is washing cars. The equation $m = 2c$ represents the money they make, m, for washing c cars. Identify the dependent variable and the independent variable and explain.

Step 1 Identify the dependent variable.

Ask: Which variable depends on the other?

The amount of money the spirit squad makes ***depends*** on the number of cars they wash. The dependent variable is m.

Step 2 Identify the independent variable.

Ask: Which variable causes the change?

The number of cars washed changes the amount of money made. The independent variable is c.

Remember to think about how the values of the variables affect each other.

Identify the dependent variable and the independent variable in each situation.

1. The distance traveled, d, and the speed, s

2. The calories, c, in a snack and the amount of the snack, a

3. The amount of money you have spent, s, and how much money you have left, m

Set B pages 233–238, 239–244

Find the rule that shows the pattern. Then use the rule to complete the table.

x	3	4	6	7	8
y	12	16	24	28	32

Step 1 Find the rule and write an equation.

Think: 12 is 3×4
16 is 4×4
24 is 6×4

Rule: The value of y is 4 times the value of x.

Equation: $y = 4x$

Step 2 Evaluate the equation for $x = 7$ and $x = 8$.

$y = 4(7) = 28$

$y = 4(8) = 32$

Remember to look for patterns between two related variables to find rules and write equations.

1. Write a rule and an equation to fit the pattern in the table. Then use the rule to complete the table.

x	0	2	10	16	20
y	0	1	5		

2. Use the equation to complete the table.

$y = 6x + 1$

x	1	2	3	4	5
y					

Set C pages 245–250, 251–256

Graph the equation $y = x + 1$.

Step 1 Make a table. Include at least 3 x-values.

x	y
0	1
2	3
3	4

Step 2 Graph each ordered pair on a coordinate plane. Then draw a line through the points. Extend the line to show more values that make the equation true.

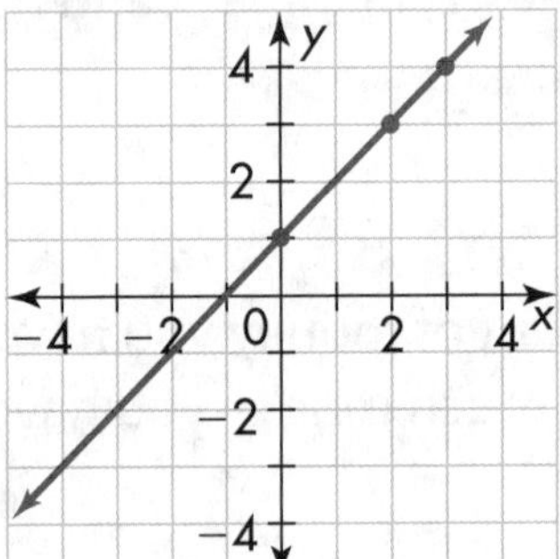

Remember that ordered pairs that make an equation true can be used to graph the equation.

Graph each equation on the coordinate plane.

1. $y = x + 3$ **2.** $y = 3x - 1$

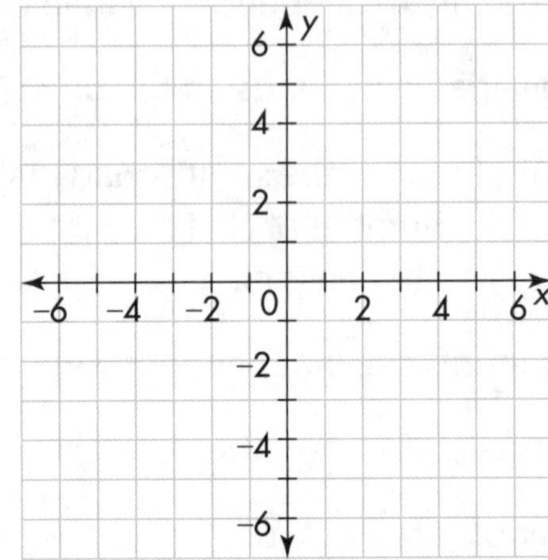

Set D pages 257–262

Think about these questions to help you **model with math**.

Thinking Habits

- How can I use math I know to help solve this problem?
- How can I use pictures, objects, or an equation to represent the problem?
- How can I use numbers, words, and symbols to solve the problem?

Remember that a table, equation, or graph can be used to show the relationship between the quantities in a problem.

Alex is making puppets for a show. He bought string for $125. It costs $18 for the remaining materials needed to make each puppet. What is the total cost to make 50 puppets?

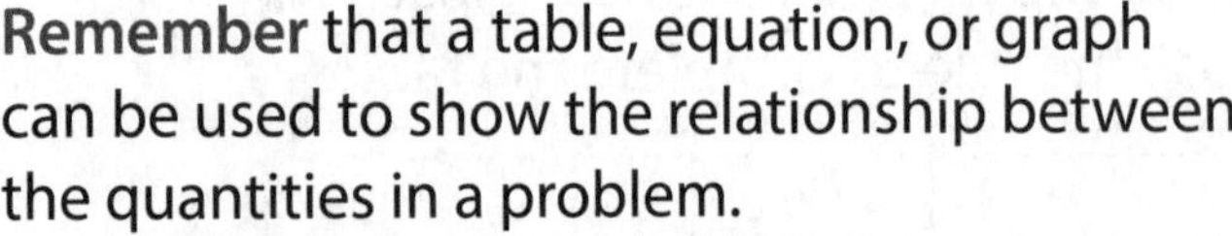

1. What equation can you write to represent the problem?

2. Explain how to use the equation to solve the problem. Then solve.

© Pearson Education, Inc. 6

Name ______________________________

1. The manager of a water park keeps track of the amount of money collected, m, and the number of tickets sold, t, each day. Which best describes the variables m and t?

Ⓐ The variable m is the independent variable because it depends on the number of tickets sold, t.

Ⓑ The variable t is the dependent variable because it depends on the amount of money collected, m, each day.

Ⓒ The variable t is the independent variable because it affects the amount of money collected, m, each day.

Ⓓ The variable m is independent of variable t, and variable t is independent of variable m.

2. For questions 2a–2e, choose Yes or No to indicate which of the equations can be used to describe the pattern in the table.

a	5	6	7	8	9
b	0	1	2	3	4

2a. $b + a = 5$ ○ Yes ○ No

2b. $b = a + 5$ ○ Yes ○ No

2c. $b = a - 5$ ○ Yes ○ No

2d. $a = b - 5$ ○ Yes ○ No

2e. $a - b = 5$ ○ Yes ○ No

3. Which equation can be used to describe the pattern in the table?

x	8	10	12	14	16
y	3	4	5	6	7

Ⓐ $y = 2x - 13$

Ⓑ $y = x \div 2$

Ⓒ $y = x \div 2 + 1$

Ⓓ $y = x \div 2 - 1$

4. April pays a dog-walking service \$30 each week to walk her dog. Complete the table to show how many dollars, d, April spends on dog-walking in w weeks.

w	1	2			5
d	30		90	120	

5. Rhonda graphed the equations listed below. For questions 5a–5d, choose Yes or No to indicate which of the equations include the point (1.25, 2.5).

5a. $y = 2x$ ○ Yes ○ No

5b. $y = x + 1$ ○ Yes ○ No

5c. $y = x + 1.25$ ○ Yes ○ No

5d. $y = 1\frac{1}{4} + x$ ○ Yes ○ No

6. Part A

Which of the following equations was used to graph the line shown?

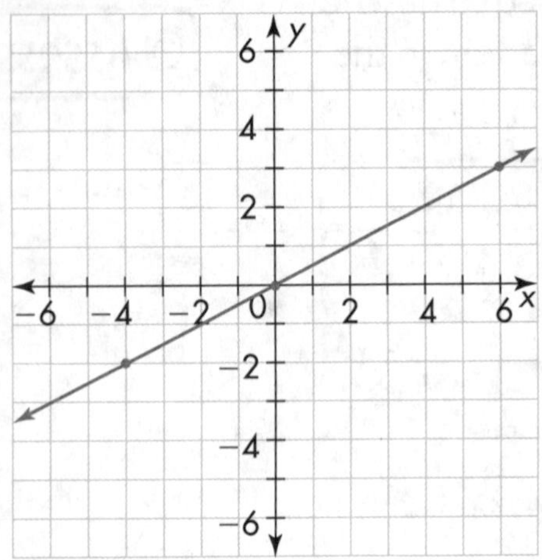

Ⓐ $y = 2x$

Ⓑ $y = x \div 2$

Ⓒ $y = x + 2$

Ⓓ $y = x - 2$

Part B

Write 2 ordered pairs for points that are on the graph of the line.

7. An amusement park charges $2 for admittance and $1.50 for each ride.

Part A

Write an equation to represent the total cost, *C*, based on the number of rides, *R*, you go on.

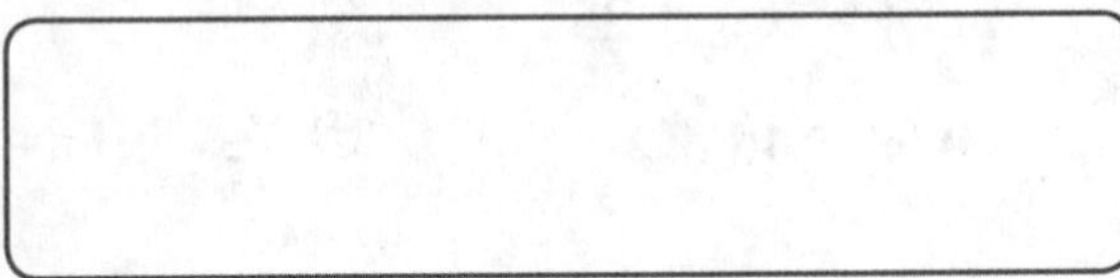

Part B

Complete the table for your equation.

R	4	7	10
C			

8. A softball team plans to buy ball caps for each player. Each cap costs the same amount. The team buys *c* caps for *d* dollars. Which variable is the independent variable and which is the dependent variable? Explain how you identified each variable.

9. Forensic scientists can use the length of the thighbone, or femur, to estimate the height of a skeleton. One equation that they may use is $h = 2.6f + 65$, where *f* is the length of the femur in centimeters and *h* is the height of the skeleton. Complete the table to find the height of a skeleton with a femur that is 37 cm long.

f	34	35	36	37
h	153.4	156	158.6	

© Pearson Education, Inc. 6

Name ______________________________

TOPIC 5

Performance Assessment

Life on a Ranch

Mr. Hart owns a small horse ranch. He also raises dogs on the ranch to help with the horses.

1. Mr. Hart wants to increase the number of horses and dogs on the ranch.

Part A

He would like to keep the same relationship between horses and dogs shown in the table when he increases their numbers.

Complete the table to show the relationship between the number of horses, *h*, and the numbers of dogs, *d*, on the ranch.

d	*h*
1	5
2	8
3	
4	
5	

Part B

Describe the relationship between the number of dogs and the number of horses on the ranch. Then write an equation that models this relationship.

Equation: ____________

2. Part A

Complete and label the graph to show the relationship between horses and dogs.

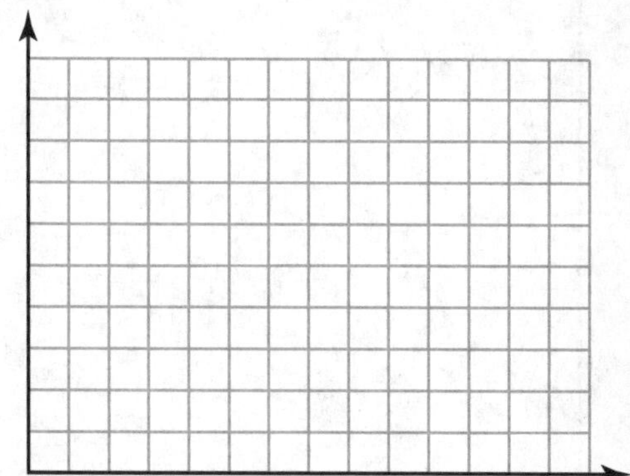

Part B

Mr. Hart would like to increase the number of dogs to 6. Extend the graph. What ordered pair represents the number of horses, *h*, when there are 6 dogs? How many horses will there be?

3. Mr. Hart estimated the cost of buying the horses and dogs.

- cost for each horse: $1,500
- cost for each dog: $500
- one-time fee for transporting horses: $2,000
- one-time fee for transporting dogs: $500

Write an equation that represents the cost to buy a horse. Write another equation that shows the cost to buy a dog. Identify the variables in the equations.

4. Mr. Hart has a total budget of $30,000 to buy horses and dogs for the ranch. How many horses and dogs can Mr. Hart buy for his ranch if the relationship stays the same? Explain your reasoning. Show your work.

© Pearson Education, Inc. 6

TOPIC 6

Fluently Divide Whole Numbers

Essential Question: How are quotients of multi-digit numbers found?

We use water to grow and process food, to produce energy, and to make all sorts of products, from bricks to cell phones.

As populations grow, so does the need for water.

How much water does the average person really use per day? Let's find out. Here's a project on water use. You will use division in the calculations needed for your report.

Math and Science Project: Water Consumption

Do Research Use the Internet or other sources to learn more about water consumption. This includes daily actions, food, objects, and technology that require water.

Journal: Write a Report Include what you found. Also in your report:

- Include how much water one person uses per day. Can one person use more than 1 gallon per hour?
- How much water does a family of four use per day? Per hour? Per minute?
- How does population affect water consumption?

Name ______________________________

Review What You Know

Vocabulary

Choose the best term from the box. Write it on the blank.

- compatible numbers
- dividend
- divisor
- estimate
- quotient

1. To find an approximate answer or solution is to __________.

2. The number being divided by another number is the __________.

3. ____________________ are numbers that are easy to compute mentally.

4. In the equation $20 \div 4 = 5$, the number 5 is the __________.

Division

Find each quotient.

5. $4\overline{)432}$

6. $691 \div 7$

7. $2\overline{)374}$

8. $872 \div 8$

9. $3\overline{)2{,}184}$

10. $1{,}135 \div 6$

Evaluating Expressions

Evaluate each expression for $x = 5$ and $x = 9$.

11. $7x$

12. $50 - 5x$

13. $12x \div 3$

14. $135 \div x$

15. $6x + 15 \div 3$

16. $5 + 4x \div 2$

Using Estimation

17. A small theater has 154 seats in 11 rows. How can Sam estimate the number of seats in each row?

© Pearson Education, Inc. 6

Name ___________________________________

Lesson 6-1

Estimate Quotients Involving Whole Numbers

I can ...
estimate quotients.

Content Standard 6.NS.B.2
Mathematical Practices MP.2, MP.3, MP.8

Solve & Share

Your school needs to buy chairs for the cafeteria. The budget for the chairs is $1,489. About how many of these chairs can your school buy for the cafeteria? ***Solve this problem any way you choose.***

Use reasoning and compatible numbers that you can divide mentally.

Look Back! **MP.8 Generalize** How can you check to see if your estimate is reasonable?

How Can You Use Compatible Numbers to Estimate Quotients?

A

A theater sold 3,084 tickets for a show. The seating in the theater is divided into sections. About how many sections will be used to seat all the ticket holders?

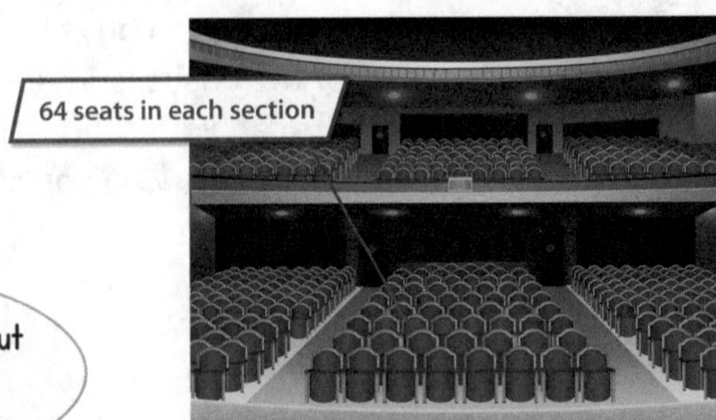

64 seats in each section

The question asks "about how many." So you can estimate.

B

Step 1

You know the number of seats in each section and the total number of tickets sold.

Divide to find the number of sections needed to seat all the ticket holders.

Find compatible numbers for 3,084 and 64.

Think...30 can be divided easily by 6.

3,000 and 60 are close to 3,084 and 64.

3,000 and 60 are compatible numbers.

C

Step 2

Divide.

$3{,}000 \div 60 = 50.$

About 50 sections will be used to seat all the ticket holders.

You can use multiplication to check your answer.

Check for reasonableness.

$50 \times 60 = 3{,}000$

Convince Me! **MP.2 Reasoning** Suppose each section of the theater has 96 seats. About how many sections would be used to seat all the ticket holders? Use estimation to explain.

© Pearson Education, Inc. 6

Name ______________________________

Guided Practice*

Do You Understand?

1. **MP.2 Reasoning** To estimate 2,265 ÷ 74, would division with the compatible numbers 2,400 and 80 give a reasonable estimate? Is there another pair of compatible numbers you can use for a good estimate? Explain both answers.

2. **MP.3 Critique Reasoning** Cesar and his crew have 765 bottles of water to put into cases. They put 24 bottles into each case. Cesar thinks they will need about 40 cases. Is this the best estimate? Why or why not?

Do You Know How?

In **3–8**, estimate using compatible numbers.

3. 2,863 ÷ 43 **4.** 3,277 ÷ 12

5. 468 ÷ 61 **6.** 146 ÷ 9

7. 6,927 ÷ 73 **8.** 1,218 ÷ 38

Independent Practice

In **9–20**, estimate using compatible numbers.

9. 4,112 ÷ 83 **10.** 2,924 ÷ 53 **11.** 48,958 ÷ 74

12. 2,243 ÷ 18 **13.** 91,002 ÷ 61 **14.** 7,618 ÷ 52

15. 5,410 ÷ 59 **16.** 3,551 ÷ 6 **17.** 2,728 ÷ 66

18. 29,089 ÷ 8 **19.** 276 ÷ 38 **20.** 4,605 ÷ 9

*For another example, see Set A on page 311.

Math Practices and Problem Solving

21. A high school volleyball team has made it to the state tournament championship game. There are 965 students who want to go, and 53 students can fit on each bus. About how many buses are needed?

22. The school auditorium has 642 seats. Twenty-three of these are reserved for special guests. Adam used the equation $23 + t = 642$ to find the number of tickets, t, that could be sold to the school play. How many tickets was it possible to sell?

23. Leon bought 6 DVDs on sale for $78. At the regular price he would have spent $108. How much did Leon save per DVD at the sale price?

24. **MP.8 Generalize** Summer needs to estimate the quotient $8,173 \div 92$. Explain how she can use compatible numbers to make a reasonable estimate.

25. **MP.2 Reasoning** The money Percy saved is about how many times as great as the money Bethany has saved?

26. **MP.2 Reasoning** The money Emily saved is about how many times as great as the money Percy has saved?

Fifth-Grade Trip to Washington, D.C.

Student	Amount Saved
Percy	$1,256
Emily	$2,345
Bethany	$401

27. At a department store, a box of 12 water filters costs $55.50. Estimate how much each filter costs.

28. **Higher Order Thinking** There are x cages at the zoo for 2,878 birds. Each cage can house between 140 and 160 birds. What would be a reasonable value for x? Justify your reasoning.

Common Core Assessment

29. Which of the following are reasonable estimates for $4,325 \div 56$?

- ☐ $5,000 \div 50 = 100$
- ☐ $4,200 \div 60 = 70$
- ☐ $4,000 \div 50 = 80$
- ☐ $3,600 \div 60 = 60$

30. Which of the following are **NOT** reasonable estimates for $2,432 \div 47$?

- ☐ $50 = 2,500 \div 50$
- ☐ $30 = 1,500 \div 50$
- ☐ $3,000 \div 50 = 60$
- ☐ $2,400 \div 50 = 48$

© Pearson Education, Inc. 6

Name ______________________

Help Practice Buddy Tools Games

Homework & Practice 6-1

Estimate Quotients Involving Whole Numbers

Another Look!

There are 32 buses in which the same number of people will ride to go to a technology convention. There are 1,759 people signed up to go. About how many people will ride on each bus?

Step 1

Find compatible numbers for 1,759 and 32.

32 is close to 30.

1,759 is close to 1,800.

1,800 and 30 are compatible numbers.

Step 2

Rewrite the division with the compatible numbers and then divide.

$1{,}800 \div 30 = 60$

Think: 18 can be easily divided by 3.

Step 3

Use the same compatible numbers to check for reasonableness:

$60 \times \mathbf{30} = \mathbf{1{,}800}$

So, a good estimate of $1{,}759 \div 32$ is 60.

About 60 people will ride on each bus.

In **1–15**, estimate using compatible numbers.

1. $1{,}832 \div 22$
$1{,}800 \div$ ☐
☐

2. $552 \div 36$
$600 \div$ ☐
☐

3. $9{,}002 \div 28$
☐ $\div$ ☐
☐

4. $2{,}983 \div 25$

5. $5{,}491 \div 77$

6. $29{,}589 \div 15$

7. $4{,}622 \div 9$

8. $1{,}447 \div 48$

9. $5{,}564 \div 91$

10. $488 \div 12$

11. $5{,}879 \div 46$

12. $89{,}078 \div 93$

13. $3{,}579 \div 89$

14. $63{,}204 \div 8$

15. $875 \div 9$

16. A school has 1,030 students. There are 42 teachers. About how times as great as the number of teachers is the number of students?

17. In the 16 years that a college has had a women's basketball team, the athletic department sold 3,140 season tickets. What is a reasonable estimate of how many season tickets they sold each year? Write the compatible numbers you used for your estimate.

18. **MP.2 Reasoning** The number of bikes rented from Shop B is about how many times as great as the number from Shop D?

19. **MP.2 Reasoning** The number of bikes rented from Shop C is about how many times as great as the number from Shop A?

Bicycles rented (May)	
Rental Shop	**Bikes rented**
Shop A	68
Shop B	785
Shop C	1,410
Shop D	191

20. **MP.3 Critique Reasoning** Kyle has 3,104 stamps in his collection. He is placing his stamps in an album with pages that each hold 42 stamps. He estimates he will need about 80 pages. Is his estimate reasonable? Why or why not?

21. **Algebra** Delilah is making batches of muffins for a bake sale. Each batch has 12 muffins. Write an inequality to represent the number of batches, *b*, she needs to make in order to have at least 130 muffins for the bake sale.

22. A-Z **Vocabulary** Find the value for *x* that makes the equation true: $x \div 50 = 300$. Then tell if the variable, *x*, is the divisor, dividend, or quotient in the equation.

Common Core Assessment

23. Which of the following are reasonable estimates for $4{,}739 \div 92$?

- ☐ $4{,}800 \div 100 = 48$
- ☐ $4{,}500 \div 90 = 50$
- ☐ $4{,}800 \div 80 = 60$
- ☐ $4{,}400 \div 110 = 40$

24. Which of the following are **NOT** reasonable estimates for $4{,}108 \div 63$?

- ☐ $3{,}800 \div 50 = 76$
- ☐ $4{,}500 \div 50 = 90$
- ☐ $41 = 4{,}100 \div 100$
- ☐ $70 = 4{,}200 \div 60$

© Pearson Education, Inc. 6

Name ____________________

Lesson 6-2
Divide Whole Numbers

I can ...
find the quotient of two whole numbers and solve division problems.

Content Standard 6.NS.B.2
Mathematical Practices MP.2, MP.3, MP.6, MP.7, MP.8

Solve & Share An office-supply warehouse is going to ship 1,715 staplers. How many boxes are needed? How many boxes will be filled? ***Solve this problem any way you choose.***

You can use reasoning to decide what operation can be used to find the number of boxes that each have 16 staplers.

Look Back! **MP.6 Be Precise** How many more staplers could be put in the partly filled box so that each box has 16 staplers? Explain your answer.

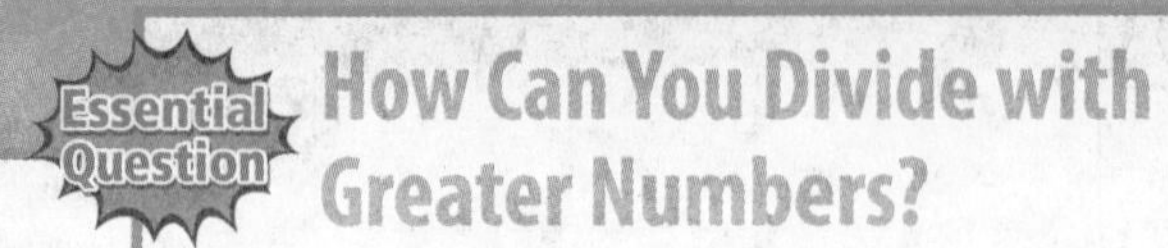

How Can You Divide with Greater Numbers?

A

A tortilla bakery makes 863 packages of tortillas to sell to restaurants. Each restaurant receives the same number of packages as a complete order. How many restaurants can receive a complete order?

Use place-value structure to divide 863 by 18.

B

Use compatible numbers to estimate 863 ÷ 18.
900 ÷ 20 = 45

The quotient is about 45, so the first digit of the quotient will be in the tens place.
Start by dividing the tens.

$$\begin{array}{r} 4 \\ 18\overline{)863} \\ -72 \\ \hline 14 \end{array}$$

Step 1 Divide
Step 2 Multiply
Step 3 Subtract
Step 4 Compare

C

Next, bring down the ones. Repeat the steps as needed to complete the division.

$$\begin{array}{r} 47 \text{ R17} \\ 18\overline{)863} \\ -72 \\ \hline 143 \\ -126 \\ \hline 17 \end{array}$$

The answer is reasonable since 47 is close to the estimate, 45.

The bakery can sell complete orders to 47 restaurants.

Convince Me! **MP.3 Construct Arguments** How can you check that the quotient above is correct? Explain your answer.

© Pearson Education, Inc. 6

Name

Practice Buddy Tools Assessment

Guided Practice*

Do You Understand?

1. MP.2 Reasoning Theo needs to put 2,405 toy cars into bins with 45 cars in each bin. He divided and got 53 R 20. How many bins will he fill?

2. MP.7 Use Structure Explain how you can decide where to place the first digit of the quotient for 6,139 ÷ 153.

Do You Know How?

In **3** and **4**, divide. Write the missing numbers.

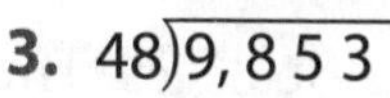

3. 48)9,853

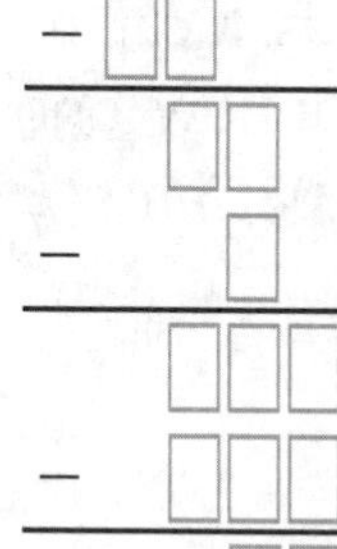

4. 36)2,789

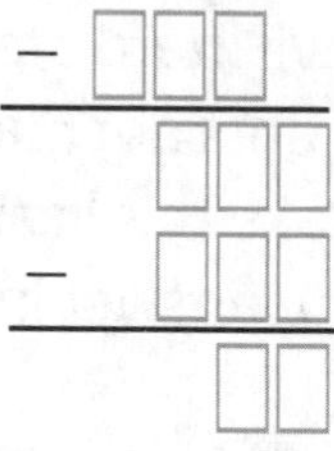

Independent Practice

In **5–7**, divide. Write the missing numbers.

5. 62)5,841

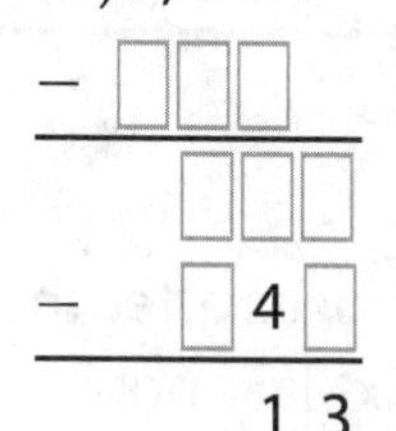

6. 84)80,304

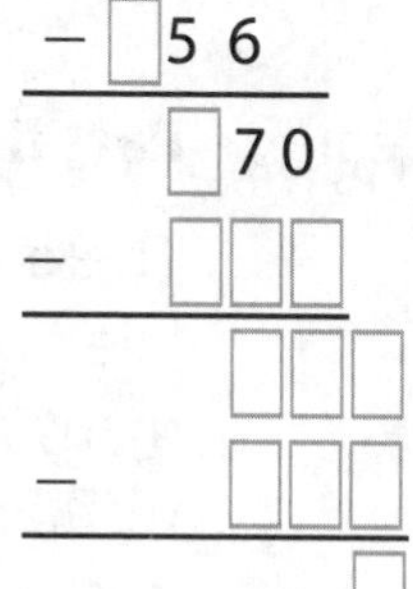

7. 55)6,784

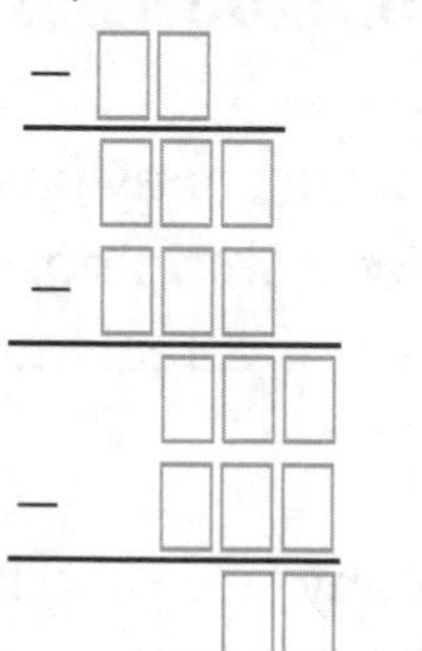

In **8–13**, divide. Check each answer by multiplying.

8. 21)2,593

9. 19)6,927

10. 8)15,284

11. 9)2,483

12. 12)9,519

13. 38)968

*For another example, see Set B on page 311.

Math Practices and Problem Solving

14. **MP.6 Be Precise** Julita bought lunch for herself and a friend. She bought two sandwiches that cost $3.50 each, two bottles of juice that were $1.75 each, and a fruit salad for $4.95. The tax was $1.35. She paid with a $20 bill. How much change did she get?

15. Henri needs to find the quotient 6,273 ÷ 82. Explain how he can use compatible numbers to make a reasonable estimate.

16. **Number Sense** Ants are one of the Thorny Devil lizard's favorite foods. It can eat up to 45 ants per minute. About how long would it take this lizard to eat 1,080 ants? Express your answer in minutes.

17. What compatible numbers can you use to estimate 4,134 ÷ 67?

18. **Higher Order Thinking** The area of a park is 1,176 square miles. If the park is divided into 58 equal parts, each containing the same whole number of square miles, how large would each part be? How large would the remaining area be?

Common Core Assessment

19. A cereal company has 1,364 boxes of cereal to pack for shipping. Workers can pack 24 boxes of cereal into one shipping box.

Part A

How many shipping boxes can be completely filled? Show how you know.

Part B

There are left over cereal boxes after the filled boxes are shipped. Explain how many more cereal boxes are needed so the workers can fill another shipping box.

© Pearson Education, Inc. 6

Name ______________________

 Help  Practice Buddy  Tools  Games

Homework & Practice 6-2

Divide Whole Numbers

Another Look!

Maggie's Orange Grove sells orange gift cartons. They have 3,987 oranges to pack into gift cartons. If 22 oranges can fit into each gift carton, how many cartons can they fill?

Use compatible numbers to estimate 3,987 ÷ 22. You can use 4,000 ÷ 20 = 200.

Use an estimate to place the first digit in the quotient.

```
     2
22)3,987
  − 44     ← The estimate is too high because 44 > 39.
```

Try 1.

```
     1
22)3,987
  − 22
```

Complete the division.

```
     181 R5
22)3,987
  − 22
    178
  − 176
     27
   − 22
      5
```

They can fill 181 cartons and have 5 oranges left over.

181 is close to the estimate.

I know the estimate is too high, so the answer is reasonable.

In **1–3**, divide. Write the missing numbers.

1. 112 R☐ — 39)4,372
2. ☐☐☐ R3 — 24)6,315
3. ☐☐☐ R☐ — 26)23,901

In **4–15**, divide. Check each answer by multiplying.

4. 13)1,722
5. 44)6,668
6. 48)4,896
7. 65)99,521
8. 99)8,624
9. 17)1,727
10. 51)6,001
11. 87)1,920
12. 8)64,218
13. 7)1,222
14. 34)968
15. 77)7,098

16. **MP.8 Generalize** Roberto needs to estimate the quotient $59{,}563 \div 57$. Explain how he can use compatible numbers to make a reasonable estimate.

17. **MP.3 Construct Arguments** April has 905 baseball cards. She wants to organize them on pages that hold 18 cards each. She has 50 pages. Does April have enough pages to organize all her cards? Explain.

18. **Higher Order Thinking** The school student council sponsored a Switch Week where students were able to switch classes every 20 minutes. The students are in school for 7 hours each day, Monday through Friday. If a student switched as often as possible, how many times in all did that student switch classes?

19. **MP.6 Be Precise** Use the coordinate plane below to find the distance between the points $(-6, 4)$ and $(3, 4)$.

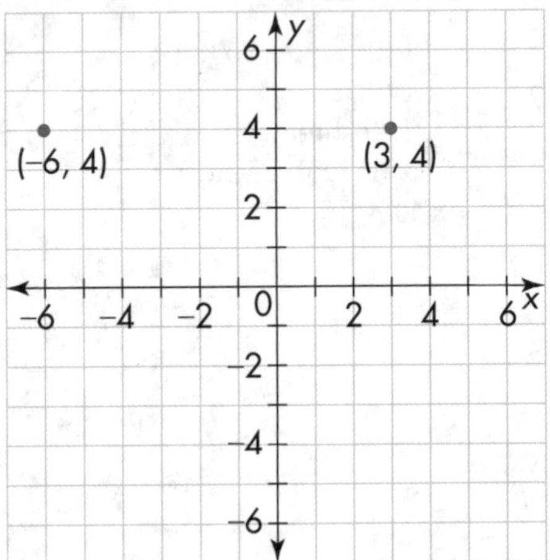

Common Core Assessment

20. A pickup truck can haul 75 plants each trip from a nursery to a garden center. There are 1,440 plants to be transported.

Part A

How many trips with a full load of plants can the pickup make? Show how you know.

Part B

How many more plants does the nursery need to fill another truck? Explain your reasoning.

© Pearson Education, Inc. 6

Name ______________________________

Lesson 6-3
Continue to Divide Whole Numbers

I can ...
fluently divide greater whole numbers.

Content Standard 6.NS.B.2
Mathematical Practices MP.1, MP.2, MP.3, MP.4, MP.6, MP.7, MP.8

Solve & Share

Last year, 24 students volunteered at the City Science Museum. Each student worked the same number of hours. If the students worked a total of 1,164 hours, did each student work at least 48 hours? ***Solve this problem any way you choose.***

Generalize and estimate before you solve the problem. Then use the estimate to check the reasonableness of your solution.

Look Back! **MP.2 Reasoning** How many total full hours would each of the 24 students need to work in order for the group to work at least 1,338 total hours? Explain your answer.

How Can You Solve Problems Involving Division of Greater Numbers?

A

A rock band records 8,944 minutes of music in 16 days. They record the same number of minutes of music each day. How many minutes of music does the band record in one day?

Make sense of the problem and decide which operation you can use to solve it.

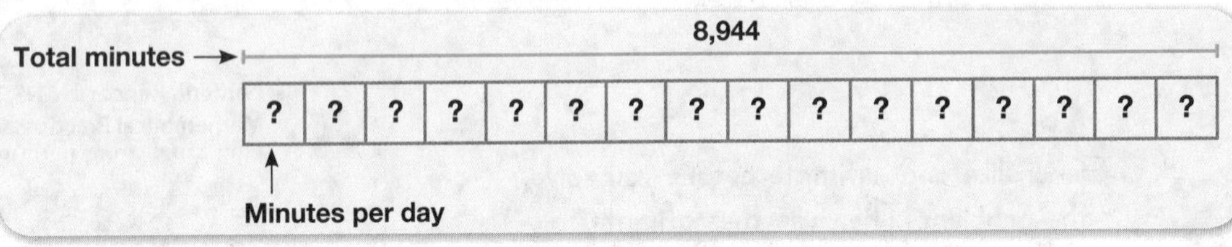

B

Step 1

Use compatible numbers to estimate.

8,944 ÷ 16 is close to 9,000 ÷ 15.

9,000 ÷ 15 = 600, so the quotient should be close to 600.

Because the estimated quotient is 600, the first digit of the quotient will be in the hundreds place.

C

Step 2

Divide.

$$\begin{array}{r} 559 \\ 16\overline{)8,944} \\ -80 \\ \hline 94 \\ -80 \\ \hline 144 \\ -144 \\ \hline 0 \end{array}$$

559 is close to the estimate, so it is reasonable.

The band recorded 559 minutes of music each day.

Convince Me! © **MP.7 Use Structure** A jazz group recorded 8,232 minutes of music in 21 days. They recorded the same number of minutes of music each day. Estimate the number of minutes of music recorded each day. Then find the exact number of minutes the band recorded each day.

© Pearson Education, Inc. 6

Name ___________________________

Practice Buddy   Tools   Assessment

Guided Practice*

Do You Understand?

1. MP.8 Generalize When finding the quotient 4,676 ÷ 64, in which place would you begin dividing? How do you know?

2. MP.2 Reasoning Another rock band recorded 8,944 minutes of music in just 12 days. On average, how many minutes did the band spend recording each day?

Do You Know How?

In **3–8**, estimate first. Then find the quotient.

3. $22\overline{)3,192}$ 4. $58\overline{)6,355}$ 5. $17\overline{)62,345}$

6. $62\overline{)5,804}$ 7. $8\overline{)9,137}$ 8. $48\overline{)3,952}$

Independent Practice

In **9–23**, estimate first. Then find the quotient.

9. 4,392 ÷ 33

10. 9,257 ÷ 82

11. 54,308 ÷ 63

12. 7,687 ÷ 74

13. 7,376 ÷ 26

14. 15,845 ÷ 82

15. 3,754 ÷ 63

16. 8,741 ÷ 22

17. 1,225 ÷ 12

18. 3,826 ÷ 8

19. 9,512 ÷ 54

20. 18,411 ÷ 9

21. 3,001 ÷ 64

22. 8,900 ÷ 87

23. 97,658 ÷ 19

*For another example, see Set B on page 311.

Math Practices and Problem Solving

In **24** and **25**, use the data table.

24. **MP.6 Be Precise** The total student entry fees paid for a chess tournament were $3,312. How many students participated?

25. There are about ten times as many students as adults registered for the tournament. About how many adults are registered?

DATA

Chess Tournament	
Student entry fee	$16
Adult entry fee	$18
Reserve a chess board	$12

26. **MP.4 Model with Math** Tabitha's class is making a flash card for each of the 1,422 words for a spelling bee. The work of making the flash cards is divided equally among 6 teams. How many flash cards will each team need to make?

1,422 flash cards

?	?	?	?	?	?

Flash cards each team makes

27. **Higher Order Thinking** Darci wants to buy a computer that costs $1,308. She has saved $350 already and works at a grocery store where she earns $11 an hour. How many hours will she have to work to earn enough money to purchase the computer?

Common Core Assessment

28. Carly and her family drove from Colby, Kansas, to Boston, Massachusetts. The total distance was 1,808 miles, which they completed in 16 equal segments.

Part A

What was the average distance driven for each segment of the trip? Show how you know.

Part B

Explain how you know that your answer is reasonable.

© Pearson Education, Inc. 6

Name ____________________

Homework & Practice 6-3

Continue to Divide Whole Numbers

Another Look!

Find 8,037 ÷ 77.

You can use estimation to check that a quotient is reasonable.

Step 1

Use compatible numbers to estimate.

8,037 ÷ 77
↓ ↓
8,000 ÷ 80 = 100

The quotient should be close to 100.

Step 2

Now, find the quotient.

$$\begin{array}{r} 104 \text{ R}29 \\ 77\overline{)8{,}037} \\ -\underline{77} \\ 33 \\ -\underline{0} \\ 337 \\ -\underline{308} \\ 29 \end{array}$$

Step 3

104 R29 is close to the estimate, 100, so the answer is reasonable.

In **1–15**, estimate first. Then find the quotient.

1. $78\overline{)3{,}796}$

2. $51\overline{)2{,}588}$

3. $38\overline{)22{,}952}$

4. $37\overline{)7{,}492}$

5. $46\overline{)6{,}725}$

6. $62\overline{)9{,}911}$

7. 869 ÷ 3

8. 7,727 ÷ 41

9. 8,905 ÷ 33

10. 6,025 ÷ 18

11. 4,900 ÷ 88

12. 90,503 ÷ 9

13. 608 ÷ 30

14. 8,855 ÷ 6

15. 49,790 ÷ 54

In **16** and **17**, use the data table.

16. **MP.6 Be Precise** It took the Riger family 6 hours to travel from San Francisco to New York. How many kilometers did they travel per hour?

17. **MP.3 Critique Reasoning** Chris said that to get from New Delhi to Tokyo in 8 hours, the plane would need to travel 650 kilometers per hour. Do you agree? Why or why not?

DATA

Distances by Plane

Route	Distance
San Francisco to New York	4,140 km
New York to Rome	6,907 km
Rome to New Delhi	5,929 km
New Delhi to Tokyo	5,857 km

18. A baseball team has hit a total of 10,009 home runs over the past 72 seasons. How many home runs has the team averaged per season?

19. **Higher Order Thinking** Zak wants to buy a used car that costs $2,625. He works at a bank where he earns $15 an hour. He has already saved $880 for the car. How many hours will he have to work to earn enough money to purchase the car?

20. **Algebra** Evaluate the following expression for $m = 2$. $5m + 2(m + 8) + 3$

21. There are 12 inches in 1 foot. How many inches are there in 120 feet?

Common Core Assessment

22. Percy and his family drove from Durham, North Carolina, to Omaha, Nebraska. The total distance was 1,235 miles, which they completed in 13 equal segments.

Part A

What is the average number of miles they drove for each segment of the trip? Show how you know.

Part B

Explain how you know your answer is reasonable.

© Pearson Education, Inc. 6

Name ____

Solve

Lesson 6-4

Evaluate Expressions

I can ...
substitute given numbers in a formula to find a missing value.

Content Standards 6.EE.A.2c, 6.NS.B.2
Mathematical Practices MP.3, MP.4, MP.7

Solve & Share

Mr. Brown wants to use the formula $s = \frac{d}{t}$ to find his average speed, s, on a business trip. He knows that d is the distance he drove and t is the number of hours he drove. If he drove 504 miles in 8 hours, what was his average speed? ***Solve this problem any way you choose.***

When you substitute values to evaluate expressions and solve formulas, you are using structure.

Look Back! **MP.7 Use Structure** If you know the distance driven and the number of hours needed to drive that distance, how can you use the formula $s = \frac{d}{t}$ to help you find the average speed?

How Can You Evaluate Formulas that Involve Division?

A

Julie's family took a 4-day trip. They recorded the miles driven and the gallons of gasoline bought each day in the table.

Julie's mother wrote an equation to calculate their gas mileage, m, in miles per gallon. Let d = the number of total miles driven on the 4-day trip. Let g = the total number of gallons used for the trip.

$$m = \frac{d}{g}$$

What was the gas mileage for the 4-day trip?

Day of Trip	Miles Driven Each Day	Number of Gallons of Gas Bought
Day 1	476	15
Day 2	439	13.5
Day 3	382	15.4
Day 4	263	16.1

How can you use the values of the variables you know to find the value of *m*?

B

Step 1

Identify the values of the variables *d* and *g*.

Find the value of *d*.

$$d = 476 + 439 + 382 + 263 = 1{,}560$$

Find the value of *g*.

$$g = 15 + 13.5 + 15.4 + 16.1 = 60$$

C

Step 2

Substitute the values of the variables into the formula and evaluate.

$$m = \frac{1{,}560}{60}$$
$$= 26$$

The gas mileage for the trip was 26 miles per gallon.

Convince Me! **MP.7 Use Structure** Evaluate the expression $3 + 12a \div 4$ for $a = 10$.

© Pearson Education, Inc. 6

Name ____

Practice Buddy | Tools | Assessment

Guided Practice*

Do You Understand?

1. **MP.3 Construct Arguments** Why is it important to use the order of operations to evaluate algebraic expressions?

2. In the problem on the previous page, suppose you were given the gas mileage and the total gallons of gas used. How could you find the total number of miles driven?

Do You Know How?

In **3–6**, use substitution to evaluate each expression for the value given.

3. $z \div 4; z = 824$

4. $6t \div 9 - 22; t = 60$

5. $44 + 2{,}640 \div x; x = 12$

6. $62{,}450 \div 50 - 3w; w = 5$

Independent Practice

Leveled Practice In **7–12**, evaluate each expression for $x = 8$, $x = 12$, and $x = 23$.

7. $450x \div 25$

8. $623 \div 89 + x^2$

9. $34 + \frac{350}{2 + x}$

10. $371 - 224x \div 14 - 3$

11. $\frac{10{,}005 - 5x}{5} + 32{,}123$

12. $\frac{4x^3}{2}$

13. Evaluate the expression for the values of t.

t	2	4	7	9	12
$4{,}984t \div 4$					

14. Evaluate the expression for the values of z.

z	3	6	9	12	15
$\frac{z^4}{81}$					

*For another example, see Set C on page 311.

Math Practices and Problem Solving

In **15** and **16**, use the diagram of the cube.

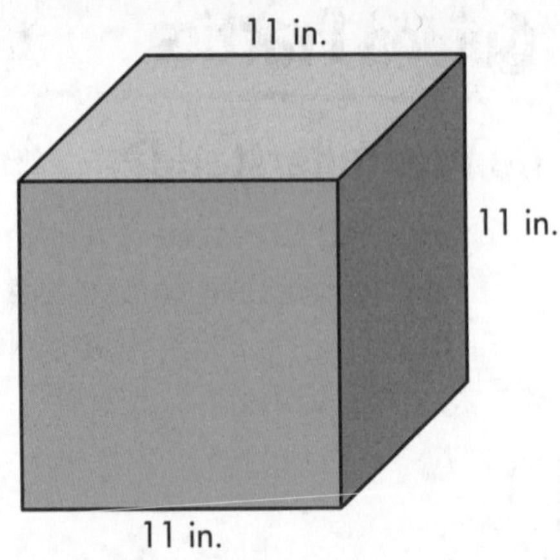

15. The formula $V = s^3$ can be used to find the volume, V, of a cube with side lengths s. Use the formula to find the volume of the cube.

16. **MP.7 Use Structure** The formula $A = 6s^2$ can be used to find the total surface area, A, of a cube. Use the formula to find the surface area of the cube.

17. **MP.3 Critique Reasoning** Katrina says that the expression $5{,}432 + 4{,}564 + 13{,}908 \div n$ can be evaluated by adding $5{,}432 + 4{,}564 + 13{,}908$ and then dividing by the value of n. Do you agree? Explain.

18. **Math and Science** The density, d, of an object can be found by using the formula $d = \frac{m}{v}$, where m is the mass of the object and v is its volume. What is the density of an object that has a mass of 73,430 kilograms and a volume of 7 m^3?

19. **Higher Order Thinking** Patriot Middle School has decided there should be one student council representative for every 24 students in the school. There are four sixth-grade classes with a, b, c, and d students in each class.

a. Write an equation to show how many representatives, r, the sixth grade will have.

b. Suppose the four sixth-grade classes have 24, 22, 23, and 27 students in them. Use your equation to find the number of sixth-grade student council members. Does your answer make sense? Explain.

Common Core Assessment

20. Which of the following expressions have a value of 240 when $w = 3$?

- ☐ $\frac{62{,}640}{87w}$
- ☐ $99 \div 3 + 207w \div 3$
- ☐ $42w \times 2 - 12$
- ☐ $13 + 7w + 180$
- ☐ $w^3 \times 32 - \frac{1{,}200}{25}$

21. Which of the following expressions have a value of 26 when $t = 14$?

- ☐ $173t - 364 + 490 \div 98$
- ☐ $7 + 60t - 13{,}136 \div 16$
- ☐ $\frac{26t}{13}$
- ☐ $t^2 + 10$
- ☐ $5t - 44$

© Pearson Education, Inc. 6

Name ______________________

Help Practice Buddy Tools Games

Homework & Practice 6-4
Evaluate Expressions

Another Look!

The cost, c, to attend the annual class trip is given by the equation

$$c = 2a + 3b + 3c + d \div 48$$

where a is the cost of a room for one night, b is the cost of meals for one day, c is the cost of tickets for one day, and d is the cost for the bus rental. There are 48 students.

6th Grade
CLASS TRIP COSTS

Room $50 PER NIGHT
Meals $40 PER DAY
Tickets $20 PER DAY
Bus $1,392

What will it cost each student to go on the class trip?

Remember to use the order of operations when evaluating the equation.

Step 1

Identify the value of each variable.

$a = 50$

$b = 40$

$c = 20$

$d = 1{,}392$

Step 2

Substitute the value of each variable into the equation and evaluate.

$c = 2 \cdot 50 + 3 \cdot 40 + 3 \cdot 20 + 1{,}392 \div 48$

$c = 100 + 120 + 60 + 29$

$c = 309$

It will cost each student $309 to go on the class trip.

In **1–7**, evaluate each expression for $z = 3$, $z = 7$, and $z = 12$.

1. $\frac{14{,}952 - 6z}{3}$

2. $378z \div 7$

3. $(7 \cdot 24) \div z$

4. $34 + 34z \div 17$

5. $45z + 4{,}565 + 9{,}078 \div 89$

6. $\frac{156 + 84z + 144}{12}$

7. $\frac{4z^4 + 26}{10}$

8. Evaluate the expression for the values of x.

x	2	3	5	7	9
$\frac{48x + 16 + 35}{3}$					

9. Evaluate the expression for the values of t.

t	2	4	8	9	21
$\frac{26{,}418}{5t - 3}$					

10. Higher Order Thinking A school district can send a representative to the state spelling bee for every 50 students in the school district. There are 5 schools with *a*, *b*, *c*, *d*, and *e* students in each school.

a. Write an equation to show how many representatives, *r*, the school district will have.

b. Suppose there are 1,587, 985, 2,052, 824, and 752 students, respectively, in each of the schools. Use your equation to find the number of students the school district can send to the state spelling bee. Does your answer make sense? Explain.

In **11** and **12**, use the menu.

11. MP.4 Model with Math Two friends ordered 2 steaks, 2 drinks, and some Caesar salads. Write an expression that shows the cost per person when the total cost is split equally between the two friends.

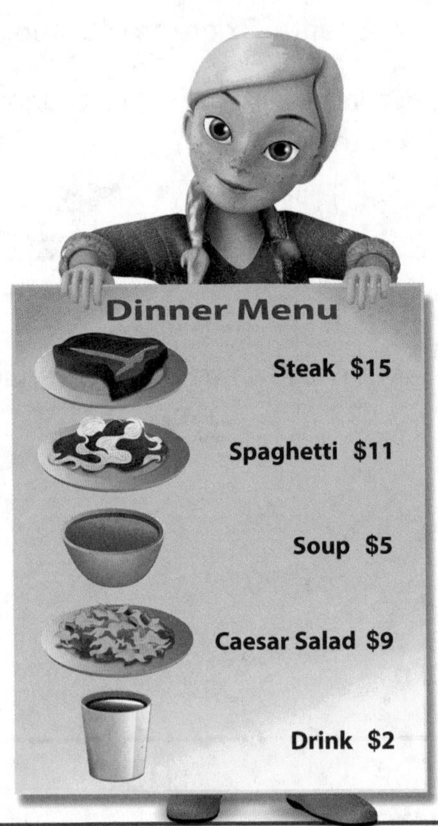

12. The 24 members of the middle school swim team ordered 9 steaks, 13 orders of spaghetti, 16 drinks, and some bowls of soup. Write an expression that shows the total cost of their order split equally among the 24 members.

Common Core Assessment

13. Which of the following expressions have a value of 13 when $n = 5$?

- ☐ $3n - 2$
- ☐ $9n \div 3 - 6 \div 3$
- ☐ $13n \times 2 - 10$
- ☐ $13 + 7n - 2$
- ☐ $\frac{n^5 - 1{,}838}{99}$

14. Which of the following expressions have a value of 112 when $z = 7$?

- ☐ $732 \div 12 + z^2$
- ☐ $7z + 3{,}136 \div 49 - 3$
- ☐ $103 + 27z \div 21$
- ☐ $67 + z^2 - 4$
- ☐ $\frac{707 - 5z}{6}$

© Pearson Education, Inc. 6

Name ______________________

Lesson 6-5
Solve Division Equations

I can ...
write and solve equations that involve division.

Content Standards 6.EE.B.7, 6.NS.B.2
Mathematical Practices MP.2, MP.3, MP.4, MP.7, MP.8

Solve & Share

A school group is planning a trip to New York City. There are 29 people going on the trip. They have agreed to share the total cost of the trip equally. Let *s* equal each person's share of the cost. What is each person's share of the cost? ***Solve the problem any way you choose.***

You can generalize by using what you know about dividing smaller numbers to write equations and solve problems involving larger numbers.

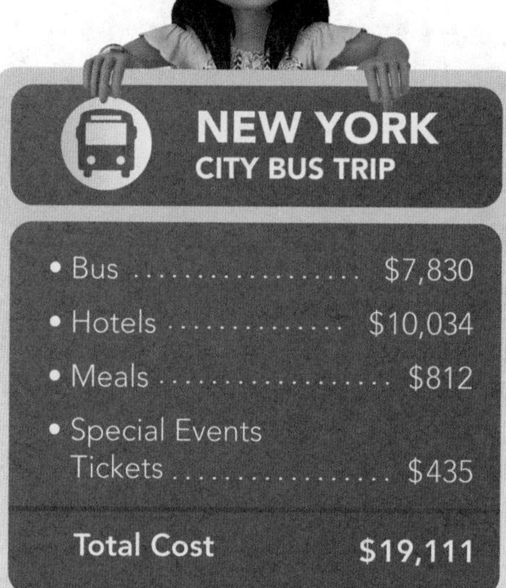

NEW YORK
CITY BUS TRIP
• Bus $7,830
• Hotels $10,034
• Meals $812
• Special Events Tickets $435
Total Cost $19,111

Look Back! **MP.3 Construct Arguments** Can you use the same strategy you used above to find each person's share of the hotel bill? Explain your reasoning.

How Can You Use Variables to Write and Solve Division Equations?

A

Helen has 2,375 stickers. She wants to put them in an album. Each page in the album can hold 25 stickers. How many pages, p, can she fill?

2,375 stickers

25 — *p* pages filled

Stickers on each page

You are using structure when you divide a quantity into equal-sized groups.

B Write an equation to represent this situation. Let p = the number of album pages Helen can fill with 25 stickers.

$$\frac{2{,}375}{25} = p \quad \text{or} \quad \frac{2{,}375}{p} = 25$$

Divide to solve for p.

$$\begin{array}{r} 95 \\ 25\overline{)2375} \\ -225 \\ \hline 125 \\ -125 \\ \hline 0 \end{array}$$

$p = 95$

Helen can fill 95 album pages.

C Use multiplication to check the division.

Represent the problem as a multiplication equation and evaluate the equation for $p = 95$.

$25p = 2{,}375$
$25 \times 95 = 2{,}375$

The math is correct.

Helen can fill 95 album pages.

Convince Me! **MP.7 Look for Relationships** What similarities do you see between the division equation $2{,}375 \div 25 = p$ and the multiplication equation $25p = 2{,}375$? Explain why both can be used to find how many album pages Helen can fill.

© Pearson Education, Inc. 6

Name ____________________

Practice Buddy Tools Assessment

Guided Practice*

Do You Understand?

1. **MP.2 Reasoning** Darius used the multiplication equation $14t = 3{,}010$ to solve a problem. Can he write a division equation to solve the same problem? Explain.

2. **MP.4 Model with Math** Emily flew 2,184 miles in 12 hours. Her plane flew an equal number of miles each hour. Let *m* stand for the miles flown each hour. Write an equation to represent one way you can find how many miles Emily's plane flew each hour.

Do You Know How?

In **3–5**, use the multiplication equation to write a division equation. Then solve each equation.

3. $23d = 2{,}392$

4. $74f = 6{,}179$

5. $11y = 10{,}857$

Independent Practice

In **6** and **7**, write a division equation and a multiplication equation to represent each problem.

6. Lolo typed 1,125 words in 15 minutes. Let *w* represent the words typed each minute. If Lolo typed the same number of words each minute, how many words did she type in 1 minute?

7. In 12 weeks Felipé earns $4,500 doing yard work. He earns the same amount each week. Let *m* stand for the amount earned each week. How much does Felipé make in 1 week?

In **8–10**, solve each division equation and use a multiplication equation to check your answer. Show your work.

8. $36{,}762 \div 33 = c$

9. $4{,}868 \div n = 16$

10. $7{,}254 \div 62 = q$

*For another example, see Set D on page 312.

Math Practices and Problem Solving

11. MP.4 Model with Math Abel has 3,330 toothpicks. He wants to use them all to make a floor mat with 18 equal rows. Use the bar diagram to write a division equation. Then solve the equation to find how many toothpicks Abel should use in each row.

3,330 toothpicks

18 | *t* toothpicks in each row

Number of rows

12. MP.8 Generalize A movie theater sells 11,550 tickets for 50 sold-out showings of the same movie. Write a division equation you can use to find the number of people who bought tickets for each showing. Use what you know about dividing with larger numbers to solve the equation.

13. MP.3 Critique Reasoning The school auditorium can seat 1,650 people. It has 30 rows of seats with an equal number of seats in each row. Valerie writes the equation $1{,}650 \div 30 = e$ to show one way you can find how many seats are in each row. Lucas says he can write a multiplication equation to represent the same problem. Is he correct? Explain.

14. Number Sense Write the integer that is the opposite of the absolute value of -75.

15. Higher Order Thinking A youth group spent $575 on 46 pizzas. Use the equation $575 \div 46 = x$ to find the cost of each pizza. If the youth group orders 3 more pizzas at the same cost for each, what is the total cost? Show your work.

Common Core Assessment

16. In February, Calvin's school used 4,920 pounds of rock salt to melt ice on its sidewalks. One bag contains 40 pounds of rock salt.

Choose **Yes** or **No** to tell which of the following equations can be used to find how many bags of rock salt, *b*, Calvin's school used in February.

16a. $4{,}920b = 40$ ○ Yes ○ No

16b. $40b = 4{,}920$ ○ Yes ○ No

16c. $4{,}920 \div 40 = b$ ○ Yes ○ No

16d. $4{,}920 \div b = 40$ ○ Yes ○ No

© Pearson Education, Inc. 6

Name ______________________

Help Practice Buddy Tools Games

Homework & Practice 6-5

Solve Division Equations

Another Look!

A book club purchased 27 copies of the same book. Each member gets 1 book. The total number of pages is 9,450. If all of the book club members complete the book, how many pages will each person read?

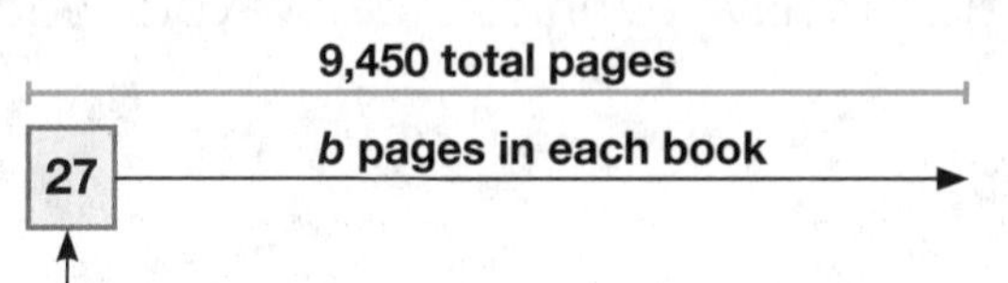

You can use a variable to represent an unknown quantity when writing equations to solve real-world problems.

Write an equation to represent the problem. Let b = the number of pages in each book.

Divide to solve for *b*.

$9{,}450 \div 27 = b$

```
     350
27)9,450   Divide the hundreds.
  - 81     Multiply and subtract.
    135    Continue the process.
  - 135
      0
```

$b = 350$

Multiply to check your work.

$27b = 9{,}450$. Let $b = 350$.

So, 27×350 pages $= 9{,}450$ pages.

The math is correct.

Each person will read 350 pages.

In **1** and **2**, write a division equation and a multiplication equation to represent each problem.

1. Gillian read 3,135 words in 19 minutes. Let w represent the words read each minute. If Gillian read the same number of words each minute, how many words did she read in one minute?

2. Colin is a math tutor. He charges the same amount, s, for every tutoring session. After 21 sessions he has earned $1,575. How much does Colin charge for one tutoring session?

In **3–5**, solve each division equation and use a multiplication equation to check your answer. Show your work.

3. $9{,}522 \div 9 = k$

4. $7{,}848 \div w = 36$

5. $56{,}259 \div 57 = i$

6. **MP.2 Reasoning** On a calm day, the 32 windmills on the Bosley family wind farm each complete 120 revolutions every minute. Which operation would you use to find the total number of revolutions the 32 windmills complete in one minute? Explain.

7. **Higher Order Thinking** The Columbus junior soccer league is selling raffle tickets to raise money for new uniforms and equipment. So far league members have earned $1,218 and sold 84 tickets. Use the equation $1,218 \div 84 = r$ to find the cost of each raffle ticket. Then use the answer to find the total earnings after 90 raffle tickets have been sold. Show your work.

8. **MP.4 Model with Math** The 46 golf balls in Stavin's golf bag have 15,180 dimples on them. Each golf ball has the same number of dimples. Complete the bar diagram. Then write and solve an equation to find the number of dimples on each ball in Stavin's bag.

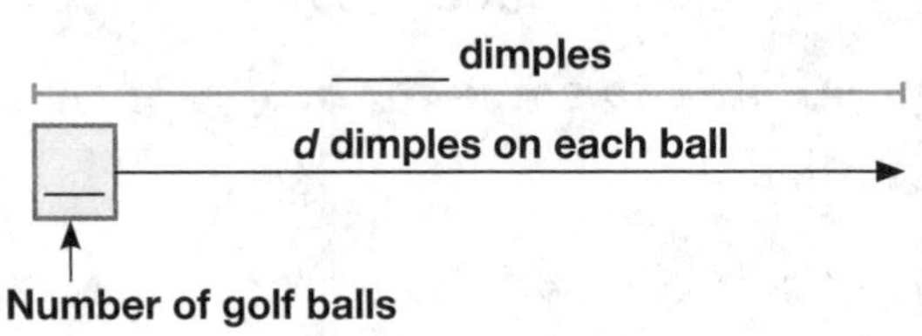

9. **Vocabulary** The mathematical phrase $\$13.25 \times w$ is an example of what type of expression?

10. **Math and Science** There are 45 houses in Grey's Lake subdivision. Each house uses 400 gallons of water each day. Write a division equation to represent the total number of gallons of water used daily in Grey's Lake subdivision.

Common Core Assessment

11. In May, a landscaping crew used 8,500 pounds of potting soil. One bag contains 50 pounds of potting soil.

Choose **Yes** or **No** to tell which of the following equations can be used to find how many bags of potting soil the landscaping crew used in May.

11a. $8,500 \div 50 = p$ ○ Yes ○ No

11b. $50p = 8,500$ ○ Yes ○ No

11c. $8,500p = 50$ ○ Yes ○ No

11d. $50 \div p = 8,500$ ○ Yes ○ No

© Pearson Education, Inc. 6

Name ____________________

Solve

Solve & Share

You want to make a curtain that is 76 inches long. Fabric is sold by the yard (36 inches), but the least you can buy is a quarter of a yard. How much does it cost to buy the needed fabric?

Directions: Ordering Fabric for a Curtain

- Find the total length of the curtain.
- Double that length.
- Add 1 foot.

$\frac{1}{4}$ yard costs $15

Math Practices and Problem Solving

Lesson 6-6

Precision

I can ...
be precise when solving math problems.

Mathematical Practices MP.6, MP.1, MP.2, MP.3
Content Standards 6.EE.A.2c, 6.NS.B.2

Thinking Habits

Be a good thinker! These questions can help you.

- Am I using numbers, units, and symbols correctly?
- Am I using the correct definitions?
- Am I calculating accurately?
- Is my answer clear?

Look Back! **MP.6 Be Precise** How did you decide how much fabric to order?

How Can You Be Precise When Solving Math Problems?

A

A class made 474 candy apples for an auction.

If they must use at least one of each size of box, what is the least cost to pack all of the apples?

What do I need to do to solve this problem?

I need to be precise in my calculations and how I interpret the remainders.

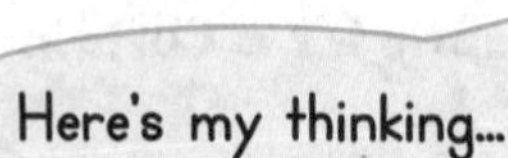

B

How can I be precise in solving this problem?

I can

- correctly use the information given.
- calculate accurately.
- interpret remainders correctly.
- use appropriate units.
- be sure my answer is clear and appropriate.

C

I must use at least 1 large, 1 medium, and 1 small box.

$25 + 15 + 5 = 45$

There are 429 apples left to pack.

I use a table to compare costs. It costs the least to use the greatest number of large boxes possible.

Number of Apples	Box Description	Cost
25	1 Large	$6.50
25	5 Small	$10.00
30	2 Medium	$9.50
30	6 Small	$12.00
75	3 Large	$19.50
75	5 medium	$23.75

$429 \div 25 = 17 \text{ R4}$ I need 17 more large boxes and 1 more small box for the 4 remaining apples.

I use an equation to find the total cost, t, of the boxes.

$$(18 \times \$6.50) + (1 \times \$4.75) + (2 \times \$2.00) = t$$

$$\$125.75 = t$$

It will cost $125.75 for the boxes needed to pack 474 candy apples.

Convince Me! © **MP.6 Be Precise** How many places in the last box are empty?

© Pearson Education, Inc. 6

Name ______________________________

Practice Buddy Tools Assessment

Guided Practice*

MP.6 Be Precise

Kaley's class is donating cans of soup to a food bank. She can buy cans in packs as shown. She wants to buy at least one of each pack size. What combination of packs should she get to spend the least amount of money on 120 cans of soup?

Number of Cans	Price per Pack
48-pack	$58.00
16-pack	$32.50
6-pack	$13.50

1. How can you attend to precision when using numbers, units, and symbols to solve the problem?

2. How many of each pack should Kaley buy to get 120 cans at the least possible cost? Complete the table and explain how you found your answer.

Pack Description	Number of Packs	Number of Cans	Cost
48-pack	1	48	$58.00
	2	96	
16-pack	1	16	$32.50
	2		
	3		
6-pack	1	6	$13.50
	2		
	8		

Independent Practice

MP.6 Be Precise

Two sixth-grade classes of 22 students each are going on a field trip to a museum. One teacher and 5 chaperones will go with each class. Tours are offered for up to 25 people at a time. What is the least amount of money that can be spent for everyone to go on a tour?

Size of Group	Price per Person
1 to 6	$15
7 to15	$12
16 to 25	$10

3. Can you use the equation $p = 2 \cdot (22 + 6)$, where $p =$ the total number of people, to represent and solve this problem? Explain.

4. Tom says the total cost is represented by the equation $2 \times \$10 + \$15 = \$35$. Did he use the information in the problem appropriately? Explain.

*For another example, see Set E on page 312.

Math Practices and Problem Solving

Common Core Performance Assessment

Tiling a Hallway

Mrs. Wu wants to tile her hallway, which is twice the size of the pattern of tiles shown. She needs to buy boxes of tiles. She cannot buy a partial box.

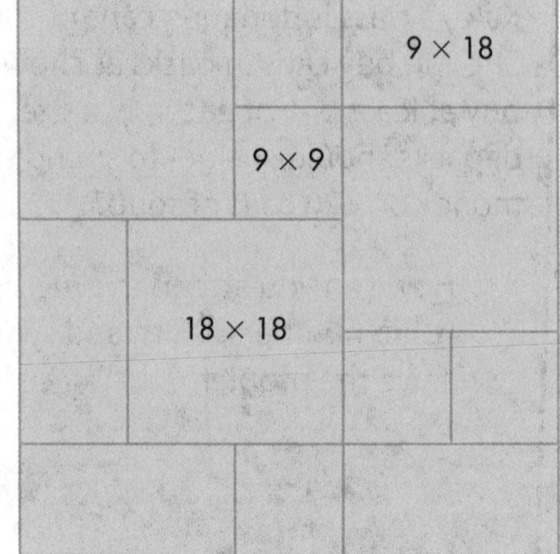

To find the least she could spend to buy enough tiles for the hallway, Mrs. Wu made a table. Then she wrote the equation $t = (2 \times \$5) + (3 \times \$5.25) + (3 \times \$4)$. She determined she will spend $37.75 on the tiles. Do you agree with her calculations?

Tile size (inches)	Number of tiles Needed	Number in Box	Price per Box
9 × 9	10	6	$5.00
9 × 18	8	3	$5.25
18 × 18	6	2	$4.00

When you critique reasoning, you ask questions to help you understand someone's thinking.

5. **MP.1 Make Sense and Persevere** How did Mrs. Wu figure out the number of tiles of each size she needed? Explain.

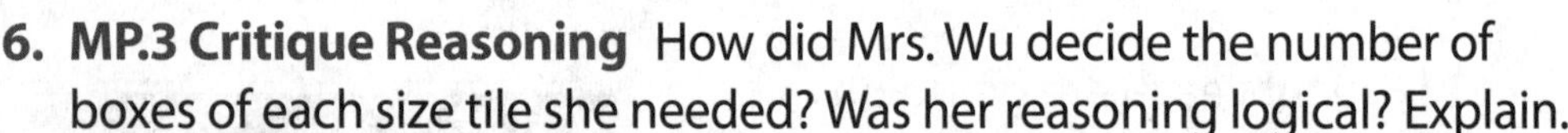

6. **MP.3 Critique Reasoning** How did Mrs. Wu decide the number of boxes of each size tile she needed? Was her reasoning logical? Explain.

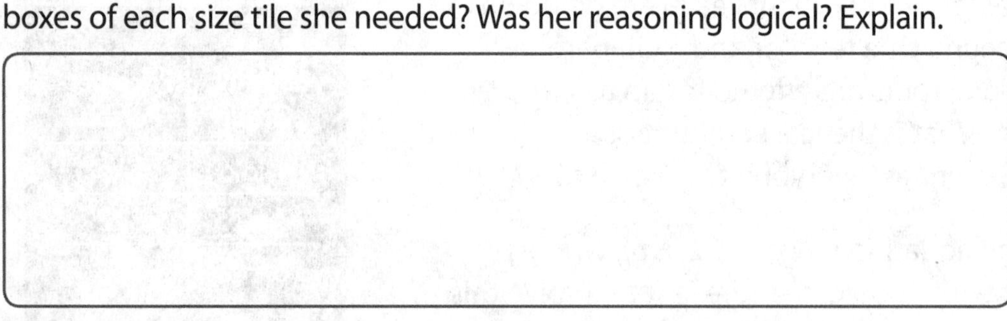

7. **MP.6 Be Precise** Is the equation that Mrs. Wu wrote accurate? Explain.

© Pearson Education, Inc. 6

Name ______________________________

Homework & Practice 6-6

Precision

Another Look!

Ethan wants to make apple pies for a banquet. He needs enough pie to serve 75 people. Which size baskets of apples can he buy for $25 or less to make enough apple pies?

How can you be precise when solving this problem?

- I can use units, numbers, and symbols correctly to find the number of pies and pounds of apples needed to serve 75 people.
- I can check my work when using a table and writing equations to find a way Ethan can serve everyone for $25 or less.

Number of pounds of basket	Number of Baskets	Total Cost
$2\frac{1}{2}$	12	$30.00
5	6	$24.60
12	3	$33.00

Attend to precision when solving the problem.

I can divide to find the number of pies needed to serve 75 people:
$75 \div 8 = 9$ R3. The remainder means Ethan will need 10 pies, or 30 lb of apples.
Buying six 5-lb baskets of apples is the cheapest option.
I can multiply to find the total cost: $6 \times \$4.10 = \$24.60$. The total cost is $0.40 less than $25.

MP.6 Be Precise

A school has 218 sixth-grade students. The town predicts that in 10 years there will be $\frac{1}{4}$ more sixth-grade students. If a maximum of 25 students can fit in a classroom, how many classes of sixth graders would there be in 10 years?

When you are precise, you pay attention to what the remainder means in a problem and use it correctly.

1. How can you find the predicted number of students in 10 years? Explain.

2. Steve says that there will be 10 sixth-grade classes in 10 years. Is he correct? Explain your answer.

© Common Core Performance Assessment

Mixing Paint

Mia painted several rooms in her house. She has paint left over that she wants to use for the play room. The room has 2 windows and 2 doors. If Mia mixes together all of her leftover paint, does she have enough paint for the walls of the room?

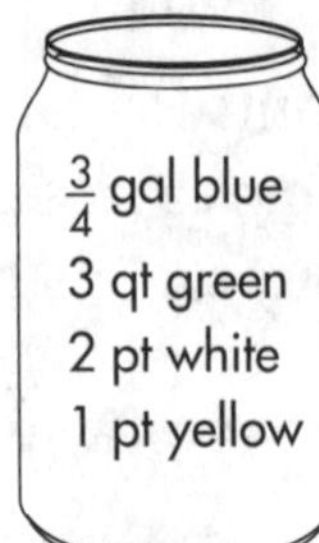

$\frac{3}{4}$ gal blue
3 qt green
2 pt white
1 pt yellow

Directions: Find the number of square feet to be painted using the formula $A = 2(\ell \cdot h) + 2(w \cdot h)$, where A = area of the four walls, ℓ = length, w = width, and h = height.

Subtract 20 square feet for each door.

Subtract 15 square feet for each window.

Each quart covers $87\frac{1}{2}$ square feet.

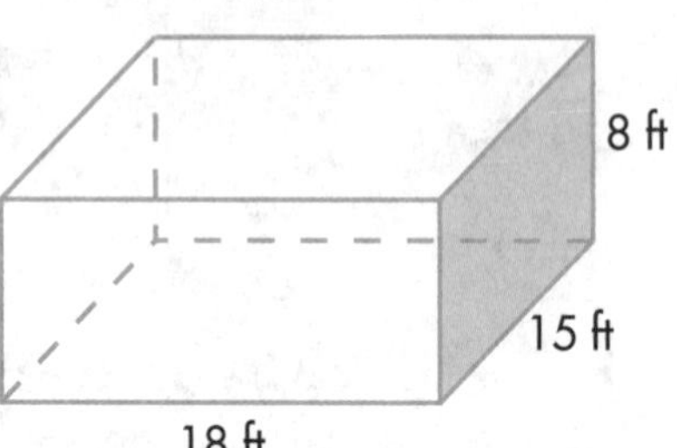

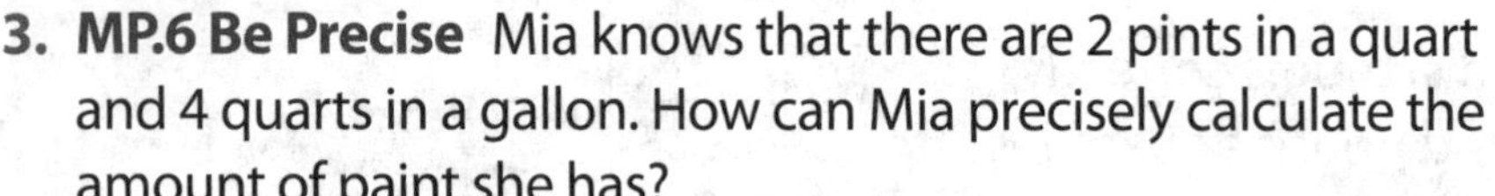

3. **MP.6 Be Precise** Mia knows that there are 2 pints in a quart and 4 quarts in a gallon. How can Mia precisely calculate the amount of paint she has?

4. **MP.3 Critique Reasoning** Mia wrote the equation $8(15 + 15 + 18 + 18) = 528$ to find the area she needs to paint without considering the doors and windows. Is it correct? Explain.

Be precise by converting measurements accurately.

5. **MP.2 Construct Arguments** Mia decided that she did not have enough paint. Do you agree? Explain.

© Pearson Education, Inc. 6

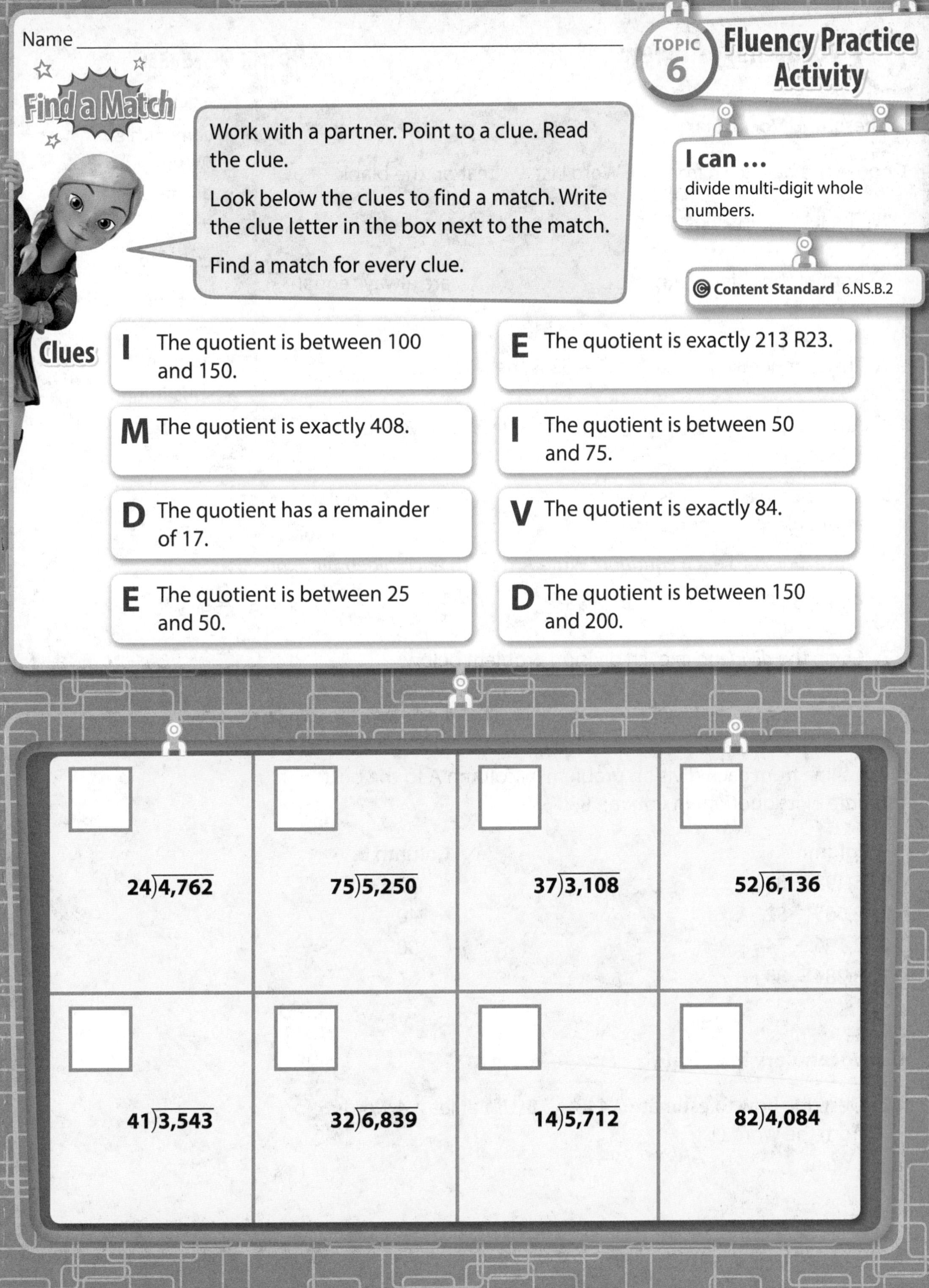

Name ___

TOPIC 6 Fluency Practice Activity

Find a Match

Work with a partner. Point to a clue. Read the clue.

Look below the clues to find a match. Write the clue letter in the box next to the match.

Find a match for every clue.

I can ...
divide multi-digit whole numbers.

Content Standard 6.NS.B.2

Clues

I The quotient is between 100 and 150.

E The quotient is exactly 213 R23.

M The quotient is exactly 408.

I The quotient is between 50 and 75.

D The quotient has a remainder of 17.

V The quotient is exactly 84.

E The quotient is between 25 and 50.

D The quotient is between 150 and 200.

☐ $24\overline{)4{,}762}$	☐ $75\overline{)5{,}250}$	☐ $37\overline{)3{,}108}$	☐ $52\overline{)6{,}136}$
☐ $41\overline{)3{,}543}$	☐ $32\overline{)6{,}839}$	☐ $14\overline{)5{,}712}$	☐ $82\overline{)4{,}084}$

TOPIC 6

Vocabulary Review

A-Z Glossary

Word List

- algebraic expression
- compatible numbers
- dividend
- divisor
- estimate
- equation
- evaluate
- quotient
- substitution
- variable

Understand Vocabulary

Choose the best term from the Word List. Write it on the blank.

1. The letter p in $2{,}064 \div 2p = 24$ is the ______________.

2. Both of the sides of a(n) ______________ are always equal in value.

3. The number 37 in $1{,}924 \div 37 = 52$ is the ______________.

4. A(n) ______________ has at least one variable and one operation.

5. To evaluate an expression, use ______________ to replace a variable with a number.

6. Write **E** next to each *equation*. Write **A** next to each *algebraic expression*.

   $44p = 3{,}784$ ____ $225n \div 35$ ____ $\frac{26x^2}{14}$ ____ $5{,}712 \div 56 = q$ ____

7. Circle the *dividend* in each division problem below.

   $3{,}645 \div 45 = p$ $\frac{18{,}904}{34w}$ $36\overline{)3{,}312}$ (quotient 92) $2{,}518 \div 63 = 39\text{ R}61$

Draw a line from each division problem in Column A to the best *estimate* of its quotient in Column B.

	Column A	Column B
8.	$5{,}498 \div 87$	30
9.	$2{,}605 \div 52$	40
10.	$2{,}196 \div 74$	50
11.	$3{,}284 \div 83$	60

Use Vocabulary in Writing

12. Describe how to estimate $2{,}448 \div 78$. Use at least 4 words from the Word List.

© Pearson Education, Inc. 6

Name ______________________________

Reteaching

Set A pages 273–278

Estimate $3{,}614 \div 57$.

Use compatible numbers to estimate.

$3{,}614 \div 57$
↓ ↓
$3{,}600 \div 60 = 60$

So, $3{,}614 \div 57$ is about 60.

Remember that compatible numbers are numbers that are easy to compute in your head.

Estimate using compatible numbers.

1. $1{,}683 \div 45$
2. $5{,}249 \div 96$
3. $3{,}798 \div 63$
4. $2{,}341 \div 72$
5. $\$6{,}134 \div 93$
6. $\$7{,}421 \div 92$

Set B pages 279–284, 285–290

Find $4{,}612 \div 50$.

Estimate to decide where to put the first digit in the quotient.

Use compatible numbers. $4{,}500 \div 50 = 90$

Start dividing the tens. Multiply and subtract. Compare the remainder to the divisor.

$$\begin{array}{r} 92 \text{ R12} \\ 50\overline{)4{,}612} \\ -\ 4\,50 \\ \hline 112 \\ -\ 100 \\ \hline 12 \end{array}$$

To check, compare the quotient to your estimate.

Remember that you can check your answer by multiplying the quotient by the divisor, and then adding the remainder to that product. The sum should be your dividend.

Estimate first. Then find the quotient.

1. $20\overline{)4{,}283}$
2. $50\overline{)6{,}532}$
3. $83\overline{)6{,}983}$
4. $93\overline{)8{,}496}$
5. $42\overline{)5{,}235}$
6. $47\overline{)5{,}190}$

Set C pages 291–296

Evaluate $18 + 40k \div 8$ for $k = 6$.

Substitute the number given for the variable and evaluate the expression.

For $k = 6$, substitute 6 for k.

$18 + 40(6) \div 8$
$= 18 + 240 \div 8$
$= 18 + 30$
$= 48$

Remember to use the order of operations when evaluating an expression.

Evaluate each expression for $t = 4$, $t = 9$, and $t = 12$.

1. $168t \div 6$
2. $36 + 2{,}304 \div t$
3. $49t + 4{,}672 \div 73$
4. $\frac{18t^2}{3}$

Set D pages 297–302

A company packs and ships games to a store. Forty-eight games fit in a box. How many boxes are needed for 2,448 games? Write a division equation to represent the problem. Then solve the equation.

Let n represent the number of boxes.
$2{,}448 \div 48 = n$ or $2{,}448 \div n = 48$

Divide to solve for n.

$$\begin{array}{r} 51 \\ 48\overline{)2{,}448} \\ -\,2\,40 \\ \hline 48 \\ -\;\;48 \\ \hline 0 \end{array}$$

Divide the tens.
Multiply and subtract.
Continue the process.

$n = 51$
The company needs 51 boxes to pack the games.

Remember that you can use a multiplication equation to check your answer.

Write a division equation to represent each problem. Then solve the equation.

1. An online movie store made $1,494 on poster sales last week. It charged $18 for each poster. How many posters did the store sell?

2. A bicycle club logged 9,860 miles. If the 29 members of the club each rode the same number of miles, how many miles did each member ride?

Set E pages 303–308

Think about these questions to help you **attend to precision.**

Thinking Habits

- Am I using numbers, units, and symbols correctly?
- Am I using the correct definitions?
- Am I calculating accurately?
- Is my answer clear?

Remember that you need to interpret the remainder to be precise.

Four teachers, 7 assistants, and three classes of 24 students each are going to a kite festival. Each person gets a kite. What is the least amount of money they can spend?

Kite Bundles	Cost per Kite
1 kite	$18
20 kites	$15
30 kites	$12

1. How can you find the least total cost?

2. Write and solve an equation to find the least total cost.

© Pearson Education, Inc. 6

Name ______________________

TOPIC 6

Assessment

1. Which of the following results is the most reasonable estimate of $4,875 \div 64$?

Ⓐ $6,000 \div 60$

Ⓑ $5,000 \div 60$

Ⓒ $4,900 \div 70$

Ⓓ $4,800 \div 70$

2. Eliana started a new bank account and saved the same amount each week for a year. Now she has $2,860 in her account. Let *a* be the amount she saved each week.

Part A

Write an equation to represent how much Eliana saved each week.

Part B

Solve your equation to find how much Eliana saved each week.

3. Select each expression that has a value of 15 when $x = 15$.

☐ $\frac{x}{3} + 10$

☐ $15,521 \div x$

☐ $(3,015 \div x) - 186$

☐ $20x^2 \div 30$

☐ $\frac{2x^2}{5} - 25$

4. Chloe served 320 cups of lemonade at a family reunion. There are 4 cups in a quart and 4 quarts in a gallon. How many gallons of lemonade did she serve? Explain how you solved the problem.

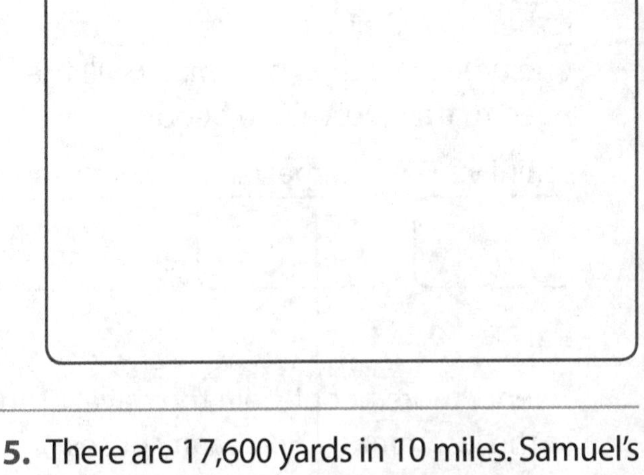

5. There are 17,600 yards in 10 miles. Samuel's father can run 10 miles in 65 minutes. If he runs the same speed for the entire distance, about how many yards does Samuel's father run each minute?

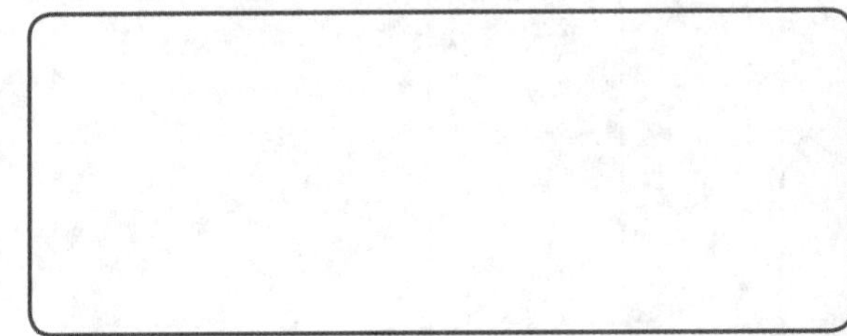

6. A city has 1,242 law enforcement officers in the police department. If the officers are equally divided into 18 groups, how many officers will be in each group?

Ⓐ 60 officers

Ⓑ 68 officers

Ⓒ 69 officers

Ⓓ 70 officers

7. There are 1,070 people going on a trip to New York City. The travel group organizing the trip can use any of the vehicles shown in the table.

Type of Vehicle	Number of Passengers	Cost
Mini Van	8	$35
Large Van	12	$50
Bus	40	$120

Part A

If the travel group decides to use only one type of vehicle, how many will they need to transport 1,070 people?

mini vans | large vans | buses

Part B

Twenty more people join the travel group at the last minute. How many buses does the group need now? Is there a less expensive option than transporting everyone by bus? Explain.

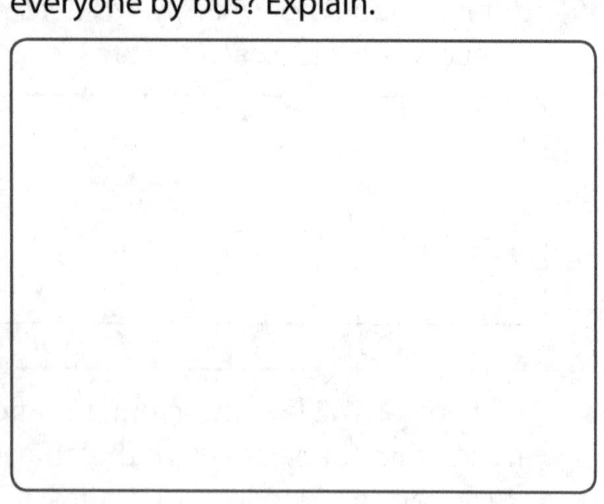

8. The table shows the number of employees going to a conference. Read each of the following problem situations. Draw lines to match each number to the question it answers.

DATA

Group	Number of Employees
Accounting	521
Marketing	536
Central Office	172

45

46

33

If 27 employees can sit in each row of chairs, how many rows of chairs will they need if each employee sits in one chair?

All of the central office and accounting employees go to special break-out sessions. The same number of people attend each of 21 sessions. How many people attend each break-out session?

For the final session, the employees are divided into 26 equal groups. If 59 people could not attend the final session, how many employees are in each group?

© Pearson Education, Inc. 6

Name ______________________________

TOPIC 6

Performance Assessment

Pizza Money

Gavin's basketball team needs to raise $13,800 to pay for their uniforms and travel expenses. There are 12 players on the team. The coach has decided to sell pizzas to raise the money they need.

1. Each player agrees to raise the same amount of money. At least how much money does each player need to raise for an equal share?

2. The pizzas to be sold are purchased in kits with 6 small pizzas or 4 large pizzas in each. The team intends to make a profit of $5 on each small pizza and $6 on each large pizza sold.

Part A

Let $p =$ the profit made on each pizza. Complete the table by evaluating the expression $k \div n + p$ to find the selling price for one of each type of pizza.

Pizza Type	Pizzas in Each Kit (n)	Cost of Kit (k)	Selling Price Each Pizza ($k \div n + p$)
Small Cheese	6	$30	
Small Pepperoni	6	$36	
Large Cheese	4	$32	
Large Pepperoni	4	$36	

Part B

Let $c =$ the selling price of 1 large cheese pizza. Solve the equation $4c = t$ to find the total selling price, t, of 1 large cheese pizza kit.

3. Gavin wrote the expression $5s + 6l$ to represent the profit he can make selling a combination of small and large pizzas, where $s =$ the number of small pizzas and $l =$ the number of large pizzas.

- Evaluate his expression for $s = 72$ and $l = 60$ to find how much he has raised so far. Show your work.
- Use the answer to find the amount of money Gavin still needs to raise to meet his share of the $13,800 goal.

4. Write an equation that describes the least number of small pepperoni pizzas Gavin can sell to raise the remainder of his share (your answer to Problem 3). Let z stand for the number of small pepperoni pizzas. If he sells the pizzas in kits of 6, what is the least number of kits he must sell? Explain.

5. The team is still $1,536 short of its goal. They decide to host a pizza night at Gavin's school. The team sells 3 times as many large pizzas as small pizzas and makes more than the goal amount. Write an inequality that can be used to find possible numbers of large and small pizzas sold on pizza night. Find one possible solution.

© Pearson Education, Inc. 6

Fluently Add, Subtract, Multiply, and Divide Decimals

Essential Question: How can you fluently add, subtract, multiply, and divide decimals?

Analyzing data on the properties of substances, such as freezing points, can help you understand how substances change.
You can analyze the properties of pure water and a salt water solution, called brine, to determine whether adding salt to water results in a chemical reaction.
We may need lots of salt this winter! Here's a project on freezing points and decimals.

Math and Science Project: Freezing Points

Do Research Use the Internet or other sources to learn more about freezing points. List some of the properties of water and salt, including the freezing point of water. Then find the freezing points of saturated brine, 5% brine, 10% brine, and 20% brine. Round to the nearest hundredth °C.

Journal: Write a Report Include what you found. Also in your report:

- How much colder is the freezing point of saturated brine than pure water? 5% brine? 10% brine? 20% brine? What is the difference in the freezing points of 5% brine and 20% brine?
- Review the properties of salt water and explain whether you think that combining salt and water is a chemical change or a physical change.

Name ____________________

Review What You Know

Vocabulary

Choose the best term from the box. Write it on the blank.

- compatible numbers
- decimal
- difference
- estimate
- product
- quotient
- sum

1. The result of multiplying two numbers is called the ____________.

2. A(n) ____________ is an approximate answer.

3. Numbers that are easy to compute mentally are ____________________.

4. In the equation 497 − 265 = 232, the number 232 is the ____________.

Whole Number Operations

Calculate each value.

5. $4\overline{)348}$

6. 9,007 − 3,128

7. 35 × 17

8. 7,964 + 3,872

9. $22\overline{)4,638}$

10. 181 × 42

Evaluating Expressions

Evaluate each expression for $x = 3$ and $x = 7$.

11. $5x$

12. $84 - 2x$

13. $4 + 21 \div x$

14. $3x + 98 \div 14$

15. $6x \div x - 2$

16. $28 + 4x \div 2$

Decimals

17. What decimal does this model represent? Explain how you know.

© Pearson Education, Inc. 6

Name ____________________ Solve

Lesson 7-1
Estimate Sums and Differences

I can ...
estimate the sums and differences of decimals.

Content Standard 6.NS.B.3
Mathematical Practices MP.1, MP.2, MP.3, MP.4, MP.6, MP.7

Solve & Share During the day, 13.9 inches of snow fell. Later that evening, another 6.4 inches fell. About how much snow did the town receive altogether that day? ***Solve this problem any way you choose.***

You can use structure to round decimals when estimating sums.

Look Back! **MP.1 Make Sense and Persevere** The next year, the same town has 4.8 inches of snow fall in the morning, 3.9 inches of snow fall in the afternoon, and 6.2 inches of snow fall in the evening. About how much more did it snow in one day the year before?

Learn Glossary

Essential Question

How Can You Estimate with Decimals?

A

The men's 100-meter dash record was broken in the 2012 Olympics with a winning time of 9.63 seconds. Mrs. Carlson, the gym teacher, ran the 100 meters in 14.7 seconds. About how much faster was the 2012 Olympic time than Mrs. Carlson's time?

To estimate means to find an approximate answer or solution.

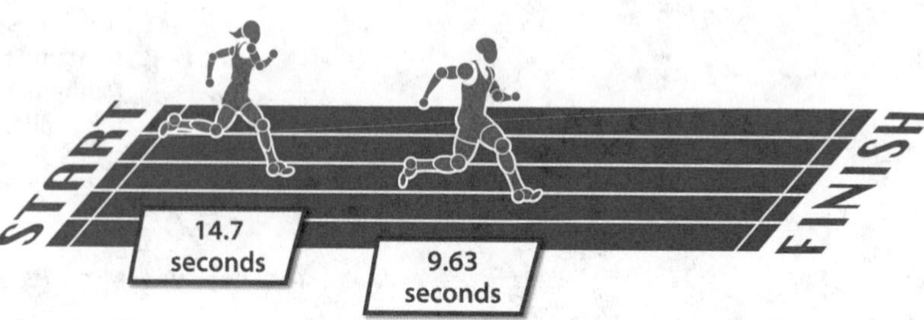

B One Way

Use rounding to estimate sums and differences. Round each number to the same place value.

Round each number to the nearest whole number.

$$\begin{array}{r} 14.7 \\ -\ 9.63 \\ \hline \end{array} \rightarrow \begin{array}{r} 15 \\ -\ 10 \\ \hline 5 \end{array}$$

The difference is about 5 seconds.

C Another Way

Use compatible numbers that are easy to compute with mentally.

$$\begin{array}{r} 14.7 \\ -\ 9.63 \\ \hline \end{array} \rightarrow \begin{array}{r} 14.7 \\ -\ 9.7 \\ \hline 5.0 \end{array}$$

The difference is about 5.0 seconds.

Convince Me! **MP.1 Make Sense and Persevere** Emma is in charge of buying the awards for the science fair. The cost for each award is \$5.43 and the frame for the award is \$3.82. She is given a budget of \$100. Emma estimated the total cost for each award and said she will have enough money for 10 awards. Is Emma's estimate reasonable? Show how you know.

© Pearson Education, Inc. 6

Name ______________________________

Practice Buddy Tools Assessment

Guided Practice*

Do You Understand?

1. When might you want to estimate an answer?

2. ◎ **MP.3 Construct Arguments** Was Emma's estimate from page 320 an overestimate or an underestimate? Explain.

3. ◎ **MP.4 Model with Math** Write your own real-world problem that would be appropriate for estimating the sum or difference of decimals.

Do You Know How?

In **4** and **5**, complete each estimate with numbers easy to compute with mentally.

4. 1.769 + 0.686
1.___ + 0.___ = ___.5

5. 20.45 − 13.15
_____ − 13.2 = _____

In **6** and **7**, round each number to the nearest whole number to estimate.

6. 1.456 + 5.4 + 14.08 = ____

7. 72.43 − 59.8 = ____

Independent Practice

In **8–13**, round to the nearest whole number to estimate.

8. 20.791 + 5.25 + 3.84

9. \$10.10 − \$3.69

10. 376.52 − 9.14

11. 34 − 12.23 + 11.8

12. 28.321 − 14.2

13. 1.01 + 0.98 + 3.784

In **14–19**, use compatible numbers to the tenths place to estimate.

14. 7.12 + 2.501 + 9.2

15. 91.26 − 31.32

16. \$3.79 − \$1.22

17. 314.53 − 34.5

18. 15.663 − 1.03 + 10.80

19. 28.02 + 2.83 + 5.008

*For another example, see Set A on page 381.

Math Practices and Problem Solving

20. Number Sense Rachel is shopping and needs to buy bread, lunchmeat, and pretzels to make lunch. She has a ten-dollar bill. Use estimation to find whether she will have enough money. Explain your reasoning.

21. Cooper, a 2-year-old stallion, ran a lap in 8.71 seconds. He ran a second lap in 7.32 seconds. Estimate Cooper's combined time to the nearest second.

22. **MP.3 Construct Arguments** Camilla estimated the sum of $8.614 + 3.099 + 7.301$ to be about 19. She added $8.6 + 3.1 + 7.3$ to get the sum. Is her estimate an overestimate or an underestimate? Explain your reasoning.

23. The jeweler made a new crown for the Queen. It was made with an 8.74-carat diamond, a 7.086-carat ruby, and a 4.93-carat sapphire. What is the approximate total weight, in carats, of all the gems in the Queen's crown?

24. Higher Order Thinking In a certain manufacturing process, a chemical must be heated to exactly 236.75°F. If the temperature showed 210.964°F, would you use an estimate to find the needed increase in temperature? Explain.

Common Core Assessment

25. Kira wants to buy a movie ticket, popcorn, and a drink. The movie ticket costs $7.75, and the snack and drink combo costs $2.85. If Kira brings $10, will she have enough money for the ticket and snack combo? Estimate to explain your reasoning.

© Pearson Education, Inc. 6

Name ______________________________

Homework & Practice 7-1

Estimate Sums and Differences

Another Look!

Ms. Danos wrote the following expressions on the board. How can you use estimation to find the approximate value of each expression?

$7.382 + 4.97$

$12.57 - 6.806$

$3.847 + 11.22$

The ≈ symbol means *about*. It can be used to estimate or show approximate values.

Estimate: $7.382 + 4.97$

Round each number to the nearest tenth.

$7.382 + 4.97$
↓ ↓
$7.4 + 5$

Add to estimate:

$7.4 + 5 = 12.4$

$7.382 + 4.97 \approx 12.4$

Estimate: $12.57 - 6.806$

Round each number to the nearest whole number.

$12.57 - 6.806$
↓ ↓
$13 - 7$

Subtract to estimate:

$13 - 7 = 6$

$12.57 - 6.806 \approx 6$

Estimate: $3.847 + 11.22$

Estimate by breaking apart the whole number and decimal.

$3.847 \rightarrow 3 \quad .8$

$+ 11.22 \rightarrow + 11 \quad .2$

↓ ↓

$14 + 1.0 = 15$

$3.847 + 11.22 \approx 15$

In **1–9**, round to the nearest whole number to estimate.

1. $4.38 + 9.179$

2. $62.873 - 12.7$

3. $52.83 + 97.288$

4. $131.049 - 82.604$

5. $79.14 + 32.546$

6. $48.468 + 63.029$

7. $112.658 - 81.903$

8. $586.735 - 204.63$

9. $107.139 + 90.621$

In **10–15**, use compatible numbers to the tenths place to estimate.

10. $9.13 - 5.1$

11. $\$15.56 + \$2.19$

12. $20.22 + 22.81 + 25.278$

13. $89.36 + 253.5$

14. $25.6 - 12.22 + 10.8$

15. $86.89 - 45.69$

16. **MP.6 Be Precise** In baseball, an earned run average (ERA) is the average of earned runs given up by a pitcher every nine innings pitched.

a Order the ERAs in the table from greatest to least.

b About how many tenths difference is there between the lowest and highest ERAs in the table?

DATA

Player	Earned Run Average (ERA)
Eddie	1.82
John	2.10
Mario	2.06
Scott	2.04
Josh	1.89

17. **MP.2 Reasoning** Alexis has a $5-bill, two $10-bills, and a $20-bill. She wants to buy a DVD for $17.89, a mug for $5.12, and a shirt for $12.99. Estimate the sum to the nearest dollar. Tell which bills she should hand to the cashier to pay for her items.

18. **Higher Order Thinking** When rounding to the nearest whole number, the decimal 9.5 would typically be rounded to 10. How would you round the numbers 9.5 and 7.5 in the equation $9.5 + 4.7 + 3.2 + 7.5 = x$ if you want your estimate to be as close as possible to the actual sum?

19. **Algebra** When evaluating the expression $8(4 + 6^2) \div 20 - (3^2 + 3)$, James said its value was 40. Is he correct? Use the order of operations to explain how you know.

20. The area of the Garrett's living room is 18.087 square yards. Their bedroom has an area of 15.98 square yards. Round to the nearest tenth and estimate the total amount of carpet they need for both rooms.

Common Core Assessment

21. Bill, Tory, and Jessica ran a 300-meter relay race. Each ran 100 meters. Bill ran his leg of the race in 13.73 seconds, Tory ran hers in 14.22 seconds, and Jessica ran the final leg in 15.09 seconds. Bill estimates that they beat the 44.2-second time they ran last year. Estimate to show whether or not Bill is correct.

© Pearson Education, Inc. 6

Name ______________________________ Solve

Solve & Share

Julie and Doug are building a tree house out of wood boards. Julie has a board that is 1.15 meters long and Doug has a board that is 0.7 meter long. What is the combined length of their boards? ***Solve this problem any way you choose.***

Lesson 7-2
Add and Subtract Decimals

I can ...
find the sum or difference of problems involving decimals.

Content Standard 6.NS.B.3
Mathematical Practices MP.1, MP.3, MP.6, MP.7, MP.8

You can use structure to add or subtract decimals by lining up place values.

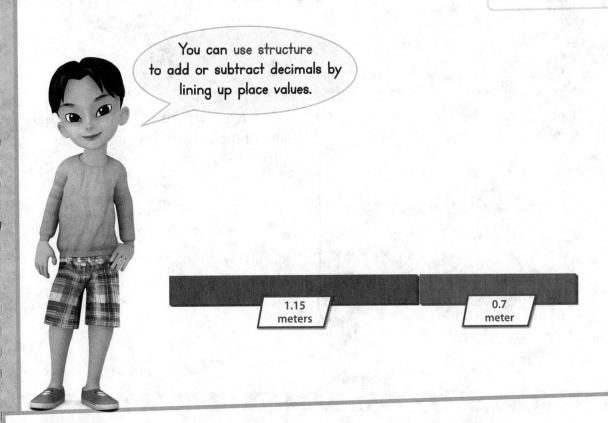

1.15 meters

0.7 meter

Look Back! **MP.7 Use Structure** A board the same size as Doug's board is cut from Julie's board. What is the length of the piece of Julie's board that is left?

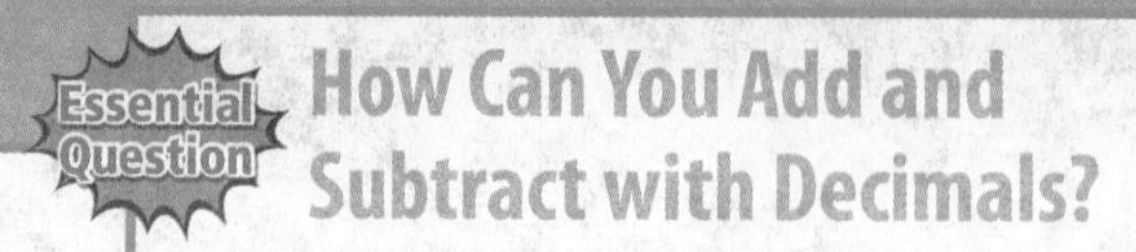

How Can You Add and Subtract with Decimals?

A

Kim and Martin swam 50 meters. Martin took 0.26 of a second longer than Kim. What was Martin's time in the race?

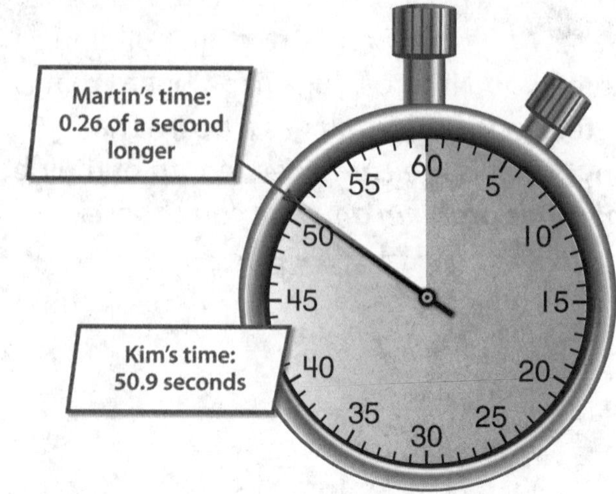

Always be precise when working with decimals.

B Find 50.9 + 0.26. Estimate first by rounding each addend.

$$51 + 0.3 = 51.3$$

Find the sum. Annex a zero so that each place has a digit.

$$\begin{array}{r} 50.90 \\ +\ 0.26 \\ \hline \end{array}$$

Remember to line up the place values to add or subtract.

C Add each place. You can regroup the sum of nine tenths and two tenths.

$$\begin{array}{r} \overset{1}{5}0.90 \\ +\ 0.26 \\ \hline 51.16 \end{array}$$

Martin swam the race in 51.16 seconds. The sum 51.16 is close to the estimate, 51.3.

Convince Me! **MP.7 Use Structure** Suppose that Martin finished the race 0.26 of a second before Kim. What was Martin's time in the race? Use an estimate to check that your answer is reasonable.

© Pearson Education, Inc. 6

Name ____________________

You can use estimation to check if your answer is reasonable.

Practice Buddy Tools Assessment

Another Example

Amy ran a race in 20.7 seconds. Katie finished the race 0.258 second before Amy. How long did it take Katie to run the race?

Find 20.7 − 0.258.
Estimate the difference by rounding.

$$20.7 - 0.3 = 20.4$$

To find the difference, line up the place values.

$$\begin{array}{r} 20.700 \\ -\ \ 0.258 \\ \hline \end{array}$$

← Annex zeros as placeholders.

Subtract each place. Regroup as needed to subtract.

$$\begin{array}{r} \overset{6\,\overset{9}{\cancel{10}}\,10}{20.7\cancel{0}\cancel{0}} \\ -\ 0.258 \\ \hline 20.442 \end{array}$$

Katie ran the race in 20.442 seconds. 20.442 is close to the estimate 20.4.

Guided Practice*

Do You Understand?

1. **MP.8 Generalize** How is adding and subtracting decimals similar to and different from adding and subtracting whole numbers?

Do You Know How?

In **2–5**, find each sum or difference.

2. 5.9 + 2.7
3. 4.01 − 2.95
4. 2.57 + 7.706
5. 15 − 6.108

Independent Practice

In **6–13**, find each sum or difference.

6. 2.17 − 0.8
7. 4.3 + 4.16
8. 46.91 − 28.7
9. 4.815 + 2.17
10. 5.1 − 0.48
11. 27 + 0.185
12. 9.501 − 9.45
13. 14 + 9.8

*For another example, see Set A on page 381.

Math Practices and Problem Solving

14. MP.6 Be Precise The U.S. Census Bureau tracks travel times to work. Use the information in the table to compare the travel time to work in New York to the travel time to work in Chicago. Write an equation to show your work.

DATA

Location	Average Travel Time to Work (minutes)
United States	23.2
Los Angeles, CA	26.5
Chicago, IL	29.1
New York, NY	35.3

15. Algebra Anna's running time for a race was 23.1 seconds. Another runner's time was 5.86 seconds faster. Write and evaluate an equation with a variable to find the difference between Anna's time and the other runner's time.

16. Higher Order Thinking Matthew bought a jersey for \$39.99, a pennant for \$10.25, and a hat for \$13.75. He paid with a \$50 bill and the rest he borrowed from his friend. If Matthew got \$6.01 in change from the cashier, how much did he borrow from his friend to pay for all the items?

Common Core Assessment

17. Use the information in the table to solve each problem. Use estimation to check that your answers are reasonable.

DATA

Trails in Joshua Tree National Park	
Trail	**Length (kilometers)**
Lost Horse Mine	6.4
Lost Palms Oasis	11.6
Mastodon Peak	4.8
Skull Rock	2.7

Part A

What is the combined length of the Lost Horse Mine trail and the Mastodon Peak trail?

Part B

How much longer is the Lost Palms Oasis trail than the Skull Rock trail?

© Pearson Education, Inc. 6

Name ______________________________

Homework & Practice 7-2

Add and Subtract Decimals

Another Look!

Three friends ran a 50-kilometer relay race. For the first two legs, Tamika ran 16.93 kilometers and Felix ran 21.6 kilometers. How many kilometers did Isaac run for the third leg?

Use place-value knowledge to add and subtract decimals.

50		
16.93	21.6	?

Add to find the total distance Tamika and Felix ran.

Estimate: $16.93 \approx 17$ and $21.6 \approx 22$

$17 + 22 = 39$

$$\begin{array}{r} \overset{1}{1}6.93 \\ +\ 21.60 \\ \hline 38.53 \end{array}$$ ← Annex a zero.

38.53 is close to 39, so the answer is reasonable.

Subtract to find how far Isaac ran.

Estimate: $38.53 \approx 39$

$50 - 39 = 11$

$$\begin{array}{r} \overset{4\ 9}{\cancel{5}\cancel{0}}.\overset{9\ 10}{\cancel{0}\cancel{0}} \\ -\ 38.53 \\ \hline 11.47 \end{array}$$ ← Annex 2 zeros.

11.47 is close to 11, so the answer is reasonable.

Isaac ran 11.47 kilometers.

In **1–15**, find each sum or difference.

1. $45.6 + 26.3$

2. $14.25 - 5.14$

3. $17.2 + 6.08$

4. $24.84 - 22.7$

5. $13.64 - 8.3$

6. $0.214 + 15.9$

7. $3.652 - 1.41$

8. $18.06 + 9.798$

9. $8.006 - 6.38$

10. $34.89 - 12.2$

11. $22.31 - 4.22$

12. $1.01 + 3.69$

13. $87.5 + 85.05$

14. $1.09 - 1.03$

15. $100.02 - 64.58$

16. © **MP.7 Look for Relationships** Complete the sequence of numbers in this set. Explain the pattern.

7.5 6.25 5 ____ ____

17. © **MP.3 Critique Reasoning** Jaime wrote $4.4 - 0.33 = 1.1$. Is his answer reasonable? Explain why or why not.

18. The weights of 3 kittens at one week old were 3.6 ounces, 4.2 ounces, and 3.3 ounces. If each kitten gained 2.3 ounces, how much would each of the kittens weigh?

19. A movie theater is having a special. If a group of four pays $7.25 each for tickets, each person can get popcorn and a drink for $5.75. Use the expression $4(5.75 + 7.25)$ to find the total cost for 4 friends.

20. © **MP.1 Make Sense and Persevere** A factory makes parts for toys in different quantities as shown in the table. How much would 11 parts cost?

Number of Parts	2	7	12	15
Cost	$0.90	$3.15	$5.40	$6.75

21. **Higher Order Thinking** The perimeter of a 5-sided figure is 45.56 meters. Two of the sides have the same length. The sum of the other three side lengths is 24.2 meters. About how long is each of the same-length sides? Explain how you decided.

© Common Core Assessment

22. Use the information in the table to solve each problem. Use estimation to check that your answers are reasonable.

Craft Supplies	
Poster board	$1.29/sheet
Markers	$4.50/pack
Tape	$1.99/roll
Glue	$2.39/tube
Construction paper	$3.79/pack

Part A

How much more does 1 tube of glue cost than 1 roll of tape?

Part B

What is the total cost for 2 packs of markers and a pack of construction paper?

© Pearson Education, Inc. 6

Name ______________________________________

Lesson 7-3
Estimate Products

I can . . .
estimate the products of decimals.

Content Standard 6.NS.B.3
Mathematical Practices MP.1, MP.2, MP.3, MP.6

Solve & Share The table shows ticket prices at a museum. About how much money would the school save by paying the group rate for 54 students and adults to visit the museum on a field trip rather than the regular rate? ***Solve this problem any way you choose.***

You can use reasoning to estimate the products of whole numbers.

Museum Tickets	
Ticket	**Cost Per Person**
Regular	\$8.95
Group	\$7.65
Season Pass	\$84.50

Look Back! **MP.2 Reasoning** Six of the people on the field trip decided to buy season passes. Estimate the total cost of 6 season passes. Explain your reasoning.

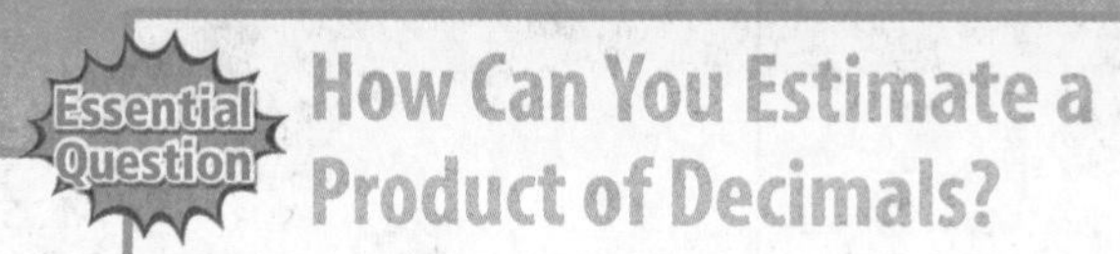

How Can You Estimate a Product of Decimals?

A

The students at Waldron Middle School are selling tins of popcorn to raise money for new uniforms. They sold 42 tins in the first week. About how much money did they make in the first week?

There is more than one way to estimate a product.

B Estimate by rounding each factor.

$$42 \times \$9.25$$
$$\downarrow \quad \downarrow$$
$$40 \times \$9 = \$360$$

So, $42 \times \$9.25 \approx \$360$.

The students raised about $360 the first week.

C Estimate by using compatible numbers.

$$42 \times \$9.25$$
$$\downarrow \quad \downarrow$$
$$42 \times \$10 = \$420.$$

So, $42 \times \$9.25 \approx \$420$.

The students raised about $420 the first week.

You can use reasoning to decide which strategy will give you the better estimate.

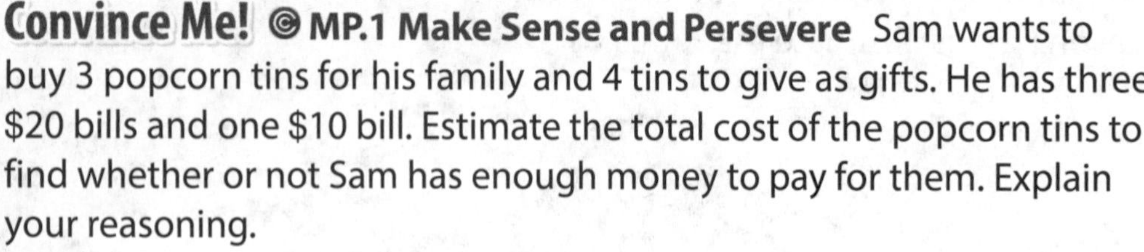

Convince Me! **MP.1 Make Sense and Persevere** Sam wants to buy 3 popcorn tins for his family and 4 tins to give as gifts. He has three $20 bills and one $10 bill. Estimate the total cost of the popcorn tins to find whether or not Sam has enough money to pay for them. Explain your reasoning.

© Pearson Education, Inc. 6

Name ______________________

Practice Buddy Tools Assessment

Another Example

How can you estimate to find a product of two decimals?

Use Rounding

Estimate 7.83 × 3.8.

$$\begin{array}{ccc} 7.83 & \times & 3.8 \\ \downarrow & & \downarrow \\ 8 & \times & 4 = 32 \end{array}$$

So, 7.83 × 3.8 ≈ 32.

Use estimation to find numbers that are easy to compute mentally.

Use Compatible Numbers

Estimate 44.3 × 6.71.

$$\begin{array}{ccc} 44.3 & \times & 6.71 \\ \downarrow & & \downarrow \\ 50 & \times & 6 = 300 \end{array}$$

So, 44.3 × 6.71 ≈ 300.

Guided Practice*

Do You Understand?

1. Which method is easier to use to estimate the amount of money the students will raise from page 332 if they sell 112 tins of popcorn?

2. **MP.3 Construct Arguments** In the examples about selling popcorn, are the estimates overestimates or underestimates? Explain.

Do You Know How?

In **3–8**, estimate each product using rounding or compatible numbers.

3. 6.8 × 53
4. 518 × 6.82
5. 65.13 × 2.89
6. 2,386.25 × 40.1
7. 9.34 × 0.68
8. 35.7 × 8.9

Independent Practice

In **9–16**, estimate each product.

9. 615 × 5.3
10. 12.10 × 3.69
11. 376.52 × 9.94
12. 20.2 × 1.96
13. 412 × 2.421
14. 98.2 × 33.46
15. 73.6 × 7.16
16. $73.09 × 0.88

For another example, see Set B on page 381.

Math Practices and Problem Solving

17. Latrell is buying clothes for school. He has \$150. He wants to buy two pairs of jeans for \$38 each and 2 shirts for \$25 each. Simplify the expression $150 - [(2 \times 38) + (2 \times 25)]$ to find whether he has enough money.

18. **Higher Order Thinking** Damon used compatible numbers to estimate the product of 12.65×55. He tried two different combinations of factors and got the same estimate both times. What numbers did he multiply?

In **19** and **20**, use the information in the diagram.

Lafayette dollar
Diameter is 38.1 mm.
Washington dollar
Diameter is 26.5 mm.
Hint: It takes 1,000 millimeters to equal 1 meter.

19. Patti used rounding to estimate the length of six Lafayette dollars laid side-by-side. Is her estimate an overestimate or an underestimate? Explain.

$$38.1 \times 6 \approx 40 \times 6$$
$$\approx 240 \text{ mm}$$

20. **MP.1 Make Sense and Persevere** The width of a table is 1 meter. If 30 Washington dollars are laid side-by-side, will the total length of the dollars be greater than or less than the width of the table? Use an estimate and explain your thinking.

Common Core Assessment

21. A sixth grade class ordered 19 veggie pizzas for a party. The regular price for the pizza is \$9.79. They have a coupon for \$1.10 off each pizza. About how much money will the sixth grade class need to pay for the pizzas?

Which of the expressions gives a reasonable estimate of the answer?

Ⓐ $10 × 20
Ⓑ $9 × 15
Ⓒ $9 × 20
Ⓓ $8 × 15

© Pearson Education, Inc. 6

Name ____________________

Homework & Practice 7-3

Estimate Products

Another Look!

In 15 minutes, a food vendor at the ball game sold 28 hot dogs. Each hot dog costs $4.25. How much money did the vendor make selling hot dogs in 15 minutes?

Rounding:

Round each factor to the nearest ten or whole number.

$28 \times \$4.25$

$\downarrow \quad \downarrow$

$30 \times \$4 = \$120$

So, $28 \times \$4.25 \approx \$120$.

The vendor made about $120 selling hot dogs in 15 minutes.

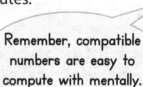

Remember, compatible numbers are easy to compute with mentally.

Compatible Numbers:

Find compatible numbers and multiply.

28×4.25

$\downarrow \quad \downarrow$

$25 \times \$4 = \$100$

So, $28 \times \$4.25 \approx \$100$.

The vendor made about $100 selling hot dogs in 15 minutes.

In **1–12**, estimate each product.

1. 3.73×8.16

2. 35.518×9.722

3. 7.349×5.62

4. 4.178×12.513

5. 8.498×5.602

6. 24.534×7.96

7. 55.93×8.34

8. 61.438×8.72

9. 122.899×5.36

10. 16.954×3.5

11. 17.158×8.99

12. 38.753×8.461

In **13** and **14**, use the diagram to solve.

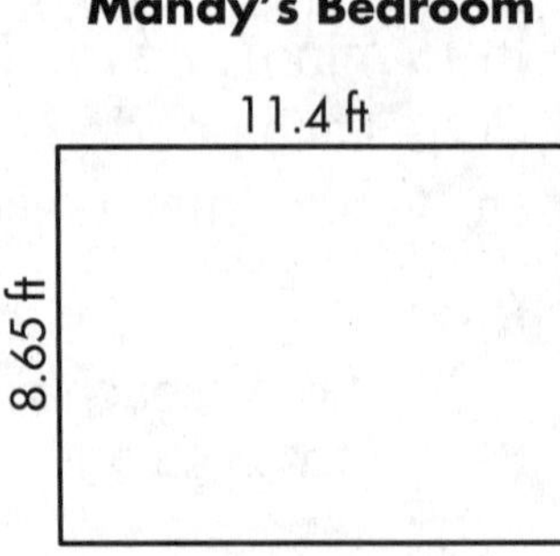

13. MP.6 Be Precise Estimate the area of Mandy's bedroom. Tell which estimation strategy you used and why.

14. Higher Order Thinking Mandy needs carpet for her bedroom. Why should the estimate for the area be an overestimate instead of an underestimate?

15. Julie estimates that she can produce 28 puzzles in one week. She sells each puzzle for $12.25. Estimate the amount of money Julie can earn in a month. Tell which estimation technique you used.

16. MP.1 Make Sense and Persevere The length of a library bookshelf is 46.725 inches. It was designed for their new MP3 audio book players. When the MP3 players arrived, the librarian found that each of the 24 cases was 1.65 inches. Will all 24 cases fit on the shelf? Use estimation to explain your reasoning.

Common Core Assessment

17. At a food manufacturer, 8.8 pounds of peanuts are added to other fruits, grains, and nuts to make one batch of granola bars. About how many pounds of peanuts are needed to make 54 batches of granola bars?

Which of the expressions would **NOT** give a reasonable estimate of the answer?

Ⓐ 8×50

Ⓑ 10×100

Ⓒ 10×50

Ⓓ 9×50

© Pearson Education, Inc. 6

Name ______________________________ Solve

Lesson 7-4
Multiply Decimals

I can …
multiply decimals.

Content Standard 6.NS.B.3
Mathematical Practices MP.2, MP.3, MP.5, MP.7, MP.8

Solve & Share Maxine is making a model windmill for a science fair. She is connecting 4 cardboard tubes together vertically. Each tube is 0.28 meter in length. What is the combined measure of the connected tubes? ***Solve this problem any way you choose.***

You can use tools, like decimal grids, to calculate with decimals.

Look Back! **MP.7 Look for Relationships** Suppose that Maxine made another windmill model by connecting 4 cardboard tubes that are 2.8 meters long. What is the combined measure of this model? What relationships do you see in the factors you used here and above? Explain how this helps you solve the problem.

Learn Glossary

How Can You Multiply Decimals?

A

What is the area of this antique map?

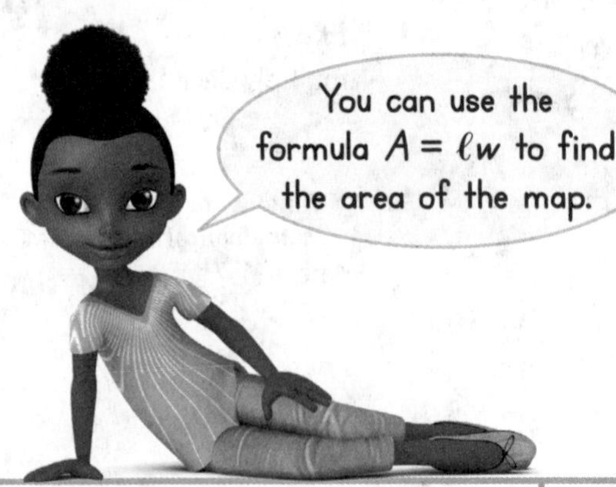

You can use the formula $A = \ell w$ to find the area of the map.

2.5 ft

3.25 ft

B One Way

Write each decimal as a fraction, then multiply.

$$\begin{aligned} A &= \ell w \\ &= 2.5 \cdot 3.25 \\ &= \frac{25}{10} \cdot \frac{325}{100} \\ &= \frac{8{,}125}{1{,}000} \\ &= 8.125 \end{aligned}$$

Remember, a tenth times a hundredth is a thousandth.

The area of the map is 8.125 ft^2.

C Another Way

Multiply as you would whole numbers. Then place the decimal point in the product.

$$\begin{array}{r} 3.25 \\ \times\ 2.5 \\ \hline 1{,}625 \\ +\ 6{,}500 \\ \hline 8.125 \end{array}$$

3.25 ⟵ 2 decimal places (hundredths)

× 2.5 ⟵ 1 decimal place (tenths)

8.125 ⟵ 3 decimal places

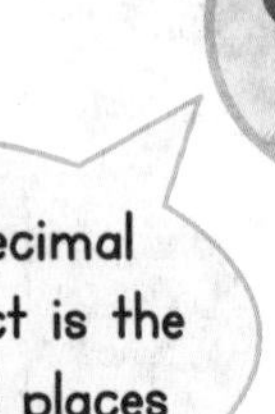

The number of decimal places in the product is the sum of the decimal places in the factors.

The area of the map is 8.125 ft^2.

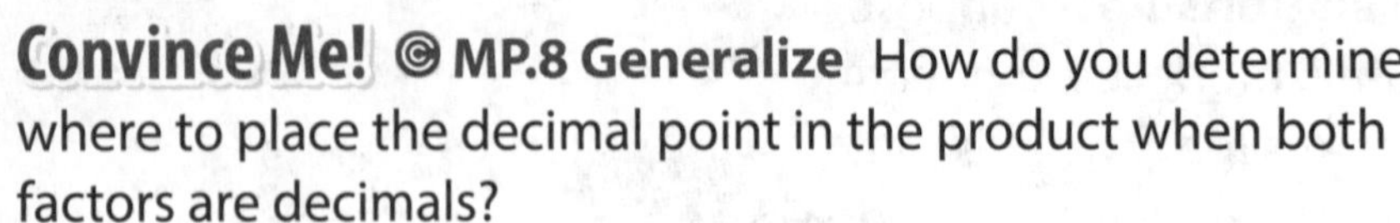

Convince Me! **MP.8 Generalize** How do you determine where to place the decimal point in the product when both factors are decimals?

© Pearson Education, Inc. 6

Name ______________________________

Practice Buddy | Tools | Assessment

Another Example

What is 48 × 3.9? What is 0.43 × 0.2?

Multiply a Whole Number and a Decimal

Find 48 × 3.9.

Estimate: 50 × 4 = 200

```
   48  ←  0 decimal places
×  3.9 ←  + 1 decimal place
  432
1,440
187.2  ←  1 decimal place
```

48 × 3.9 = 187.2

Annex Zeros in the Product

Find 0.43 × 0.2.

```
  0.43  ←  2 decimal places
×  0.2  ←  + 1 decimal place
 0.086  ←  3 decimal places
```

0.43 × 0.2 = 0.086

When you multiply hundredths by tenths, the product is thousandths.

Guided Practice*

Do You Understand?

1. What can you do if a decimal product has final zeros to the right of the decimal point?

2. **MP.3 Critique Reasoning** Diego says that the product of 0.51 × 2.427 will have five decimal places. Is Diego correct? Explain why or why not.

Do You Know How?

In **3–8**, place the decimal point in the product.

3. 4 × 0.94 = 376

4. 5 × 0.487 = 2435

5. 3.4 × 6.8 = 2312

6. 3.9 × 0.08 = 312

7. 0.9 × 0.22 = 198

8. 9 × 1.2 = 108

Independent Practice

In **9–14**, find each product.

9. 7 × 0.5

10. 12 × 0.08

11. 24 × 0.17

12. 0.4 × 0.17

13. 1.9 × 0.46

14. 3.42 × 5.15

*For another example, see Set B on page 381.

Math Practices and Problem Solving

15. **Number Sense** Write a number sentence that illustrates the following. A number with two decimal places multiplied by a number with one decimal place. The product has only two nonzero digits.

16. The Bright-O Shampoo factory includes 1.078 ounces of vanilla oil in a 6.35-ounce bottle of shampoo. How much of the bottle of shampoo is **NOT** vanilla oil?

17. Write the expanded form of the expression 8^5 and then evaluate the expression.

18. **Higher Order Thinking** Explain why 0.25×0.4 has only one decimal place in the product.

In **19–21**, use the graph to solve.

19. The fastest speed a table tennis ball has been hit is about 13.07 times as fast as the speed for the fastest swimming. What is the speed for the table tennis ball?

20. **MP.7 Look for Relationships** How fast would 1.5 times the fastest rowing speed be? Before you solve, tell the number of decimal places in your answer.

21. Which activity has a recorded speed about 7 times as fast as the fastest rowing speed?

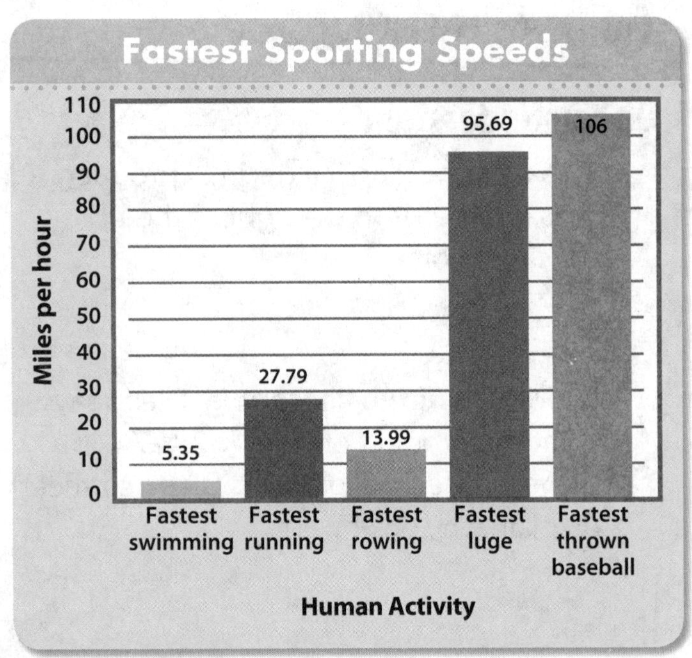

Common Core Assessment

22. The wings of some hummingbirds beat 52 times per second.

Part A

If a hummingbird hovers for 35.5 seconds, how many times do its wings beat?

Part B

Estimate the number of times its wings would beat in a minute.

© Pearson Education, Inc. 6

Name ______________________

Help | Practice Buddy | Tools | Games

Homework & Practice 7-4
Multiply Decimals

Another Look!

You can use the same algorithm to multiply whole numbers and to multiply decimals.

Find 0.72 × 23 and 0.45 × 0.8.

Ignore the decimal points. Multiply as you would with two whole numbers.

The number of decimal places in the product is the sum of the decimal places in the factors.

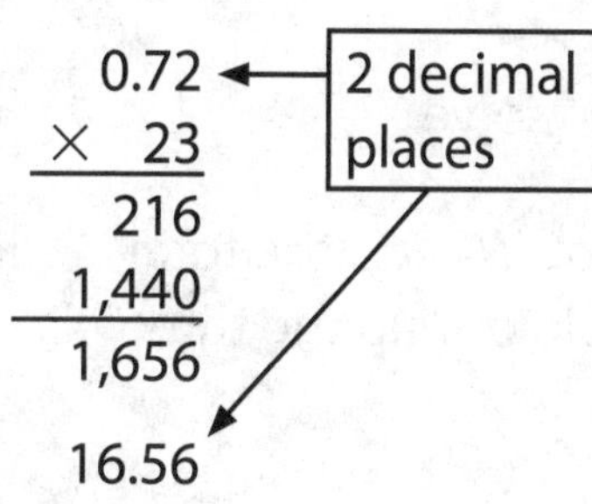

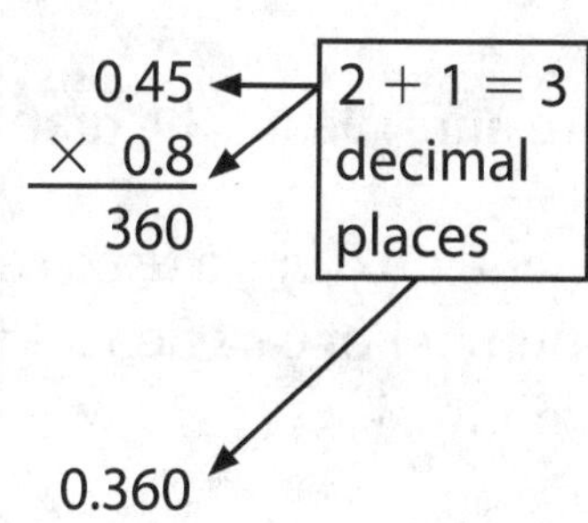

In **1–3**, place the decimal point in each product.

1. 1.2 × 3.6 = 432

2. 5.5 × 3.77 = 20735

3. 4.4 × 2.333 = 102652

In **4–15**, find each product.

4. 532.1 × 4.2

5. 47.50 × 0.03

6. 210.7 × 17.4

7. 4.3 × 2.1 =

8. 40.45 × 0.01 =

9. 6.1 × 0.3 =

10. 4.89 × 2.2

11. 2.01 × 0.43

12. 54.1 × 0.69

13. 0.5 × 0.05

14. 14.09 × 1.3

15. 10.92 × 4.08

16. **MP.2 Reasoning** If you multiply two decimals less than 1, can you predict whether the product will be less than or greater than either of the factors? Explain.

17. **Number Sense** Two factors are multiplied and their product is 34.44. One factor is a whole number. How many decimal places are in the other factor? Tell how you know.

In **18** and **19**, use the graph to solve.

18. Renaldo owns a used car lot. What is the total number of cars Renaldo sold during the three months?

19. Renaldo makes $956.75 for each car that he sells. Estimate how much money he made during the three months.

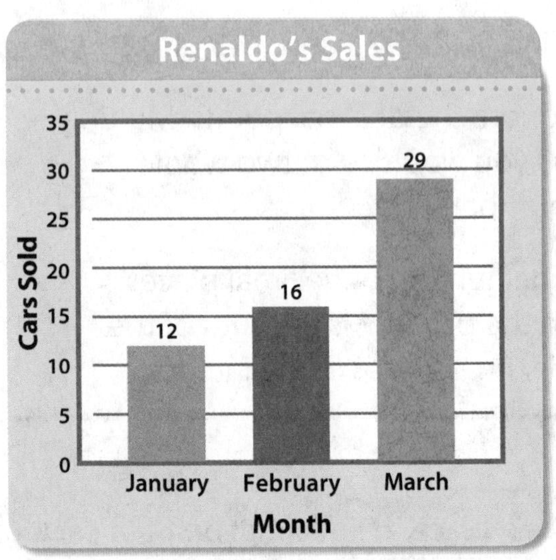

20. **MP.3 Critique Reasoning** Kim multiplied 8×0.952 and got 76.16. How can you use estimation to show that Kim's answer is wrong?

21. **Higher Order Thinking** The decimal 104.3 becomes 1,043 when multiplied by 10. The same number becomes 10.43 when mulitplied by 0.10. Explain why.

Common Core Assessment

22. A wolf is able to hear the howl of another wolf in the forest up to 1.8 kilometers away. Wolves are also very quick and can jump up to 4.5 meters.

Part A

If a kangaroo can jump 1.68 times that of a wolf, how many meters can a kangaroo jump?

Part B

An elephant is able to hear 5.4 times the distance of a wolf's hearing ability. How many kilometers away is that?

© Pearson Education, Inc. 6

Name ______________________________________

Lesson 7-5
Divide Decimals by a Whole Number

I can ...
divide decimals by whole numbers.

Content Standards 6.NS.B.2, 6.NS.B.3
Mathematical Practices MP.2, MP.3, MP.7

Solve & Share Lola, Tanisha, Sarita, and Tia receive the bill for a snack and drinks. If they share the cost equally, how much does each girl owe? ***Solve this problem any way you choose.***

You can reason about how the quantities are related to determine which operation to use to solve the problem.

Bill of Sale	
1 veggie plate	2.99
4 medium drinks	7.16
Tax	0.81
Total	$ 10.96

Look Back! **MP.3 Construct Arguments** Explain how to use estimation to check that your answer is reasonable.

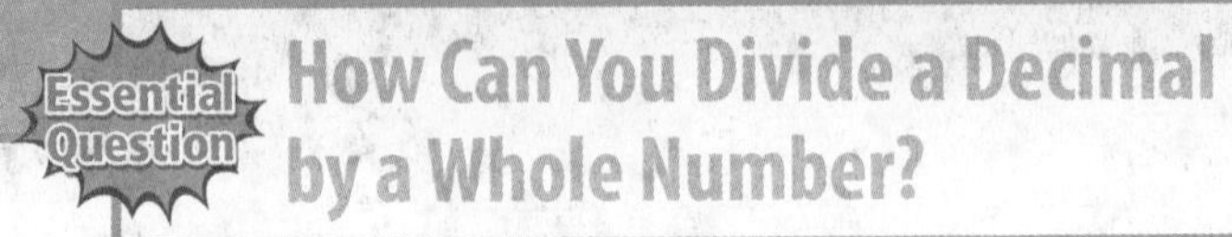

How Can You Divide a Decimal by a Whole Number?

A

Gina will make 12 equal payments to pay for her new computer. How much is Gina's monthly payment?

Use what you know about division to find the monthly payments.

B

Step 1

Estimate the quotient to help decide where to place the first digit.

Use compatible numbers to estimate.

809.40 is close to 840.
$840 \div 12 = 70$

Write the division problem using the standard algorithm.

$12\overline{)809.40}$

Because the estimate is 70, start dividing in the tens place.

C

Step 2

Divide.

$$\begin{array}{r} 67.45 \\ 12\overline{)809.40} \\ -72 \\ \hline 89 \\ -84 \\ \hline 54 \\ -48 \\ \hline 60 \\ -60 \\ \hline 0 \end{array}$$

Place the decimal point in the quotient above the decimal point in the dividend.

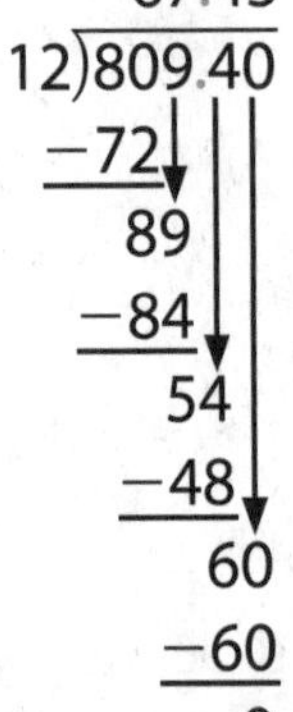

D

Step 3

Check that your answer is reasonable.

The quotient 67.45 is close to the estimate of 70, so the answer is reasonable.

Gina's monthly payment is $67.45.

Convince Me! **MP.7 Use Structure** How can you use multiplication to check the answer to the problem above?

© Pearson Education, Inc. 6

Name ______________________________

Another Example

How can you write a decimal quotient when dividing whole numbers?

Find 180 ÷ 8.
Estimate. Because 180 ÷ 10 = 18, start dividing in the tens place.

Divide the tens and ones.

```
   22
8)180
 - 16
   20
 - 16
    4
```

Write the remainder as a decimal. Place the decimal point and annex a 0 in the tenths place.

Then complete the division.

```
   22.5   Place the decimal.
8)180.0   Annex a zero.
 - 16
   20
 - 16
    40
  - 40
     0
```

Guided Practice*

Do You Understand?

1. MP.7 Use Structure How do you know where to place the decimal point in the quotient when dividing by a whole number with decimals?

2. MP.2 Reasoning How would you estimate the quotient of \$722 ÷ 89? In which place would you start dividing?

Do You Know How?

In **3** and **4**, complete each divison problem.

3.
```
   □.9□
5)34.75
 - 30
   □□
 -  45
    □□
 -   25
      □
```

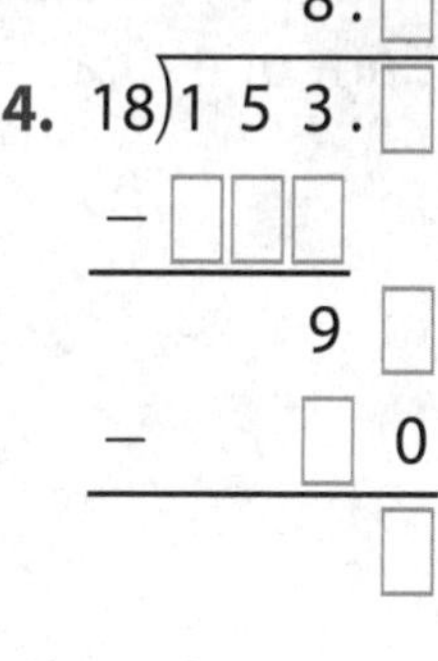
4.
```
     8.□
18)153.□
 - □□□
     9□
  -  □0
      □
```

Independent Practice

In **5–12**, find each quotient.

5. 6)\$54.18

6. 5)56

7. 6)86.1

8. 8)187.2

9. 22.34 ÷ 10

10. 6.3 ÷ 7

11. \$2.75 ÷ 25

12. 232 ÷ 40

*For another example, see Set C on page 381.

Math Practices and Problem Solving

13. **Vocabulary** Write an example of a *formula*.

14. The longest spin of a basketball on one finger is 255 minutes. How many hours is this?

15. **MP.3 Critique Reasoning** Henrieta divided 0.80 by 20 as shown. Is her work correct? If not, explain why and give a correct response.

$$\begin{array}{r} 0.40 \\ 20\overline{)0.80} \\ -\ 80 \\ \hline 0 \end{array}$$

16. Which brand of fruit snacks costs less per pound? How much less?

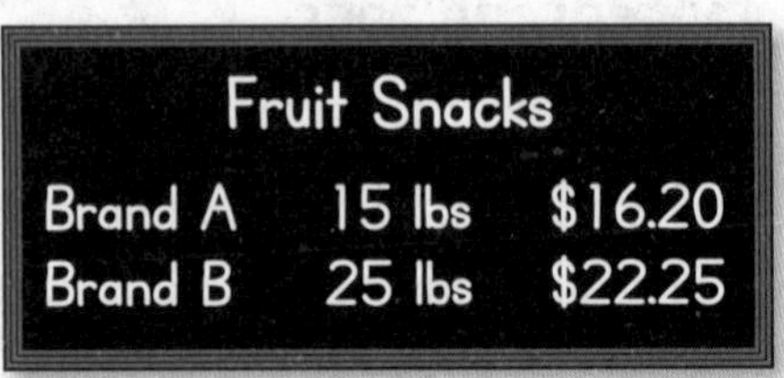

Fruit Snacks		
Brand A	15 lbs	\$16.20
Brand B	25 lbs	\$22.25

17. How might you best estimate the quotient of 479.25 ÷ 24?

18. **Higher Order Thinking** Kendra has 5.5 pounds of popcorn and wants to package it equally in 50 bags. How can she use place-value reasoning to find the amount of popcorn to put in each bag?

Common Core Assessment

19. Draw lines to connect each division expression in Column A with its quotient in Column B.

Column A	Column B
21.6 ÷ 3	7.2
315.7 ÷ 41	7.5
90 ÷ 12	7.7

© Pearson Education, Inc. 6

Name ____________________

Help | Practice Buddy | Tools | Games

Homework & Practice 7-5

Divide Decimals by a Whole Number

Another Look!

The school Gaming Club spent $196.80 on snacks and prizes for a party. There are 32 members in the club. Each agrees to pay an equal share for the snacks and prizes. Find 196.8 divided by 32.

Step 1

Put the decimal point in the quotient right above the decimal point in the dividend. Divide. Subtract.

$$\begin{array}{r} 6. \\ 32\overline{)196.8} \\ -\,192 \\ \hline 4 \end{array}$$

Remember, you can use estimation to see if your answer is reasonable.
$180 \div 30 = 6$

Step 2

Fill in the next place value with the 8. Divide. Subtract.

$$\begin{array}{r} 6.1 \\ 32\overline{)196.8} \\ -\,192 \\ \hline 48 \\ -\,32 \\ \hline 16 \end{array}$$

Step 3

Annex a zero to the end of the dividend. Divide. Subtract.

$$\begin{array}{r} 6.15 \\ 32\overline{)196.80} \\ -\,192 \\ \hline 48 \\ -\,32 \\ \hline 160 \\ -\,160 \\ \hline 0 \end{array}$$

Each member pays $6.15.

In **1–16**, find each quotient.

1. $12\overline{)\$44.40}$ **2.** $9\overline{)20.7}$ **3.** $4\overline{)26}$ **4.** $7\overline{)22.61}$

5. $42.78 ÷ 3 **6.** 73.5 ÷ 6 **7.** 34 ÷ 10 **8.** 59.6 ÷ 8

9. 188.4 ÷ 60 **10.** 9 ÷ 90 **11.** 231 ÷ 42 **12.** 11.2 ÷ 25

13. 32.9 ÷ 5 **14.** 0.34 ÷ 34 **15.** 12.8 ÷ 64 **16.** 31 ÷ 62

17. Yolanda bought 8 tickets to a concert for \$214. What was the cost of each ticket?

18. **Number Sense** Vicky makes jewelry. She uses 42 beads for each necklace she makes and has 500 beads. How many necklaces can she make? Explain.

19. **MP.3 Critique Reasoning** Dana said that $0.6 \div 30 = 0.02$. Is she correct? Explain how you know.

20. Which bag of potatoes costs more per pound? How much more?

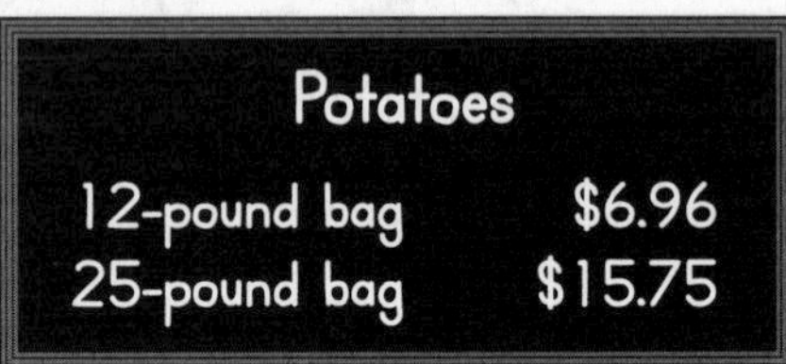

Potatoes	
12-pound bag	\$6.96
25-pound bag	\$15.75

21. Tony bought a 72-ounce box of dog biscuits. How many pounds of dog biscuits did he buy?

Remember,
1 pound = 16 ounces.

22. **Higher Order Thinking** When you divide 7.7 by 700, how many decimal places will the quotient have? Use place-value reasoning to explain how you know.

Common Core Assessment

23. Draw lines to connect each division expression in Column A with its quotient in Column B.

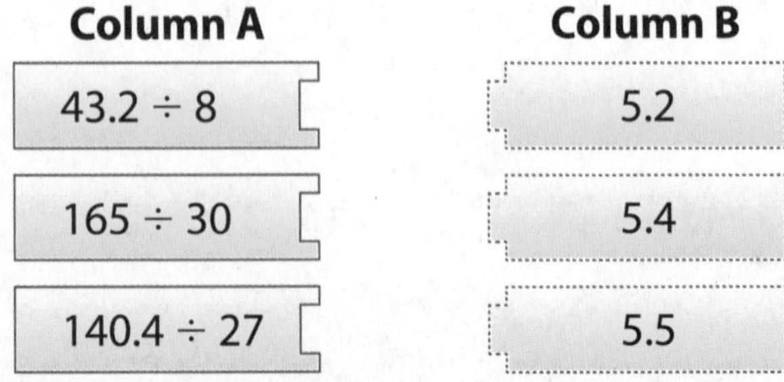

Column A	Column B
$43.2 \div 8$	5.2
$165 \div 30$	5.4
$140.4 \div 27$	5.5

© Pearson Education, Inc. 6

Name ____________________

Lesson 7-6
Divide Decimals

Solve & Share Tara bought special beads to use in a bracelet she is making. Each bead costs $0.30. The total cost of the beads was $1.50. How many beads did Tara buy? ***Solve this problem any way you choose.***

I can ...
use different strategies to divide decimals.

Content Standards 6.NS.B.2, 6.NS.B.3
Mathematical Practices MP.2, MP.4, MP.6, MP.7

Model with math by drawing a picture that can help you solve the problem.

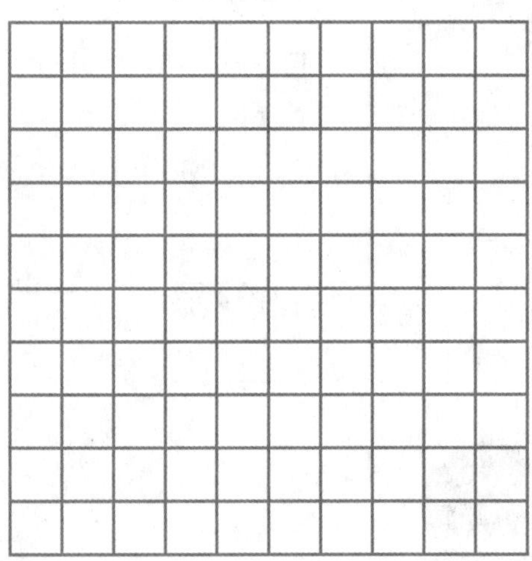

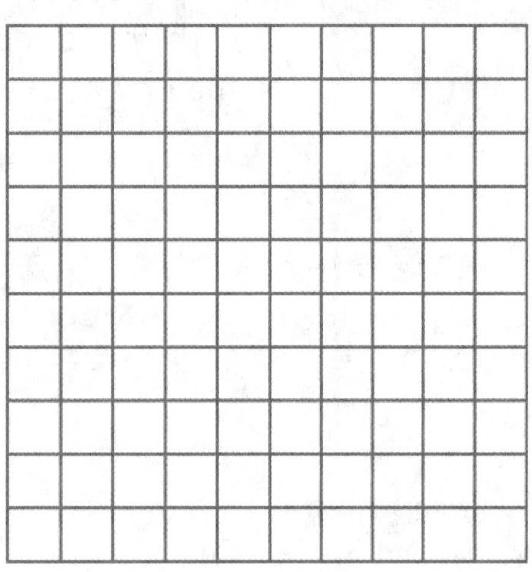

Look Back! **MP.2 Reasoning** Think of the cost of the beads as 150 cents rather than $1.50. How might this make the division easier? Explain your reasoning.

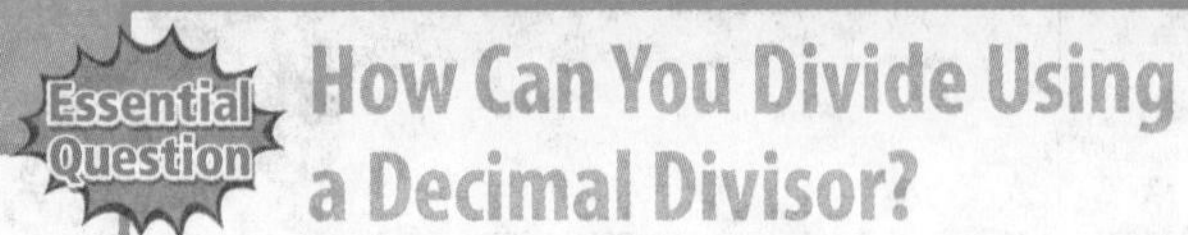

How Can You Divide Using a Decimal Divisor?

A

Tyler purchased several songs to download to his MP3 player. Before tax, the total cost was $4.20 and the cost of each song was $1.40. How many songs did he buy?

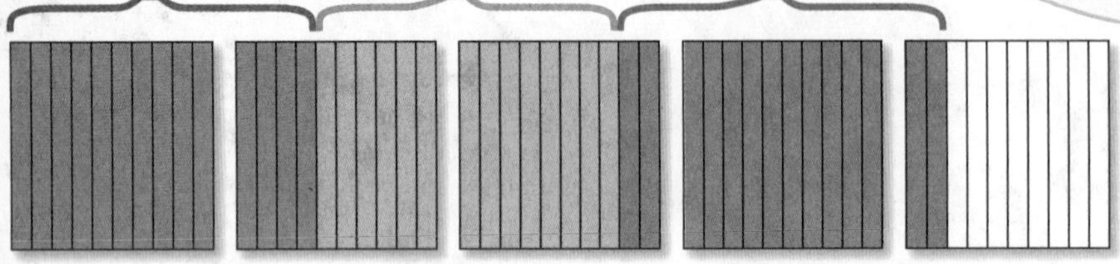

You use structure when you divide decimals. Place value is based on powers of 10.

B

Step 1

Estimate: $4 \div 1 = 4$

Think of a power of 10 that will make the divisor a whole number.

$$1.40\overline{)4.20}$$

Multiply 1.40 by 10^2 or 100.

C

Step 2

Multiply both the divisor and the dividend by the same power of 10.

$$1.40\overline{)4.20}$$

Multiplying both the divisor and dividend by the same power of 10 keeps the math the same.

D

Step 3

Find $420 \div 140$.

Divide. Place the decimal in the quotient, if needed.

$$\begin{array}{r} 3 \\ 140\overline{)420} \\ -\ 420 \\ \hline 0 \end{array}$$

3 is close to 4, so the answer is reasonable.

Tyler purchased 3 songs.

Convince Me! **MP.7 Use Structure** In the division problem $41.75\overline{)250.5}$, how do you make the divisor a whole number? Write a new division problem with a whole number divisor.

© Pearson Education, Inc. 6

Name ___________________________

Practice Buddy Tools Assessment

Another Example

Find 0.021 ÷ 0.35.

Multiply the divisor and dividend by the same power of 10 that will make the divisor a whole number. Then place the decimal in the quotient.

$0.35\overline{)0.021} = 35\overline{)2.1}$

Divide. Annex zeros as needed.

$$\begin{array}{r} 0.06 \\ 35\overline{)2.10} \\ -\ 2\,10 \\ \hline 0 \end{array}$$

So, 0.021 ÷ 0.35 = 0.06.

Guided Practice*

Do You Understand?

1. **MP.7 Look for Relationships** When dividing 55.8 by 2.325, by which power of 10 would you multiply the divisor and dividend? How many places would the decimal point move in the divisor and dividend?

2. In Another Example above, why is a 0 annexed in the dividend?

Do You Know How?

In **3–6**, find each quotient.

3. $3\overline{)0.6}$

4. $0.50\overline{)2.50}$

5. 3.6 ÷ 0.9

6. 8.8 ÷ 0.4

Independent Practice

In **7–14**, find each quotient.

7. $0.8\overline{)64}$

8. $0.03\overline{)33.9}$

9. $0.005\overline{)0.04}$

10. $0.6\overline{)0.024}$

11. 52.6 ÷ 0.08

12. 1.275 ÷ 0.03

13. 52.056 ÷ 7.23

14. 9.089 ÷ 0.745

*For another example, see Set C on page 381.

Math Practices and Problem Solving

15. An electric company charges $0.15 for each kilowatt-hour of electricity. If your electric bill is $67.50, how many kilowatt-hours of electricity did you use?

16. **Number Sense** How can you decide which quotient is greater, 127.34 ÷ 0.673 or 127.34 ÷ 0.671, without doing the division?

17. **MP.6 Be Precise** How many times as much does each item cost in 2010 as in 1960?

Movie ticket ____________

Regular popcorn ____________

Regular drink ____________

DATA

Item	1960 Cost	2010 Cost
Movie Ticket	$0.75	$9.75
Regular Popcorn	$0.25	$4.10
Regular drink	$0.35	$3.08

18. **Higher Order Thinking** You and a friend are paid $38.25 for doing yard work. You worked 2.5 hours and your friend worked 2 hours. You split the money according to the amount of time each of you worked. How much is your share of the money? Explain.

Common Core Assessment

19. A farmer harvested 634.5 bushels of sweet corn from a 4.5 acre corn field. If the same number of bushels were harvested from each acre, how many bushels are there per acre?

Explain how to find 634.5 ÷ 4.5.

© Pearson Education, Inc. 6

Name ____________________

Homework & Practice 7-6
Divide Decimals

Another Look!

Find 2.48 ÷ 0.8.

When you divide by a decimal, rewrite the dividend and the divisor so that you are dividing by a whole number.

To make the divisor a whole number, multiply the divisor and the dividend by the same power of 10.

Place the decimal in the quotient and divide as you would with whole numbers.

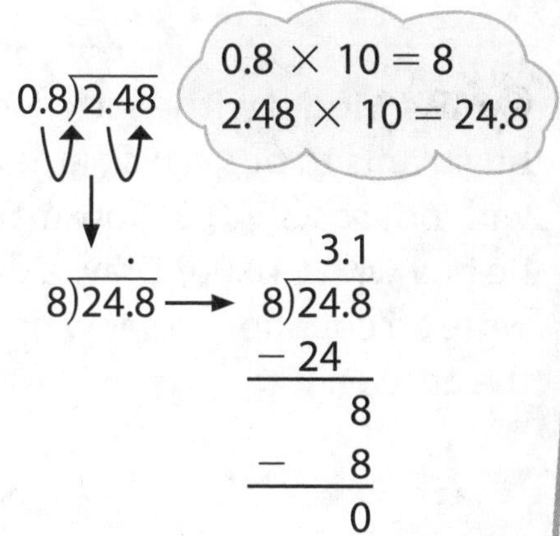

In **1–22**, find each quotient.

Remember, sometimes you need to annex zeros to complete your division.

1. 0.6)0.36 **2.** 0.2)1.5

3. 8.4 ÷ 0.3 **4.** 10.5 ÷ 1.5 **5.** 7.28 ÷ 1.4 **6.** 2.87 ÷ 0.01

7. 66.15 ÷ 0.63 **8.** 0.86 ÷ 0.004 **9.** 14.36 ÷ 0.4 **10.** 78.32 ÷ 2.2

11. 36.4 ÷ 0.52 **12.** 0.4462 ÷ 9.7 **13.** 4.8 ÷ 0.6 **14.** 6.588 ÷ 0.54

15. 23.6 ÷ 5 **16.** 89.54 ÷ 11 **17.** 21 ÷ 0.2 **18.** 100.8 ÷ 8.4

19. 10.25 ÷ 4.1 **20.** 76.23 ÷ 0.03 **21.** 2.8 ÷ 1.4 **22.** 9.3 ÷ 3.1

23. **Math and Science** Alec researched the melting points of different elements. Sodium melts at 97.72°C. Lead melts at 327.5°C. How much hotter is the melting point of lead than sodium?

24. **Higher Order Thinking** How do you know that $1.016 \div 4.064 \neq 0.025$ without doing the division?

25. **MP.4 Model with Math** Ricky wants to buy plants to put in his garden. Each plant with pot costs $1.60. How many plants can he buy with $10.00? Draw a picture and write an equation to show how you can get the answer.

26. Mr. Timm rented a truck for $39.95 for the day, plus $0.54 for each mile he drives. His total bill, not including gasoline, was $72.62. How many miles did he drive?

Common Core Assessment

27. A farmer harvested 1,627.5 bushels of soybeans from 38.75 acres. If the same number of bushels were harvested from each acre, how many bushels are there per acre?

Explain how to find $1{,}627.5 \div 38.75$.

© Pearson Education, Inc. 6

Name ____________________

Solve

Lesson 7-7
Continue to Divide Decimals

I can . . .
divide decimals to find solutions to real-world problems.

Content Standards 6.NS.B.2, 6.NS.B.3
Mathematical Practices MP.1, MP.2, MP.4, MP.7

Solve & Share Some friends went to lunch and split the bill equally. If each person paid $6.75, how many people went to lunch? Use a diagram or equation to explain your thinking. ***Solve this problem any way you choose.***

You can use reasoning to solve the problem.
RECEIPT
Food $$$
Drinks $$$
Total $27

Look Back! **MP.2 Reasoning** Suppose $7.00 was added to the bill for a dessert that everyone shared. How much more does each person have to pay? Explain how you found the answer.

Learn Glossary

Essential Question How Can You Divide a Decimal by a Decimal?

A

The area of Josie's rectangular flowerbed is 7.75 square meters. How long is Josie's flowerbed?

$A = \ell \cdot w$

$7.75 = \ell \cdot 1.25$ ← Divide both sides by 1.25.

$7.75 \div 1.25 = \ell$

Find $7.75 \div 1.25$.

You can use the area formula to write a division expression to find the length.

B

Step 1

Multiply the divisor by a power of 10 that makes it a whole number. Multiply by 10^2 or 100.

$1.25 \cdot 100 = 125$

Multiply the dividend by the same power of 10.

$7.75 \cdot 100 = 775$

Find $125\overline{)775}$.

When you divide by a decimal, rewrite the divisor so that you are dividing by a whole number. The answers are the same.

C

Step 2

Place the decimal in the quotient and divide.

$$\begin{array}{r} 6.2 \\ 125\overline{)775.000} \\ -750 \\ 250 \\ -250 \\ 0 \end{array}$$

The quotient 6.2 is close to the estimate of 6, so the answer is reasonable.

D

Step 3

Multiply the length you found by the width to check your answer.

$6.2 \cdot 1.25 = 7.75$

The area of 7.75 square meters checks.

The length of Josie's garden is 6.2 meters.

Convince Me! **MP.2 Reasoning** Henry has a flower garden. All the sides measure 0.006 kilometer. The garden's perimeter is 0.03 kilometer. How many sides does Henry's garden have? Explain how you found the answer.

© Pearson Education, Inc. 6

Name ____________________

Practice Buddy Tools Assessment

Guided Practice*

Do You Understand?

1. MP.7 Look for Relationships When the divisor is a decimal, how do you know which power of 10 to multiply it by in order to make it a whole number?

2. Why is it necessary to multiply both the divisor and the dividend by the same power of 10?

Do You Know How?

In **3–6**, find each quotient.

3. $2.7 \div 0.3$

4. $1.6 \div 0.004$

5. $8.1 \div 0.03$

6. $2.25 \div 0.05$

You use place-value structure when you multiply and divide decimals.

Independent Practice

Leveled Practice In **7–14**, find each quotient.

7. $0.03\overline{)1.5}$

8. $0.008\overline{)0.64}$

9. $0.04\overline{)9.6}$

10. $0.02\overline{)5.74}$

11. $13.76 \div 0.32$

12. $0.116 \div 0.004$

13. $73.8 \div 0.9$

14. $3.91 \div 0.23$

*For another example, see Set C on page 381.

Math Practices and Problem Solving

The mass of each winning vegetable at a state fair is recorded in the table.

State Fair Vegetable Contest Results			
Vegetable	Mass	Vegetable	Mass
Carrot	7.5 kg	Pumpkin	652 kg
Cabbage	32.6 kg	Broccoli	14.8 kg
Cauliflower	13.7 kg	Sweet Potato	10.6 kg

15. How many times as great is the mass of the pumpkin than the mass of the cabbage?

16. Gina's wagon will hold up to 135 kilograms. How many prize-winning carrots can the wagon safely hold?

17. Last year, the winning cauliflower had a mass of 12.9 kg. How much more mass does this year's winning cauliflower have than last year's cauliflower?

Remember to use estimation to see if your answers are reasonable.

18. Helen has a flash drive with 8 megabytes of storage. She wants to use the flash drive to save photos from her class trip. Each photo takes up 0.36 megabyte of storage space. How many photos can she save on her flash drive? How much storage space will be left?

19. **Higher Order Thinking** A jar filled with marbles has a mass of 8.65 kilograms. When the jar is empty it has a mass of 0.9 kilogram. Each marble is 0.025 kilogram. Can you find the number of marbles in the jar without counting each one? Explain.

Common Core Assessment

20. Choose all of the equations that are true.

- ☐ $161.6 \div 5.05 = 32$
- ☐ $6.12 \div 0.68 = 90$
- ☐ $0.06 \div 0.005 = 12$
- ☐ $90.2 \div 2.2 = 410$

21. Choose all of the equations that are **NOT** true.

- ☐ $10.8 \div 3 = 3.6$
- ☐ $814 \div 3.7 = 202$
- ☐ $4.03 \div 32.5 = 1.24$
- ☐ $5.418 \div 1.4 = 3.87$

© Pearson Education, Inc. 6

Name ____________________

Help | Practice Buddy | Tools | Games

Homework & Practice 7-7

Continue to Divide Decimals

Another Look!

If all the plastic bottles collected by the Quinn family for recycling during a given month were laid end to end, they would measure 35.2 meters long. How many plastic bottles were collected if each plastic bottle measures 0.16 meter?

Find 35.2 ÷ 0.16.

When you divide by a decimal, rewrite the divisor so that you are dividing by a whole number.

Step 1 Make the divisor a whole number. Multiply the divisor and the dividend by the same power of 10. Place the decimal in the quotient.

$$\begin{array}{r} 220 \\ 0.16\overline{)35.20} \\ -32 \\ \hline 32 \\ -32 \\ \hline 0 \end{array}$$

0.16 × 100 = 16
35.2 × 100 = 3,520

Step 2 Divide as you would with whole numbers. Remember that sometimes you may need to annex zeros.

Step 3 Multiply to check that your answer is reasonable.

220 × 0.16 = 35.2
220 bottles is reasonable.

There is no remainder, so there are no decimal places in the quotient.

In **1–8**, find each quotient.

1. $0.25\overline{)500}$ **2.** $0.68\overline{)0.816}$ **3.** $0.9\overline{)0.36}$ **4.** $0.5\overline{)0.004}$

5. 15.4 ÷ 0.308 **6.** 7.37 ÷ 0.67 **7.** 4.848 ÷ 0.4 **8.** 1.16 ÷ 0.008

Samantha visits her local farm market to buy apples and oranges to make a fruit salad. She has $10.00 to spend.

9. If Samanatha buys only apples, how many can she buy?

10. If Samantha buys only oranges, how many can she buy?

11. **Higher Order Thinking** Samantha decides to buy both apples and oranges. Give two different solutions to tell how many apples and how many oranges she might buy.

12. **MP.4 Model with Math** Jared draws several figures that each have equal side lengths of 1.4 meters. He records the perimeter, in meters, of each figure in the table below.

Let n = the number of sides of each figure. Write an equation to represent the perimeter and complete the table.

Number of Sides, n	3	4	5	6	8
Perimeter	4.2		7		

13. **MP.1 Make Sense and Persevere** You have $15.60 to buy juice boxes for the school picnic. Each juice box costs $0.80. How many juice boxes can you buy? Should you expect to get change when you pay for the juice boxes? If so, how much?

Common Core Assessment

14. Choose all of the equations that are true.

- ☐ $157.59 \div 35.02 = 4$
- ☐ $2.244 \div 3.4 = 0.66$
- ☐ $222.5 \div 0.89 = 25$
- ☐ $4.428 \div 1.2 = 3.69$

15. Choose all of the equations that are **NOT** true.

- ☐ $8.5 \div 2.5 = 0.34$
- ☐ $5.60 \div 7.0 = 8$
- ☐ $3.311 \div 1.4 = 2.365$
- ☐ $2.58 \div 0.3 = 8.6$

© Pearson Education, Inc. 6

Name ____________________

Solve

Lesson 7-8
Evaluate Expressions with Decimals

I can ...
evaluate an algebraic expression with decimals.

Content Standards 6.EE.A.2a, 6.EE.A.2c, 6.NS.B.2, 6.NS.B.3
Mathematical Practices MP.3, MP.4, MP.6, MP.7, MP.8

Solve & Share A bike shop charges by the hour to rent a bike. Related items are rented for flat fees. Write an expression that represents how much it will cost to rent a bike and helmet for *h* hours. How much would it cost to rent a bike and a helmet for 3 hours? ***Solve this problem any way you choose.***

Model with math. You can write an algebraic expression with decimals the same way you do with whole numbers.

Rental	Cost
Bike	$12.50 (per hour)
Helmet	$5.25
Lock	$1.75
Basket	$2.25

Look Back! **MP.7 Use Structure** Write an expression that represents renting a bike, lock, and basket for *h* hours. What is the cost of renting this equipment for 4 hours?

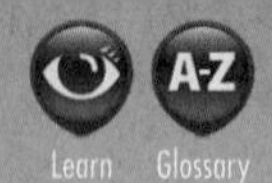

How Can You Write and Evaluate Algebraic Expressions with Decimals?

A

Sarah and her brother buy tickets to the school play for their family. They decide to share the cost equally.

Write an algebraic expression that shows Sarah's share of the cost. Then use the expression to find Sarah's share of the cost if there are 6 people in her family.

School Play Ticket Prices	
All Ages	\$4.25

Be precise. You can use a variable to represent an unknown value.

B

Step 1

Write the algebraic expression.

Let x = the number of tickets bought.

Each ticket costs \$4.25, so the expression $4.25x$ represents the total cost of the tickets.

Sarah and her brother share the cost equally, so use division to find the equal parts.

$$4.25x \div 2$$

Think about which operation should be performed first in the algebraic expression.

C

Step 2

Evaluate the algebraic expression.

Use substitution to evaluate the expression.

Evaluate $4.25x \div 2$ for $x = 6$.

$$4.25(6) \div 2$$
$$= 25.50 \div 2$$
$$= 12.75$$

Sarah will pay \$12.75 for her family's tickets.

Convince Me! **MP.7 Use Structure** Suppose that groups over 10 people can purchase tickets at a discounted price of \$4.00 per ticket. Write an algebraic expression that shows Sarah's cost if she buys tickets for more than 10 family members. Explain what each term of the expression represents.

© Pearson Education, Inc. 6

Name ______________________________

Guided Practice*

Practice Buddy | Tools | Assessment

Do You Understand?

1. MP.8 Generalize What does it mean to *evaluate* an expression by using *substitution*?

2. MP.7 Use Structure Suppose the play tickets cost $5.50 each. Write an algebraic expression to represent the amount that Sarah would pay for her family's tickets. How much would Sarah pay if there are 3 people in her family?

Do You Know How?

In **3–6**, evaluate each expression.

3. $r \div 2.4; r = 16.8$

4. $9.85 \times s; s = 4$

5. $4f - 7; f = 12.6$

6. $6y + (y \div 2); y = 6.1$

Remember to use the order of operations when you evaluate expressions.

Independent Practice

In **7–15**, evaluate each expression for $x = 1.8$, $x = 5$, and $x = 6.4$.

7. $x \div 4$

8. $x(3.35)$

9. $2x + 3.1$

10. $6.7(x \div 2)$

11. $x \div x$

12. $2x + x^2$

13. $(1.3x + 8.9) \times 0$

14. $3x + 1.2x$

15. $x^2 \div 1 + 1$

16. Evaluate the expression for the values of *t*.

t	0.02	6	11.2
$6.32 + 4.2 \div t$			

17. Evaluate the expression for the values of *p*.

p	69.08	25	0.008
$p \div 8 + 0(p)$			

18. Evaluate the expression for the values of *b*.

b	8.9	5.1	0.2
$b(3) + 20.4$			

19. Evaluate the expression for the values of *n*.

n	13.8	45.16	53.004
$n \div 2 - 4.15$			

*For another example, see Set D on page 382.

Math Practices and Problem Solving

In **20** and **21**, use the table to solve.

Necklace length	Cost of Chain	Cost of Pendant
Long	\$2.25	\$4.50
Medium	\$1.80	\$3.72
Short	\$1.15	\$2.39

20. **MP.4 Model with Math** Tamara is making a medium-length necklace. Write an expression that shows how much it will cost Tamara for the chain, pendant, and for b beads that cost \$0.25 each. Then find the total cost of the necklace if Tamara uses 30 beads.

21. **Higher Order Thinking** Ronnie is making short and long necklaces with only one chain and one pendant per necklace. Write an expression that shows how much it will cost Ronnie to make s short and n long necklaces. Then find the cost for 3 short necklaces and 2 long necklaces.

22. **MP.3 Critique Reasoning** A chemist uses the expression $g \div 2.25 + 2.25$ to find the number of grams of a chemical needed for a mixture. When $g = 4.5$, David said the answer is 1. What mistake did David make? What is the correct value of the expression for $g = 4.5$?

23. Katie is evaluating the expression $15.75 \div p + 3p$ when $p = 3.15$. Explain each step she should follow.

Common Core Assessment

24. Choose the correct values from the box below to complete the table that follows. Evaluate the expression for each value of the variable in the table.

0.32 **0.48** **27.2** **28.8** **38.4**

x	0.09	5.1	7.2
$5x + (x \div 3)$			

© Pearson Education, Inc. 6

Name ______________________________

Homework & Practice 7-8

Evaluate Expressions with Decimals

Another Look!

To evaluate an expression with decimals, substitute the variable with the given value. Then use the order of operations to calculate.

Evaluate $5.1 + 3n$ for $n = 2.6$.

Replace n with 2.6. → $5.1 + 3(2.6)$

Multiply first. → $5.1 + 7.8$

Then add. → 12.9

The value of the expression is 12.9.

Evaluate $x^2 + 2x - x \div 3$ for $x = 3.3$.

Replace x with 3.3. → $3.3^2 + 2(3.3) - 3.3 \div 3$

Evaluate terms with exponents first. → $10.89 + 2(3.3) - 3.3 \div 3$

Then multiply and divide. → $10.89 + 6.6 - 1.1$

Then add and subtract. → 16.39

The value of the expression is 16.39.

In **1–3**, evaluate each expression by using substitution.

1. $6n$; $n = 2.3$

2. $3x - 8.1$; $x = 6.4$

3. $r + 53.3 \div r$; $r = 6.5$

In **4–9**, evaluate each expression for $x = 3.1$, $x = 6.2$, and $x = 8.3$.

4. $5x$

5. $8.2 + x \div 2$

6. $2x + 1.5x$

7. $12x - 14.5$

8. $(0.85 + x) \div 5$

9. $8.92 - (x + 0.47)$

10. Evaluate the expression for the values of f.

f	0.6	24	100
$2.6f + f \div 8$			

11. Evaluate the expression for the values of v.

v	1.8	13.2	200.89
$v - 0.8 + 0.5 \cdot v$			

12. Evaluate the expression for the values of s.

s	0.002	2.89	34.74
$4.09s \div s$			

13. Evaluate the expression for the values of t.

t	0.01	1	2.5
$\frac{9.5}{t} + 3.2t$			

14. Higher Order Thinking The deli sells ham for \$3.95 per pound, turkey for \$4.30 per pound, and cheese for \$3.10 per pound. Write an expression that shows how much it will cost to buy h pounds of ham, t pounds of turkey, and c pounds of cheese. Then find the cost for 1 pound of ham, 1.5 pounds of turkey, and 2.3 pounds of cheese.

15. MP.4 Model with Math Juan rented a paddleboard for \$5.75 per hour plus a \$17.50 fee. Write an expression that shows how much it will cost Juan to rent the paddleboard for x hours. Then evaluate the expression for 3 hours.

16. MP.6 Be Precise The table shows how much a frozen yogurt shop charges for its yogurt. Write an expression to show how much it costs to buy a small yogurt with no toppings and a large yogurt with x toppings. Then find the total cost for a small yogurt with no toppings and a large yogurt with 3 toppings.

DATA

Size of cup	Cost of cup	Cost per topping
Small	\$2.85	\$0.25
Medium	\$3.75	\$0.30
Large	\$4.65	\$0.35

17. Math and Science The heart of an adult human being pumps about 83.3 gallons of blood per hour. Write an expression to tell how many gallons of blood an adult heart pumps in h hours.

18. Evaluate the expression from Exercise 17 to find how many gallons of blood the heart of an adult human being pumps in 3 hours and in 10 hours.

19. A-Z Vocabulary Multiplication and division have an *inverse relationship*. How are multiplication and division related?

20. Order the follow numbers from least to greatest.

$\frac{3}{4}, -\frac{1}{8}, \left|\frac{1}{4}\right|, -3, -\frac{1}{2}, |-1|$

Common Core Assessment

21. Choose the correct values from the box below to complete the table that follows. Evaluate the expression for each value of the variable in the table.

0.71	0.97	3.13	3.73	4.13

r	0.59	1.8	2.3
$3r - (r + 0.47)$			

© Pearson Education, Inc. 6

Name ____________________

Lesson 7-9
Solve Equations with Decimals

I can ...
solve algebraic equations that include decimals.

Content Standards 6.EE.B.7, 6.NS.B.2, 6.NS.B.3
Mathematical Practices MP.2, MP.3, MP.4, MP.7

Solve & Share

The Shore Coast Trail is a popular hiking trail. One family on vacation hiked 22.2 miles on the trail. How many times did they hike the trail during their vacation? ***Solve this problem any way you choose.***

Can you use numbers and symbols to show your reasoning?

Look Back! **MP.2 Reasoning** How can you use estimation to check your answer for reasonableness? Explain.

Learn Glossary

Essential Question

How Can You Solve Equations with Decimals?

A

Molly bought these oranges for \$7.15. She pays the same amount for each orange.

Let m equal the cost of each orange. Solve the equation 13m = 7.15 to find what Molly paid for each orange.

Use structure to decide how to solve the equation.

B Use inverse relationships to solve the equation.

The variable m is multiplied by 13. To get m alone on one side of the equation, use the inverse of multiplying by 13.

Divide both sides of the equation by 13.

$$13m = 7.15$$

$$13m \div 13 = 7.15 \div 13$$

$$m = 0.55$$

C To check the solution, substitute 0.55 for m.

$$13(0.55) = 7.15$$
$$7.15 = 7.15$$

It checks!

Molly paid \$0.55 for each orange.

Convince Me! **MP.4 Model with Math** Molly also buys a bag of 8 apples for \$3.60. Write and solve an equation to find how much Molly paid for each apple.

© Pearson Education, Inc. 6

Name ___

Practice Buddy Tools Assessment

Another Example

Use inverse relationships to solve each equation.

$m + 5.43 = 9.28$	$x \div 2.5 = 40$	$y - 6.2 = 2.9$
$m + 5.43 - 5.43 = 9.28 - 5.43$	$x \div 2.5 \times 2.5 = 40 \times 2.5$	$y - 6.2 + 6.2 = 2.9 + 6.2$
$m = 3.85$	$x = 100$	$y = 9.1$

Guided Practice*

Do You Understand?

1. **MP.3 Construct Arguments** Why are inverse relationships important to solving equations?

2. **MP.3 Critique Reasoning** Johnny says that he solved the equation $x - 3.5 = 7.2$ by adding 3.5 to the left side of the equation. Explain whether Johnny is correct.

Do You Know How?

In **3–6**, solve each equation and check your solution.

3. $13.27 = t - 24.45$
4. $17.3 + v = 22.32$
5. $1.8x = 40.14$
6. $r \div 5.5 = 18.2$

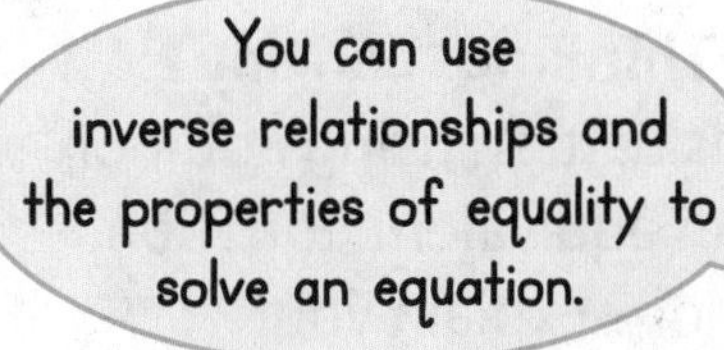

You can use inverse relationships and the properties of equality to solve an equation.

Independent Practice

Leveled Practice In **7–11**, solve each equation and check your solution.

7. $w - 3.2 = 5.6$
$w - 3.2 +$ ___ $= 5.6 +$ ___
$w =$ ___

8. $9.6 = 1.6y$
$9.6 \div$ ___ $= 1.6y \div$ ___
___ $= y$

9. $48.55 + k = 61.77$

10. $m \div 3.54 = 1.5$

11. $45.3 = 3g$

*For another example, see Set D on page 382.

Math Practices and Problem Solving

12. **Math and Science** The scientific name for the little bumps on your tongue is *fungiform papillae*. Each bump can contain many taste buds. The number of taste buds a person has varies. There are three general classifications of taste: supertaster, medium taster, and nontaster. Suppose a supertaster has 8,640 taste buds. Solve the equation $4.5n = 8{,}640$ to find the number, n, of taste buds a nontaster may have.

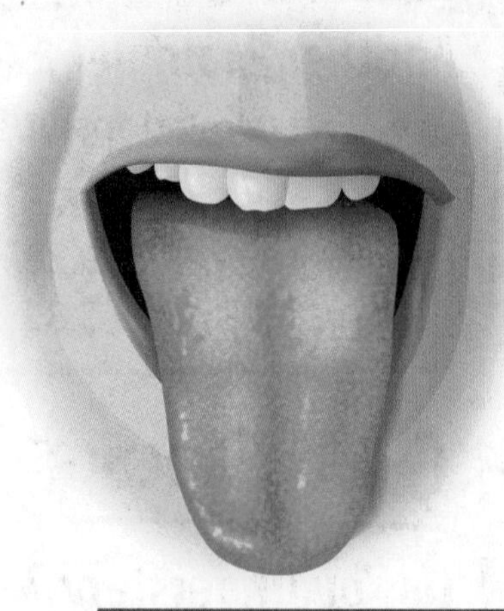

A supertaster may have 4.5 times as many taste buds as a nontaster.

13. **MP.4 Model with Math** In one study, the number of women classified as supertasters was 2.25 times the number of men classified as supertasters. Suppose 72 women were classified as supertasters. Write an equation that represents the number of men, m, who were classified as supertasters. Then solve the equation you wrote. How many men were classified as supertasters?

14. **Higher Order Thinking** Can any equation that is written using addition be written as an equivalent equation using subtraction? Explain your reasoning and give an example that has decimals that shows your reasoning.

15. **MP.3 Critique Reasoning** Oscar is 12 years old, and his little sister is 6. Oscar uses a to represent his age. He says that he can use the expression $a \div 2$ to always know his sister's age. Do you agree? Explain.

Common Core Assessment

16. Which is the solution to the equation below?

$0.26y = 0.676$

Ⓐ $y = 0.17576$

Ⓑ $y = 0.26$

Ⓒ $y = 2.6$

Ⓓ $y = 26$

17. Which is the solution to the equation below?

$0.435 + x = 0.92$

Ⓐ $x = 1.355$

Ⓑ $x = 0.595$

Ⓒ $x = 0.495$

Ⓓ $x = 0.485$

© Pearson Education, Inc. 6

Name ______________________

Help | Practice Buddy | Tools | Games

Homework & Practice 7-9

Solve Equations with Decimals

Another Look!

Equations can be solved by using inverse relationships and the properties of equality to get a variable alone on one side of the equation.

Remember that you need to do the same thing to both sides of the equation to keep the equation equal.

Solve the equation $5.2 + c = 13.6$.

To get c alone, undo adding 5.2 by subtracting 5.2 from both sides.

$$5.2 + c = 13.6$$
$$5.2 + c - \mathbf{5.2} = 13.6 - \mathbf{5.2}$$
$$c = 8.4$$

Check your solution by substituting 8.4 for c in the equation.

$$5.2 + c = 13.6$$
$$5.2 + 8.4 = 13.6$$
$$13.6 = 13.6 \quad \text{It checks.}$$

Solve the equation $t \div 2.5 = 11.7$.

To get t alone, undo dividing by 2.5 by multiplying by 2.5 on both sides.

$$t \div 2.5 = 11.7$$
$$t \div 2.5 \times \mathbf{2.5} = 11.7 \times \mathbf{2.5}$$
$$t = 29.25$$

Check your solution by substituting 29.25 for t in the equation.

$$t \div 2.5 = 11.7$$
$$29.25 \div 2.5 = 11.7$$
$$11.7 = 11.7 \quad \text{It checks.}$$

In **1–14**, solve each equation and check your solution.

1. $t \div 5.4 = 9.01$

$t \div 5.4 \times$ ____ $= 9.01 \times$ ____

$t =$ ________

2. $43.9 = m + 8.84$

$43.9 -$ ______ $= m + 8.84 -$ ______

$m =$ ______

3. $w \div 1.9 = 9$

4. $10.4 = 0.2t$

5. $51 = b \div 3.25$

6. $\frac{v}{2.6} = 88.9$

7. $x \div 3.25 = 5.6$

8. $2.7k = 54.0$

9. $5.89 + j = 9.34$

10. $m - 7.62 = 9.5$

11. $k + 24.75 = 36.12$

12. $x \div 45.2 = 2.3$

13. $12.85 = x - 4.34$

14. $15.95 = 3.19n$

15. In a 400-meter relay race, 4 runners pass a baton, each running 100 meters of the race. The table shows the split times for the first 3 runners of a relay team. Suppose the team has set a goal of running the race in 210 seconds. Solve the equation $(53.715 + 51.3 + 52.62) + n = 210$ to find the number of seconds, n, the 4th runner must run to meet their goal.

DATA

400 Meter Relay Team Split Times (seconds)	
1st runner	53.715
2nd runner	51.3
3rd runner	52.62
4th runner	n

16. **Number Sense** Suppose the team in Exercise 15 meets their goal and runs the race in 210 seconds. Write 210 seconds as a decimal in minutes. Then write 210 seconds as minutes and seconds.

17. **MP.4 Model with Math** The winning team in a 400 meter relay race had a time of 198.608 seconds. Suppose all 4 of the split times were the same. Write an equation to find the split times. Then solve the equation you wrote. What was the split time for each runner?

18. **Higher Order Thinking** Can any equation that is written using multiplication be written as an equivalent equation using division? Explain your reasoning and give an example that has decimals that shows your reasoning.

19. **MP.7 Use Structure** Teresa placed parentheses in the expression below so that its value was greater than 80. Write the expression to show where Teresa placed the parentheses.

$$10.5 + 9.5 \times 3 - 1 \times 2.5$$

Common Core Assessment

20. Which is the solution to the equation below?

$y \div 2.5 = 1.95$

Ⓐ $y = 0.78$

Ⓑ $y = 4.875$

Ⓒ $y = 48.75$

Ⓓ $y = 4{,}875$

21. Which is the solution to the equation below?

$x - 4.21 = 6.047$

Ⓐ $x = 10.68$

Ⓑ $x = 10.257$

Ⓒ $x = 10.247$

Ⓓ $x = 1.837$

© Pearson Education, Inc. 6

Name ____________________

Math Practices and Problem Solving

Lesson 7-10

Use Appropriate Tools

I can …
choose an appropriate tool and use it strategically to solve a problem.

Mathematical Practices MP.5, MP.4, MP.7, MP.8
Content Standards 6.NS.B.2, 6.NS.B.3

Solve & Share You are going to play a math game called Magic Squares. You will solve a magic square by finding the missing values so that each row, column, and diagonal has the same sum, known as the magic number. Find the missing numbers using the most efficient and accurate way to solve.

Choose an appropriate tool to help you solve this problem.

Magic Number: 21

	7	
	10	4.75

Thinking Habits

Be a good thinker!
These questions can help you.

- Which tools can I use?
- Why should I use this tool to help me solve the problem?
- Is there a different tool I could use?
- Am I using the tool appropriately?

Look Back! **MP.5 Use Appropriate Tools** Suppose the values in each square of the magic square were fractions and the magic number was a mixed number. Would the tool you used to find the decimal values be appropriate to find the fraction values? Explain why or why not.

How Can You Choose an Appropriate Tool?

A

James, a coin collector, saves quarters in paper sleeves or rolls. Each roll has the same number of quarters. He measures each roll and finds the total width of all the rolls. How many quarters does James have?

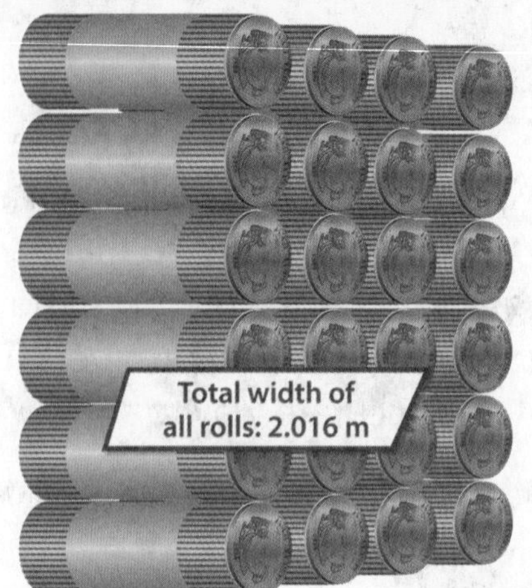

What do I need to do?

Use appropriate tools and apply what I know about money to solve the problem.

Here's my thinking...

B

Which tools can I use to help me solve this problem?

I can

- decide which tool is appropriate.
- use technology to solve this problem.
- use the tool correctly.

C

I can use the Internet to find the width of one quarter.

Then convert 2.016 meters into millimeters, so that the units are the same.

1 meter = 1,000 millimeters
2.016 meters = 2,016 millimeters

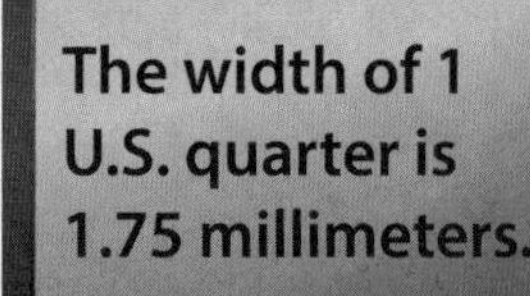

The width of 1 U.S. quarter is 1.75 millimeters.

Find the total number of quarters using the standard algorithm.

Divide. $2{,}016 \div 1.75 = 1{,}152$

James has 1,152 quarters.

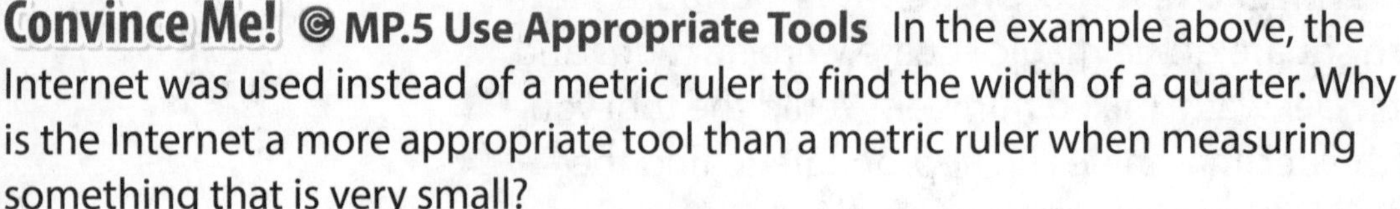

Convince Me! **MP.5 Use Appropriate Tools** In the example above, the Internet was used instead of a metric ruler to find the width of a quarter. Why is the Internet a more appropriate tool than a metric ruler when measuring something that is very small?

© Pearson Education, Inc. 6

Name

Practice Buddy Tools Assessment

Guided Practice*

MP.5 Use Appropriate Tools

May made a pan of lasagna. She evenly spread 2.45 pounds of cheese in the pan for the recipe. If May cuts the lasagna into 10 equal pieces, how many ounces of cheese are there in each piece of lasagna?

1. What tool can help you solve this problem?

2. Explain why the tool you chose is appropriate. Then solve the problem.

Independent Practice

MP.5 Use Appropriate Tools

Patty has a length of ribbon measuring 100 inches. She wants to cut the ribbon into 16 equal pieces. To the nearest $\frac{1}{4}$-inch, what is the length each piece of ribbon should measure?

3. What tool can you use to make sure the 16 pieces of ribbon are cut in equal lengths?

4. Why is this tool appropriate for solving the problem? Explain how you can use it strategically to make 16 equal lengths of ribbon.

When you use tools strategically, you are using them in ways that make sense and help you solve the problem correctly.

5. Can you use a different tool to solve this problem another way? Explain your reasoning.

*For another example, see Set E on page 382.

Math Practices and Problem Solving

Common Core Performance Assessment

Swim Competition

A swim team has six members: Jordan, Allison, Kylie, Oscar, Matt, and Luis. Each competed in two races at a swim meet. The fastest swimmer had the lowest combined time. Complete the chart to find the fastest swimmer on the team.

Swimmer	First Race (seconds)	Second Race (seconds)	Combined Time (seconds)
	42.11	42.55	
	39.65	40.03	
	43.03	42.94	
	39.25	39.14	
	41.8	41.83	
	40.82	40.29	

- Jordan's combined time was 81.11 seconds.
- Allison finished four tenths of a second behind the fastest swimmer on the team in the first race.
- Kylie's time for the first race was 0.11 of a second slower than her time for the second race.
- Luis took 0.03 of a second longer to finish the second race than to finish the first race.
- It took Oscar about 43 seconds to complete the first race.

You use structure when you add or subtract decimals.

6. **MP.5 Use Appropriate Tools** Can the table help you solve the problem? Explain.

7. **MP.7 Use Structure** How can you use place-value relationships to solve the clues and find the fastest swimmer on the team?

© Pearson Education, Inc. 6

Name ___________________________

Homework & Practice 7-10

Use Appropriate Tools

Another Look!

Deidre wants to cover all the sides and the top of a cube with blue denim fabric. She calculates the surface area to be covered. Then she rounds to the next $\frac{1}{4}$ yard to make sure she has enough fabric. How much fabric does Deidre need to buy?

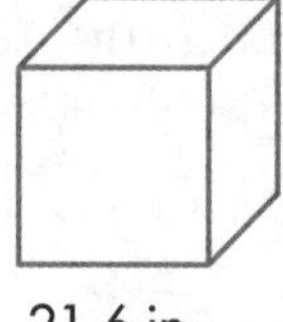

Tell how you can use tools to solve the problem.

- I can use paper and pencil to diagram the problem.

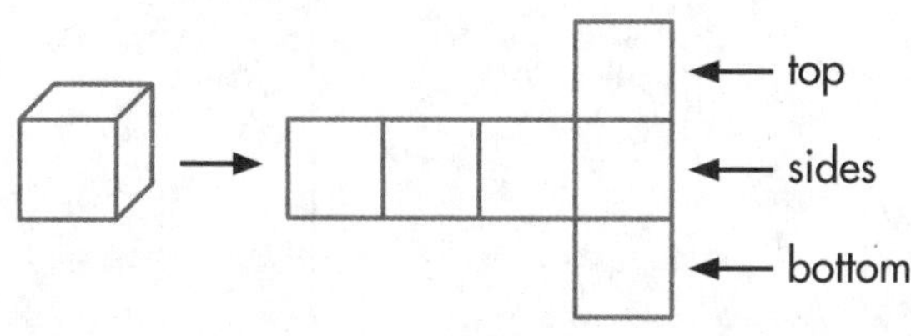

- I can use a conversion chart or the Internet to make sure that 36 inches = 1 yard.

Solve the problem. Explain how to use the tools strategically to find the solution.

The diagram shows 5 square sides that need to be covered. Multiply to find the total area.
$5 \times 21.6 \times 21.6 = 2{,}332.8$ square inches

Fabric is sold in yard lengths that are 60 inches wide. Multiply to find the number of square inches in 1 yard of fabric.
1 yard = 36 inches
$36 \times 60 = 2{,}160$ square inches

Divide to find the number of yards of fabric needed.
$2{,}332.8 \div 2{,}160 = 1.08$
Deidre needs 1.08 yards, so she will have to buy 1.25 yards of fabric.

MP.5 Use Appropriate Tools

Harris has a laptop that takes up an area of 135.9 in^2 when closed. He receives a computer sleeve that measures 15.75 inches by 13.2 inches as a gift. Will the sleeve work with his computer? Explain how you decided.

When you use appropriate tools, such as technology, be sure to use them correctly.

1. What tool can help you solve this problem? Why would you use this tool?

2. Explain how to use this tool strategically to solve the problem.

Common Core Performance Assessment

Money Measures

Zack found this table on the Internet. He has a stack of quarters and dimes that is 12 mm tall. Three of the coins are quarters, the rest are dimes. What is the value of his stack of coins? What is the mass of his coins?

	Penny	Nickel	Dime	Quarter	Half Dollar
Mass	2.500 g	5.000 g	2.268 g	5.670 g	11.340 g
Thickness	1.52 mm	1.95 mm	1.35 mm	1.75 mm	2.15 mm

3. **MP.5 Use Appropriate Tools** How can you use the table strategically to help solve the problem?

4. **MP.4 Model with Math** Explain how you can use words, numbers, and symbols to find the number and value of Zack's coins.

You can write and solve equations to model with math.

5. **MP.8 Generalize** Can you use the same strategy to find the total mass of Zack's coins? Explain your reasoning.

© Pearson Education, Inc. 6

Name ______________________________

Follow the Path

Shade a path from **START** to **FINISH**. Follow the products and quotients in which the digit in the hundredths place is greater than the digit in the tenths place. You can only move up, down, right, or left.

I can ...
multiply and divide multi-digit decimals.

Content Standard 6.NS.B.3

Start				
22.04×9	$7.2\overline{)42.12}$	53.08×2.4	0.18×1.5	$7\overline{)0.28}$
$25\overline{)28}$	3.71×0.6	$2.5\overline{)23.35}$	$9\overline{)0.954}$	0.9×0.27
12.4×14.6	$1.3\overline{)2.314}$	86.35×7	$0.4\overline{)1.06}$	$6\overline{)72.72}$
$1.2\overline{)0.9}$	1.05×1.05	$2.4\overline{)8.7}$	7.2×0.06	$75\overline{)18}$
86.3×0.4	$16\overline{)0.04}$	$8\overline{)4.4}$	5.2×3.8	22.3×1.8
				Finish

TOPIC 7

Vocabulary Review

Glossary

Word List

- compatible numbers
- decimal
- difference
- equation
- estimate
- evaluate
- inverse relationship
- product
- quotient
- round
- sum

Understand Vocabulary

Choose the best term from the Word List. Write it on the blank.

1. A number that is close to an exact answer is a(n) ________________.

2. A mathematical sentence stating that two expressions are equal is a(n) ________________.

3. A number with one or more digits to the right of the decimal point is a(n) ________________.

4. The answer to an addition problem is called a(n) ________________.

5. ________________ an expression to find its value.

Which operation represents the *inverse relationship* that can be used to solve each equation? Write *addition, subtraction, multiplication,* or *division*.

6. $3n = 4.8$ ________________

7. $a - 0.52 = 1.02$ ________________

8. $3.8 + z = 5.55$ ________________

9. $0.4 \div d = 0.16$ ________________

Draw a line from each *equation* in Column A to its solution in Column B.

Column A	Column B
10. $x \div 0.5 = 0.2$	$x = 0.01$
11. $3x = 3.3$	$x = 0.1$
12. $1 - x = 0.99$	$x = 1.1$

Use Vocabulary in Writing

13. Explain two ways to estimate $12.741 - 9.8$. Use at least 4 words from the Word List.

© Pearson Education, Inc. 6

Name ______________________

TOPIC 7

Reteaching

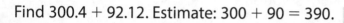

Set A pages 319–324, 325–330

Find 300.4 + 92.12. Estimate: 300 + 90 = 390.

Find 90.23 − 7.8. Estimate: 90 − 8 = 82.

Write the numbers. Line up the decimal points. Annex zeros as placeholders if needed. Then add or subtract.

$$\begin{array}{r} 300.40 \\ +\ 92.12 \\ \hline 392.52 \end{array} \qquad \begin{array}{r} \overset{8}{\cancel{9}}\overset{9}{\cancel{0}}.\cancel{2}\overset{12}{3} \\ -\ 7.80 \\ \hline 82.43 \end{array}$$

392.52 is close to 390. 82.43 is close to 82. The answers are reasonable.

Remember that you can estimate sums and differences of decimals by rounding or using compatible numbers.

Estimate each answer. Then find the sum or difference.

1. 91.2 + 89.9
2. 902.3 − 8.8
3. 62.99 − 10.83
4. 423.22 + 98.30
5. 24.52 − 9.6
6. 369.45 + 32.42

Set B pages 331–336, 337–342

Find 52.5 × 1.9. Estimate: 50 × 2 = 100.

$$\begin{array}{r} 52.5 \\ \times\ 1.9 \\ \hline 4725 \\ 5250 \\ \hline 99.75 \end{array}$$

52.5 ← 1 decimal place

1.9 ← + 1 decimal place

99.75 ← 2 decimal places

The answer is reasonable because 99.75 is close to 100.

Remember that you can estimate products using rounding or compatible numbers.

Find each product.

1. 5 × 98.2
2. 4 × 0.21
3. 4.4 × 6
4. 7 × 21.6
5. 12.5 × 163.2
6. 16 × 52.3

Set C pages 343–348, 349–354, 355–360

Divide 2.75 ÷ 0.05.

Estimate 300 ÷ 5 = 60.

$$\begin{array}{r} 55. \\ 5\overline{)275.} \\ -\ 25 \\ \hline 25 \\ -\ 25 \\ \hline 0 \end{array}$$

Multiply the divisor and dividend by the same power of 10 to divide with whole numbers.

Place the decimal point in the quotient and divide.

55 is close to 60 so the answer is reasonable.

Remember to think of a power of 10 that will make the divisor a whole number.

Find each quotient.

1. 9.6 ÷ 1.6
2. 48.4 ÷ 0.4
3. 13.2 ÷ 0.006
4. 10.8 ÷ 0.09
5. 1.26 ÷ 0.2
6. 2.24 ÷ 3.2
7. 35.75 ÷ 55
8. 120.4 ÷ 602

Set D pages 361–366, 367–372

Evaluate $2.4 \cdot m$ for $m = 6$.

Substitute 6 for the value of m in the expression.

$$2.4 \cdot m = 2.4 \cdot 6 = 14.4$$

Solve $x \div 5.3 = 6.2$. Use inverse operations to get the variable by itself on one side of the equation.

$$x \div 5.3 = 6.2$$

$$x \div 5.3 \times 5.3 = 6.2 \times 5.3$$ ← **Multiply both sides by 5.3.**

$$x = 32.86$$

Remember to use substitution and check your solution.

In **1–3**, evaluate each expression.

1. $6.7 + x$; $x = 2$

2. $x(3.4)$; $x = 5.4$

3. $5n^2 + 2d \div 4$; $n = 3, d = 6$

In **4** and **5**, solve each equation.

4. $x \div 7.9 = 50.56$

5. $0.02x = 0.82$

Set E pages 373–378

Think about these questions to help you **use appropriate tools strategically**.

Thinking Habits

- Which tools can I use?
- Why should I use this tool to help me solve the problem?
- Is there a different tool I could use?
- Am I using the tool appropriately?

Remember to choose the tool that is most helpful in solving the problem.

Eva joins a gym for 12 months and wants 5 training sessions. Option A is \$45 per month and \$79 per training session. Option B is \$55 per month plus \$245 for 5 training sessions. Which is the better option for Eva?

1. What tool can help you solve the problem?

2. Use the tool to solve the problem.

© Pearson Education, Inc. 6

Name ______________________________

1. The table gives the areas of 3 parks. Which is the best estimate of the difference between the sizes of Shady Heights and Pine Island?

DATA

Park Area	Size in Acres
Shady Heights	58.38
Pine Island	27.5
Oak Woods	792.84

Ⓐ 30 acres

Ⓑ 35 acres

Ⓒ 38 acres

Ⓓ 40 acres

2. Mrs. Jenks bought 53 erasers for the students in her class. Mr. Bailey bought 9 more erasers than Mrs. Jenks bought. Each eraser cost \$0.14. How much did the teachers spend for the erasers? Explain how you found your answer.

3. Russ has a car that averages 9.8 miles per gallon. Mike's car averages 39.2 miles per gallon. How many times more miles per gallon does Mike's car average than Russ's car?

4. Write the correct solution for each equation. Choose the numbers from the box below.

$n - 3.1 = 1.6$ $n =$

$2.9t = 10.73$ $t =$

$9.1 = 7.6 + s$ $s =$

$38.74 = 14.9p$ $p =$

1.1 1.5 4.7 3.7 0.5 2.6

5. Choose all the expressions that have a quotient of 0.7.

- ☐ $1.61 \div 0.23$
- ☐ $1.61 \div 2.3$
- ☐ $2.87 \div 4.1$
- ☐ $0.287 \div 41$

6. Chris and Jeff sold 15.5 pounds of trail mix. They sold the trail mix for \$3.98 per pound. How much money did they collect? Explain how you found your answer.

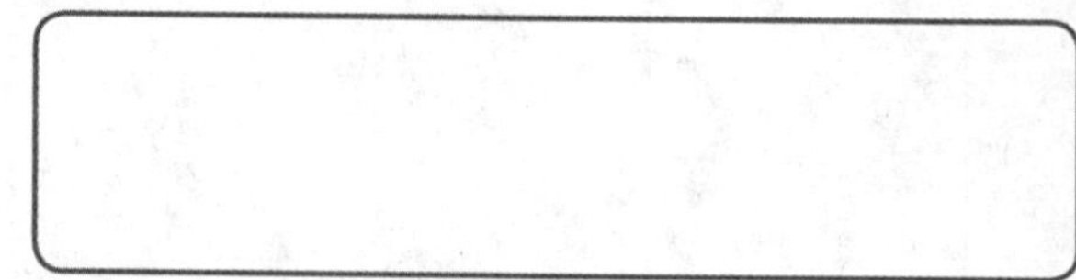

7. Ilana needs d more dollars to buy a new scrapbook that costs \$8.35. She has \$4.88. Solve the equation $\$4.88 + d = \$8.35$ to find how much more money Ilana needs.

Ⓐ $d = \$3.57$

Ⓑ $d = \$3.47$

Ⓒ $d = \$3.42$

Ⓓ $d = \$4.12$

8. Evaluate the expression $6.908 - g$ for $g = 0.173$.

9. Draw lines to connect each division expression in Column A with its quotient in Column B.

Column A	Column B
$32.8 \div 8$	4.1
$436.1 \div 89$	4.2
$37.8 \div 9$	4.5
$54 \div 12$	4.9

10. Diego and Ashley estimated the product 23.879×2.995. Diego estimated $25 \times 3 = 75$. Ashley estimated $23 \times 3 = 69$.

What method did each student use? Are they both correct? Explain.

11. Abby, Brianna, and Maria competed in a figure skating competition. The table shows how one judge scored each skater on a scale from 0 to 6.0. Which statements about their scores are true? Select all that apply.

Skater	Scores	
Abby	Technical	5.8
	Presentation	5.9
Brianna	Technical	5.7
	Presentation	5.6
Maria	Technical	5.8
	Presentation	5.4

- ☐ Brianna has the lowest combined score.
- ☐ The difference between Brianna's and Abby's combined scores is 0.4.
- ☐ The difference between Abby's and Maria's combined scores is 0.05.
- ☐ Maria's technical score is 0.1 more than Brianna's technical score.

12. Milo wants to ship both items shown below. He finds out that a special rate is available for a large box as long as no dimension is greater than 30.48 cm. Will his items fit in one large box? Explain.

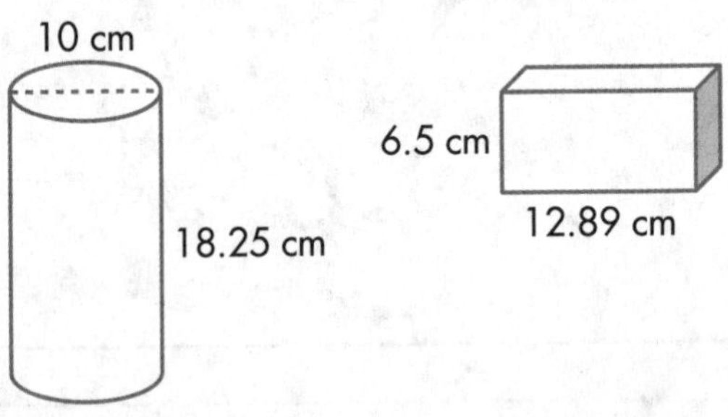

© Pearson Education, Inc. 6

Name ____________________

TOPIC 7

Performance Assessment

Food Bank

Volunteers at the Food Bank package meals to feed a family of four. The table shows the foods that are available, the number of people served by each food, and the weight of the food.

- One selection from each category is packed into a box.
- Each box can hold a maximum of 3.5 pounds, or 56 ounces.

DATA

Main Course			**Side Dish**		
Food	**Serves**	**Weight**	**Food**	**Serves**	**Weight**
Roast Beef	4	16 oz	Potato	1	4 oz
Chicken	2	12.6 oz	Cole Slaw	4	12.4 oz
Stew	1	5.2 oz	Green salad	2	5.6 oz
Lasagna	4	28 oz	Baked beans	4	14.2 oz
Chili	1	8.6 oz	Pasta	2	5.2 oz
Vegetables			**Dessert**		
Carrots	2	6 oz	Custard cup	1	3.2 oz
Corn	2	5.8 oz	Carrot cake	4	10.4 oz
Green beans	1	3.2 oz	Frozen yogurt	2	2.7 oz
Peas	4	14.8 oz	Apple	1	5 oz

1. Suppose you pack 2 carrots, 4 potatoes, and 2 frozen yogurts.

Part A

Write an equation for the number of ounces that are still available for a main course. Let $x =$ the number of ounces.

Part B

Which main dishes can you use to complete the meal under the food bank's guidelines? Explain how you know.

2. Describe a meal that you could make that weighs 3.5 pounds or less. Include the number of servings and total weight of each food.

3. The Food Bank has 110.9 pounds, or 1,774.4 ounces, of chicken. To the nearest whole number, how many servings of chicken does this provide?

4. If donations to the Food Bank increase, they will be able to offer meals for a family of six, too.

Part A

Would boxes with a weight limit of 5.1 pounds, or 81.6 ounces, be enough to make good meals for 6 people? Explain your thinking.

Part B

Decide on a weight limit for each box for a family of six. Justify your choice. Then make a meal that will fit in the box.

© Pearson Education, Inc. 6

Common Factors and Multiples

Essential Question: How can you find common factors and multiples of numbers?

Cryptology is the science of making and breaking codes. Cryptographers use large prime numbers to encrypt and decode secret messages. You will do a project to learn more about this.

Did you know that you can find prime numbers all around you?

Prime numbers are found in nature. Cicadas have 13-year or 17-year life spans and human DNA is made up of 23 chromosomes.

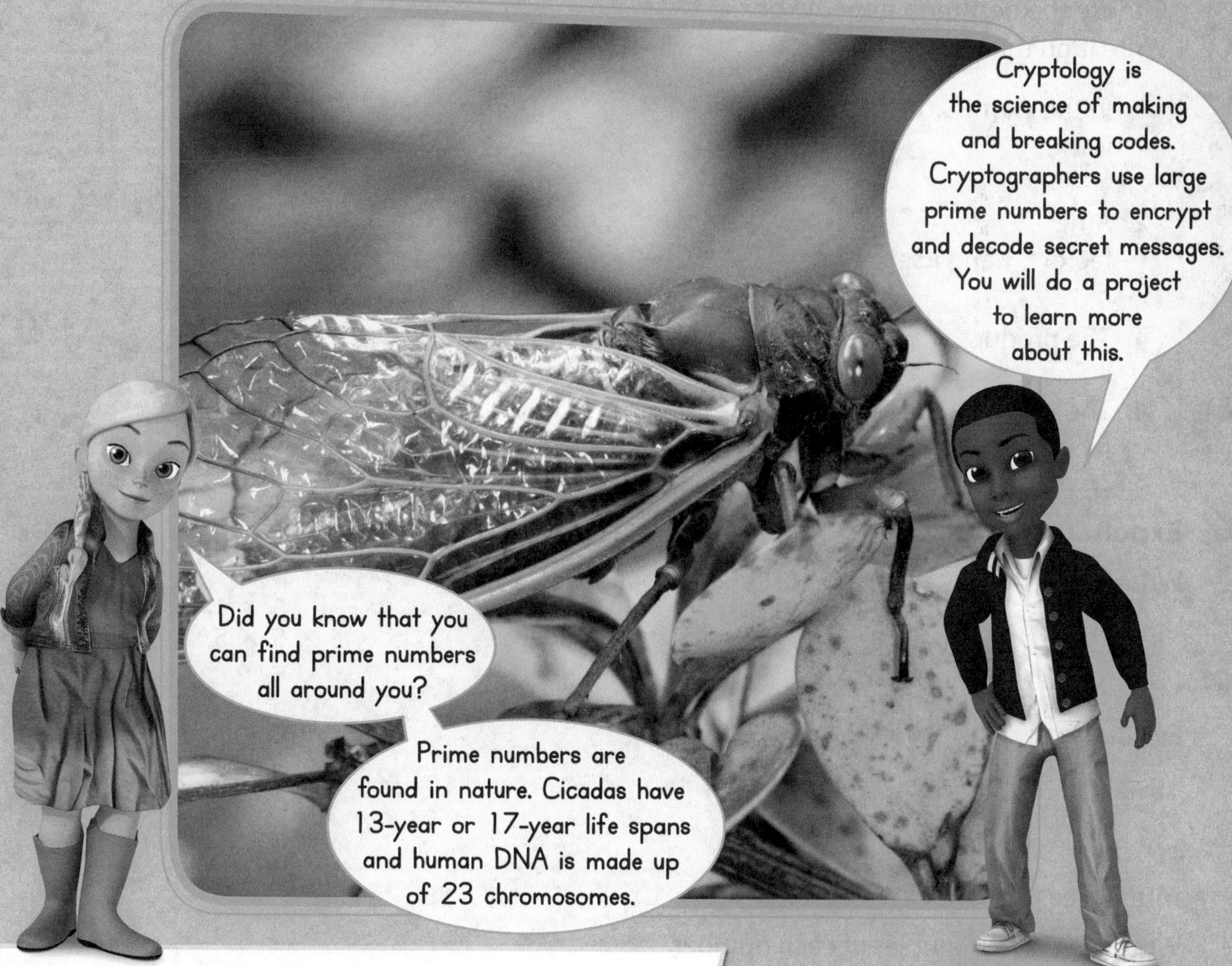

Math and Science Project: Cryptography

Do Research Use the Internet or other sources to learn about various encryption techniques. Find examples of techniques that are easy to reproduce.

Journal: Write a Report Include what you found. Also in your report:

- Describe at least three basic encryption techniques.
- Choose one of the encryption techniques you described to encrypt a secret message. State the secret message and then show its encrypted form.

Name ______________________________

Review What You Know

Vocabulary

Choose the best term from the box. Write it on the blank.

- base
- composite number
- exponent
- factor
- multiple
- prime number

1. In the expression 4^3, the number 3 is the ______________.

2. A(n) ______________ is a whole number greater than 1 that has exactly two factors, 1 and itself.

3. The product of a given factor and any whole number is a(n) ______________.

4. The number 12 is a(n) ______________ because it has more than two factors.

Exponents

Write an equivalent expression using an exponent.

5. $8 \times 8 \times 8$

6. 7×7

7. $5 \times 5 \times 5 \times 5$

Evaluate each expression.

8. 3^3

9. 2^5

10. 5^2

Multiples

Write the first 5 multiples of each number.

11. 8

12. 9

13. 6

14. 4

Factors

15. How can you find the factors of 12 and 15? Explain.

© Pearson Education, Inc. 6

A-Z Glossary

My Word Cards

Use the examples for each word on the front of the card to help complete the definitions on the back.

prime factorization

24

6×4

$2 \times 3 \times 2 \times 2$

$2^3 \times 3$

factor tree

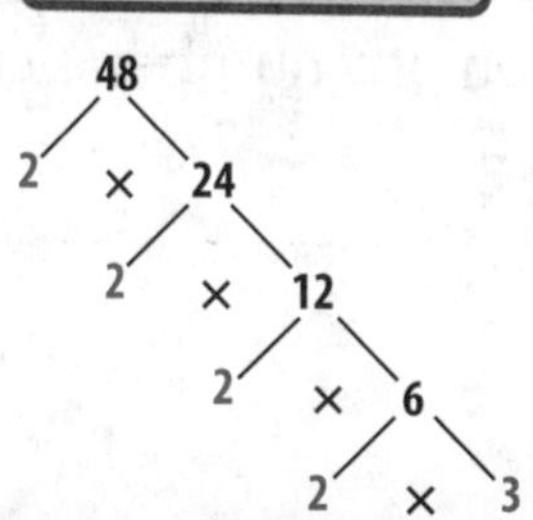

greatest common factor (GCF)

factors of 30: 1, **2**, 3, 5, (6), 10, 15, 30
factors of 24: 1, **2**, 3, 4, (6), 8, 12, 24

2 and 6 are common factors of 30 and 24.

6 is the **greatest common factor (GCF)**.

common multiple

multiples of 4: 4, 8, 12, 16, (20), 24, 28, 32, 36, (40)
multiples of 5: 5, 10, 15, (20), 25, 30, 35, (40)

20 and **40** are **common multiples** of 4 and 5.

least common multiple (LCM)

multiples of 4: 4, 8, 12, 16, (20), 24, 28, 32, 36, 40
multiples of 5: 5, 10, 15, (20), 25, 30, 35, 40

20 and 40 are common multiples of 4 and 5.

20 is the **least common multiple**.

counterexample

Statement: All odd numbers are prime numbers.
Example: 3 is a prime number.
Counterexample: 9 is **NOT** a prime number.

My Word Cards

Complete the definition. Extend learning by writing your own definitions.

A diagram that shows the prime factorization of a number is called a

_______________.

A number written as a product of prime factors is called a

_______________.

A multiple of two or more numbers is a

_______________.

The greatest number that is a factor of two or more numbers is the

____

_______________.

An example that shows that a statement is false is a

_______________.

The least number, not including 0, that is a common multiple of two or more numbers is the

____

_______________.

© Pearson Education, Inc. 6

Name ______________________________

Lesson 8-1

Prime and Composite Numbers

I can ...
identify prime and composite numbers and write the prime factorization of a number.

Content Standard 6.NS.B.4
Mathematical Practices MP.2, MP.3, MP.6, MP.7

Solve & Share

A garden has an area of 24 square units. The length and width of the garden are whole numbers. What are the possible dimensions of the garden? ***Solve this problem any way you choose.***

You can look for structure to find all possible dimensions of the garden.

Look Back! **MP.2 Reasoning** A rectangular garden has an area of 17 square yards. Its sides are whole numbers of yards. What dimensions are possible?

Essential Question

How Can You Use Prime and Composite Numbers to Write the Prime Factorization of a Number?

A

Whole numbers greater than 1 are either prime or composite numbers. A composite number can be written as a product of its prime factors, called its prime factorization.

How can you find the prime factorization of 48?

12 is a composite number because it has more than two factors.

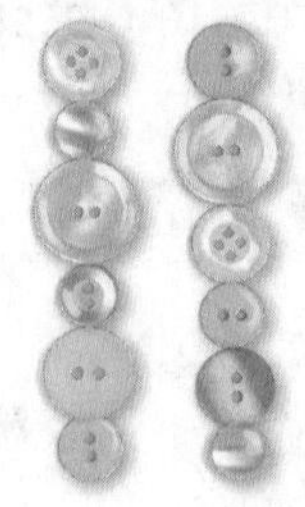

$1 \times 12 = 12$
$2 \times 6 = 12$
$3 \times 4 = 12$

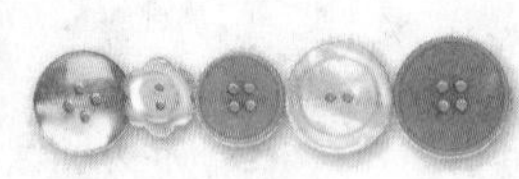

$1 \times 5 = 5$

5 is a prime number because the only factors of 5 are 1 and 5.

B One Way

To find the prime factorization of 48, write its factors. It is sometimes helpful to start with the least prime factor.

$48 = 2 \times 24$ ← 2 is the least prime factor of 48.

$= 2 \times 2 \times 12$ ← Continue using prime factors.

$= 2 \times 2 \times 2 \times 6$

$= 2 \times 2 \times 2 \times 2 \times 3$

The prime factorization of 48 is $2 \times 2 \times 2 \times 2 \times 3$ or $2^4 \times 3$.

C Another Way

A **factor tree** shows the prime factorization of a composite number. You can use a factor tree to find the prime factorization of 48.

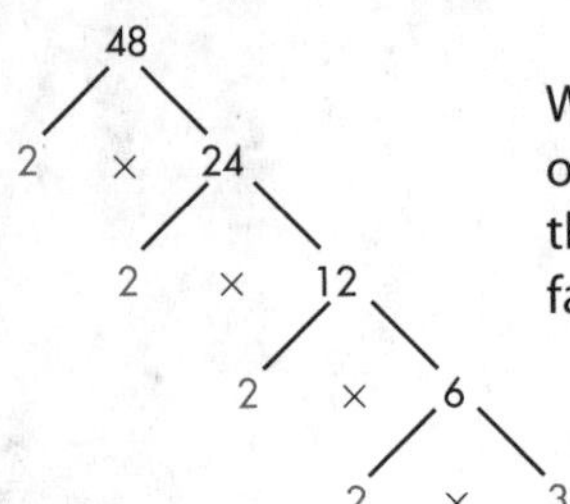

Write 48 as the product of two factors. Continue the process until all of the factors are prime factors.

The prime factorization of 48 is $2 \times 2 \times 2 \times 2 \times 3$ or $2^4 \times 3$.

Convince Me! **MP.6 Be Precise** Lucero is thinking of a number. The number is greater than 2 and it has 2 as a factor. Is the number prime or composite?

© Pearson Education, Inc. 6

Name ______________________________

Practice Buddy Tools Assessment

Another Example

Li and Tim each wrote the prime factorization of 72. Who is correct?

Li's Work

To find the prime factorization of 72, Li began with any two factors.

$72 = 8 \times 9$
$= 2 \times 4 \times 9$
$= 2 \times 2 \times 2 \times 9$
$= 2 \times 2 \times 2 \times 3 \times 3$

Tim's Work

To find the prime factorization of 72, Tim made a factor tree.

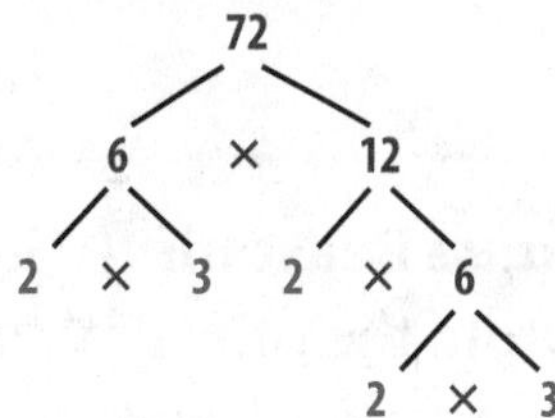

The prime factorization is $2 \times 2 \times 2 \times 3 \times 3$ or $2^3 \times 3^2$.

Li and Tim are both correct. There is only one prime factorization for any number.

Guided Practice*

Do You Understand?

1. **MP.6 Be Precise** Linda begins with the factors 4 and 18 to find the prime factorization of 72. Will Linda find the same prime factorization for 72 as Li and Tim? Explain how you know.

2. Juan says that the prime factorization of 36 is $2 \times 3 \times 6$. Is he correct? Explain.

Do You Know How?

In **3–8**, write the prime factorization of each number. If the number is prime, write *prime*.

3. 33 **4.** 23

5. 32 **6.** 45

7. 49 **8.** 19

Independent Practice

In **9–14**, find the prime factorization of each number. If it is prime, write *prime*.

9. 26 **10.** 8 **11.** 42

12. 27 **13.** 30 **14.** 47

*For another example, see Set A on page 417.

Math Practices and Problem Solving

15. A triangle has a 60°, a 30°, and a 90° angle. Is the triangle acute, right, or obtuse?

16. Chris says that the expression $31{,}521g \div 61 - 15{,}205 + 13{,}908$ can be evaluated by dividing $31{,}521g$ by 61, then subtracting 15,205, and finally adding 13,908. Do you agree? Explain.

17. **MP.3 Critique Reasoning** Gabrielle and John each wrote the prime factorization of 64. Analyze their work and explain any errors.

Gabrielle's Work

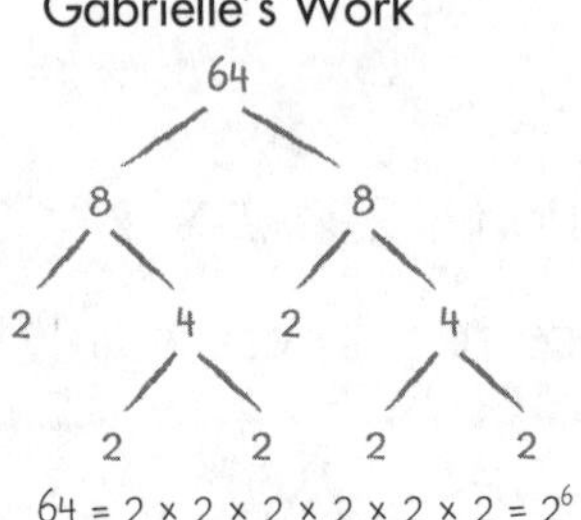

John's Work

$64 = 2 \times 32$
$= 2 \times 2 \times 16$
$= 2 \times 2 \times 2 \times 8$
$= 2 \times 2 \times 2 \times 2 \times 4$
$= 2 \times 2 \times 2 \times 2 \times 2 \times 2$

18. What are the first ten prime numbers? Explain how you know that each is a prime number.

19. **MP.3 Construct Arguments** Is the number 1 prime, composite, or neither? Explain.

20. Stephen ordered 3 pounds of oranges at \$2 per pound, and 4 pounds of pears at \$3 per pound. He had to pay \$6.25 for shipping. What was his total cost?

21. **Higher Order Thinking** Raul says that every odd number greater than 3 can be expressed as the sum of two primes. Use the prime number 11 to provide a counterexample and explain that Raul is incorrect.

Common Core Assessment

22. The Furius Baco is a roller coaster that reaches a maximum speed of 84 miles per hour. Write the prime factorization of 84.

23. Janie's grandmother is 76 years old. What is the prime factorization of 76?

© Pearson Education, Inc. 6

Name ______________________

Help | Practice Buddy | Tools | Games

Homework & Practice 8-1
Prime and Composite Numbers

Another Look!

You can find the prime factorization of a composite number by breaking it down into prime factors or by using a factor tree. Find the prime factorization of 36.

$36 = \mathbf{2} \times 18$
$= 2 \times \mathbf{2} \times 9$
$= 2 \times 2 \times \mathbf{3} \times \mathbf{3}$

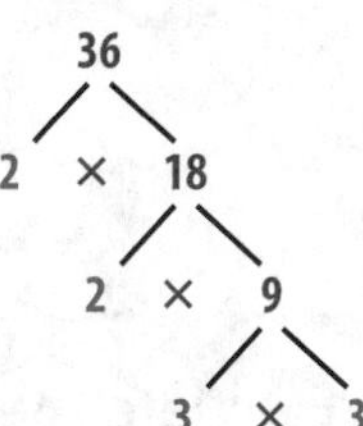

Remember, a prime number has exactly two factors, 1 and itself. A composite number has more than two factors.

The prime factorization of 36 is $2 \times 2 \times 3 \times 3$ or $2^2 \times 3^2$.

In **1–18**, find the prime factorization of each number. If it is prime, write *prime*.

1. 38 | **2.** 75 | **3.** 20

4. 90 | **5.** 66 | **6.** 52

7. 86 | **8.** 27 | **9.** 99

10. 25 | **11.** 49 | **12.** 50

13. 68 | **14.** 85 | **15.** 7

16. 97 | **17.** 41 | **18.** 100

19. **MP.6 Be Precise** A sports car goes from 15 feet per second to 110 feet per second in 5 seconds. Use the formula $a = \frac{(f - s)}{t}$, where a is the acceleration, f is the final speed, s is the starting speed, and t is the time it takes to make the change. What is the acceleration (in feet per second squared) of the sports car?

20. **Number Sense** Write the next three numbers in this pattern. Then describe the pattern.

7 3 11 7 15 11 19 15 23

21. **MP.2 Reasoning** Alisa's birthdate is a prime number in December. The date is between December 15 and December 20. What are Alisa's possible birthdates?

22. Evaluate the expression $(5^3 + 9) - 12 \div \frac{6}{2}$.

23. **MP.2 Reasoning** Mrs. James displayed the factor tree at the right on the board. Complete the factor tree to find the number that has a prime factorization of $2^4 \times 3$.

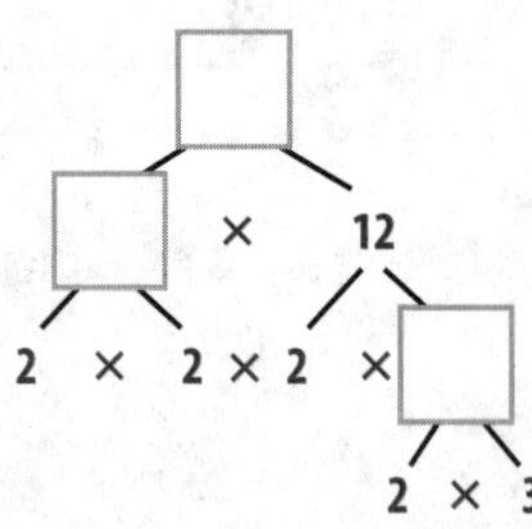

24. **MP.3 Construct Arguments** Tricia says that 2 is the only even prime number. Explain why Tricia is correct.

25. **Higher Order Thinking** Martise says that the first 5 odd numbers greater than 2 are prime numbers. Provide a counterexample and explain why Martise is incorrect.

Common Core Assessment

26. An average sixth grader takes 18 breaths per minute. What is the prime factorization of 18?

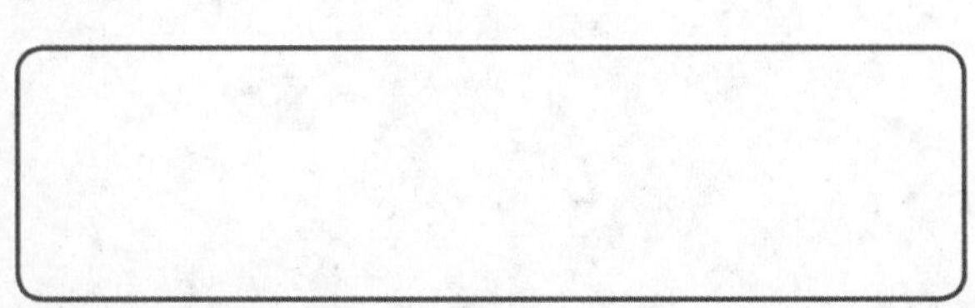

27. A jaguar at the local zoo weighs 100 kilograms. What is the prime factorization of 100?

© Pearson Education, Inc. 6

Name ____________________

Lesson 8-2

Find the Greatest Common Factor

I can ...
find the greatest common factor of two numbers.

Content Standard 6.NS.B.4
Mathematical Practices MP.1, MP.2, MP.4, MP.5, MP.8

Solve & Share There are 16 sixth graders and 20 seventh graders in the rocket club. Students will be arranged in equal groups to build models, but each group will have only sixth graders or only seventh graders. What is the greatest number of students who can be in each group? ***Solve this problem any way you choose.***

You can use reasoning to find a relationship between the number of equal groups of sixth graders and seventh graders.

16 Sixth Graders		20 Seventh Graders	
Number of Groups	Number of Sixth Graders in Each Group	Number of Groups	Number of Seventh Graders in Each Group

Look Back! **MP.1 Make Sense and Persevere** Suppose that 4 more seventh graders join the rocket club. Now what is the greatest number of students who can be in each group?

How Can You Find the Greatest Common Factor of Two Numbers?

A

Keesha is putting together bags of supplies. She puts an equal number of craft sticks and an equal number of glue bottles in each bag. There are none left over. What is the greatest number of bags of supplies that Keesha can make?

12 bottles of glue

42 craft sticks

The number of craft sticks and the number of glue bottles in each bag will not be the same. How can you use factors to find how many of each go in each bag?

B One Way

List and compare the factors of each number.

Factors of 12: 1, 2, 3, 4, 6, 12

Factors of 42: 1, 2, 3, 6, 7, 14, 21, 42

1, 2, 3, and 6 are common factors of 12 and 42.

Identify the greatest common factor (GCF) of 12 and 42. The GCF is the greatest number that is a factor of two or more numbers.

The GCF of 12 and 42 is 6. So 6 is the greatest number that divides into both 12 and 42 with none left over. So Keesha can make 6 bags of supplies.

C Another Way

Use prime factorization to find the GCF.

Use factor trees to find the prime factorizations.

Find the prime factorizations.

$12 = 2 \cdot 2 \cdot 3$
$42 = 2 \cdot 3 \cdot 7$

Multiply the common prime factors.

$2 \cdot 3 = 6$

The GCF of 12 and 42 is 6. So Keesha can make 6 bags of supplies.

Convince Me! **MP.2 Reasoning** Keesha has 24 beads to add equally to each bag. Can she still make 6 bags and have no supplies left over? Explain how you know.

© Pearson Education, Inc. 6

Name ______________________

Practice Buddy Tools Assessment

Another Example

You can use the GCF and the Distributive Property to write:

$$32 + 56 = 8 \cdot 4 + 8 \cdot 7 = 8(4 + 7)$$

Find the sum of 18 and 24.

The greatest number that is a factor of both 18 and 24 is 2 • 3. So the GCF is 6.

Step 1 Find the GCF of 18 and 24.

$18 = 2 \cdot 3 \cdot 3$

$24 = 2 \cdot 2 \cdot 2 \cdot 3$

Step 2 Write each number as a product using the GCF as a factor, and apply the Distributive Property.

$18 + 24 = 6 \cdot 3 + 6 \cdot 4 = 6(3 + 4) = 6(7) = 42$

Guided Practice*

Do You Understand?

1. How are the two ways shown to find the GCF for a set of numbers different?

2. MP.8 Generalize Why is the GCF of two prime numbers always 1? Explain your reasoning.

Do You Know How?

In **3–8**, find the GCF for each pair of numbers.

3. 18, 36
4. 14, 35
5. 22, 55
6. 29, 57
7. 100, 48
8. 30, 70

Independent Practice

In **9–12**, find the GCF for each pair of numbers.

9. 21, 49
10. 8, 52
11. 20, 35
12. 32, 81

In **13–16**, use the GCF and the Distributive Property to find each sum.

13. 30 + 66
14. 34 + 51
15. 15 + 36
16. 45 + 27

For another example, see Set B on page 417.

Math Practices and Problem Solving

17. **MP.4 Model with Math** The Venn diagram to the right shows the factors of 24 and 40.

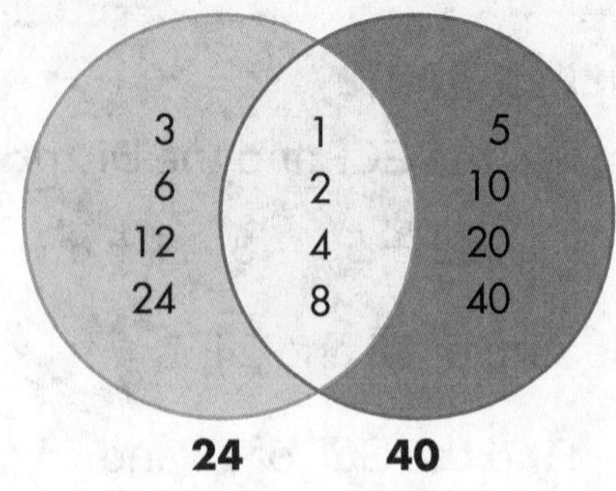

a. What is the meaning of each of the three shaded regions?

b. Explain how you use the Venn diagram to find the GCF of 24 and 40. What is the GCF of 24 and 40?

18. **MP.2 Reasoning** You have 50 blueberry scones and 75 cranberry scones. Make as many identical bags of scones as possible. Each bag should have an equal number of blueberry scones and an equal number of cranberry scones. What is the greatest number of bags you can fill? Explain how you know.

19. **Algebra** The equation $3.2p = 16$ represents the total cost of p pounds of fruit that Jamal bought at a farmer's market. Solve for p to find the number of pounds of fruit Jamal bought.

20. **Math and Science** Periodical cicada species emerge in large numbers from their larval stage at intervals in years that are prime numbers, 13 or 17. What is the GCF of the years?

21. **Higher Order Thinking** Gena has 28 trading cards, Sam has 91 trading cards, and Tiffany has 49 trading cards. Use the GCF and the Distributive Property to find the total number of trading cards Gena, Sam, and Tiffany have.

Common Core Assessment

22. Write the pairs of numbers in the correct box.

18, 72   57, 71
24, 60   12, 48
9, 51   17, 31

GCF = 1	GCF = 3
GCF = 12	**GCF = 18**

© Pearson Education, Inc. 6

Name ______________________________

Homework & Practice 8-2

Find the Greatest Common Factor

Another Look!

Find the GCF of 12 and 40.

The greatest number that divides into two numbers is the greatest common factor (GCF) of the two numbers.

List the Factors

Step 1 List the factors of each number.

12: 1, 2, 3, 4, 6, 12

40: 1, 2, 4, 5, 8, 10, 20, 40

Step 2 Circle the factors that are common to both numbers.

12: 1, (2), 3, (4), 6, 12

40: 1, (2), (4), 5, 8, 10, 20, 40

Step 3 Choose the greatest factor that is common to both numbers. Both 2 and 4 are common factors, but 4 is greater. The GCF is 4.

Use Prime Factorization

Step 1 Write the prime factorization of each number.

12: $2 \times 2 \times 3$

40: $2 \times 2 \times 2 \times 5$

Step 2 Circle the prime factors that the numbers have in common.

12: $2 \times 2 \times 3$

40: $2 \times 2 \times 2 \times 5$

Step 3 Multiply the common factors.

$2 \times 2 = 4$ The GCF is 4.

In **1–8**, find the GCF for each pair of numbers.

1. 45, 60

2. 24, 100

3. 19, 22

4. 14, 28

5. 12, 18

6. 60, 100

7. 55, 99

8. 83, 91

In **9–14**, use the GCF and the Distributive Property to find each sum.

9. $32 + 48$

10. $15 + 57$

11. $98 + 14$

12. $55 + 88$

13. $45 + 75$

14. $81 + 99$

15. **MP.5 Use Appropriate Tools** Complete the Venn diagram to show the common factors of 36 and 54. What is the GCF?

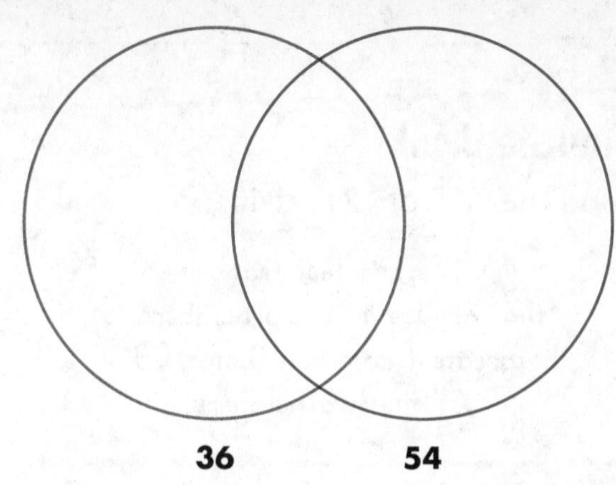

16. Al's garden is 18 feet long and 30 feet wide. He wants to put fence posts the same distance apart along all sides of the garden. What is the greatest distance apart that he can place the fence posts?

17. **Vocabulary** How does finding the *prime factorizations* of two numbers help you find their GCF? Use an example to illustrate.

18. **Higher Order Thinking** The student council was preparing for the school bake sale. The members divided each type of the donated items equally onto plates. Each plate contained only one type of item and every plate had exactly the same number of items. There were no leftovers. What is the greatest number of items that could have been placed on each plate?

Bake Sale Donations	
Muffins	96
Breadsticks	48
Rolls	84

Common Core Assessment

19. Write the pairs of numbers in the correct box.

25, 30   51, 85
98, 84   10, 95
27, 45   42, 70

GCF = 5	GCF = 9
GCF = 14	GCF = 17

© Pearson Education, Inc. 6

Name ______________________________

Solve

Lesson 8-3
Least Common Multiple

I can ...
find the least common multiple of two numbers.

Content Standard 6.NS.B.4
Mathematical Practices MP.3, MP.7, MP.8

Solve & Share

Mark sets the dinner table every 2 days and dries the dishes every 3 days. If he sets the table on Day 2 and dries the dishes on Day 3, on what day would Mark first perform both chores on the same day? ***Solve this problem any way you choose.***

You can look for relationships as you record Mark's chores for each day.

Day	Chore

Look Back! **MP.8 Generalize** On what day will Mark do both chores on the same day again? How can you find on which days Mark does both chores without making a list?

How Can You Find the Least Common Multiple of Two Numbers?

A

Grant is making picnic lunches. He wants to buy as many juice bottles as applesauce cups, but no more than he needs to have an equal number of each.

How many packages of each should Grant buy?

Remember, a multiple is the product of a given factor and any nonzero whole number.

B

One Way

List the multiples of each pack size.

6: 6, 12, 18, 24, 30, 36, 42, 48 . . .
8: 8, 16, 24, 32, 40, 48 . . .

24 and 48 are common multiples of 6 and 8. The least common multiple (LCM) is the least multiple common to both numbers. 24 is the LCM of 6 and 8.

$6 \times 4 = 24$ $8 \times 3 = 24$

Grant should buy 4 packages of juice and 3 packages of applesauce.

C

Another Way

You can use prime factorization to find the LCM of two numbers.

$6 = 2 \times 3$
$8 = 2 \times 2 \times 2$

List the greatest number of times each factor appears in either prime factorization. Multiply these factors.

$3 \times 2 \times 2 \times 2 = 24$

$6 \times 4 = 24$ $8 \times 3 = 24$

Grant should buy 4 packages of juice and 3 packages of applesauce.

Convince Me! **MP.7 Use Structure** Grant also buys bottled water and juice drinks for the picnic. There are 12 bottles of water in each case and 10 juice pouches in each box. He wants to buy the least amount but still have as many bottles of water as juice pouches. How many of each should Grant buy? Explain how you know.

© Pearson Education, Inc. 6

Name ____________________

Practice Buddy · Tools · Assessment

Guided Practice*

Do You Understand?

1. **MP.3 Construct Arguments** Grant finds juice bottles that come in packages of 3, but can only find applesauce in packages of 8. Will the LCM change? Explain.

2. **MP.3 Critique Reasoning** Sarah says that you find the LCM of any two whole numbers by multiplying them together. Provide a counterexample to show that Sarah is incorrect.

Do You Know How?

In **3** and **4**, find the LCM of each number by listing their multiples.

3. 2, 5

4. 6, 10

In **5** and **6**, use prime factorization to find the LCM of each number.

5. 8, 12

6. 6, 9

Independent Practice

Leveled Practice In **7–16**, find the LCM for each pair of numbers.

7. 4, 10

Multiples of 4: 4, 8, ______, ______, ______, …

Multiples of 10: 10, ______, …

LCM: ______

There may be more than one factor tree for a composite number, but there is only one prime factorization.

8. 9, 12

9 = ______ × ______

12 = ______ × ______ × ______

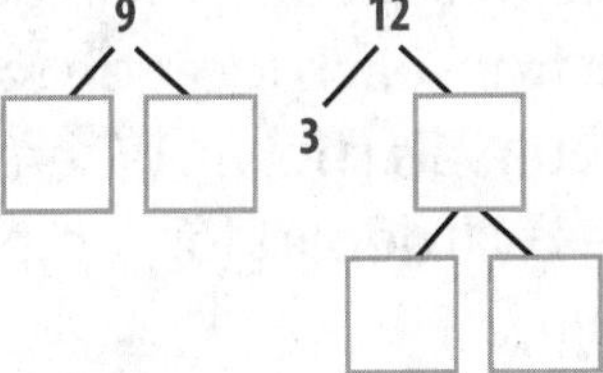

LCM = 2 × 2 × 3 × 3 = ______

9. 12, 11

10. 4, 12

11. 5, 8

12. 7, 11

13. 8, 10

14. 7, 12

15. 3, 5

16. 7, 8

*For another example, see Set C on page 418.

Math Practices and Problem Solving

17. Math and Science Find the LCM of the two numbers. Then use the LCM to find the corresponding letter in the key. Write that letter in the box. What word did you decode?

2 and 3	3 and 7	2 and 7

Decryption Key

A = 1	B = 2	C = 3	D = 4	E = 5
F = 6	G = 7	H = 8	I = 9	J = 10
K = 11	L = 12	M = 13	N = 14	O = 15
P = 16	Q = 17	R = 18	S = 19	T = 20
U = 21	V = 22	W = 23	X = 24	Y = 25
Z = 26				

18. Linda is sending out cards. If envelopes come in boxes of 12 and stamps come in packs of 10, what is the least number of stamps and envelopes she can buy to get one stamp for each envelope?

Are your answers reasonable? Do your answers make sense?

19. Rami has swimming lessons every 3 days and guitar lessons every 7 days. If he has both lessons the first day of the month, in how many days will he have both lessons on the same day again?

20. Vocabulary Identify three *common multiples* of 3 and 5.

21. Number Sense A number is between 58 and 68. It has prime factors of 2, 3, and 5. What is the number?

22. Higher Order Thinking A college offers shuttle service from Dickson Hall or Lot B to its campus quad. Both shuttles first depart their locations at 9:10 A.M. They run from each location to campus and back at the intervals shown. When is the next time both shuttles will depart for campus at the same time? Explain.

DATA

College Shuttle

Shuttle Name	Running Time
Lot B	Every 15 minutes
Dickson Hall	Every 12 minutes

Common Core Assessment

23. Mr. Jenkins bought the same number of blue pencils as green pencils. Blue pencils come in packs of 5, and green pencils come in packs of 4. What is the least number of blue or green pencils Mr. Jenkins could have bought?

Ⓐ 10 pencils Ⓑ 15 pencils Ⓒ 20 pencils Ⓓ 40 pencils

© Pearson Education, Inc. 6

Name ______________________

Homework & Practice 8-3

Least Common Multiple

Another Look!

Find the LCM of 4 and 5.

You can find the least common multiple (LCM) in different ways.

List Multiples

Step 1 List multiples of each number.

4: 4, 8, 12, 16, 20, 24, 28, 32, 36, 40, 44, 48...

5: 5, 10, 15, 20, 25, 30, 35, 40, 45, 50...

Step 2 Circle the multiples the numbers have in common.

4: 4, 8, 12, 16, (20), 24, 28, 32, 36, (40), 44, 48...

5: 5, 10, 15, (20), 25, 30, 35, (40), 45, 50...

Step 3 Determine which of the common multiples is the least.

20 and 40 are both common multiples, but 20 is the least.

The LCM of 4 and 5 is 20.

Use Prime Factors

Step 1 List the prime factors of each number.

4: 2×2

5: 5

Step 2 Circle the greatest number of times each different factor appears.

4: (2×2)

5: (5)

Step 3 Find the product of the factors you circled.

$2 \times 2 \times 5 = 20$

The LCM of 4 and 5 is 20.

In **1–12**, find the LCM of each pair of numbers.

1. 8, 12

2. 6, 7

3. 3, 4

4. 4, 9

5. 3, 8

6. 5, 11

7. 4, 8

8. 5, 6

9. 3, 6

10. 2, 4

11. 10, 11

12. 3, 7

13. **MP.3 Critique Reasoning** Ron is trying to find the LCM of 4 and 6. His work is shown at the right. What is Ron's mistake? Explain how to find the correct LCM of 4 and 6.

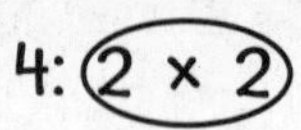

6: 2 × 3

2 × 2 × 2 × 3 = 24, so the LCM of 4 and 6 is 24.

---

14. Peanuts are sold in 8-ounce and 12-ounce packages. What is the least number of ounces you can buy of each package to have equal amounts of each package size?

15. **Algebra** A certain substance begins to melt at temperatures above 42°F. Write an inequality that represents the temperatures at which the substance will not melt. Show this on a number line.

---

16. At what times between 10:00 A.M. and 5:00 P.M. do the chemistry presentation and the recycling presentation start at the same time?

Science Museum
— Show Schedule —
Chemistry — Every 10 minutes
Electricity — Every 20 minutes
Recycling — Every 6 minutes
Fossils — Every 45 minutes
The first showing for all shows is at 10:00 A.M.

17. **Higher Order Thinking** The museum performs shows in schools every Monday and shows in public libraries every fifth day (on both weekdays and weekends). If the museum did both a school show and a library show on Monday, how many days will it be until it does both shows on the same day again?

Common Core Assessment

18. The different kinds of beads Casey is using to make purses come in packages of 3 and 9. What is the least number of each kind of bead Casey can buy to have an equal number of each of the different kinds of beads?

Ⓐ 90 Ⓑ 27 Ⓒ 9 Ⓓ 6

© Pearson Education, Inc. 6

Name ______________________________________

Solve & Share

Sam is exploring patterns with prime numbers. He starts with the number 1 and then adds consecutive odd prime numbers. He says that the sum of 1 and consecutive odd prime numbers is always a square number.

Critique Sam's reasoning and explain whether his statement is correct.

$1 = 1$

$1 + 3 = 4$

$1 + 3 + 5 = 9$

Math Practices and Problem Solving

Lesson 8-4

Critique Reasoning

I can ...

critique the reasoning of others using what I know about factors and multiples.

Mathematical Practices MP.3, MP.1, MP.6, MP.7
Content Standard 6.NS.B.4

Thinking Habits

Be a good thinker! These questions can help you.

- What questions can I ask to understand other people's thinking?
- Are there mistakes in other people's thinking?
- Can I improve other people's thinking?

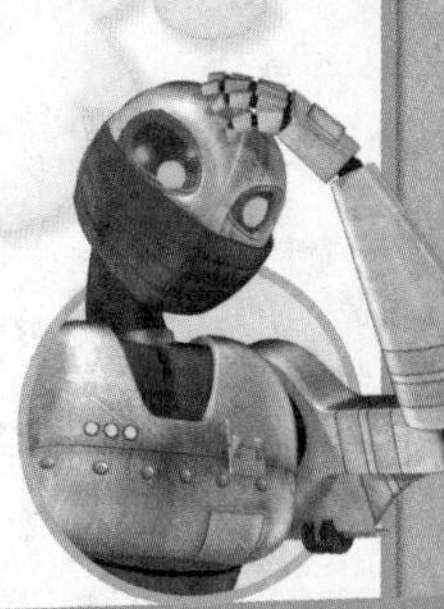

Look Back! **MP.3 Critique Reasoning** How can I improve Sam's thinking?

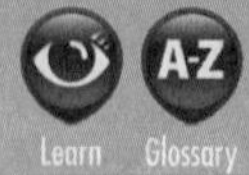

Essential Question

How Can You Critique the Reasoning of Others?

A

Sara lists the factors of each square number less than 100.

She says that the GCF of any two of these square numbers is 1.

1: 1

4: 1, 2, 4

9: 1, 3, 9

16: 1, 2, 4, 8, 16

25: 1, 5, 25

36: 1, 2, 3, 4, 6, 9, 12, 18, 36

49: 1, 7, 49

64: 1, 2, 4, 8, 16, 32, 64

81: 1, 3, 9, 27, 81

100: 1, 2, 4, 5, 10, 20, 25, 50, 100

You can critique the reasoning of others by using what you know about factors.

What is Sara's reasoning to support her statement?

Sara's reasoning is based on her analysis of the list of factors of each square number less than 100.

B

How can I critique the reasoning of others?

I can

- ask questions for clarification.
- decide if the strategy used makes sense.
- look for flaws in estimates or calculations.

C

Here's my thinking...

Sara's reasoning is flawed because a counterexample can show that Sara's statement is not true for all square numbers less than 100. A counterexample is an example that shows that a statement is not true.

The GCF of 4 and 16 is 4.

Sara's reasoning is incomplete and her statement is not correct.

Convince Me! **MP.3 Critique Reasoning** Sara revised her statement. She says that the GCF of any two consecutive square numbers less than 100 is 1. Critique Sara's reasoning and explain whether she is correct.

© Pearson Education, Inc. 6

Name ______________________________

Guided Practice*

MP.3 Critique Reasoning

An athletic director schedules the use of the gym for May. The gym can be used for only one activity each day. The director reasons that if he starts on May 1 and schedules basketball practice every 3 days and soccer practice every 4 days, the two practices will not occur on the same day. He checks the calendar and finds that basketball practice will occur on May 3, 6, and 9 and soccer practice will occur on May 4, 8, and 12.

You can critique reasoning by using what you know about math concepts, such as multiples, factors, and the GCF or LCM.

1. What is the director's reasoning to support his statement?

2. Does the director's reasoning make sense? Use an example or a counterexample to critique his reasoning.

Independent Practice

MP.3 Critique Reasoning

Sadie says that the Venn diagram shows the common factors of 8 and 12 in the center section. She concludes that the GCF is 8 because $1 \times 2 \times 4 = 8$.

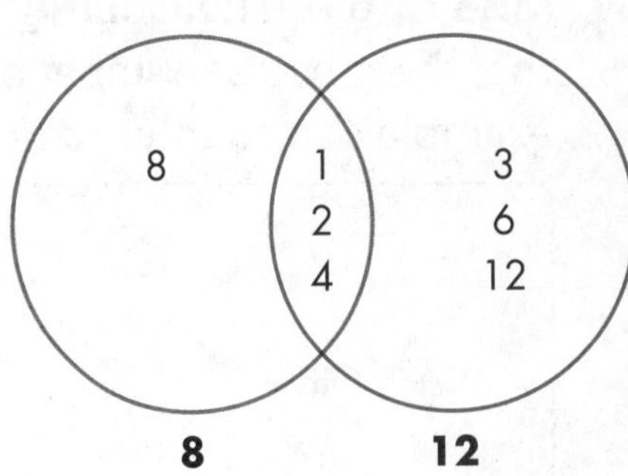

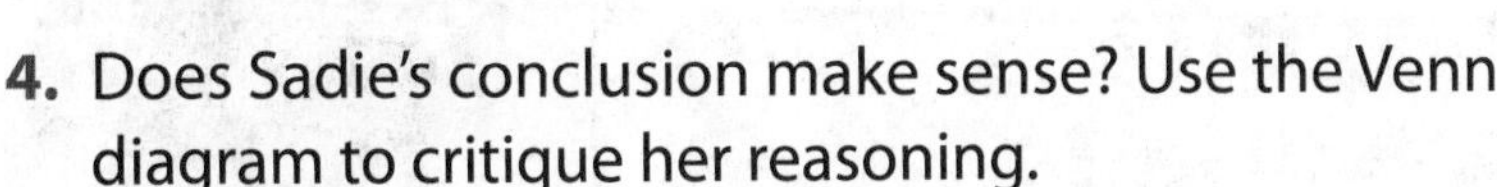

3. How does Sadie support her conclusion?

4. Does Sadie's conclusion make sense? Use the Venn diagram to critique her reasoning.

5. What mistake did Sadie make?

*For another example, see Set D on page 418.

Math Practices and Problem Solving

Common Core Performance Assessment

Walk-a-Thon Snack Bags

Juan is making snack bags for a walk-a-thon. He plans to put the same number of bottles of water and the same number of energy bars in each bag. He wants to make the greatest number of bags that he can with none of the supplies left over. Juan claims that the greatest number of bags he can make is 14, with 6 bottles of water and 4 energy bars in each bag.

bottles of water	84
energy bars	56

$84 + 56 = 14(6 + 4)$

14 snack bags: 6 bottles of water and 4 energy bars

6. **MP.7 Use Structure** How does Juan use the relationship between addition and multiplication to support his claim?

7. **MP.1 Make Sense and Persevere** How can you use Juan's math to check that his strategy makes sense?

When you critique reasoning, you can use math to explain why other people's work is correct or incorrect.

8. **MP.3 Critique Reasoning** Does Juan's math support his claim that the greatest number of bags he can make is 14? Use an example or a counterexample to justify your answer.

9. **MP.6 Be Precise** How many bottles of water and energy bars can Juan put in each bag? Justify your answer.

© Pearson Education, Inc. 6

Name ____________________

Help | Practice Buddy | Tools | Games

Homework & Practice 8-4

Critique Reasoning

Another Look!

Jim notices that 18 and 27 are multiples of 9 and that the sum of 18 and 27 is 45, which is also a multiple of 9. He reasons that for any two numbers that are multiples of 9, their sum will also be a multiple of 9. Explain whether Jim's reasoning makes sense.

$9 \times 3 = 27$

$9 \times 2 = 18$

$18 + 27 = 45$ $45 = 9 \times 5$

You can critique reasoning by analyzing a person's thinking and then testing or questioning their approaches.

Critique Jim's reasoning by testing more examples.

$9 \times 6 = 54$ $9 \times 8 = 72$	$9 \times 1 = 9$ $9 \times 4 = 36$
$54 + 72 = 126$	$9 + 36 = 45$
$126 = 9 \times 14$	$45 = 9 \times 5$

Use the Distributive Property to show why this works.

$9 \times 6 + 9 \times 8 = 9(6 + 8) = 9(14)$
$9 \times 1 + 9 \times 4 = 9(1 + 4) = 9(5)$

Writing the expressions using the Distributive Property shows that the sum of two numbers with a GCF of 9 will always be a multiple of 9.

Jim's reasoning makes sense.

MP.3 Critique Reasoning

Eva says the LCM of two odd numbers is the product of the two numbers.

Multiples of 3: 3, 6, 9, (15)
Multiples of 5: 5, 10, (15)

Multiples of 7: 7, 14, 21, 28, 35, 42, 49, 56, (63)
Multiples of 9: 9, 18, 27, 36, 45, 54, (63)

Remember, when you critique reasoning, just one counterexample proves the conjecture is incorrect.

1. How does Eva support her conjecture?

2. Critique Eva's reasoning by testing more examples. Is there a counterexample that proves her conjecture is not true?

Common Core Performance Assessment

Balloons

Jane is making balloon centerpieces for a school banquet. She wants to use $\frac{1}{3}$-pack of each balloon type per centerpiece. Jane states that the least number of centerpieces she can make with no balloons left over is 54.

6: 2×3
9: 3×3
LCM: $2 \times 3 \times 3 \times 3 = 54$

Type of Balloon	Number of Balloons per Pack
Latex (6 pks.)	9
Mylar (6 pks.)	6

3. MP.1 Make Sense and Persevere What is Jane's argument and how does she support it?

When you critique reasoning, you can look for flaws in calculations.

4. MP.3 Critique Reasoning How can you tell whether Jane's argument is correct?

5. MP.3 Construct Arguments Is Jane's math correct?

© Pearson Education, Inc. 6

Name ____________________

Fluency Practice Activity

Find a partner. Get paper and a pencil. Each partner chooses a different color: light blue or dark blue.

Partner 1 and Partner 2 each point to a black number at the same time. Each partner divides the greater number by the lesser number.

If the answer is on your color, you get a tally mark. Work until one partner has twelve tally marks.

I can ...

divide multi-digit whole numbers.

Content Standard 6.NS.B.2

Partner 1
1,080
3,168
2,215
6,048
4,048

44	137 R17	88	67 R28
112 R16	84	262 R22	176
46 R22	96 R7	60	100 R48
336	30	52 R48	168
61 R19	18	56 R16	15
30 R55	224 R16	36 R55	123 R1

Partner 2
36
18
72
23
60

Tally Marks for Partner 1	Tally Marks for Partner 2

TOPIC 8

Vocabulary Review

Word List

- common multiple
- composite number
- counterexample
- factor tree
- greatest common factor (GCF)
- least common multiple (LCM)
- prime factorization
- prime number

Understand Vocabulary

Choose the best term from the Word List. Write it on the blank.

1. Every composite number can be written as a product of prime factors called its ____________________.

2. The number 5 is the ____________ of 10 and 15.

3. A diagram that shows the prime factors of a composite number is a ____________________.

4. A number that has more than two factors is a ____________________.

5. Write **P** next to each *prime number*. Write **C** next to each *composite number*.

   2____ 9____ 65____ 73____

6. Circle the *common multiples* of 8 and 12.

   2 12 24 48 72 4 16 36 60

Draw a line from each pair of numbers in Column A to the *least common multiple* (*LCM*) of the numbers in Column B.

Column A	Column B
7. 9, 7	36
8. 9, 12	56
9. 8, 7	63

Use Vocabulary in Writing

10. Describe two ways to find the *prime factorization* of 16. Use at least 3 words from the Word List in your explanation.

© Pearson Education, Inc. 6

Name ______________________________

TOPIC 8

Reteaching

Set A pages 391–396

Find the prime factorization of 24.

Start with any two factors.
Keep finding factors until all factors are prime.

$24 = 4 \times 6$
$= 2 \times 2 \times 6$
$= 2 \times 2 \times 2 \times 3$

The prime factorization of 24 is $2 \times 2 \times 2 \times 3$ or $2^3 \times 3$.

You can also use a factor tree. Start with any two factors.

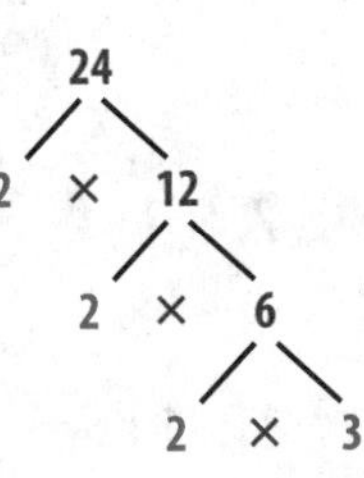

The factor tree shows that the prime factorization of 24 is $2 \times 2 \times 2 \times 3$ or $2^3 \times 3$.

Remember that a number is prime when its only factors are 1 and the number itself.

Write the prime factorization of each number. If the number is prime, write *prime*.

1. 39

2. 56

3. 83

4. 64

5. 42

6. 75

7. 29

Set B pages 397–402

Find the greatest common factor, or GCF, of 24 and 66 by using prime factorization. Then use the GCF and the Distributive Property to find the sum of 24 and 66.

Step 1 Find the prime factorization of each number.

$24 = 2 \times 2 \times 2 \times 3$ $\quad$ $66 = 2 \times 3 \times 11$

Step 2 Multiply the common, prime factors. The GCF of 24 and 66 is $2 \times 3 = 6$.

Step 3 Use the GCF and the Distributive Property to find the sum of 24 and 66.

$24 + 66 = 6 \times 4 + 6 \times 11 = 6(4 + 11)$
$= 6(15) = 90.$

Remember that to find the GCF, you can also list all of the factors for each number, and then choose the greatest factor they have in common.

Find the GCF for each pair of numbers. Then use the GCF and the Distributive Property to find the sum of each pair of numbers.

1. 30, 100 $\quad$ **2.** 8, 52

3. 28, 42 $\quad$ **4.** 37, 67

5. 75, 89 $\quad$ **6.** 48, 72

Set C pages 403–408

Find the least common multiple (LCM) of 10 and 6.

List multiples of each number.

10: 10, 20, 30 . . .   6: 6, 12, 18, 24, 30 . . .

The LCM is 30.

You can also use prime factorization to find the least common multiple.

10: ②×⑤

6: ②×③

List the greatest number of times each factor appears in either prime factorization. Then multiply the factors.

$2 \times 5 \times 3 = 30$

Remember that you multiply a given number by any whole number to find a multiple.

Find the LCM for each pair of numbers.

1. 4, 9

2. 3, 6

3. 8, 10

4. 3, 5

5. 4, 12

6. 6, 11

7. 9, 12

8. 4, 10

9. 7, 8

10. 9, 7

11. 12, 11

12. 10, 2

Set D pages 409–414

Think about these questions to help you **critique the reasoning of others**.

Thinking Habits

- What questions can I ask to understand other people's thinking?
- Are there mistakes in other people's thinking?
- Can I improve other people's thinking?

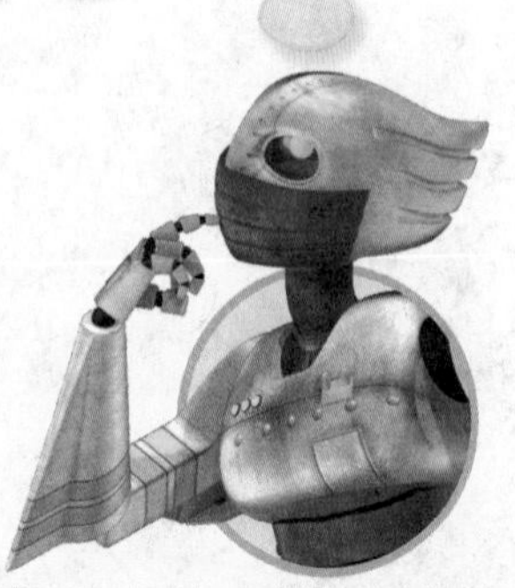

Remember that you can critique reasoning by offering a counterexample.

Ms. Davis schedules after-school group activities for 18 girls and 24 boys. She wants to make equal groups with the same number of girls and the same number of boys in each group. Ms. Davis says that the greatest number of equal groups she can make is 3.

1. Is Ms. Davis correct? Use an example or counterexample to critique Ms. Davis's statement.

2. What mistake did Ms. Davis make?

© Pearson Education, Inc. 6

Name ____________________

1. Kristen buys sheets of elephant stickers and sheets of tiger stickers. There are 12 elephant stickers on each sheet and 10 tiger stickers on each sheet.

Part A

What is the least number of each type of sticker that Kristen can buy so that she has an equal number of each type of sticker? Show how you know.

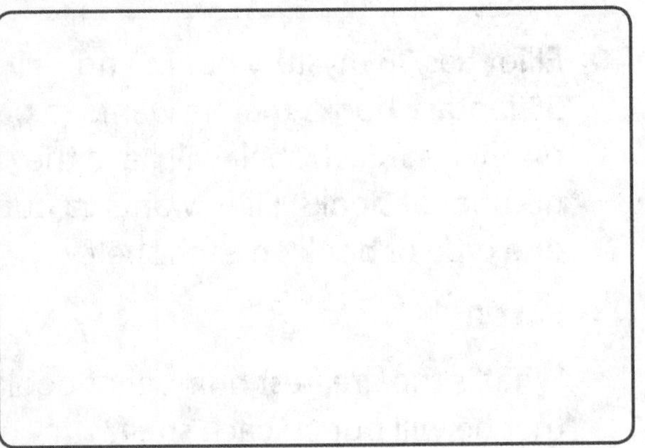

Part B

How many sheets of each type of sticker should she buy? Show how you know.

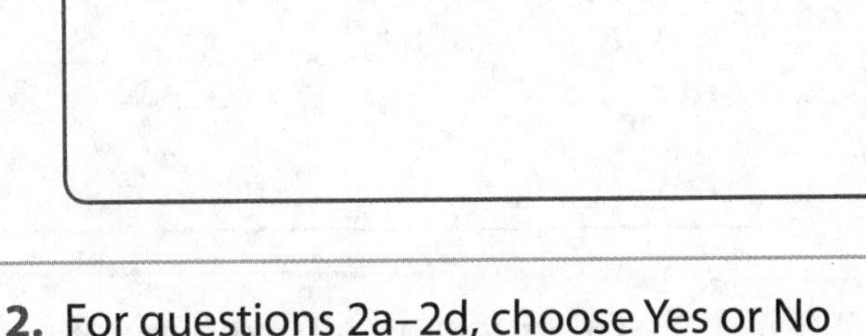

2. For questions 2a–2d, choose Yes or No to tell whether 3 is the GCF of the pair of numbers.

2a. 9, 15 ○ Yes ○ No

2b. 12, 18 ○ Yes ○ No

2c. 15, 27 ○ Yes ○ No

2d. 30, 45 ○ Yes ○ No

3. Ziva notices a pattern when finding the LCM of two prime numbers. She reasons that because the only factors of each prime number are 1 and itself, the LCM of two prime numbers is always the product of the numbers.

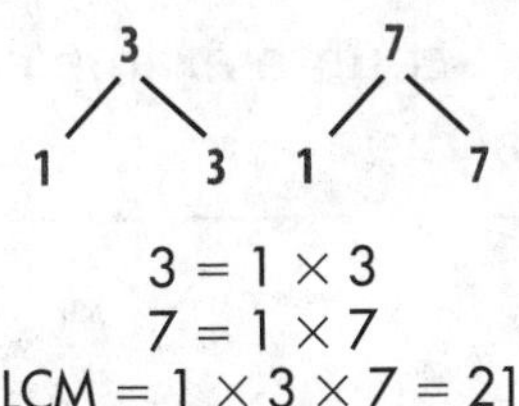

$3 = 1 \times 3$

$7 = 1 \times 7$

$\text{LCM} = 1 \times 3 \times 7 = 21$

Does Ziva's reasoning make sense? Explain how you know.

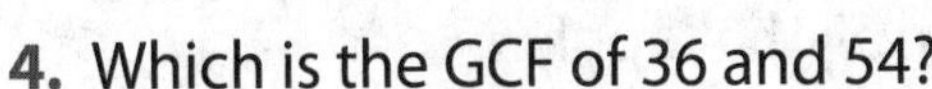

4. Which is the GCF of 36 and 54?

Ⓐ 2

Ⓑ 6

Ⓒ 9

Ⓓ 18

5. Jamie volunteers at the pet shelter every 3 days and at the food pantry every 6 days. This month he volunteers at the pet shelter on the 3rd day of the month and the food pantry on the 6th day of the month. Jamie says that the first time he will volunteer at both places will be the 18th day of the month because the LCM of 3 and 6 is 18.

Does Jamie's reasoning make sense? Use an example or a counterexample to explain your analysis.

6. Use the GCF and the Distributive Property to find the sum of 49 + 56. Show your work.

7. Jase wrote the prime factorization of 99. Which expression could he have written? Choose all that apply.

- ☐ $3^2 \times 11$
- ☐ 9×9
- ☐ $3 \times 3 \times 3 \times 11$
- ☐ 3^4
- ☐ $3 \times 3 \times 11$

8. Draw lines to match each pair of numbers on the left to the LCM of the numbers on the right.

4, 10	12
2, 12	15
3, 8	18
6, 9	20
5, 15	24

9. Elliot has 28 mystery books and 35 fantasy books that he wants to put on shelves. Each shelf will have the same number of books. Elliot wants to put only one type of book on each shelf.

Part A

What is the greatest number of books that he will put on each shelf?

Part B

How many shelves will there be of mystery books? How many shelves will there be of fantasy books?

10. Find the GCF of 9 and 12. Explain your method.

© Pearson Education, Inc. 6

Name ____________________

TOPIC 8

Performance Assessment

The Cookout

Ali is planning a cookout for family and friends. There will be 24 people at her cookout.

1. Ali is renting tables for the cookout and wants to seat an equal number of people at each table. She needs to decide how many tables to get. How could she arrange the seating so that a reasonable and equal number of people sit at each table? Explain your reasoning.

2. Ali has invited 18 adults and 6 children. Mo, Ali's best friend, suggests that Ali seat an equal number of adults and an equal number of children at each table. What is the greatest number of tables Ali would need? How many adults and children would be seated at each table? Explain how you found your answer.

3. Ali wants to buy an equal number of each of the items in the table. She wants to avoid leftovers.

Item	Number of Items per Package
Veggie Hot Dogs	6
Hot Dog Buns	8

Part A

What is the least number of items Ali needs to buy so there is an equal number of each? Explain your reasoning.

Part B

How many packages of each item does Ali need to buy? Explain how you decided.

4. At the last minute, Mo invites 6 of her friends to Ali's cookout. There are 4 more adults and 2 more children. How can Ali use what she has learned about seating the adults and children to arrange seating for all the invited guests? Explain your reasoning.

© Pearson Education, Inc. 6

Glossary

absolute deviation The total distance between each data point and the mean.

absolute value The distance that an integer is from zero on the number line.

acute angle An angle with a measure greater than 0° but less than 90°.

acute triangle A triangle with three acute angles.

adjacent angles A pair of angles with a common vertex and a common side but no common interior points. *Example:* ∠*RSP* and ∠*PST*

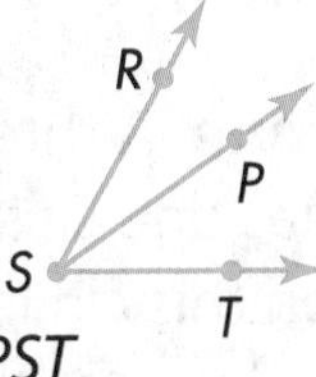

algebraic expression A mathematical phrase that has at least one variable and operation. *Example:* $10 \times n$ or $10n$

angle Two rays with the same endpoint.

arc A part of a circle connecting two points on a circle.

area The number of square units needed to cover a surface or figure.

associative properties Properties that state the way in which addends or factors are grouped does not affect the sum or product.

average The sum of the values in a data set divided by the number of data values in the set. Also called the *mean*.

axis (*pl.* axes) Either of the two perpendicular lines of a coordinate plane that intersect at the origin.

bar graph A graph that uses bars to show and compare data.

base (in geometry) A designated side of a polygon that is perpendicular to the height of the polygon; one of the two parallel faces on a prism; a particular flat surface of a solid, such as a cylinder or cone.

base (in numeration) A number multiplied by itself the number of times shown by an exponent. *Example:* $4 \times 4 \times 4 = 4^3$, where 4 is the base.

box plot A diagram that shows the distribution of data values using the median, quartiles, least value, and greatest value on a number line.

capacity The volume of a container measured in liquid units.

Celsius (°C) A scale for measuring temperature in the metric system.

center (in geometry) The interior point from which all points of a circle are equally distant.

center (in statistics) The part of a data set where the middle values are concentrated.

centi- Prefix meaning $\frac{1}{100}$.

central angle An angle with its vertex at the center of a circle.

chord A line segment with both endpoints on a circle.

circle A closed plane figure with all points the same distance from a given point called the center.

circle graph A graph that represents a total divided into parts.

circumference The distance around a circle.

cluster An interval with a greater frequency compared to the rest of the data set.

coefficient The number that is multiplied by a variable in an algebraic expression. *Example:* For $6x + 5$, the coefficient is 6.

common denominator A denominator that is the same in two or more fractions.

common factor A factor that is the same for two or more numbers.

common multiple A multiple that is the same for two or more numbers.

commutative properties The properties that state the order of addends or the order of factors does not affect the sum or product.

compatible numbers Numbers that are easy to compute mentally.

composite number A natural number greater than one that has more than two factors.

cone A three-dimensional figure that has one circular base. The points on this circle are joined to one point outside the base called the vertex.

conjecture A generalization that you think is true.

constant speed A rate of speed that stays the same over time.

conversion factor A rate that compares equivalent measures. *Examples:*

$\frac{4 \text{ cups}}{1 \text{ quart}}$ $\frac{12 \text{ inches}}{1 \text{ foot}}$ $\frac{1{,}000 \text{ meters}}{1 \text{ kilometer}}$

coordinate plane A two-dimensional system in which a location is described by its distances from two perpendicular number lines called the *x*-axis and the *y*-axis.

© Pearson Education, Inc. 6

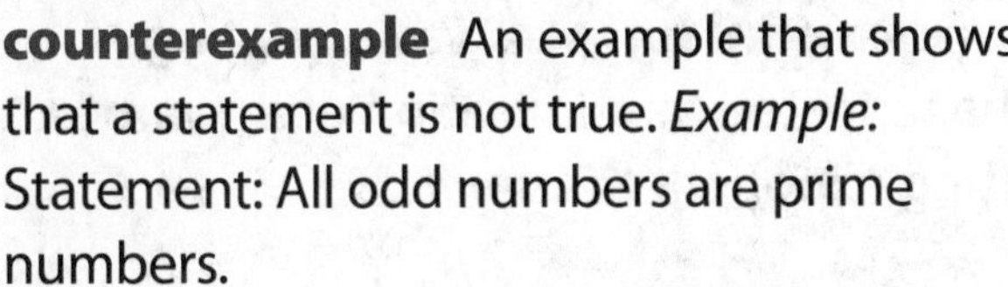

counterexample An example that shows that a statement is not true. *Example:* Statement: All odd numbers are prime numbers.
Counterexample: 9 is an odd number but is not a prime number.

cubic unit A unit measuring volume, consisting of a cube with edges one unit long.

cylinder A three-dimensional figure that has two circular bases which are parallel and identical.

data Information that is gathered.

data distribution How data values are arranged.

decagon A polygon with ten sides.

decimal A number with one or more digits to the right of the decimal point.

decimal point A dot used to separate dollars from cents in money or ones from tenths in a number.

degree (°) A unit for measuring angles or temperatures.

denominator The number below the fraction bar in a fraction; the total number of equal parts in all.

dependent variable A variable that changes in response to another variable.

diagonal A line segment that connects two vertices of a polygon and is not a side.

diameter A line segment that passes through the center of a circle and has both endpoints on the circle.

dimensional analysis A method that uses conversion factors to convert one unit of measure to another unit of measure. *Example:*

$$64\ \cancel{\text{ounces}} \times \frac{1\text{ cup}}{8\ \cancel{\text{ounces}}} = \frac{64}{8}\text{ cups} = 8\text{ cups}$$

Distributive Property Multiplying a sum by a number produces the same result as multiplying each addend by the number and adding the products.
Example: $2 \times (3 + 4) = (2 \times 3) + (2 \times 4)$

dividend The number being divided by another number. *Example:* In $12 \div 3 = 4$, 12 is the dividend.

divisible A number is divisible by another number if its quotient is a whole number and the remainder is zero.

divisor The number used to divide another number. *Example:* In $12 \div 3 = 4$, 3 is the divisor.

dot plot A display of data values where each data value is shown as a dot above a number line. See also *line plot*.

edge The line segment where two faces of a polyhedron meet.

equation A mathematical sentence stating that two expressions are equal.

equilateral triangle A triangle with three sides of the same length.

equivalent expressions Expressions that have the same value regardless of which number is substituted for the same variable.

equivalent fractions Fractions that name the same amount.

estimate To find a number that is close to an exact answer.

evaluate To find the value of an algebraic expression by replacing each variable with a given value. *Example:* Evaluate $2n + 5$ when $n = 3$; $2(3) + 5 = 11$.

expanded form using exponents A number written in expanded form with the place values written in exponential form. *Example:* $3{,}246 = (3 \times 10^3) + (2 \times 10^2) + (4 \times 10^1) + (6 \times 10^0)$

exponent The number that tells how many times the base is being multiplied by itself. *Example:* $8^3 = 8 \times 8 \times 8$, where 3 is the exponent and 8 is the base.

exponential form A way of writing the repeated multiplication of a number using exponents. *Example:* 2^5

expression A mathematical phrase that can contain numbers, variables, and operations. *Example:* $12 - x$

face A flat surface of a polyhedron.

factor A number that is multiplied by another to get a product.

factor tree A diagram that shows the prime factorization of a number.

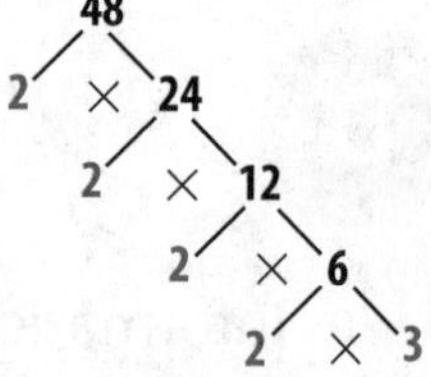

Fahrenheit (°F) A scale for measuring temperature in the customary system.

formula A rule that uses symbols to relate two or more quantities.

fraction A number that can be used to describe a part of a whole, a part of a set, a location on a number line, or a division of whole numbers.

frequency table A table that shows the number of times a data value or range of values occurs in a data set.

© Pearson Education, Inc. 6

gap An interval with a lesser frequency compared to the rest of the data set.

gram (g) Metric unit of mass.

greatest common factor (GCF) The greatest number that is a factor of two or more numbers.

height The segment from a vertex perpendicular to the line containing the opposite side; the perpendicular distance between the bases of a solid.

heptagon A polygon with seven sides.

hexagon A polygon with six sides.

histogram A graph that uses bars to show the frequency of equal intervals.

identity properties The properties that state the sum of any number and zero is that number and the product of any number and one is that number.

independent variable The variable that causes the dependent variable to change.

inequality A statement that contains $>$ (greater than), $<$ (less than), $\geq$ (greater than or equal to), $\leq$ (less than or equal to), or $\neq$ (is not equal to) to compare two expressions.

input/output table A table of related values.

integers The counting numbers, their opposites, and zero.

interquartile range (IQR) A measure of variability that is the difference between the third quartile and the first quartile.

interval A range of numbers used to represent data.

inverse relationships Relationships between operations that "undo" each other, such as addition and subtraction, or multiplication and division (except multiplication or division by 0).

isosceles triangle A triangle with at least two identical sides.

kilo- Prefix meaning 1,000.

kite A quadrilateral with two pairs of adjacent sides that are equal in length.

least common denominator (LCD) The least common multiple of the denominators of two or more fractions. *Example:* 12 is the LCD of $\frac{1}{4}$ and $\frac{1}{6}$.

least common multiple (LCM) The least number, other than zero, that is a multiple of two or more numbers.

like denominators Denominators in two or more fractions that are the same.

like terms Terms that have the same variable, such as y and $2y$.

line A straight path of points that goes on forever in two directions.

line plot A display of data values where each data value is shown as a mark above a number line. See also *dot plot*.

line segment Part of a line that has two endpoints.

linear equation An equation whose graph is a straight line.

liter (L) Metric unit of capacity.

mass Measure of the amount of matter of an object.

maximum The greatest data value in a data set.

mean The sum of the values in a data set divided by the number of values in the set. Also called the *average*.

mean absolute deviation (MAD) The mean of the absolute deviations of a set of data.

measure of center A single number that summarizes the center of a data set. *Example:* mean or median

measure of variability A single number that summarizes the variability of a data set. *Example:* interquartile range

median The middle data value in a data set.

meter (m) Metric unit of length.

metric system (of measurement) A system using decimals and powers of 10 to measure length, mass, and capacity.

midpoint The point that divides a segment into two segments of equal length.

milli- Prefix meaning $\frac{1}{1000}$.

minimum The least data value in a data set.

mixed number A number that combines a whole number and a fraction.

mode The data value that occurs most often in a data set.

multiple The product of a given whole number and any non-zero whole number.

© Pearson Education, Inc. 6

net A plane figure pattern that, when folded, makes a solid.

nonagon A polygon with nine sides.

numerator The number above the fraction bar in a fraction; the number of objects or equal parts being considered.

numerical data Data where each value is a number.

numerical expression An expression that contains only numerical values and operations.

obtuse angle An angle with a measure greater than 90° but less than 180°.

obtuse triangle A triangle with an obtuse angle.

octagon A polygon with eight sides.

opposites Integers on opposite sides of zero and the same distance from zero on a number line. *Example:* 7 and −7 are opposites.

order of operations A set of rules mathematicians use to determine the order in which operations are performed.

ordered pair A pair of numbers (x, y) used to locate a point on a coordinate plane.

origin The point (0, 0), where the x- and y-axes of a coordinate plane intersect.

outlier An extreme value with few data points located near it.

parallel lines Lines in the same plane that do not intersect.

parallelogram A quadrilateral with both pairs of opposite sides parallel.

pentagon A polygon with five sides.

percent A rate in which the first term is compared to 100.

perimeter Distance around a figure.

perpendicular bisector A line, ray, or segment that intersects a segment at its midpoint and is perpendicular to it.

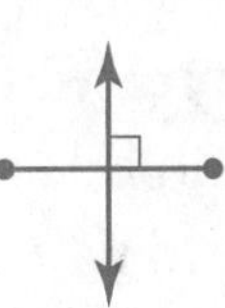

perpendicular lines Intersecting lines that form right angles.

plane A flat surface that extends forever in all directions.

point An exact location in space.

polygon A closed plane figure made up of three or more line segments.

polyhedron A three-dimensional figure made of flat surfaces that are polygons.

power The value of the base and exponent written as a numerical expression.

prime factorization The set of prime factors whose product is a given composite number. *Example:* $60 = 2^2 \times 3 \times 5$

prime number A whole number greater than 1 with exactly two factors, 1 and itself.

prism A polyhedron with two identical and parallel polygon-shaped faces.

properties of equality Properties that state performing the same operation to both sides of an equation keeps the equation balanced.

proportion A statement that two ratios are equal.

pyramid A polyhedron whose base can be any polygon and whose faces are triangles.

quadrant One of the four regions into which the x- and y-axes divide the coordinate plane. The axes are not parts of the quadrant.

quadrilateral A polygon with four sides.

quartiles Values that divide a data set into four equal parts.

quotient The answer in a division problem. *Example:* In $45 \div 9 = 5$, 5 is the quotient.

radius Any line segment that connects the center of the circle to a point on the circle.

range The difference between the greatest and least values in a data set.

rate A ratio that compares two quantities with different units of measure.

ratio A relationship where for every x units of one quantity there are y units of another quantity.

rational number Any number that can be written as a quotient $\frac{a}{b}$, where a and b are integers and $b \neq 0$.

ray Part of a line with one endpoint, extending forever in only one direction.

reciprocals Two numbers whose product is one. *Example:* The reciprocal of $\frac{3}{4}$ is $\frac{4}{3}$ because $\frac{3}{4} \times \frac{4}{3} = 1$.

rectangle A parallelogram with four right angles.

reflection The change in the position of a figure or point that gives a mirror image over a line.

© Pearson Education, Inc. 6

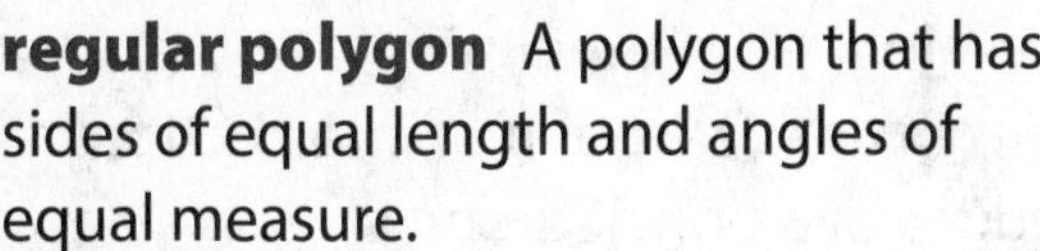

regular polygon A polygon that has sides of equal length and angles of equal measure.

repeating decimal A decimal in which a digit or digits repeat endlessly.

rhombus A parallelogram with four equal sides.

right angle An angle that measures 90°.

right triangle A triangle with one right angle.

S

scale The ratio of the measurements in a drawing to the actual measurements of the object.

scale drawing A drawing made so that distances in the drawing are proportional to actual distances.

scalene triangle A triangle with all sides of different lengths.

sector A region bounded by two radii and an arc.

side A segment used to form a polygon; a ray used to form an angle.

simplify To use operations to combine like terms in an expression.

solution (of an equation) A value that makes an equation true.

sphere A three-dimensional figure such that every point is the same distance from the center.

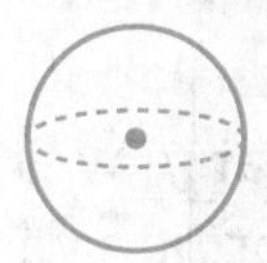

square A rectangle with four equal sides.

squared When a number has been multiplied by itself.
Example: 5 squared $= 5^2 = 5 \times 5 = 25$

statistical question A question which anticipates that there will be different answers in the data.

straight angle An angle that measures 180°.

substitution The replacement of the variable of an expression with a number.

surface area (SA) The sum of the area of each face of a polyhedron.

symmetric data Data distributed equally on both sides of the center.

T

terminating decimal A decimal with a finite number of digits.
Example: 0.375

terms The quantities *x* and *y* in a ratio. Also, each part of an expression that is separated by a plus or minus sign.

transformation A move such as a translation, reflection, or rotation that moves a figure to a new position without changing its size or shape.

trapezoid A quadrilateral with exactly one pair of opposite sides parallel.

triangle A polygon with three sides.

unit price A unit rate that gives the price of one item.

unit rate A rate in which the comparison is to one unit. *Example:* 25 feet per second

unlike denominators Denominators in two or more fractions that are different.

variability A measure of the spread of values in a data set.

variable A quantity that changes or varies, often represented with a letter.

vertex (in an angle) The common endpoint of two rays that form an angle.

vertex (in a polygon) (*pl.* vertices) The point of intersection of two sides of a polygon.

vertex (in a polyhedron) (*pl.* vertices) The point of intersection of the edges of a polyhedron.

volume The number of cubic units needed to fill a solid figure.

weight A measure of how heavy an object is.

***x*-axis** The horizontal line on a coordinate plane.

***x*-coordinate** The first number in an ordered pair that tells the position left or right of the *y*-axis.

***y*-axis** The vertical line on a coordinate plane.

***y*-coordinate** The second number in an ordered pair that tells the position above or below the *x*-axis.

© Pearson Education, Inc. 6

Photographs

Photo locators denoted as follows: Top (T), Center (C), Bottom (B), Left (L), Right (R), Background (Bkgd)

001 Irin-k/Shutterstock; **013** Pearson Education; **079** Tlorna/Shutterstock; **139** Brykaylo Yuriy/Shutterstock; **146B** Sebastian French/Fotolia; **146CL** Corbis; **146CR** Corbis; **146T** Nicola_G/Fotolia; **223** Solarseven/Shutterstock; **228** Pearson Education; **256** Stockbyte/Getty Images; **271** Ginger Livingston Sanders/Shutterstock; **280** Pearson Education; **282** Steve Lovegrove/Fotolia; **317** Volodymyr Goinyk/Shutterstock; **332** Pearson Education; **344** Mikiekwoods/Shutterstock; **387** Chris Alcock/Shutterstock; **404** Pearson Education; **423** NatalieJean/Shutterstock; **428BC** Massimo Cattaneo/Shutterstock; **428BL** Pearson Education; **428BR** Ysbrand Cosijn/Shutterstock; **428TC** Capture Light/Shutterstock; **428TL** Rebeccaashworth/Shutterstock; **428TR** Marcel Jancovic/Shutterstock; **500** Sascha Hahn/Shutterstock; **504** Dmitry Nikolaev/Fotolia; **537** Wasu Watcharadachaphong/Shutterstock; **591** Sly/Fotolia; **602C** Jupiter Images; **602L** Jupiter Images; **602R** hotshotsworldwide/Fotolia; **604** Dmitri Gomon/Shutterstock; **655** TFoxFoto/Shutterstock; **664B** Carmen Steiner/Fotolia; **664T** johnnyraff/Shutterstock; **703** Ermess/Fotolia; **745** Razlomov/Shutterstock; **770** Nerthuz/Shutterstock; **781** Real Deal Photo/Shutterstock; **804T** Pearson Education; **804B** Pearson Education; **840** Inga Nielsen/Shutterstock; **849L** Image Source/Getty Images; **849R** Getty Images.